Sailor *from* Oklahoma

Sailor *from* Oklahoma

one man's two-ocean war

by Floyd Beaver

NAVAL INSTITUTE PRESS
Annapolis, Maryland

Naval Institute Press
291 Wood Road
Annapolis, MD 21402

Library of Congress Cataloging-in-Publication Data
Beaver, Floyd.
  Sailor from Oklahoma : one man's two-ocean war / Floyd Beaver.
      p. cm.
  Includes bibliographical references and index.
  ISBN 978-1-59114-060-3 (alk. paper)
  1. World War, 1939-1945—Naval operations, American. 2. Beaver, Floyd. 3. World
War, 1939-1945—Personal narratives, American. 4. United States. Navy—Biography. 5.
Sailors—United States—Biography. I. Title.
  D773.B39 2009
  940.54'5973092—dc22
  [B]
                                                              2009020375

Printed in the United States of America on acid-free paper

14 13 12 11 10 09   9 8 7 6 5 4 3 2
First printing

All photos are from the author's personal collection.

To All the Old Ones

◦ Contents ◦

⟶ Introduction ⟵

TOO OFTEN HISTORY IS little more than a barren recital of events, dates, and names, written by those too young to have known or to remember the events they chronicle, all gleaned from the pages of books already written by others about, and often by, the great and powerful. But the full color of the history of a time and of a people shows only when the hard white light of fact is passed through a prism of living memory. To provide that prism, the author writes this account while a living memory of World War II, though greatly diminished by time, does still persist.

With the exception of an immaterial observation now and then, nothing exists in these pages that was not first seen by the author's eyes. Therefore, do not look for studies of grand strategy or for brilliance of tactics or for learned discussion of logistics. Look instead for all those men, now so fondly recalled by the author, whose individual endurance and devotion to duty combined to make up the collective merit that sustained our nation through a time of great trial by bloody war.

> When anchor chains in hawsepipes rattle
> and tattered colors flutter down,
> when sailors rest from sea and battle,
> the long gray ships are home.
>
> When evening stars begin to glimmer
> and seabirds settle for the night,
> when thoughts of war grow dim and dimmer,
> the long gray ships are home.
>
> It's then that sailors look with yearning
> to shore lights shining through the mist,
> and reckon not the tide's new turning.
> The long gray ships are home.

Note: Verse composed by author.

1
Escape from Oklahoma

SOMETIMES BETWEEN ACTS in a theater a rumbling can be heard behind drawn curtains as scenery for past acts is rolled offstage and that for the acts to come is rolled on. This has always been for me a most evocative sound, and one that never fails to remind me of another rumbling I heard once a long time ago.

The rumbling that time was of train wheels on a bridge over the Arkansas River at Tulsa, Oklahoma. It was June 6, 1939. I was then nineteen years old. The scenery being rolled offstage was that of eastern Oklahoma's Osage Hills and creek bottoms in which all my life to that time had been played. The scenery being rolled on was that of oceans and foreign lands and ships of the American and British navies, in which I would spend the next six-plus years of my life.

Except for Japan's adventures in China and Italy's recent invasion of Ethiopia, there was not then much discernible sign in the whole world of the bloody war to come—certainly not in my innocent country boy's mind at the time. The only apprehension I felt was that of leaving one's home and family for the first time. I was leaving behind everything of love and comfort and support I could remember in my life—for a future I knew absolutely nothing about.

My father and stepmother Cora—out of a misguided sense of loyalty to my dead mother, I unforgivably refused to call Cora anything other than her name, although I knew she longed to be called Mother—and my two sisters, Flora and Zena Mae, had come to Tulsa's then neat and glistening Union Station to see me off to the Navy. Recruiting Chief Petty Officer C. L. Barnett was there as well, but he was decent enough to stand to one side and leave us alone for our final few minutes together.

Dad did not wear his suit; instead he wore a clean shirt with a necktie—and the hard, flat-brimmed straw hat he was never without in summer. Cora wore her best print dress. Her thinning red hair was still damp from being spit curled in my honor. Her sentimental Irish eyes were wet, and she held close to me in a kind

1

of desperate effort to put off the inevitable for as long as she could. Flo, then only eighteen, and Zena Mae, fourteen, stood to one side, saying little but watching me as though expecting me to vanish into thin air even before the train arrived.

We were a few minutes early. We were always early for things because Dad was never sure his old car would start—or how far it would go if it did. I don't think he even owned a watch. It was probably long since hocked. As was usual in our little family, words did not come easy in the waiting. People in the Oklahoma of that time were not demonstrative. I am sure we all felt the pain of parting, but none of us could find a way to put it into words. At least I had the excitement of the coming unknown to lighten me, but the others had nothing but the prospect of depression and Dust Bowl–era hard times staring them in their faces—and without whatever support and comfort I had ever been able to bring them.

There, too, was the unspoken thought of dangers to come. The American submarine *Squalus* had sunk only a few days before and a number of sailors had lost their lives. Dad had brought up the subject the night before I left and had used it in one last try to have me stay home. He did not mention it that morning at the station, but I knew it was in his mind. He wanted me to stay home and learn his painter's trade.

The waiting was spent mostly in uneasy silence as we groped for things to say, knowing that if we did slip into any expression of love or of the loneliness to come we might lose control and display emotions that some people might see as normal but that we, I suspect, would have seen as weakness.

It was a great relief when the train did come. The big black locomotive rolled slowly past, the bell tolling and warm wet steam spewing over our legs, causing the platform itself to tremble. Flo and Zena pressed close to Dad, and Cora clutched me harder than ever. My resolve to go took a sudden, sickening dive. The thought of running away to sea became not nearly so exciting.

Chief Barnett handed me a manila envelope printed with the Navy seal—the first of many such official packets I would see in the years to come. The Navy would meet me in Dallas, he said. He wished me luck and stepped back again to let us say our family good-byes. Cora was openly crying by that time, and Flo and Zena pressed even closer to Dad, staring at the waiting train as though it were some huge black monster fixing to swallow their only brother. Dad smiled at me, and we shook hands. "Be careful, Son," he said. "Don't volunteer for anything."

That was the sum of Dad's advice from his experience in the Army during World War I, and he gave it to me freely. He also left a wadded five-dollar bill in my hand as he backed away. That brought my capital to seven dollars and fifty-five cents, a sum that would have to see me through until I arrived in San Diego and drew my first month's Navy pay—twenty-one dollars, less twenty cents or so as a hospitalization fee.

I quickly boarded the train—the first train I ever rode—and took a seat from which I could see all the love and warmth there was for me in the world, huddled together as it was on the platform outside. But already I was cut off from my family by the thick sealed glass of the train window and could not hear anything they said. We smiled to each other through the glass and made little, tentative waving motions with our hands.

I longed for the train to move, anything to put an end to the strain. I did not know how much longer I could hold the pose of brave young man setting out into a strange and possibly threatening world. But when the train did start, it was in such a smoothly effortless glide that its movement became apparent only when my family slipped silently backward, out of sight. A sudden panic struck hard in me, and I half rose from my seat. But it was too late by that time. The train was moving. I was on my way. I had never felt so alone in my life.

Even now, a half century and more later, I can remember the awful sense of desolation that came over me. Not least of all I felt a great sense of guilt for deserting the only people in the world I loved. Mama had died almost ten years before, and Cora, a woman with the biggest heart I ever knew in a human being, had come into our lives to marry Dad and to make it possible for us to stay together as a family. The Depression, although none of us knew it at the time, was beginning to come to an end, under the impetus of rearmament. We had lived through the worst of the hard times, and now that things were about to become better, I was running off and leaving my family to live or die on its own. I was not proud of myself.

Dad had provided for us by working at whatever menial jobs he could get. I can remember his walking—his old car long since gone—the six long miles home from Tulsa with a sack of what was then called relief food over his shoulder—flour, cornmeal, and sugar in cloth bags; lard; and canned meat in bronze-colored cans that we would bury when they were empty so there would be no betraying sign in our garbage of the fact we were on relief.

Cora had worked, too, at whatever she could find. She was a good cook and had worked at one time in the cook shacks of early day Idaho lumber camps. She cooked and scrimped and made do for us. Our underwear, for instance, she made for us from empty flour sacks. She even pawned, and never saw again, her beloved rings, the pitifully small store of jewelry she had had before marrying Dad. For Decoration Day, she gathered wildflowers and made them into pretty wreaths and sprays for our real mother's grave, though out of delicacy she would not go to the cemetery with us.

Even Flo and Zena worked. They picked fruit and berries on neighboring farms. Blackberries and strawberries were the hardest, blackberries because of their thorns and strawberries because they grew so low to the ground. I had a newspaper route and did whatever else I could find to do. Sometimes I helped Dad cut firewood for sale in Tulsa. And when he did find work as a painter I helped him with that too.

In this way we found it possible to see me through my freshman year at the University of Tulsa. I worked on campus in a federal program painting campus buildings, for the most part, in order to earn my tuition for the following year. I also ran an elevator at the Tulsa *Tribune* and sometimes wrote small things for money. But there were still times when I had to ask Dad for money for books and lab fees and other incidentals. He never failed to help me however he could, although he did not really want me to go to college. As I have said, he wanted me to stay in Tulsa and learn a trade, preferably his own trade of house painting and paperhanging.

Despite all this, however, the strain proved too much, and I dropped out of college after only one year. The elevator work at the *Tribune* had grown into a full-time job on the paper's wire desk, but that ended early on because the editor had to let someone go. All the other men in the newsroom had wives and children to support. I was the only one in the office without dependents. That was often how it was done during the Depression: the man without dependents was the one to go.

The only other job I could get after months of looking for work was clerking in a Safeway grocery store—at eighteen dollars a week for six twelve-hour days. We worked even longer hours on Saturdays, when produce bins had to be cleaned after the store closed.

Worst of all, there was no indication in the world that anything would ever be different. I was going to spend the rest of my life stacking cans, piling bags, and sweeping sawdust-covered wooden floors. It is not all that hard for me now to understand the frustration and despair felt today by young people in our inner cities. There were times, I think now, when I might have been induced to shoot somebody.

Around this time a professor at the University of Tulsa told me about a Navy program that saw a hundred enlisted men taken each year from the fleet for enrollment in the Naval Academy at Annapolis. I lacked the family contacts for an appointment to the Academy or the education to pass competitive examinations, but I had demonstrated a fair academic facility in high school and my freshman year in college and the Navy provided special prep schools for the enlisted men it selected. The professor felt I stood a better than average chance. Given my frustration in the grocery industry, I did not much care what my chances were; I would take them.

I began to haunt Chief Barnett's recruiting office on the second floor of Tulsa's old post office building on South Boulder Avenue. I hated the Safeway store with an irrational passion, and I was then romantic enough to see running off to sea as a perfect solution to all my problems. I had read every Joseph Conrad and Jack London book ever printed, I suppose, and was completely enamored of everything to do with the sea. That I was utterly ignorant of any water bigger than Bird Creek or Tulsa's Mohawk Lake did not slow me down at all.

But Chief Barnett did. It was not easy to get into the Navy in those days. There were fewer than 90,000 officers and men in the entire Navy then, he said, and those who were in were not getting out. The Navy could pick and choose, and Chief Barnett made it clear it was not likely to pick me, given a choice. I was far under the weight required. My chest expansion did not measure up either, and my ribs were deformed from the effects of the childhood disease rickets. Most damning of all, I had an all but disabling speech impediment.

For more than a year, I ate everything I could get my hands on. I spent hours chinning myself to build up my chest measurements, and I drove people crazy by talking with my mouth full of marbles because someone had told me it would help my stuttering. Ironically, it was this long delay that resulted in my not going to Annapolis, for I was too old for the Academy when I did get into the Navy.

Despite all my trying, I could not meet the Navy's physical standards. I did get my weight close. My chest expansion was nearly enough. And I could speak without stuttering if I talked slowly enough and concentrated hard enough. But I was still not what the Navy, in its infinite wisdom, was looking for in the way of seagoing warriors.

I had all but given up and was thinking of hopping a freight train for California—or anywhere else—when, on May 24, 1939, I received a penny postcard announcing my acceptance. I thought then that Chief Barnett had probably felt sorry for me, but a more likely explanation is that the Navy was beginning its expansion for the war and had lowered its standards. Regardless, I was in! I can still remember the feeling of escape that swept over me as I read that postcard—and the gloating elation I felt upon telling a certain Safeway store manager what he could do with his store, if he had the anatomical capacity for it. I had never felt so free in my life.

From that day until the morning I boarded the train in Tulsa, I thought of nothing else but my own satisfaction in at last getting away. I didn't give a thought to Dad and Cora and Flo and Zena Mae. It was sheer selfish exultation—until I saw them huddled together on the station platform and slipping out of my sight as the train began to move.

Then I felt guilt in all its tormenting forms for running away and leaving them after all they had done for me. The train moved slowly past the backsides of buildings and weed-grown vacant lots, all the trashy things American towns showed then to rail passengers. I sank lower and lower in my seat.

It was not until the train rumbled out onto the bridge over the Arkansas River—an appropriately gloomy sound that I am reminded of now when I hear stage scenery being moved about behind drawn curtains—that I realized the full enormity of what I had done. That rumbling sound seemed to cut off with a terrible finality all that was known and familiar to me in the world, leaving a dark and menacing future among strange and uncaring people. But I was young then, and the young do not long feel guilt. (They will feel it later, but it does not last long at the time.) It helped when the conductor took my Navy voucher and joked with me about joining the Navy. Nearby passengers looked at me with open interest then, and I began to feel a little better.

It was the first time in my life that strangers had looked at me as though I might be human. Some of them even smiled at me. I pretended not to notice, but it felt good to see them do that. I was going thousands of miles away and would see oceans and ships and foreign lands. The people on the train were going to stay right there in Oklahoma. Some of them would probably even work in grocery stores.

I began to take some interest in the country outside my window. It was early summer. Everything was still fresh and green with new growth, not yet seared and dusty with Oklahoma's hot summer sun and winds. It was not much different from the country where I had grown up, rolling wooded hills with slow brown rivers sunk deep in muddy banks. But it was an increasingly poor country as we went south. Few farm buildings showed sign of ever having been painted. Fences were down in many places. Some fields were not planted at all, and others were cruelly gashed by uncontrolled erosion.

There were still horse-drawn wagons to be seen on the roads of Oklahoma then, and teams of horses working in the fields. There were few tractors and not many trucks. Men at work in the fields moved slowly and did not look up as we went past. Only the young paid much attention to the train. New colts and calves raced away with their tails in the air, and children waved and shouted silent shouts beyond the insulating window glass.

One thing I remember most clearly is the sight of people walking the country roads. Few roads were paved then. Fence rows and roadside ditches were overgrown with weeds and young hackberry trees. People walked singly or in groups of as many as four or five at a time. A lot of them carried sacks over their shoulders or bundles in their arms. As many seemed to be going in one direction as in another.

I had seen photographs of primitive peoples in *National Geographic* magazines in TU's McFarlin Library. The people I saw that morning in Oklahoma looked much like those I had seen in the magazine pictures. Seen through the occasional clouds of steam and smoke that swept past my window, the country seemed already exotic and foreign to me.

The towns we passed through were strange too. I had passed that way in an Army truck during my time in the National Guard, but on that passage we had usually skirted the main parts of town. Trains, on the other hand, stopped in those days in the middle of small towns. Passengers could see the wide, empty streets with cars angled into curbside parking places like tethered horses, and people idly strolling the sidewalks or standing in groups to talk.

The towns themselves during the Depression were slow and lacking in life. Cars were dull with dust and caked-on mud from unpaved roads. Men were colorless in faded blue bib overalls, and women drab in print dresses gone limp from too many washings. About the only animation showing at all was that at the railway station itself. People came to see who was coming or going or simply on the off chance that something might happen. They stared curiously at those of us they could see behind our windows, as though we were specimens of some kind. I would later see people stare at fish in aquariums in much the same way.

Through the thick glass of the train window nothing could be heard, of course. It all looked detached and sterile, and I came to feel that I was already a long way from home, although I was not really far at all. And Dallas, when we came to it, seemed little different from Tulsa. It was larger, I suppose, but the streets and the buildings and the residential areas we passed through seemed much like those in Tulsa. The railway station was not even as nice as Tulsa's neat little gem.

A Navy sailor in whites collected me and added me to a group of four or five others who got off the same train I had been on. They must have been on the train before I boarded or got on somewhere along the way without my noticing. The sailor recognized us by the manila envelopes we carried, I suppose, for we had nothing else in common that I could see. Without the official envelopes we would have been like any other group of young men of the time, dressed in poor clothes and wearing puzzled expressions of mingled dread and excitement.

The Navy's main recruiting station for the region was in Dallas. It was there we would actually be taken into the Navy. The office in Tulsa had been merely a substation. Since there had been no doctor in Tulsa, my physical there was perfunctory at best. We would get our final physical examination in Dallas before we were officially accepted into the Navy. There was still a chance we would be rejected.

We met still more recruits at the Dallas recruiting station itself until there were some fifteen or twenty of us. We were processed smoothly, almost mechanically. A real doctor examined us, and enlisted men in spotless whites entered us onto the paper forms, which, though we did not know it then, would measure and regulate our lives as long as we were in the Navy. There was about as much warmth and human feeling in it all as there had been in the Safeway butcher's checking in of his morning's meat delivery.

The mood changed, though, when the mechanics were completed. The doctor rejected two of us for some unannounced reason, but a full lieutenant in dress blues, brass buttons, and golden stripes emerged from an inner office and gave the rest of us the oath of enlistment. He was a tall, well setup man of impressive dignity. I looked hungrily at his fine uniform, thinking already of the time when I would wear a uniform like his. My heart swelled, and the frustration and anger of my life to that time fell away.

The lieutenant gave us a little speech before he administered the oath. I bought it all, lock, stock, and barrel. He reminded us of the great and noble calling into which we were entering for the service of God and country. He talked about the grandeur of sacrifice and duty. And he did it all as though he really meant it. His simple faith might well be questioned now, in light of modern thinking, but then it all seemed reasonable and very much worth doing.

There was a dramatic pause before the oath itself was administered. The office became still, and the sailors working there waited in silence out of respect for the great event taking place. Even the typewriters fell silent. The lieutenant cleared his throat and looked at each of us in turn. I no longer remember the actual words, but the feeling is still warm in me at the thought my great country was willing to trust me with the awesome responsibilities of an apprentice seaman in the U.S. Navy—and was going to feed and bed me, and pay me twenty-one dollars a month besides!

In return I was asked only to be willing to expose myself to unknown forms of death, mutilation, and extreme discomfort at any time my lawful superiors thought fit to order it—orders I agreed never to question and to obey no matter the cost or peril to my own precious body. In the heedless rush of the young, I did not think it a bad bargain at all. It beat the hell out of Safeway grocery stores, for one thing. Of course, it never occurred to me that I might someday actually be exposed to any of that bad stuff. War was the furthest possible thing from my mind.

By the time it was all done, it was late afternoon, and a good deal of time still remained before our train would leave for San Diego. The Navy, already accepting its duty toward its newest members, treated us to a swim in a nearby YMCA pool—and fed us a good restaurant meal. All my troubles in becoming accepted were beginning to seem more and more worthwhile.

Of course, I did not then, nor do I now, know how to swim—but the big indoor pool was impressive. At Tulsa I had helped paint the pool room in Harwell Gymnasium, but I had never gone into the water. The pool was drained while we were painting, and I was always too shy to go into the water while I was a student, even if I had had a bathing suit.

That was another thing: In the Dallas Y, none of us had swimsuits. We went in bare as radishes. Oddly, I was not the only one who was uncomfortable taking off my clothes in front of all those strangers. The boys I had grown up with in Osage County and I had sometimes gone naked into the cow ponds and muddy pools of Flat Rock Creek, but that was with friends and out in the open air. It was different, somehow, to be naked indoors and with a lot of guys I did not know. Besides, the water was so clear and clean it seemed wrong to get into it naked.

Any sensitivity to male nudity any of us may have had was something the Navy took care of entirely before it was through with us. From that day on, our bathing, clothes laundering, and even sitting on the toilet trough were done in full public view and naked as jaybirds, in the country vernacular. We would see and be seen in all our physical glory, whatever it might be.

With the exception of two or three loners, we quickly warmed to each other in the shared excitement of adventure and our common fate in an unknown future. We learned each other's names and where we came from. The restaurant meal that followed the swimming—our first naval dinner—took on a party feeling of easy talking and laughing and self-conscious posturing before the civilians eating there with us. We talked and laughed too loud, I suppose, but at least we could laugh. There was something exhilarating in the realization that we need not ever again be hungry. Nor worry for fear we could not pay for food. The lifting of personal responsibility was exciting in a way.

The Texas and Pacific—called the T&P everywhere in Texas—train we boarded sometime that night was pulled by a big black steam locomotive like the one for the train I had ridden from Tulsa to Dallas. We were put into a Pullman car of our own for the long ride to the West Coast. We did not know then just how long it would be, but we would not have cared anyway. We already were on the Navy's payroll, and someone was going to feed us when we became hungry and provide a bed when we grew tired. To us, nothing else much mattered. Again, I felt freedom from personal responsibility as an almost physical release. It is hard now to remember how strong that feeling was.

It had been a long and wearing day. Most of us, I think, were ready when the porter came to make up our berths. I know I was. It seemed days ago that I had risen from my pallet on the floor of our little house in the Bird Creek bottoms north of Tulsa. There had been then the sounds of birds and cows and oil field pump stations. Now it was the clack and clatter of a train on rough Texas tracks. Even the bitter memory of saying good-bye on the Tulsa station platform seemed a long time ago. Each new experience had erased, in part, what had gone before. And, strangely, each new experience fired a hunger for what would come next.

I was lucky enough to draw a lower berth—there were not nearly enough of us to fill the car—and could lie, once the lights were out, and watch the passing country outside. Of course, since it was Texas, there was not much to see. Just seemingly endless miles of dark nothingness, with, now and then, a dim and lonely window of yellow lamp light or the almost equally lonely lights of small and dusty towns, where we would stop for far longer than seemed justified.

I wanted to stay awake longer, but sleep did come finally and I woke only once during the night. I was unsure, for a time, where I was. The clattering racket of the car and its rough up-and-down and hard side-to-side motion made the whole world seem a strange and violent place. Once I put my head out through the green curtains of the berth with its crisply clean sheets and looked along the long and dimly lighted aisle, where the curtains of other berths swayed and bulged to either side like shifting and unsteady walls of a hallway through a dark and vaguely menacing underworld.

Uneasy, I pulled back into my berth and looked out the window for reassurance. But there was none there. We were then, I suppose, somewhere out onto the great empty mesquite plains of Texas, where there was less to see even than before. Memories of home and family, reborn of my sudden fears, struck hard then, and I found myself crying for what seemed lost. I was grateful for the train noises, which would mask my sobbing and keep the others from hearing. And, without knowing exactly when, I went back to sleep.

The next morning we were out onto open grasslands with little to do until lunchtime. None of us had thought to bring books or other amusements. Someone had brought a deck of cards, though, and a game was started that lasted more or less continuously until we reached Los Angeles. Few of us had any money, and what there was quickly found its way into the hands of three or four men who then had to play for it among themselves. The rest of us became spectators.

Watching the endless country was amusement enough for me. It had never occurred to me that the world beyond Oklahoma's Osage County could be so big. We would go for miles sometimes in a perfectly straight line; the land was so flat no curves at all were needed to maintain a grade. Late in the afternoon, when we neared El Paso, the land finally did begin to rise and change in ways that were new to us. The grass grew even shorter and its clumps became farther and farther apart, leaving expanses of bare dry ground with no cover at all. And, far off beyond the horizon, we saw mountains stained blue by distance.

Here and there we could see adobes, small, flat-roofed, and square houses, looking as though they had grown out of the earth—as, in fact, they had in a sense. They were made of earthen blocks dug from the ground and dried in the sun. Sometimes we saw people, either on poorish horses or walking the hard ground.

Closer to El Paso the houses became more and more frequent. Some of them were made of wood, and there were roads we could see. There were even occasional cars and trucks, each streaming a boiling horizontal plume of white dust behind it.

El Paso itself was unlike Dallas or Tulsa, dribbled down as it was on the slopes of hills flanking the Rio Grande. Its central buildings were solid piles of real bricks and cut stone, with frequent white stone trims arched like startled eyebrows over doors and windows. Lawns, where there were any, were dry, flowerless, and softened only by the thin shade of scattered cottonwoods and other dry-country trees and shrubs.

The most exciting thing for me was that, on the other side of the unimpressive river, the mountains of Mexico rose into a dusty sky. They were tawny brown slopes fading off into the pale blue of distance. Juarez, a town then much smaller than El Paso, huddled its dun-colored clutter at the far end of an international bridge. All of it was colorless and lacking in the drama and excitement I had always dreamed of as the mark of an alien land. But it was my first foreign country, and a fevered imagination can build its own drama from the most unpromising materials. I looked on Mexico that day with far more interest than I would feel for the truly exotic lands I would later see.

As it happened, we had some hours before our train continued on. The man in charge of us—another recruit, but much older, probably in his mid- to late twenties—had been in the Army before, I think. He warned us to be careful and—especially—not to go over into Mexico. He could have said nothing, of course, more likely to get us to do just that.

The streets of El Paso were eye-openers for us. Spanish was heard almost as often as English, and dark Mexican faces were everywhere. The clothes we saw were far different too from the faded blue bib overalls and washed-out print dresses of Oklahoma. We felt ourselves to be a long way from home, especially when we were on the streets of Juarez. It felt good—and safe—to be back again on our own side of the river.

Our leader had done a good job of warning us off the Mexicans. They all carried knives, he said, and were both willing and able to use them. They were especially touchy, he warned us, about their women. This, of course, made the girls' flashing black eyes and challenging smiles all the more attractive for us, but our time was short and his warnings were not put to the test of time. How long they would have held up otherwise, I do not know, for the girls were pretty.

We did, in fact, suffer our first casualties in El Paso. Two of us failed to return to the train on time and were left behind. Whether they had decided the Navy life was not for them or had simply became lost, I don't know. We never saw them again, but I was convinced in my own mind that their lifeless bodies were lying in some Juarez alley, still bleeding from the wounds of vengeful Mexican knives. Imagination can be fun sometimes. Scary too.

That night the way west from El Paso was through rough mountains that showed as shifting and shadowy forms through the train windows, now close, now far away across open plains. In the dim light they seemed more rugged probably than they were. I found them fascinating and watched them for hours.

The others, though, after our stop in El Paso, were more rambunctious, probably emboldened by their first liberty in a foreign land. Some of them had even come up with small bottles of cheap whiskey. There really wasn't enough of it to make anyone drunk, but they certainly acted drunk.

New sailors were apt to do that, I learned. Aboard ship, I later saw it happen time and again: A young sailor would be perfectly sober until coming in sight of ship or landing, then he would become staggeringly drunk and disorderly, wanting to appear to be a real sailor. The Navy called it smoke-stacking and punished it lightly in recognition of the frailty of human nature.

We were punished more severely on the train. The porters were given such a bad time they refused to come into our car to make up the berths. We could live with that. We were used to sleeping in far worse places than an unmade Pullman berth. But when the air-conditioning failed, no one would come to repair it. We suffered.

It was June and we were just then entering the real desert. The car became a sweat box. In self-defense we forced open the windows, but that didn't work either. Instead of a relatively clean sweat box, we had a very dirty sweat box. Cinders and small rocks, bird feathers, and bits of weeds and grass blew in on us. It was unpleasant.

And it stayed unpleasant all the way to Los Angeles, then still two or three days away, as I recall. It was a slow train. Our introduction to the desert was much more realistic than we would have liked, given a choice. But there was nothing we could do about it. The only relief we found was at mealtime, when we could enjoy the dining car—briefly. The trainmen wouldn't allow us in there any longer than they had to.

The only place I had ever seen deserts before was in cowboy movies. I watched them from the balcony in Tulsa's old Lyric theater at the corner of First and Main streets. Those deserts were all in grainy black and white. The one I saw from the train was full of subtle color, but you had to look close to see it. The deserts in the movies were not hot or dirty either. The one we saw from the train was both hot and very dirty. I don't like deserts, but the one I saw from the train was impressive to my first-time eyes, especially so at night when the air cooled rapidly and the stars seemed unnaturally bright and close to earth.

I remember now few of the details of that awful ride. I do remember, after all this time, one mountain far off to the south with a Christian cross of snow caught in rock crevices near its top. I thought it was cool, in the vernacular of a later time, to see snow from the heat and dust of a desert.

I remember, too, seeing the Salton Sea. I had never seen so much water in my life. We were told it was saltier than the oceans themselves. And it was all the more dramatic for being right there in the middle of a desert. We rode along its north shore for what seemed a long time. (Everything seemed to be a long time on that ride.) I remember thinking that if the ocean was bigger than the Salton Sea, it must be really big. But one of us who had seen the ocean said the Salton Sea was nothing. We could see land all around it. On the ocean, you couldn't see land anywhere.

I didn't know whether to believe that or not, but the Salton Sea was big. And it was in California. That meant Los Angeles could not be far away. So far, though, the only difference we could see in the environment was that the desert was hotter and drier than ever. We saw the weird forms of Joshua trees and saguaro cactus and jumbled masses of huge rocks. And, always, in the far distance, blue mountains.

Towns soon became larger and closer together. We came into areas of irrigated farmlands whose bright green crops were like soothing salve to our desert-burned eyes. The towns had watered lawns and large beds of blooming flowers. Tall Imperial palms reared high and straight in the sky. This was more like it.

The near approaches to Los Angeles seemed even more exotic to us. The train made its slow way through mile after mile of orange groves and other watered crops. We could even see oranges on the trees. Snow-capped mountains looked down on us from the distance. The towns became small cities of broad palm-lined streets and beautiful gardens filled with flowers, all of which were strange to us. These cities turned, imperceptibly, into the outskirts of Los Angeles itself.

Union Station in Los Angeles was a culmination of all the wonders we had seen. Kept spotlessly clean and finished in a stucco mass of walls of some soft buff color, it was the biggest building I had ever seen. We were told sixty-four tracks came into Union Station. Little patios and gardens were scattered through it, with living orange trees and other strange-to-us plants. There were benches where people could sit apart from the hustle and bustle.

And there was hustle and bustle. People were coming and going in all directions and in all conditions of dress and manner. A streamliner, all bright and shining with stainless steel, arrived on the track next to ours, and a mob of newspapermen and cameramen with their big square Speed Graphics ran toward it, knocking people right and left. Some movie star, we were told, was coming in from the East. We gawked and craned our necks but could see nothing but the backs of the newsmen. At any rate, we were where things were happening. We would never have seen anything like that in Tulsa or Dallas.

Again, we had time before our train left for San Diego. Why should Los Angeles be different? We went out into the bright California sun, not as bright as the desert sun we had been blinking into for so long maybe, but bright enough. Olivera Street, a Mexican shopping district, was not far away. One of our group had been to Los Angeles before. He told us about Olivera Street and showed us the way.

Olivera Street was like a carnival, with booths everywhere and music and good-natured people and the quick rattling of Spanish all around us. The sightseeing was fun, but I, for one, was getting tired and wanted to get to San Diego. We had been on the way some three or four days, but it seemed much longer. I was dirty and well-sweated. I went back to the station and waited there for our train.

San Diego lies only a hundred miles or so south of Los Angeles, and we had a fast Santa Fe streamliner for that leg of our long journey. It did not take long, once we got under way. Anticipation was building in all of us by that time, and we came into San Diego's Spanish-style station at the foot of Broadway in a state of more or less controlled excitement. We would soon know, for good or bad, what we had gotten ourselves into.

Even from the train we could see streets running with sailors and Marines in uniform—our first Marines. They looked clean and well fed and moved confidently when contrasted with our little group's shambling gait and lazy posture. They were different in some hard-to-define way. Even more interesting for me, though, was the bay on the far side of a broad waterfront boulevard. The dim blue hump of Point Loma rode on the western horizon, with just the merest sight of the ocean itself over the end of North Island. It was not much, but I had seen it. I had seen the ocean I had dreamed about for so long.

Still more eye-catching, a nest of what I would later know as Bird-class minesweepers lay moored to the wharf. There were four of them, all spotlessly clean in the Navy's peacetime haze gray with the round tricolor roundel of the Mine Force and individual numbers on their bows. Bright pennants and flags fluttered from their masts and signal yards. They were among the humblest of the Navy's ships, but to me, they glistened as a mighty fleet and the men in dungarees working about their decks were gallant seamen. I felt a catch in my throat at the sight of the little ships. In memory, I can see them still as they were then.

Larger ships—some of the old four-stacker light cruisers and an auxiliary or two—were anchored offshore, but those four little minesweepers were the first Navy ships I ever saw and the ones that now remain most vivid in my recollection.

There was little time for such thoughts, though. Gray Navy buses from the training station—an installation we would come to know as boot camp—were waiting for us, and we boarded them to a chorus of boos and cries of "Suckers!" and "You'll be sorry!" from passing sailors in the street. We were in the Navy! At long last, I was in the Navy.

2
Boot Camp

IF THE SOUND OF TRAIN WHEELS on a bridge in Oklahoma can be taken as an omen of the new scenery being set for the coming drama of my life, the curtain rose for that play on the Main Gate of the U.S. Naval Training Station in San Diego in June 1939. I saw that gate for the first time from the windows of the bus that brought us there from the railway station.

It was the first of many such gates I would know in the Navy, but no other was ever so grand for me. It was flanked to either side by two small, square, tile-roofed stucco buildings connected by an ornamental wrought-iron arch over the roadway itself. These small buildings were flanked in turn by larger structures with graceful arched windows. A highly polished brass plaque on each of the two gatehouses announced the place as a naval station. Decorative iron lamps with amber-colored lenses added a formal note. A long oval of lawns and flowering beds, bordered by streets lined with what for me were exotic trees—palms and eucalyptus—and clipped shrubbery. It was the most beautiful place I had ever seen. It was prettier than the prettiest cemetery I had ever seen in Oklahoma.

The gate was the duty station for the officer of the deck and his various assistants, all in immaculate uniforms and carrying themselves with a taut military formality that made it clear this was a serious place. We paused only long enough for our papers to be filed with the officer of the deck. (The Navy refers to officers in charge, even on shore stations, as officers of the deck.) We were then driven directly to South Unit, a quarantine area that we would not be permitted to leave for four weeks—long enough to be certain we had not brought with us any diseases that might infect our betters. The definition of "betters" was anyone who had been in the Navy longer than we had been, even if only by days or hours.

The station grounds we rode through were all as impressive as those by the Main Gate itself. Barracks and classrooms were good solid two-story buildings of the same buff stucco of the gatehouses. All were spotlessly clean and roofed with heavy red tiles. Each individual building was joined to the next by arched arcades to form a continuous walkway along which men could walk dry-shod in any weather. We shared the streets with bodies of marching sailors, and whole companies drilled on the parade grounds. We could hear the shouted orders of instructors and the thumping beat of drums.

Everything was ordered and clean and beautifully secure—all adjectives I had seldom known in my life before. I felt a sudden, strange warm feeling of being at home. It was interesting that most sailors saw the high chain-link fences around naval installations as meant to keep them in. I always saw them as intended to keep the rest of the world out.

Everywhere we went on the station that day we were met by the same raucous cries of "Suckers!" or "You'll be sorry!" we had heard at the San Diego railway station. It was all good-natured ribbing, though. We took comfort from the knowledge that, within a few days, we would be able to yell the same things to those poor souls who would follow us.

South Unit was not so beautifully landscaped and maintained as was the main part of the station. It was more spartan, more like a military base might be expected to be. There were barracks, mess halls, lecture rooms, a gym with a big swimming pool, playing fields, and a paved parade ground we would get to know very well as "the grinder."

By the time we climbed down from our buses, it was late afternoon, and the Navy was content simply to feed us and to bed us down for the night. Everything else would have to wait for the next day, which promised to be long and busy.

The supper was good, although it was served cafeteria style. Dinner was "supper" in the Navy, we learned. That was no change for most of us country boys for whom dinner was always at noon anyway. The most impressive thing to me was that we could eat all we wanted. The only requirement was that we ate everything we took. The order was "Take all you want, but eat all you take." For those of us used to living on nickel Cokes and ten-cent hamburgers, the effect was boggling. Fresh milk, by the quart if we wanted it, was in itself impressive. As Cora used to say to us kids when we did have enough to eat at home, my eyes were bigger than my stomach. I had a hard time finishing off all the food I took on my tray. Some of us ate so much we were sick. Our bellies were just not used to being so full.

The Navy was quick, though, to let us know we were not there as guests. We were all told off to one duty or another in the big galley and mess hall. "Galley" is the Navy's word for kitchen. I drew the chore of shelling and veining shrimp into a big stainless steel pot. I had never seen shrimp before. They looked something like the crawdads we had in Oklahoma, except they had no claws and there was more meat to them.

After supper, I remember nothing until bedtime. We were all young then and well screened for good health, but it had been a long and stressful day. And the following days, we suspected, were going to be just as trying. We were ready to turn in. I know I was.

That first night in the Navy we slept in double-deck bunks with wire springs, but the next day we were issued hammocks—sailors then slept in hammocks. They were made of stiff white canvas, suspended from cord clews coming to single points at either end. A thin cotton mattress was provided, with a slip-over cover rather than sheets. Two beautiful blue-banded white wool blankets and a simple pillow completed our bedding, all of which could be rolled tight and secured with a length of new manila line provided for the purpose. With what sometimes seemed rare naval logic, this line was called a hammock lashing.

Once we had our seabags, our hammocks could be bent and lashed about them to make a single bundle of all our worldly goods, with our galvanized iron laundry and/or bath buckets dangling from one end. Within fifteen minutes of first notice, we could be standing at the gangway of our ships, ready in all respects to leave on whatever duty the Navy, in its wisdom, might assign us. We traveled light.

That length of manila hammock lashing, incidentally, coiled and struck without warning to bring me my first naval disciplinary punishment.

As our company commander, a veteran chief torpedoman, told us on our first complete day in the Navy, there are three ways of doing anything in the world: the right way, the wrong way, and the Navy way. We were expected to do things the Navy way. The lashing of our hammocks was no exception.

There was an eye splice in one end of the hammock lashing. In lashing your hammock the Navy way, this loop was positioned near one end of the rolled hammock. The other end of the lashing was passed through the loop, hauled taut, and then, in eight evenly spaced hitches—again logically called hammock hitches—snugged home to make a long, tight, cigar shaped bundle.

In complete innocence—and even more complete ignorance—I committed the terrible sin of passing the running part of the lashing under the standing part when it should have been passed over that part—or vice versa—I don't remember which now. I could not see that it made much difference or that it posed much of a threat to the security of the United States one way or the other. Our newly appointed company commander could, though. He did a marvelous imitation of a man in the early stages of apoplexy at my terrible error. It was clear I would have to be punished.

Another thing we did with our hammocks, other than lashing the damned things—and trying to sleep in them—was airing them. Every day, weather permitting, we opened out our bedding and arranged it over a jackstay in the open air. (A jackstay is a horizontal metal pipe.) This was a sanitary measure, and naturally, it had to be done in the Navy way too.

The chief decided that, in penance for my error in hammock lashing, I should lash, unlash, air, and lash again my bedding—all night long. I was to do this by taking my bedding down to the barracks yard, rigging it for airing, getting the duty officer to inspect and approve the job, then taking it back inside, lashing it again, and getting the duty officer to inspect and approve that too. And I was to do that over and over the whole damned night. This interfered with my getting a good night's sleep.

Old-time sailors will remember that new manila line was hard and stiff. By the time dawn came my hands were raw and bleeding from tugging and pulling on my hammock lashing. I knew, too, that I would be held accountable for the blood on my bright new hammock. After all, it was my blood. Some doubts did enter my mind that night about the wisdom of choosing a career in the Navy, but I never again lashed a hammock in any way but the Navy way.

At any rate, we were all sorted out the next day. We were formed into Recruit Company 39-13. (This meant we were the 13th Company to be processed at San Diego in the year 1939.) We were assigned one of the two-story barracks buildings, with the First Platoon on the ground floor and the Second Platoon upstairs. (There were two platoons in a company.) The barracks were large, airy, and empty rooms, spotlessly clean, with glistening waxed floors—called decks in the Navy—which we would learn, once we started falling out of our hammocks, were very, very hard.

The only furniture as such were some scrubbed wooden tables and benches down the center, where we were supposed to write letters, play games, or do rudimentary pressing with a provided electric iron in our spare time. This was all thoughtful as hell—except for the fact that we had no spare time. Wooden rifle racks were fitted near the door. The remainder of the furniture was two series of jackstays, one high and one low, from which we were to sling our hammocks and seabags. The stays for hammocks were about six feet off the floor—sorry! deck—high enough to account for a number of broken arms and other wounds until we got the hang of getting into—and staying in—our hammocks. The stays for seabags were about four feet off the deck, as I recall.

We hardly had time to appreciate the luxuriousness of our new house before we were shouted out to start a frantic round of physicals, haircuts, inoculations, dental examinations, uniform issues—all compressed on a human (?) assembly line urged on and kept moving by petty officers and chiefs who did not exhaust themselves by trying to hide their contempt for us. All movement was at the run, most conversation was shouted, and our inevitable goofs were met with withering impatience and creative punishments.

At boot camp I first heard the Navy chief's ominous pronouncement, "Maybe I can't make you do that, son, but I can sure as hell make you wish you had." I would hear it again from time to time, until I was made a chief myself.

Once we had our Navy clothes, we were given brown cardboard grocery store boxes—shades of Safeway—and the opportunity to send our civilian clothes home—at our own expense. Most of us didn't have enough of value to make sending it home worth the trouble, but to please Cora, I had worn my high school graduation suit of cheap wool in a chalk-striped black, with a pleated back and a half-belt that nipped it in at the waist behind. I never knew what Dad had had to do to buy that suit, but I sent it home. I couldn't bring myself to throw it away.

Thus, we became creatures of the Navy, made as nearly alike, at least in appearance, as possible without surgery. The haircuts, incidentally, did come close to surgery. "Hair removal" would have been a more accurate term. The barbershop floor became ankle deep in hair of every conceivable color and texture—except for kinky black. There wasn't much kinky black in the Navy of those days. We came out feeling light-headed and strangely cool on top.

There must have been breaks sometime during that day, for meals and visits to the "head," which, we learned, was the Navy's word for toilet, but I don't remember them if there were. It all became a big blur that ended that night with us standing bemused, showered, fed, shorn, and apprehensive beside the hammocks into which we were expected somehow to lift ourselves in defiance of gravity and all common sense.

Our new seabags, heavy, clean, and white canvas sacks closed by drawstrings, posed still another problem. We were expected to cram everything in the world we owned into them, including shoes, raincoats, and the thick short jackets called peacoats for cold weather. All the clothing we were issued awed us with its quality. Everything was first-rate. The whites were crisp and firm-bodied; the blues were rich in both color and texture. The peacoats, thick Melton cloth with slick satin linings, were special marvels. For those of us who had never in our lives worn any but the cheapest of things from the shelves of the cheapest stores, it was impressive.

I had never felt so rich in my life. And all of it, including two pairs of black leather shoes and rubbers for wet weather, was ours at no cost at all. At no money cost, that is. The Navy would expect payment in various ways before it was through with us.

Another, more infamous, item the Navy gave us was a pair of canvas leggings. These were like the old-fashioned spats gentlemen once wore over their shoes. They reached half to our knees. A strap with a buckle, passed under the soles of our shoes, kept them from riding up. They laced up the outer sides of our legs. They were called boots. We would wear them the entire time we were in the training station—which was why we were called "boots" and why the station itself was called "boot camp."

And it all had to be fitted into the dismayingly small seabag they gave us. Everything was new and stiff, of course, and would not fit. We were tired. We took the problem to be the Navy's. If it wanted us to cram all that stuff into one little bitty bag, it was going to have to show us how to do it. For the time being, we got it stowed as best we could and left the rest in piles here and there. All Navy clothes are stenciled with the owners' names; we could sort it out later.

For the moment, the problem was to get into the goddamned hammocks. The company commander came through and shouted us into the effort. Dutifully, we soared up into the swinging contraptions—known to sailors as fart sacks—and tried to sleep. There was a great crashing of bodies on the hard and solid deck, along with some sincere moaning—and some even more sincere country boy cussing—as some sailors missed their hammocks on takeoff.

Actually, hammocks make for good sleeping—especially on board ships, where they swing slowly in keeping with the vessel's motion in the sea. But they do take some getting used to. I was so tired from the day's exertions, both physical and emotional, that I could have slept soundly on a spool of barbed wire, had it been properly fluffed. Most of us must have been in the same state of exhaustion because, after taps, that most lovely of all bugle calls, the barracks lapsed into a silence broken only by the occasional thud of bodies falling from hammocks and the embarrassed snuffling of men choking back the sobs of homesickness.

I hadn't known our company commander cared—he had hidden the fact damned well until then—but I guess he did. After lights out, he came to the barracks door and, in the only touch of compassion he had shown all day, told us not to be ashamed for being homesick. It was seldom fatal, he said. And it was a sign that those who suffered it had good homes to miss. Hell, he almost made us feel guilty if we were not homesick.

As it happened, our expectation of even busier days to come was not disappointed. Reveille came at 5:45 in the morning. First, we lashed and aired our bedding. Next we cleaned the barracks and ourselves—in that order. This included shaving every morning, whether we needed it or not. I didn't need to. I had learned to shave with Dad's old straight razor, but straight razors were not allowed in the

Navy for obvious reasons. No one who has known the crowded washrooms in ships thrashing about in rough seas will question the logic of that rule. Most of the time in boot camp I shaved with no blade in my razor at all, but I damned well shaved.

Breakfast was at 7:30, and we fell in for infantry drill at 8:00. Dinner was at 11:30, and we drilled again until 4:00. I never understood how walking funny and flipping hands to eyebrows would make a man a better fighter, but the Navy knew more about those things than I did, I suppose. After supper, we washed a complete change of clothes, from cap to leggings—again, whether they needed washing or not.

In the paved courtyards behind the barracks there were long waist-high wooden tables. That is where we scrubbed our clothes every night, using lots of harsh soap and stiff-bristled brushes. Even the high quality of Navy uniforms did not stand up well to that kind of treatment, but they were clean.

The Navy did not use anything so simple as ordinary clothes pins. Once scrubbed, the clothes were stopped to the drying lines. Wet clothes were tied, instead of pinned, to drying lines by short lengths of line with brass tips, like shoelaces, called clothes stops. All our washables were made with small paired holes through which these clothes stops were passed and tied to the clotheslines.

The clotheslines themselves were double lengths of manila line led to the top of a tall central mast, from which they led down and out to shorter poles set in a circle around the tall center spar. When loaded, these lines were hoisted to the top of the central mast by a system of pulleys that sailors call "blocks." In the end it all looked like some kind of weird maypole or a surrealistic Indian teepee.

After scrubbing our clothes we scrubbed ourselves. There were showers and washbasins in each barracks—shining white-tiled rooms with mirrors and all the hot water we wanted. I, who had never had a shower in my life until I took one in the Dallas YMCA, was now taking a shower every day—again, whether I needed one or not. If all this sounds as though the Navy had a fetish about cleanliness, that is not far from the truth. Sometimes I thought my fingers would be permanently wrinkled from being so much in water. I recalled ruefully my family's little house in the Osage, where we had had to haul our water one barrel at a time from a distant spring.

After showering—and cleaning the barracks again—we could do whatever we wanted for the five or ten minutes before it was time to struggle up into our hammocks and try to sleep. The next day it was all to be done over again.

Virtually all we did while in South Unit was infantry drill and calisthenics, both with and without arms. Arms, in this sense, meant our rifles. The parade ground was paved with asphalt that became hot and sticky in the San Diego sun.

It was called "the grinder," for reasons that soon became obvious. We became intimate with every blessed inch of it. It was not only the stage for infantry drill and calisthenics; it was also the scene of much of our punishment for lapses. Every night shadowy white figures could be seen on the grinder, with rifle and bayonet, marching off sentences, sometimes all night long. An interesting variation was to be sentenced to scrubbing the damned thing with a toothbrush.

After only two or three days, we were issued our 1903 Model Springfield .30-caliber rifles, with cartridge belts and bayonets, the long kind of bayonets from World War I. (We didn't know it was World War I then, of course.) And, with the rifles, we received another one of those little lectures we were becoming so familiar with. The rifles were issued to us by serial number, and we were to guard them with our lives. God help the poor soul who lost his rifle or allowed it to be damaged. Hell itself would be cool in comparison to what would happen then. We also learned our rifles were not guns, or even rifles; they were pieces.

I had a head start in all this soldier stuff from my time in the National Guard and knew the basic movements of infantry drill and the Manual of Arms. The Navy recognized this great achievement and made me a recruit petty officer and leader of the First Squad, Second Platoon, of Recruit Company 39-13, an imminence I bragged about in letters home as though I had been commissioned a full lieutenant at least. Actually, recruit petty officers had little recognized authority off the grinder, but they wore rating badges like those of real sailors, except only about half as big. They had the same eagle—called "crow" in Navy slang—and inverted chevrons below. Instead of the usual specialty mark in the center, though, they had an embroidered square knot. That is why we were called "square knot admirals" and were laughed at a good deal for the airs we tended to put on. Off the drill field no one paid much attention to us. But it was my first step up on what I expected to be a long naval career.

The Navy then still used the old eight-man, two-rank squad, and the complications of its handling were baffling to most of us. I still don't understand why infantry drill was so important for men who were supposed to do their fighting in ships, but smarter men than I thought it was, I guess. After trying to fight my way through Right Front into the Line, Left and Right Oblique, and several other now obsolete intricate maneuvers, I came away with a much greater respect for chorus girls.

We spent those first few weeks in South Unit learning to stand and walk funny and how to move from one part of the grinder to another without getting lost. We learned the mysteries of military saluting too, which probably went a long way toward making us vicious fighting men. One little puzzle never explained to us was why the Navy did not salute when uncovered—that is, not wearing a hat—but the Army did. Of such things great military victories are made, I suppose.

I had been familiar with guns all my life and had had my own since my tenth birthday, but those old Springfields they gave us in the Navy were different animals altogether from the .22s and 410 shotguns I had known before. They weighed eight pounds when empty, for one thing, and they just plain looked mean. We spent hours snapping them in. This meant squeezing the trigger until the firing pin snapped forward. The goal was to do it so that you would not know when the gun was going to fire. The exact moment of firing was supposed to come as a surprise. That way, the gun would not be pulled off target, you see.

On another subject, I have read many accounts over the years of sadistic drill sergeants—especially Marine sergeants—but I saw none in the Navy. Our company commanders were veteran chief petty officers from the fleet. For some specialties—gunners mates, quartermasters, and the like—recruiting duty and boot camp assignments were about the only chance they ever had for shore duty. They could be rough. Their patience was limited. We soon learned not to play around with them. They wore the same heavy-bladed cutlasses used for hand-to-hand fighting in the old sailing ship Navy. (Officers wore swords.) They could unsnap the heavy leather scabbards from their belts and whip them across the backside of an offender, cutlass, scabbard, and all, in one swift unerring motion, to noticeable effect. But I never saw any gross abuse or pointless cruelty.

Oddly, those days I remember now as some of the happiest of my young life. Before I had been a loner and was often depressed in a world that could find no place for me other than in a grocery store. Now, I was at last part of a greater whole. I found in the welfare of my squad something more important than my own heretofore precious self. That I didn't have to worry about getting something to eat and had a warm—if dangerous—place to sleep every night helped, I suppose, but I think now it was bigger than that.

I wish I could say I was wise enough then to see through all the sham and pretense and the manipulated patriotism, the inherent idiocy of military life, but I wasn't. I bought the whole thing. I marched, postured, and saluted with the best of them. I did not doubt for a minute that I was doing something important. My marks as I went along stayed at a perfect 4.0, and I was singled out one time as best in my company. I was proud of that. I boasted in my letters home that I was a good sailor. I sometimes wish now that I had never lost the blessed innocence that led me to feel that way. Life, I suspect, would have been much more comfortable for me and my family.

Oddly, though I busted my butt in becoming the best I could in the military arts, it never occurred to me that those arts had been developed over man's long history for the purpose of killing people. When snapping in my rifle or, later, actually firing it, I never saw anything beyond the paper target. Just as I was conditioned to instant and unquestioning obedience, it never occurred to me that I would someday without hesitation obey orders to fire machine guns into a small boat crowded with Japanese soldiers.

It was all more like a game in which I tried to excel only in order to beat the competition of my colleagues, some of whom were equally gung ho. I was then still thinking of going to Annapolis, so ambition was undoubtedly a part of it. But, for the most part, it stayed a game, just as school work had always been a game for me, a game in which besting my classmates was more important than simply learning something.

Marching in formation held a special fascination for me. It was the epitome of teamwork, for one thing. Individual performance was unimportant—yet absolutely essential—to the performance of the whole. I was never very good at it. You were supposed to hear a slight difference in the drumbeat that would tell you which foot to step out on, but I never could. I stayed in step by watching the others. Still, there was an emotional high in swinging along with all those other men, all holding themselves so erect as they marched. The tread of shoes, the squeak of leather and webbing, the pulsant thumping of drums—all of it on beat, responding as blood in a living body responds to the beat of a single heart.

Later, in North Unit, we would march in dress parades every Friday. We were practiced enough by that time to be respectably good at the drill. There were bleachers beside the North Unit grinder. People came to watch us. Officers, with their gold braid and fancy swords, marched with us in those parades. Guidons and flags flapped in the wind, and there was the stirring music of a band. (We always passed in Review to the music of Sousa's "Washington Post March." I did not know until many years later that the music was written in honor of a newspaper. I always assumed it was about an Army post somewhere.) Oh, it was grand! For me who had never amounted to anything before, it was. Everyone else pretended to hate the parades, but I loved them.

The time in South Unit passed almost before we knew it. Our days—and nights—had been so programmed, with little or no idle time between events, that the time flew. It was what is now known as total immersion—with a vengeance. We were molded into what the Navy wanted so unendingly and so thoroughly it seemed we had been there for years. All the artificial stuff of standing at attention and marching and saluting had become second nature to us. Old Pavlov would have recognized us right off, I suspect. We probably salivated on hearing mess call and closed our eyes without thinking when taps was sounded.

To that time, our days had been spent in infantry drill, calisthenics, and simply becoming part of the Navy—in speech and dress, thought and act. Our civilian lives became thin memories, recalled less and less often. The Navy even tried to teach us to swim and to box—all to absolutely no effect in my case.

Being young, we forever tried to resist the Navy. As a matter of pride, if nothing else, I suppose. But we rarely won. The Navy had been in the business a lot longer than we had. I remember once another sailor and I decided getting our brains knocked out was not all that amusing. It was during boxing training.

As were all the military services of the time, the Navy was convinced that boxing was a valuable skill for its men. The Navy's way of organizing the drill was to form a company into two ranks, one behind the other. The front rank was then ordered to About Face, and we fought the man fate had positioned across from us, regardless of size, weight, skill, or anything else in the way of fairness.

My friend and I figured out that if one of us fell in behind the other, we would fight each other. Wonderful! We could spar about for a little while and come out unscarred, pretending to fight but not hitting hard at all. The scheme worked fine in theory, but in practice it became less predictable. After a few minutes of bobbing and weaving, my friend thought I hit him too hard. Escalation followed, and we were soon whacking away at each other as hard as ever we had at a stranger. We both wound up in sick bay, he with a broken jaw and I with a flattened nose. We were wearing sixteen-ounce gloves, but we were so totally ignorant of how to defend ourselves that we were both hurt in the same flailing exchange. At least it got us out of any further boxing nonsense.

I avoided swimming much the same way. The instructors had long wooden poles with metal hooks in their ends, hooks they used to snag the swim trunks of sinkers and to pull them to the surface before they drowned completely. I think the instructors simply got tired of pulling me out because one day a chief told me that if I could make it across the goddamned pool he would pass me. Swimming the length of the pool was a feat that was as far beyond me as flying the same distance would have been. But, I could hold my breath long enough to swim across the pool, and I finally did. That is how I became a Navy swimmer.

Another activity that didn't take with me was churchgoing. Every Sunday we were assembled with rifles and bayonets and marched to the chapel for what the Navy calls divine services. It seemed ironic that we should march with deadly rifles on our shoulders, stack our arms outside, then go in and listen to sermons about the Prince of Peace. We were not forced to attend divine services after we left the training station, but attendance was required in boot camp.

After my company moved to North Unit and its handsome barracks buildings, our training moved onto subjects like gunnery, boats, seamanship, and all the

other things sailors had to know then. Infantry drill became less and less important, though we did do some of it every day and we had our weekly dress parades.
We learned how to handle oars in the Navy's heavy wooden whaleboats. I pulled
number seven oar in the company crew in races against other companies and
against boats from ships that chanced to be in harbor. The most impressive thing,
I thought, was that the starting line was off North Island. We had to row all the
way across the bay just to get to the starting line. And we actually fired our rifles,
and various pistols and machine guns, at the Marines' range in La Jolla—now an
expensive beachfront suburb of San Diego, I understand. No one's nose was bleeding from the height yet, but we were moving up in the Navy.

The most dramatic change for us in North Unit was that we got liberty. On
weekends we could go to San Diego—Dago was the Navy's name for the town—
for a few hours. In navalese, "liberty" was a sailor's freedom to be away from his
duty post for up to seventy-two hours, as I recall. Anything more than that was
called "leave" and charged against the sailor's annual official allowance of thirty
days. Even though we were land-based in boot camp, we spoke of liberty as "going
ashore."

There was virtually every imaginable form of recreation on the training station grounds—all of it free—including nightly first-run movies. But we couldn't
wait to go ashore and spend our money on whatever tawdry entertainment a
few dollars would buy. The good people of San Diego were well developed in the
arts of separating sailors from their money. Boots from the training station were
especially vulnerable. Lower Broadway was a gauntlet to be run every time we
went to town. Several blocks were lined with one cheap credit jewelry store, souvenir stand, and schlock shop after another. They hired carnival-type pitchmen who
came out onto the sidewalk and fished the stream of young sailors and Marines
like bears fish salmon from a spawning river. Aggressive and forceful, these guys
would grab us by the arms and drag us into their stores as we tried to pass along
the street, pushing free matchbooks on us and signing us up for all kinds of trashy
stuff, none of which we could wear or use while in uniform.

Few of us were up to resisting altogether. I bought a sleazy black leather jacket
one time. It had a bright fake satin lining and lots of silver buttons. I couldn't wear
it, and I had no place to keep it. I finally threw the damned thing away. Some got
taken for much more than I did, signing away their pay for months or years to
come. The Navy, to its shame, sided with these vultures and restricted men who fell
behind in their payments. Even after we were assigned to ships, some commanding officers forced their men to pay up or face punishment for bringing discredit
on the Navy, for God's sake.

Boots, for the most part, enjoyed innocent forms of pleasure. We were not yet up to the hornier forms of sailor amusement, and our twenty-one dollars a month did not buy much in the way of whiskey and women. We ate junky hamburgers and skimpy milkshakes and went to movies and ballgames. Some of us, impatient to be away to sea, visited Navy ships in harbor. That was my special pleasure. I visited, at one time or another, destroyers, light cruisers, minesweepers, and auxiliaries. Once I even visited the aircraft carrier *Saratoga* at her anchorage off Coronado. I never dreamed that I would someday serve briefly in the huge ship.

The *Sara* was too big to enter San Diego Bay in those days. She was anchored out, and visiting her required a motor launch ride of probably ten miles or more, round trip. It was my longest voyage yet on the water, and my first in the open sea, where Southern California's great swells lifted and lowered the boat delightfully. The boat was spotless, of course, with new paint and much varnish and polished brass. Its crew was immaculate—ships competed then in the smartness of their boats' crews, and most of the boats were things of beauty.

The regular crewmen of the ships we visited, of course, had a lot of fun with us. They told us outlandish stories and fed us weird descriptions of life on board. But we would learn the truth soon enough. Then we could kid the pants off boots who came to visit our ships.

After my first fever to get ashore in San Diego, though, my appetite for liberty soon cooled. The sleazy leather jacket I was paying for probably had something to do with my loss of enthusiasm, but I was already coming to feel more at home with Navy men on the Navy's own grounds than I was with civilians. It would be charitable to say of San Diego's citizens that they were indifferent to us. Positive disapproval would be a more accurate description of their feelings. Certainly, they liked sailors' money, but they obviously wished we would mail it to them and not clutter up their nice streets with our bodies.

I think it was my last time ashore in San Diego as a boot that a bunch of us went out to Mission Beach one night. There was an amusement park there with rides and shooting galleries and carnival candy. Out on the broad sandy beach itself, there were driftwood fires with crowds of young people from the town roasting weenies and marshmallows and having a good time. There were girls in those crowds. They caught our attention. Some of us even made moves to join in, but we were quickly put right. Such things were not for us. Sometimes there were even fistfights between sailors and town kids.

Mission Beach was an exotic setting for those of us who were country or small town kids. Garish neon lights, loud mechanical music, the clatter and crash of carnival rides and the excited shrieks and shouts of laughter, all backed up by the blackness of the sea night and the slumping crash of surf on the sand. The crests of breakers glowed with reflected carnival lights. It was exotic, I suppose, but I never felt as lonely in my life as I did that night in Mission Beach. I never went back.

I was happier on the station. Especially in the big library, which was never crowded. There were hundreds of books and comfortable chairs and good reading lights. The high ceiling was finished with dark wooden beams. Meticulously made ship models berthed in niches and shelves all around. Everything was quiet and clean, and there was no one to tell me I was just a boot sailor.

The training in North Unit was more interesting too. For one thing, as I mentioned earlier, after all our hours of snapping in, we were allowed to fire our rifles. I shot a perfect score in initial firing with .22s, but the powerful Springfields intimidated me, I think, with the vigor of their recoil. The Colt .45 pistols were too much for me as well, as were the Thompson submachine guns. I couldn't hold them down. The air-cooled Lewis guns from the world war were easier, but I was still not very good with them. As it turned out, a Lewis gun was the only gun I ever fired in the coming war.

The Marine sergeants at the La Jolla range were intolerant of us. I had lived with guns all my life. When I was handed a five-round clip, I thumbed it into my rifle without thinking, a fact a burly Marine pointed out to me at once—and at some length. He made me jack out every one of the rounds, making sure that the whole firing line knew how stupid I had been for loading my piece before I was ordered to do so. On the firing line, we were not supposed to do anything until ordered to do it.

Other than that, though, the firing went fairly smoothly. Each of us took his turn on the line—firing from standing, sitting, and prone positions—slow and rapid fire. Then we took our turns in the butts, a depressed area behind a thick earthen embankment from which we raised and lowered the targets, each time pasting a paper patch over any hits scored. In case the poor sailor missed the target entirely—and a surprising lot of them did—we signaled that too with a round black marker on a long pole. This embarrassment was known by the old Army term "Maggie's drawers."

We fired only a few rounds from the exotic stuff—the Colt pistols and Thompson and Lewis machine guns—just enough to let us know what it was like to fire them. What it was like was scary. Even though we were warned in advance, their recoil was so violent we did little more than shoot holes in the sky.

Recoil was also a problem with the Springfields. The most natural thing in the world was to lay your thumb across the top of the stock, in the same way you would hold a pistol. We were warned over and over again not to do that, but, being human—and dumb sailors—we did it anyway. When you fired holding your gun like that the recoil slammed your thumb against your cheek hard enough sometimes to tear the skin. If lucky, you returned to the station with nothing more than a black eye and some colorful bruises.

By that point in our training, we were marching formally only about thirty minutes a day, except for the weekly dress parade on Fridays. Much of our time was spent in the hallowed naval traditions of inspections. We stood for personnel inspections, barracks inspections, seabag inspections—and probably a good many more I have forgotten. And these were just the formal inspections. Every time we fell in for a formation, we ran the critical gauntlet of the company commander's eyes—and those of any officer who happened to be in range. They liked to keep their hands in, you see. At least we could not complain of being ignored.

Still, there were times in North Unit when there was little to do. Especially on weekends when almost everyone went ashore in Dago. My letters home of that time tell of walking the bay front by the parade ground and watching the ships and the sky and the buildings of San Diego across the water—with the blue mountains of Mexico in the distance. I was still enamored of everything about the sea and cared little for the town's attractions.

During the week, we were kept occupied. The companies competed for pennants—in exactly the same way kindergarten children compete for gold stars in school. Individual companies were ranked in their order of excellence in the various areas of our training: barracks cleanliness, personnel inspection, infantry drill, and the like. Each week winning companies were awarded distinctive pennants to be flown from brackets over their barracks doors for the following seven days. We broke our necks to win these childish prizes. I was as proud as anyone can be one memorable week when our company won all the pennants. We came and went under their fluttering colors for a whole week.

There were special duties sometimes too. I remember once, owing to my exalted status as a square knot admiral, being made corporal of the guard for South Unit. The extent of this vital duty was my riding a bicycle around all the guard posts—all military installations have guard posts—and reporting back to the officer of the deck that his sentries were still alive.

There was one more onerous duty, though, for which companies were responsible. Each week, one company had to serve in the mess hall. It was hard, dirty work, but I lucked out on that too. As top man in Company 39-13, I was assigned to the officer's mess. There were only a dozen or so officers. The work was light. I had refrigerator privileges and was allowed to lounge on the soft officer chairs and read the good officer magazines any time no officers were present. The other boots envied me, but I didn't like the job. It was too much like being a servant, something no good Oklahoman of the time would stand still for.

I was aware that I was getting special attention from the boot camp officers. Some of my colleagues were aware of it too. The word already was out that I had a year of college and was on my way to Annapolis; the officers were good to me. They encouraged me and offered help. But I still did not like being a wardroom flunky, and the special attention made me suspect in the eyes of the other boots. A little coolness developed where there had been open friendship before.

By that time, we were nearing the end of our training. Everyone began thinking of boot leave. We had been promised ten days leave at the end of our training, and we were all making plans. Roundtrip rail fare to Tulsa then was $25.90 in a chair car. In my letters home I reported having twenty-six dollars, with two more paydays to come before I came home. I could afford to make the trip.

It is interesting how my Depression-born obsession with money was hanging on. On the day I went to Mission Beach, for instance, I dutifully reported in a letter home that I spent sixty cents for the entire day's outing. I proudly reported that my pay would go all the way to thirty-six dollars a month when I graduated from boot camp. Hell, I would be rich. But I did not become giddy at the prospect and do anything foolish. In token of our elevated status—once we completed training—we could have our laundry done for us for two dollars a month, but I continued to wash my own clothes long after reporting aboard ship. I was close with money.

As it happened, I inked a black border on my letter home of August 23. I would not be getting leave after all. The Navy then had advanced and more specialized schools beyond boot camp for selected men. I applied for communications school and was accepted as one of fifteen men chosen from 550 applicants—a circumstance I made clear in letters home. My life, before entering the Navy, had been so empty of the normal little triumphs of growing up that I bragged shamelessly about anything I did win.

The catch in getting the school, though, was that I would get no leave for another four months. I had wanted to go home more than I thought, I guess, for I was very much disappointed.

That happened to be around the time of the Navy's annual carnival in San Diego. This was a big-for-the-time public relations deal, and it distracted me from my no-leave blues. The carnival was staged on the training station beach. Thousands of people came.

It all started with our marching in a big dress parade. Then almost a hundred Navy fighters screamed down out of the sky in a mock raid. They were Grumman F2Fs. Tiny by today's standards—one pilot described flying them as being like having an engine in his lap and a feather in his ass—we thought they were wonderful. And I, naturally, decided then and there I would be a Navy pilot, another dream to be cruelly denied.

Many surface ships had come into the bay for the event as well. Swarms of ships' boats milled around them, bringing and taking visitors and sailors alike between ship and shore with a great dinging of bells and revving of motors. There was even a stage show and rides and booths of all kind, just like a real carnival. Movie stars made personal appearances. The atmosphere was holiday all the way.

At night things were even more spectacular. Navy planes flew over in formation, their running lights making bright new constellations in the sky. And, in the bay, ships put on what were then known as searchlight displays. Their big gunnery searchlights were trained upward and moved about according to prearranged plans to create shifting patterns of eerie blue-white wands that weaved and paused and weaved again. I would later see similar effects in the far northern skies off Iceland. It was beautiful, but I don't suppose anyone now will ever see another searchlight display. They would be pretty tame anyway, I suppose, to generations used to the light shows put on by modern rock bands.

For us newly minted seamen second class—our rate upon completing boot camp—the carnival was exciting for its noise and colors and lively activity. For me it was even headier when the girls and civilian young men looked at me with something other than the cool disinterest with which they had looked at me before. For those three or four days, I fell into the silly trap of thinking I might amount to something after all.

At any rate, the first step of our training was over. The boot camp tailor sewed the two thin stripes of seamen second onto the cuffs of our blues. And we could stow away the stigmatic boots that had marked us as the lowliest of the low. Except for those of us assigned to our ships' landing forces, we would rarely wear them again.

The barracks were full of excited chatter as seabags were packed for the last time and hammocks lashed around them, and sailors made and unmade their plans for leave. I felt a little sad. I had come to know these men. We had been through the trial of boot camp together. As happened many times to me in the Navy, I was parted from friends I would never see again. It was an unspoken tradition among Navy sailors that, once they were separated by duty, they rarely wrote letters to each other.

In my letter home of September 5, though, I began, "Gloom is so thick over the barracks you could stir it with an oar. [I used lots of salty expressions then in my letters home.] The men all had had their bags packed and their dress blues pressed ready to go home. They talked and thought of nothing else."

But, the next morning at our graduation parade, the training station commanding officer announced that all leaves were canceled. At first, I think, the sailors thought the captain was joking—we had not been in the Navy long enough to know that Navy captains don't joke.

There would be no leaves throughout the Navy until further notice. Normally, at that time, when men finished boot camp they were kept in a transfer unit for as long as a month or two before being assigned to ships and permanent duty stations. But the captain told us our class could expect to be aboard ship within three or four days.

All Navy procedures were being tightened. Civilians were limited in their access to ships and stations. A new intensity took hold. Construction work was started on enlarging the training station.

We did not know it then, but World War II had started for us.

3

Comm School

THE THING THAT KILLED Company 39-13's boot leave was Hitler's invasion of Poland. I first learned of it the night before our graduation from boot camp. The glad excitement in the barracks of those who thought they were going on leave was depressing for those of us who knew we were not. A couple of other school selectees and I decided to go ashore and catch a movie. At least we would not have to listen to all the gas about girlfriends back home and Mom's cooking.

I no longer remember what the picture was, but the theater was the ornate Fox on San Diego's F Street. Movie theaters in those days were usually full, and the Fox that night was no exception. But, not long after the feature started, the house lights came up and a man in a business suit came on stage. "All naval personnel are ordered to return to their ships and stations immediately," he announced solemnly. Then, as though to emphasize the importance of his message, he said it again.

No one knew what had happened. My first thought was that there had been some kind of disaster somewhere. The Navy was sometimes called on to help with floods and big storms and the like. Civilians in the audience did not know any more than we did, I suppose. They probably thought it was some kind of drill. Regardless, all the sailors and Marines got to their feet and filed out of the theater.

This was the second time I had seen civilians look at sailors with much respect at all. The first time had been at the Navy carnival, but then it had been little more than curiosity—and a little well-restrained envy. This time, in the theater, I think they sensed something was really wrong. Nobody envied us much at all. The people's faces were serious as they watched us hurry out. But the house lights dimmed again, and the show went on before we were out of the lobby. I assume the audience went ahead and enjoyed the show.

Once we got back to the station no one knew what to do with us. The guys who planned to go on leave the next day didn't know any more than we did. We hung around the barracks until bedtime and turned in, still not knowing what was going on.

We were told that the president had declared a state of national emergency when Hitler invaded Poland, but we could not see how the invasion had anything to do with us. Poland was on the other side of the world, and from all we knew, it would be an Army problem. At least we assumed it would be an Army problem. We couldn't see anything the Navy could do about a problem in a place like Poland.

It had still not occurred to me that I might ever become involved in a war. I suspect most of us felt that way. We went to sleep that night more resentful for having paid for a movie we did not get to see than for anything else. It would be more than two years before we were actually in the war, but we were still too new in the Navy to realize that things would never be the same again.

Leaves throughout the Navy were canceled, and my Company 39-13 ship-mates were bundled off immediately to various ships and stations around the world. For those of us going on to advanced training, nothing changed. We simply moved across the courtyard at the rear of the barracks to new berths in the school buildings.

The school buildings were exact duplicates of the North Unit barracks we had been living in. But they were fitted with double-decked bunks rather than hammocks, and we had stainless steel lockers rather than seabags for our gear. There were no rifle racks. There were classrooms and labs and study areas. We moved in with little fuss and settled in for a four-month stay.

The first month was given over to general work common to all communications rates. The final three found us specializing in radio, visual signals, quartermaster, or yeoman—the Navy's paper workers. Quartermasters in the Navy were assistants to the navigator, not the supply man as in the Army.

Our routine was completely different from that in boot camp. We no longer marched at all, not even in parades, and inspections were few. We ate in the same mess hall with the boots, but we no longer wore leggings and we had two thin white stripes on the cuffs of our dress blues and a white braid around our right sleeves at the shoulder. We were officially seamen second class, and our pay went to thirty-six dollars a month.

My preoccupation with money continued to show in letters home. On September 24 I wrote, "I should be drawing seventy-two dollars a month within a year. And that will be clear money, too. It is a simple matter to live in the Navy on ten dollars a month—I lived three months here on less than that. Next payday I will have more than sixty dollars, then my pay will be thirty-six dollars a month. If I do get leave when I graduate I will have almost $150, more money than I ever thought I would have at one time."

At the school, in fact, it was even easier to save money than it had been in boot camp—we didn't have time to spend anything. Theoretically, we had more freedom to go ashore, but our classes were from eight in the morning until nine at night, with brief recesses for dinner and supper. For the first month we were not given time even to go to the station movies. I still did my own laundry, but it was hard to find a few moments for such chores. There were forty-seven of us in our class. We were a selected group, and competition was fierce. We came not only from the San Diego boot camp, but from training stations at Newport, Norfolk, and Great Lakes as well. We quickly became, in the Navy way, shipmates and friends. Our former friends in recruit training were forgotten about equally as quickly. I don't remember seeing any of them again. Just as I would probably never again see any of my classmates in comm school once we were graduated. It was simply the Navy way.

I liked comm school even better than I had boot camp. The work was hard—much harder than any class work I had faced in college—and there were few distractions. Both instructors and students were conscientious about what they were doing. We quickly forgot our initial concern at the declaration of the state of national emergency, but a lurking seed had been planted and so we took our work seriously. At graduation, final marks for the top men had to be carried out to four decimal places to determine who was first in the class.

Our first month was spent primarily on Morse code and typing. My work in the *Tribune*'s newsroom helped with the typing. There were some lectures, but for the most part it was practice, practice, practice. It was what the Navy called basics, and it was so thoroughly drilled into my head that I can still read Morse code—if it is slow enough.

Again, in the Navy way, school work quickly became routine. We were called at six in the morning; taps sounded at ten at night—2200 in the Navy's twenty-four hour timekeeping system. Everything in between was prescribed and, necessarily, performed in the time allotted for its doing. As one result, time passed quickly.

At the end of the first month, we were assigned to our subspecialties, not always the one we wanted. Men with top marks, as an incentive, I suppose, were given their choices. I got quartermaster/signalman school and began a whole new course of study. The signaling part continued on much as it had before, but in addition I learned chart correcting and the use and care of navigating instruments and the taking of times and the like. I had always been intrigued by the mystery of how men found their ways about the oceans by means of sun and stars. In particular my interest lay in the ancients—the Arabs and Chinese—who discovered the great mysteries of the skies in the first place. My mind does not work that way.

Navy Day that year gave me a new chance to show off my pride at being in the Navy. Civilians had become limited in their visits to ships and the big air station on North Island. This meant even more visitors than before. They swarmed over us, giggling and staring and asking stupid questions. In letters home, I was very intolerant of them.

In school, we attended classes all day, but as a demonstration for our tax-paying civilian guests, I was assigned to show the form and majesty of semaphore signaling. My classmate and I were put on the roof of one building to semaphore across to other sailors on another roof. We made up our own unflattering messages about our guests and flailed them across the open space between buildings in the awkward herky-jerky motions of amateurs. The assignment kept me a welcome distance from the civilians. I felt much superior to the people watching me, their mouths rounded in appreciative oohs and ahs for my expertise—which wasn't expert at all, as I quickly learned when I joined the fleet and met real signalmen. But the civilians' awe seemed perfectly appropriate.

The pace of events in the Navy continued more hectic than before Roosevelt's emergency proclamation, but that too became routine, a phenomenon I was to learn is true of everything in the Navy. In a November 1 letter I wrote, "All the ships are out now. I don't know where they are or what they are doing. They stay out a great deal of the time now, coming in only long enough to refuel and take on provisions. The airplanes are kept busy, too. The drone of their motors fills the air continuously."

The Navy, even then, was revving up for the bloody war to come. A lot of new construction was going on at both the Navy and Marine training stations in preparation for the flood of recruits soon to come.

In another excerpt from the same letter I bragged, "I was surprised when I first joined the Navy how the boys all seemed to like me. They still do and have given me an interesting nickname." I do not remember any nicknames now and suspect I made up this anecdote for the home folks, another manifestation of the impressive inferiority complex I had developed in Depression-era Oklahoma.

Incidentally, a letter home from November 5 indicated that the Depression was still not completely over in Oklahoma. Apparently Dad had complained of being cold, for I wrote, "I left all my money on the books [a term the Navy uses for not drawing your pay] but next payday I will draw some to get you an overcoat. . . . Maybe you could get something down at Dick Bardon's." Dick Bardon's, on South Main Street, was Tulsa's pawnshop of choice.

School did progress. It was a demonstration of sailors' mobility that we moved our living quarters with every step up in the curriculum—which meant every month. We moved progressively to more desirable parts of the barracks and were given more privileges. As seniors, for instance, we got to go to the head of the chow line—with juniors, sophomores, and basics following in order.

That too was the Navy's way. The whole elaborate edifice was built on a system of privilege and precedence. Officers, of course, had more privileges than we "white hats" would ever have. But even they, among themselves, took their precedence in the order of their numbers—the date and their standing in the year of their graduation from Annapolis. Miscreant officers commonly lost some of their numbers, a punishment that moved them down on the promotions list. If he lost enough numbers, an officer might as well get out of the Navy. His career was over.

This brings up a sore point. I don't remember now who broke the news, but it was at about this time that I learned I would never go to Annapolis. I was too old. Midshipmen then could not be more than twenty years old on April 1 of the year in which they would enter the Academy. I was twenty on March 20—out by ten days. Neither Chief Barnett, the Tulsa recruiter, nor the lieutenant in Dallas whose pitch of patriotism and duty I so thoroughly bought, nor any of the training station officers who had encouraged me ever told about the age restriction. I guess they assumed I was younger than I was.

At any rate, that phase of my naval career ended before it began. It was a blow. Given my educational deficiencies, especially in math and science, it is unlikely that I could have succeeded at the Academy, but it had been such a glistening dream, such a glorious possibility for redemption after all the humiliation of trying to find a place in the world during the Depression. I was shaken when it was pulled away on what I took to be an insignificant technicality.

The pain was not eased much the next year when the age limit was raised to twenty-one. I missed again—by the same ten days. Of course, I was on the hook for four years, whether I went to Annapolis or not. I would just spend those years in what we called the enlisted men's low-necked gowns rather than in a midshipman's spiffy uniform. There was still the chance of becoming an officer by going up through the warrant officer grades, but that took twenty or thirty years even for outstanding men, periods beyond the comprehension of a nineteen-year-old. Such officers were known in the Navy as Mustangs and usually were limited in their assignments to lesser commands in tugboats, yard craft, and other humble ships of what was called the Dungaree Navy.

A faster and probably more certain way to commissioned rank was through fleet aviation. At that time, a sizable percentage of the Navy's fighter, torpedo, and utility airplanes were flown by enlisted men—men known in the Navy as dungaree pilots for the work uniform they wore in flight. Officer pilots were known as naval aviators and wore khaki with brown shoes. Enlisted flyers were called aviation pilots and wore black shoes. By means of such distinctions, the nation's safety is secured. (Floyd Bennett, Admiral Byrd's pilot in Antarctica, was an enlisted pilot. An airfield was named for him in New York.)

Another consideration was that quartermasters and radiomen, along with machinist's mates, were given preference in selection for flight training. I was going to be a quartermaster, I thought. I adjusted my sights accordingly and began to watch the Navy airplanes flying overhead with a new interest.

Oddly, too, after the first shock of learning I was barred from Annapolis, I gained a new appreciation of the men I had come to know in the Navy, enlisted or not. Almost 25 percent of the men in comm school had been to college, some of them for as long as three years. Most comforting of all, of course, was my continuing conviction that anything was better than a Tulsa Safeway store.

Another strange thing was that my relationship with other sailors improved after my dreams of Annapolis fell through. Before, when they knew I was trying for the Academy, they were encouraging and helpful, but there was a kind of reticence too. It was almost as though the gap between enlisted man and officer had already kicked in. After it became known that I was not going after all, I was just one of the guys and was accepted as such.

Another distraction at the time turned out to be the Navy's resumption of granting leaves. It became all but certain that I would get leave in January, and that fact took over much of my thinking. My family had moved to a small rented house in Tulsa since I left home, so I would not be returning to the house I remembered in the Bird Creek bottoms north of town. But the prospect of seeing Dad, Cora, Flo, and Zena was exciting.

The leave would be short. Travel time enough was granted to give each man at least four days at home. In my case that would mean a round-trip journey of some three thousand miles for a grand total of ninety-six hours at home. And it would virtually wipe out my hoarded store of money. But it never occurred to me not to go. I think most of us felt that way.

School continued to demand hard long hours, and the newness had worn off. I began to go ashore on weekends more often. My new interest in aviation made my visits to the carrier *Saratoga* more interesting than ever. I could stand on her broad flight deck and picture myself taking off and landing while lesser types watched from the bridge and other vantage points. One time I went aboard one of the old four-pipe light cruisers then based in San Diego and stayed for the movies.

Another time, a British cruiser came in to take on fuel and water. This event inspired the following strange passage in my next letter home: "It is more than likely an escort for the merchant ships taking planes for England and France out of Los Angeles. It is gone now, though. There was rust on her sides and she looked all run down. The Germans have been leading them [the British] a merry chase. I don't blame them, though. I don't like Englishmen." This is strange because I don't remember now ever disliking Englishmen. I would later serve with their Navy and come to admire both it and its sailors. The statement must have come from reading Walter Winchell and Westbrook Pegler, two syndicated columnists of the time who were rabid Anglophobes.

Even though I continued to like the Navy and the school work was interesting, the fall-through of my Annapolis dream hit harder than I suspect I realized at the time. The school barracks backed onto Rosecrans Avenue, the main thoroughfare out to San Diego's residential neighborhoods in the lee of Point Loma. Even then there were many homes out that way. We could see them from the barracks windows, neat stucco houses for the most part, with beautiful green lawns and beds of bright flowers under exotic trees with names I did not know.

I started to play a game I had once enjoyed in Tulsa. At night I would watch the windows of the houses, glowing with lamplight through their drawn shades. I imagined happy families living behind those shades and tried to think of what they might be doing. I always pictured Norman Rockwell-ish scenes of smiling faces and lots of laughter. Divorce and family fights and purely human faults had no place there.

Before dark in the evenings we could see children in the yards and mothers and fathers playing games with the kids and talking with neighbors. From what we could see of them, they could all have posed for *Good Housekeeping* ads. I would feel low then. In Tulsa I had known that a grocery store clerk would never have enough money for a nice house and family like those along Rosecrans Avenue. In San Diego I knew that an enlisted man wouldn't either. Even if I made chief petty officer—after fifteen or twenty years—my base pay would be only $126 a month. For the foreseeable future I would never earn more than $72 to $84 per month. Flight pay when I became an enlisted pilot would add 50 percent to that, but that still would not buy a house on Rosecrans.

The approach of the holidays made me feel even worse. My letters home of the time began to sound more sour notes than before. This was the low point of my young naval career but thoughts of my upcoming leave helped. I would be with my family in three or four weeks. Fortunately, I had told no one in Tulsa of my hopes for Annapolis. No one there would ever know I already had failed to achieve my main goal in joining the Navy.

There was another thing I became aware of during that time. Dad must have asked in one of his rare letters about his chances for getting work in San Diego, for I wrote back, "I don't think your chances would be very good. There are lots of Mexicans here, and you know what that means. San Diego is a well-painted town, though—all the houses and buildings are kept in good condition, but I believe it would be pretty tough for an outsider to break in. Californians don't like Oklahomans anyway."

I had become used to economic and class discrimination in my life—probably too conscious of it—but this was the first time I had met up with geographic discrimination. It was the time of the Okies and John Steinbeck's *Grapes of Wrath*. Californians didn't like Oklahomans, and they had some pretty nasty ways of showing it. I even ran into prejudice in the Navy sometimes.

All this made me even more eager to go home. The railroads and bus companies sent agents to the training station to sell tickets and help the men plan their routes. It turned out that it would take me a hundred hours and $31.50 to get to Tulsa and back. That was chair car, of course, but I was young then. I started counting the days.

According to the original plan, I was to arrive in Tulsa at 8:15 the night of January 8, but the Navy proved to have a heart after all and moved up our graduation so we could be home with our families for Christmas—and, for some of us, New Year's Eve as well. It also granted travel time enough for us to have seven full days at home. We doubled up on schoolwork to make up for that.

One of the last things we did before leaving the station was put in our ship requests. At least we could ask for the kind of ship in which we wanted to serve. There was no guarantee we would get what we wanted, but we could ask. Most of the guys asked for big ships, but I requested destroyers. Destroyers were small and fast and, with the possible exception of submarines, the hardest duty in the Navy. In rough weather destroyer sailors had to use straps simply to stay in their bunks. (Destroyer sailors did not sleep in hammocks.) And galley stoves became a problem. Sailors ate cold sandwiches.

Destroyers of the time were only about three hundred feet long and thirty wide. Living quarters were cramped. Old-timers told me I was crazy, but I was full of the romance of the sea. To me, destroyers were pert and saucy. Beside them, other ships were plodding dray horses. Of course, I didn't really know one damned thing about destroyers—or any other kind of ship, for that matter. I had never even been to sea. I made my choice with all the certain sureness of abject ignorance.

As the top man in my class, I was supposed to be given my choice of duty—if not of an individual ship, at least a ship of the class requested. Well, life is full of little disappointments—and some big ones. I already had learned that. I was ordered to the USS *Indianapolis*, a heavy cruiser and flagship for Vice Adm.

Adolphus Andrews, Commander, Scouting Force (COMSCOFOR in the Navy's cryptic shorthand), the third-ranking command afloat in the entire Navy. I did not know that then, though. We would not be given our orders until our return from leave.

Fortunately, youth is resilient, if nothing else. My disappointment at missing Annapolis was all but forgotten in the bustle of stowing our gear and getting our tickets. The barracks were full of happy laughing, joking, and horseplay. We hardly slept the night before we left. We had worked hard and lived a hard regime. The release was intoxicating.

As it happened, I had much the same luck with trains that I had had with my request for destroyers. The one I got was old and rickety and pulled by a well-rusted black steam engine. Most of all, it was slow. We left from San Diego in the slanting sun of late afternoon and headed east into desert mountains. The train was easily as slow as the one we had ridden west from Dallas, and the track rougher. I have since looked on maps for the road, but I have never found it. At one time during that first long night, the conductor told me we were actually in Mexico. Certainly, from the little we could see in the darkness, we might well have been—cactus, rocks, and blocky adobe houses with dim yellow lamplight in their little windows and narrow doors.

The next morning found us somewhere in eastern Arizona and chugging doggedly on our way. Since I was paying my own way this time, I ate in no dining cars. Nor did I sleep in any Pullman berths. I ate what fruit and candy I could buy from the butchers who hawked things through the cars. I slept as best I could in my seat. Three or four days later we arrived in Oklahoma.

It was the day before Christmas. I had left San Diego in warm sunshine, a land of irrigated green lawns and colored flowers. I arrived in an Oklahoma of winter-dead trees and brown fields, of cold winds and gray skies. The buildings and houses of little towns seemed huddled together for warmth. Cows and horses blew steam from their noses. I was home, and it was winter.

My family had moved to a small white frame house on Tulsa's East Archer Street. Its lawn was gray-brown, and its two small elm trees were naked in the cold. Dad was there, and Cora, Flo, and Zena Mae. That was all the warmth I needed. We all, true to our time and place, had never been a demonstrative family, but we did slip a little bit that time. There was a small decorated Christmas tree and the warm smells of Cora's wonderful cooking in the kitchen. We all cried through our laughter.

Dad embraced me, and Cora held onto me as though fearing I might try to get away. Flo and Zena Mae pressed close, and we all talked at the same time. It was a small, poorly furnished house, but it did have electric lights and was "modern," the

Oklahoma term for houses with indoor plumbing. My family had come up in the world. I had never known the joys of indoor plumbing before joining the Navy.

I remember little of what I did while I was home that time. I did call one girl with whom I had worked on the TU newspaper, *The Collegian*, but she pulled back when she learned I was a Navy sailor. That was a new experience, but I didn't really give much of a damn. There had been so much talk in the barracks about girls that I felt I had to give it a try, I suppose. I had never had a date with a girl in my life. I had seldom even talked with one.

All the boys with whom I had gone to high school lived out in the country, and Dad did not have a car at the time. My former classmates at TU, for one reason or another, were not around. Since I had always been a loner anyway, that did not make much difference to me. I did go to the *Tribune* and talked with the reporters and editors I had known there, but we no longer had anything in common. After a few minutes of strained exchange, I left.

In talking with other sailors later, I found that they had had much the same experience. We had become, in only a few months, separated from what to the rest of the world were normal lives. The Navy had done its job well. Even our families, in continuing on at the centers of their worlds had become, in a sense, strangers to those of us who had moved on to the new centers of ours. I know I was uneasy for much of the time I was home.

Cora, in her sentimental Irish way, made over me all the time I was home. She all but force-fed me when I was awake and tucked the covers about me when I was asleep. Dad, in his own halting way, tried to talk with me about the Navy and the strange things I had seen, but even with him I was aware of a loss of oneness. We, too, had slipped apart.

Flo and Zena were openly proud of me and tried to work me into their social lives, but I let them down, I am afraid. Young people of my own age seemed more alienated even than older people were. My few civilian clothes no longer fit at all after six months of Navy chow, and I was self-conscious in Tulsa in my dress blues and white hat.

I did take Flo and Zena to the Ritz one night. The Ritz was one of Tulsa's four first-run movie houses. The only time I had ever been there before was when I graduated from high school and the theater owner gave free tickets to graduates. When I was growing up, we had always gone to the Lyric or the Strand, where tickets did not cost so much. The Ritz was something special. Its ceiling was painted as a night sky. Special lighting effects made clouds seem to pass across the stars. To me, it was the height of sophistication, but I was ill at ease in my blues. People stared at me openly, and I imagined them to be hostile. In fact, they were probably no more than curious.

One of the things that bothered me most, I think, was the fact my family lived in town. The house I remembered—the house I had so often visited in my homesickness in the Navy—had been north of town in a land of tall red oaks and grassy fields where at night owls and coyotes could be heard. The pervasive sound of oil field pumps was a heartbeat of the world that, in some strange way, did not disturb the stillness of the night. The house sat at the end of its own road. The next nearest house was at least a half mile away.

That was the house I remembered all the time I was away, but I did not even get to see it while I was home. The rented house in Tulsa was undoubtedly more comfortable than the one in the country, but it was too close to other houses. Too many cars went by, and people were both too many and too near. The noises of the town were intrusive and remindful of the living world I was too shy to join on its terms—and it was too indifferent to have me on mine.

I was almost glad when the few days of my leave were up. This was another emotion I found often shared by other sailors in the Navy. We no longer fit into our former places. I thought of Thomas Wolfe's *You Can't Go Home Again.*

I know now my family was hurt by my failure to enjoy my leave, but it was not their fault. And there seemed to be nothing I could do about it. Finally, I think they, too, were glad when I went back to the Navy. I suppose they were as relieved as I was to have an end put to the pretense.

My luck did improve, though, in the matter of trains. My return ticket was for a Santa Fe streamliner I had to catch somewhere in Kansas. Wellington, I think. I got that far on one of the motorized railcars—half passenger and half freight— that crisscrossed much of the country in those days. I remember this one for the group of undertakers who were on it. They were returning home from a convention somewhere and had a lot of fun shocking the green young sailor with their shop talk. One of them showed me a catalog of things for their business. I remember one item: a man's burial garment. It was a dark business suit, white shirt, and sober tie, all sewed together in one piece. It was split up the back and could be simply laid over the corpse and tucked in at the sides to make the body appear to be conventionally dressed, all without need for lifting or fitting stiffened arms and legs into sleeves and pants. I was glad to get off that car.

The streamliner, when it came, was bright and shiny and pulled by a diesel engine that would have us in Los Angeles in less than a day and a half. My ticket was still for chair car only, but the seats were bigger and roomier than those in the puddle jumper I had ridden home. They reclined too, so that I could sleep almost normally. The only disconcerting thing was an incident in the dining car.

I had not spent as much money as I had thought I would in Tulsa and had several dollars left over. I decided to treat myself to dinner in the dining car. I had seen no other sailors on the train and had hoped to eat alone. The headwaiter greeted me with some reticence, I thought, but it may have been that I was beginning to look for slights by that time. He seated me at a table with a well-dressed middle-aged couple who looked up at me with what seemed mingled amusement and curiosity.

They nodded me to a seat at their table politely enough, but if I had thought they meant to make it a pleasant time for me, I was wrong. The woman immediately began a vehement discussion of how many schools, libraries, and hospitals could be built for the cost of just one battleship. I didn't know enough to doubt her facts, but I couldn't see one hell of a lot I could do about them. I hadn't attended a Washington strategy session in weeks. The man, when he could break in, reminded me that he had a brother-in-law who had been in the Navy during the world war and the experience had ruined him. He had become so used to loafing that he was never able to hold a decent job in his life.

Both man and wife were horrified to learn I had been in the Navy for seven months and had not yet been to sea. All this did little, I suppose, to help my digestion, but it was not as bad as what came next. No one else in the car could hear what the old people were saying to me, but everyone could hear the college football team that came in.

It was a Big Ten team, as I recall, and on its way to the Rose Bowl game. I think it was Ohio State, but it may not have been. Whoever they were, they were feeling good, and it occurred to them to have some fun with the sailor boy. This was at the time when college students were swallowing live goldfish and taking oaths never to take up arms in war. The Navy—and those in it, I was soon to learn—enjoyed no great respect in their eyes.

The football players made fun of what they called my monkey suit and close haircut, each trying to outdo the others in ridiculing me and, through me, the Navy. God knows I was bashful enough at the time to be an easy target, and they showed no mercy. I finally got up and left my dinner half eaten—and unpaid for. The waiter chased me down the aisle for his money, making me even more embarrassed than before.

I never went back to the dining car. I was glad when, at last, I was back behind the training station fence. That was the only time I was ever so openly set upon, but I experienced many other, less overt, instances of this disregard for sailors in those days. We had all heard stories—false or not—of signs in Norfolk, Virginia, parks warning sailors and dogs to keep off the grass. Richard McKenna, author of the great Navy novel *The Sand Pebbles* and himself a former sailor, wrote in a later nonfiction book of a chief petty officer who sued a Newport, Rhode Island, restaurant for refusing to serve him while he was in uniform.

We all quickly learned there were places where enlisted men were not wanted. Unfortunately, we learned equally well that there were places we *were* wanted: the bars, whorehouses, clip joints, and schlock shops of the world welcomed us gladly—for as long as we had money. Our welcomes seldom lasted much longer than our dollars, but the bargain was an honest one and we accepted it. It was simply the way things were. The credit jewelers on San Diego's lower Broadway were steamy cases in point.

4

The *Indianapolis*

FORTUNATELY FOR THE PURITY of my character, I had little time to sample the delights—and the moral pitfalls—of life in the stateside peacetime Navy. The first thing we did upon returning to San Diego was collect our stored seabags and fall in for delivery to our various assigned ships. I was still a lowly—very lowly—seaman second class, but I was at last to be a real member of the seagoing Navy.

As I wrote earlier, I was ordered to the *Indianapolis*, rather than the destroyers I had requested. But, man proposes and the Navy disposes. The *Indianapolis* at the time was in Mare Island Navy Yard finishing a routine yard overhaul. Those of us assigned to her and to other fleet ships were taken by boat out to where the *Cimarron*, then the newest ship in the Navy, rode to anchor in the stream for further delivery to our individual ships.

The *Cimarron* was a tanker. (Navy tankers of the time were named for rivers in oil-producing regions. By coincidence, I had grown up not far from the Cimarron River in Oklahoma.) We were to be passengers in her—and to learn the special status of passengers in Navy ships.

Although I had visited as many ships as I could while in boot camp, I was virginally ignorant of ships at sea. This was something the *Cimarron* quickly remedied. She was on her way to an overhaul of her own at Mare Island. Thus, she was empty, and empty tankers ride light—very light. She rode like a cork. And, since Navy ships in those days steamed on passage at an easy, fuel-saving ten knots, she did not have even the stabilizing effect of speed to steady her.

Once we rounded Point Loma and turned north to take the Pacific's famous long swells on her port bow, the green hands on board were in trouble. The ship's bows would rise over one swell and roll heavily to starboard. As the swell passed from beneath her, her bows would sink and she would roll to port. The effect was that of a screw being twisted over the heaving water, with devastating effects on innocent stomachs. Fortunately, I was blessed with immunity and was free to enjoy both the discomfort of my friends and the excitement of my first passage at sea.

We came to Long Beach in the late afternoon and lay to off the outer break-water. Long Beach then was the main Pacific Fleet base. As we drew near a dozen or more battleships, even more heavy cruisers, two aircraft carriers, and a number of auxiliaries became visible in the growing dusk. The only ships missing were the destroyers and old light cruisers based in San Diego.

It was a stirring sight. The battleships, like floating fortresses, lay in a long gray line, alive with flags and pennants and flashing signal lights. The cruisers were only slightly less imposing. The carriers and auxiliaries were the only jarring notes—they did not look like warships. Ironically, they would prove to be most valuable of all in the coming war—they and the submarines, none of which could be seen that day in Long Beach.

In all, the resting ships constituted a floating city of several thousand men: the city of Long Beach—and the famous Pike, a huge amusement park at the water's edge—with the inland Santa Monica and San Gabriel mountains serving as a back-drop in the opalescent pre-smog air. Los Angeles did not show at all. In those days it was miles inland.

Small boats drew a tracery of white wakes between ship and ship, and ship and beach. Lights were coming on ashore, and we could hear bands on the closer ships as evening colors were made and ships hauled down their national ensigns. It was thrilling as hell, and I was again glad for having joined the Navy. The Safeway store in Tulsa—and the dining car of the streamliner—seemed a long way off.

The *Cimarron* signaled the various ships for whom she had men, and they sent boats to get them. For more than an hour the *Cimarron* was the center of a milling lot of ships' boats, their engine bells dinging merrily as they maneuvered to come alongside. The new men, lashed hammocks and seabags on their shoulders, boarded and were taken away to the ships that would be their new homes.

Once completed, the *Cimarron* kicked ahead and we shaped a course to clear Point Firmin—sailors called it Point Hard-on for the physiological effect it had upon men first sighting it when homeward bound after a long time at sea. Those of us still on board were piped to the evening meal, and the ship settled down for the night. It would be my first night at sea.

The Navy did not then pamper passengers in its ships. We slept where we could find space—on deck or otherwise—and the next morning we were put to work chipping paint, the eternal chore for men sailing in steel ships. No self-respecting boatswain's mate of the time would have been able to sleep at night knowing he had passengers on board unless he got the last full measure of work out of them. The ship's own deck force saw passengers as gifts from a thoughtful God to be used to lighten their own workload. But I didn't give a damn; I was at sea.

It was hard to get to sleep that first night. The world of ships is full of strange noises and smells and—most of all—motions unlike anything a normal man was likely ever to have known. I was on deck far into the night, just watching the white water boiling along the sides of the ship and listening to the sounds a ship makes at sea: the boom and bump of waves hitting the side plates, the whirr and beat of pumps and blowers, the hum of night winds around masts and stays. I was far too excited to sleep.

Daylight found us off what must have been Piedras Blancas, or Point Sur, two prominent landmarks on the central California coast. As winter days are apt to be in that part of the world, that one was beautiful. The sea was a rich, coastal-waters green, and the Santa Lucia Mountains stood as a tall blue wall to the east, hiding behind it the great nation I was then sworn to defend with my life if necessary. Against what, I had no idea in the world.

We steamed all that day to the northwest at our decorous ten knots. It was not until mid-afternoon that the dark outriding clouds of an approaching front appeared in the northwest and the sea turned mean. The wind picked up and spray came aboard from time to time. For the first time, I tasted sea salt on my lips and felt the chilling cold of a sea wind. This was more like it! Things were shaping up!

The sun was gone entirely behind clouds by the time we turned east to enter the Golden Gate, and the world was growing dark. Lights were coming on in small coastal towns onshore, and we could see the headlights of cars crawling along curving Highway 1. We saw first the great lighthouse on Southeast Farallon Island. Then those of Point Bonita and on Alcatraz Island inside San Francisco Bay. The Golden Gate Bridge was then only two years old. It was an arcing line of lights joining one hilly shore to the other. We could see the patterned lights of San Francisco's streets and, more distant, those of Oakland and other East Bay communities. Directly over and just to the right of Alcatraz, the lights of the 1939 World's Fair lighted the sky over Treasure Island. Alcatraz then was still an active federal prison and was itself brightly lighted.

It was my first landfall, and it was memorable. The front we had seen approaching that afternoon overtook us as we steamed under the Golden Gate Bridge. A gentle rain sifted down, dimming the lights and turning the bay into something dark and mysterious, especially so to us innocents on board. The old-timers were sensibly under cover and keeping dry. But I would not miss a minute of it. We came left and passed inside Angel Island and steamed for another two hours or so before reaching the Navy yard. I stood on deck the full time.

Some twenty-five or thirty miles northeast of San Francisco, the Mare Island Navy Yard sits, as its name implies, on an island across the Napa River from the small town of Vallejo. It was then a relatively modest establishment—although it was the oldest Navy installation in California. There were one or two dry docks, some old Civil War–era redbrick buildings, and a handful of modern shop and foundry buildings strung along the western shore of the river just above where it empties into San Pablo Bay. Before Navy ships converted to oil, coal was kept in a broad, but low, assortment of open sheds with arched roofs. In 1939 they were used for miscellaneous storage.

It was not visible from the dock where we landed, but there was also a little village of officers' housing on the yard grounds that looked very much like the New England villages I would later see. Large, white-painted wood-frame houses with black louvered shutters at their windows stood on wide, well-tended green lawns under old trees. Later, I would be chased by Marines from the area, which I inadvertently invaded on a walk about the base. It was off-limits to white hats.

Vallejo itself, named for a Mexican general who made his peace—and a sizable fortune—by siding with the Americans then rebelling against Mexican rule, was built on low hills across the river from the Navy Yard. Its houses were more like those of East Coast mill towns than anything I had yet seen in California: square wood-framed structures with steep gabled or pyramid roofs and high narrow windows, set along steep streets that met at rigid right angles regardless of terrain. A square redbrick church tower dominated the modest skyline, along with a vertical sign for the Casa Vallejo Hotel.

Vallejo's streets were named for the states of the Union going one way, and for California's counties going the other. Down near the river was Sailor Town: Georgia and Virginia streets. This area now is a landscaped park and site of a handsome civic center. In 1939 it was a noisome collection of bars and whorehouses, tattoo parlors, and clip joints of every degraded kind conceivable to a business community dedicated to getting sailors' money away from them as efficiently as possible—while keeping the sailors themselves safely away from the better parts of town. The town of Vallejo literally lived off the Navy. Those who did not work in the yard itself preyed on those who did and on sailors off ships in for overhaul.

It was still raining when the *Cimarron* slipped alongside a Navy yard pier that night. Just ahead of her at the dock, I could see the clean, yachtlike lines of the *Indianapolis*, glistening in the rain. Dramatically underlit by the dock lights as she was, her superstructure was limned against the night sky. Beyond her high, gracefully arcing clipper bows, her six forward 8-inch guns thrust out from their rounded mounts. And, beyond the guns, the layered towers of communication and bridge decks had masts and directors and yardarm signal halyards that seemed to reach far higher than they actually did. She looked fast and powerful even while lying to a dock. I forgot all about my stupid request for destroyers.

We passengers in the *Cimarron* were called immediately to the quarterdeck, all with our lashed hammocks and seabags with galvanized wash buckets dangling from one end. From there we were transferred at once to the *Indianapolis*, walking along the rain-puddled dock for the few yards separating the ships.

The *Indianapolis'* officer of the deck, with gray mocha gloves and the telescope of his office tucked under his left arm, was personally spruce enough. So were the enlisted men of the watch. But the ship herself was an ungodly mess. Heavy black rubber hoses and electrical cables lay everywhere about her decks, which were themselves soiled and stained by the comings and goings of yard workmen in their muddy boots. I had never seen a ship in yard overhaul before. I hadn't known what to expect.

The officer of the deck took our papers and handed them to the quartermaster of the watch to be logged. After learning that we had had our evening meal in the *Cimarron*, he put us in the hands of a master at arms to be bedded down for the night wherever we could find a place. We would be sorted out and assigned to divisions the next day.

There were many empty bunks in the *Indianapolis* that night. The Navy took advantage of yard periods to give men leave during a time when they would be of little value on board. Many of them had not yet returned. Also, the *Indianapolis* was the flagship for a senior admiral, and admirals are given staffs of officers and allowances of enlisted men, most of them communications people, known collectively as the Flag. Since the admiral was not on board, neither was his Flag, which meant there were even more empty bunks. We took the first we came to and made our beds for the night.

Making our beds was simplicity itself. We simply unlashed our hammocks, stashed our seabags in a corner out of the way, and rolled out hammock, mattress, and blankets on bare bunk springs. When we got our permanent berth assignments, our hammocks would be left permanently under our mattresses, with their clews tucked in at either end for convenient stowage. We sometimes pressed our blues by smoothing them carefully between mattress and hammock and sleeping on them.

The bunks were simple pipe frames with metal springs, fitted three high to vertical stanchions in such a way that they could be folded upward when not in use in order to make more room in the compartment. Stainless steel lockers for our gear were placed wherever they would fit among the bunks. Two or three strategically placed garbage cans completed the furnishings. We lived simply in the ships.

The few men who were on board when we arrived that night complained sleepily—and profanely—about the noise we were making. Since we were boots we tried to be quiet. The washrooms and heads were two decks above the sleeping compartment, so there was a good deal of coming and going for a few minutes. Then all was quiet, and I was ready for my first night's sleep in a U.S. Navy combat ship.

I had expected to have trouble getting to sleep that night. Everything was all so new, I had waited so long to find myself where I was, and the ship was so deathly still—and cold. Ships in the yard had their engines down, and the Navy was not going to waste money on shore power simply to keep sailors warm. But, as it happened, getting to sleep was no problem at all. Before I knew anything had happened a master at arms was going through the compartment, banging on bunks and yelling the Navy's traditional wake-up cry: "Rise and shine! Show a leg, Sailors! Drop your cocks and grab your socks!" It was 5:30, time for deck force sailors to get up.

There was a good deal of grousing and commotion for a few minutes, but no more than that. Securing our bunks came first. Then a quick run to the head and washroom for shaving and washing the sleep out of our eyes. Then off to the big mess halls for breakfast. These mess halls extended from one side of the ship to the other. The camber of their decks was clearly visible. ("Camber" is the term for the arch of the ships' decks—they are higher in the middle than at the sides. It is a strength factor in ships' hulls.)

The *Indianapolis* then still fed family style in individual division messes in a pattern as old as navies themselves. Food was cooked in a central galley and delivered to the messes by men known as mess cooks. They were not cooks at all, but rather waiters who brought the food in nested metal tureens, all held in racks some three or four feet high. These tureens served as serving dishes on the scrubbed oak tables, and everyone helped himself at places that already were set.

The mess cooks also kept the mess halls clean. Between meals the tables, their wrought-iron legs folded flat, were hoisted onto overhead racks and the benches, with their legs folded as well, were slid on top of them so that the mess hall decks were left clear and unobstructed, reaching the width of the ship and extending forty to fifty feet fore and aft. The decks themselves were shiny red linoleum.

After breakfast—a large and hearty meal in the Navy—we new men were paraded on the fantail aft for a kind of slave market in which the ship's division chief petty officers selected individual sailors for their divisions. I didn't know it then, but as a school man, I was supposed to go straight to the signal bridge without putting in the traditional first few months in the deck force.

As a result of that particular piece of ignorance, I didn't object when I was picked for the Third Division, the division responsible for the aftermost deck in the ship. I spent the next few days holystoning decks, scrubbing paintwork, and polishing brass, the time-honored jobs of deck divisions, whose men were known to the rest of the Navy as deck apes or swabbies. In battle we would man the number three 8-inch gun mount, but our normal jobs were little more than housekeeping—and providing hands for endless working parties as the ship was made ready for sailing.

Most of the old hands thought that was the best way in any event. Even the specialists. They felt it wouldn't hurt us new men and might even help us appreciate the easy life and the privileges we would enjoy as watchstanders. The secretary of the Navy, however, disagreed with them, and I was taken onto the bridge when someone in the exec's office noticed I was a comm school graduate. (The exec—short for executive officer—was second in command in the ship and responsible to the captain for its day-to-day administration.)

I did not go onto the bridge before learning enough about holystoning to be damned glad I wouldn't be doing it for a living. A holystone was a heavy rectangle of sandstone about the size of a large brick. It was called a holystone because sailors once got down on their knees to use them. At the time I became acquainted with them they were manipulated by a wooden handle, like a broomstick without its broom. Each stone had a shallow depression in its top. In theory, you put the stick in the dent and slid the stone back and forth to scour the deck clean. The problem for beginners was that because the depression was so shallow the stick had to be held down with a good deal of pressure or it would jump out. But, if you pressed too hard, the damned stone wouldn't slide at all, defeating its whole purpose.

We were showed how to take the stick in our right hands, reach through with our left hands and grab our right forearms in such a way that the stick was held firmly against our shoulders. Then, by swaying our whole upper bodies, we could slide the holystone back and forth along a deck seam, making it work as a big piece of sandpaper and clean wooden decks with great efficiency. So efficiently, in fact, that holystoning was against Navy regulations. Metal deck fittings on older ships sometimes were two or three inches higher than the surrounding wooden planks—all worn away as they were by the zealous holystoning ordered by captains who wanted nice white decks on their ships.

As in most things, there was a trick in holystoning. To see a line of veteran swabbies swaying rhythmically across a snowy white teak deck striped with black caulking could be a most pleasing sight—so long as the viewer was not doing the swaying. Fortunately, I was not in a deck division long enough to learn the trick and could enjoy the view in comfort from the safe distance of the signal bridge.

At any rate, we went to sea the morning after my reporting aboard. It would have been nice to think the ship had been waiting for me, but I don't think that was the case. All the hoses and cables cluttering the decks disappeared as though by magic, and the sounds of a living ship slowly came online—the blowers and pumps and auxiliary motors that never stop unless the ship is under yard overhaul or victim of some other disaster. Yard workmen took their tools and equipment and filed ashore. The *Indianapolis* was again a living ship of the Navy.

Ships, when they finish a yard overhaul, are required to undergo what are known as yard trials. They go to the nearest open water and are put through a grueling series of tests of engines, steering gear, and all the other components of an operating vessel to ensure that the work just completed is satisfactory and that nothing more need be done.

We stood at quarters for getting under way. I was still in the Third Division so my station for getting under way was on the main deck aft. We stood in ranks, with chiefs and officers at their posts. As often happens after California's winter rains, the sky was cloudless and the air like crystal. Civilians ashore were driving to work as we slipped down the Napa River. Some of them pulled off the road and stopped to watch us go.

The river is narrow at Vallejo. The *Indianapolis* was a beautiful ship, even fouled with yard grime as she was that morning. Her graceful clipper bow and compact bridge structures were unlike the more utilitarian lines of newer ships. She was built to treaty limitations as to guns and armor—one of the ships sometimes cynically described as "paper clads" for their vulnerability—limitations that would be amply demonstrated in the coming war when she sank quickly under Japanese submarine attack. But, oh, she was beautiful slipping out to sea that morning. Again, the Safeway store in Tulsa seemed a long way off.

We had come the night before in the *Cimarron* across San Pablo and San Francisco bays, but it had been a rainy night and we could not see much of the land. San Pablo Bay, according to the sailors who sail it, is ten miles wide, ten miles long—and ten feet deep. It is like a large inland lake, with low hills all around, rising to Mount Tamalpais in the west and Mount Diablo in the east. Because it is so shallow, ships can cross it only by staying in a narrow dredged channel. The shores were not built up then as they are now, of course, and were all green from winter rains. The water was stained brown with runoff from the great rivers to the east.

We had seen more of San Francisco Bay the night before because of the lights rimming its shores in all but continuous brightness. But it, too, was even more impressive in daylight. The city's buildings, though modest enough by today's standards, seemed to me tall and grand. Unlike those of most cities, San Francisco's buildings seemed white, or nearly so. This was especially true of residential areas. Squarish houses were jammed cheek by jowl wherever they would fit along the plunging streets in a kind of cubist geometry. Here and there, brilliantly green parks broke the ranks of homes.

Our trip up the coast from San Diego in the *Cimarron* was made at a stodgy nine or ten knots, a lumbering and comfortable speed perhaps—in anything other than an empty tanker. In the *Indianapolis* we built quickly to eighteen knots, then to even more, until, for most of the day we were steaming at as much as thirty knots. It was exhilarating, with the wind tearing at our clothes and dollops of cold winter spray bursting through the lifelines from time to time. The motion was even more exciting.

Unlike the *Cimarron*'s bluff bows, the *Indianapolis* had bows like a knife. Once under the Golden Gate Bridge and beyond Point Bonita we met up with the great winter swells so often found there. Speeding as we were, our bows dug deep into the rising swells until reserve buoyancy swept us up in a rush, with spray flying and rigging all taut and straining in the wind. We pounded then into the following trough with shock enough to cause men to stagger. Our bows would dig into the next swell, and it was all done over again.

We ran our trials in the Gulf of the Farallones, a body of water off the Golden Gate, bounded by Mount Tamalpais to the north and Mount Montara to the south. The Farallon Islands—*farallones* is the Spanish word for small, rocky islands—are planted right in the middle of the gulf.

The Gulf of the Farallones can be a rough and dangerous place, as evidenced by the number of ships that have been lost there, some even in recent years. But that January morning in 1940 the scene could have been used as a recruiting poster. There were the same boldly bright colors of sea and sky used in such posters, the same simplicity of a world made of air and water, with the clean line of the horizon to mark the difference, and the blue of distant mountains the only hint of land at all. The beautiful *Indianapolis*, dashing and turning, starting and stopping, churned the water into froth as she was put through her paces.

The picture was so vividly printed onto my young mind that I remember it yet, all these years later. This is not to say, though, that I was free to savor it as I might. I was a Third Division deck ape, spending my day holyrocking the fantail teak. Any sightseeing I did was managed only by taking my eyes away from the work at hand. This, in turn, resulted in a loss of concentration that found the damned broomstick slipping from its appointed place. I would lurch then into my companion apes to either side, causing them to express their dissatisfaction with me.

Even worse, the division chief noticed my repeated lapses, and I was pulled out of the line and put to work on an isolated nook where I would not be a hindrance to others. This was a surprisingly painful punishment for someone who wanted so badly to be accepted as I did.

At any rate, we finished our trials in mid-afternoon and turned for the gate. Our captain then was physically very large. The crew, completely without affection, called him the Sea Pig. Most times this was shortened to merely the Pig. The latter part of our trials found us working our way closer to the gate so that, when the exercise was over, we were not far offshore at all. We came tearing in through the gate at some eighteen to twenty knots. Consensus among the deck apes was that the "Goddamn Pig must have a hot date in Vallejo for tonight."

Nor did we did slow at all when we went left to pass through Raccoon Straits, a narrow passage between Angel Island and the Marin County coast. Large ships were then allowed to sail those confined waters, but not at the speed we were making. That speed meant that we would be in Mare Island in little more than an hour. It also meant that our wake would play hell with shoreside structures in the little town of Tiburon on the north shore.

That disaster, at least, was avoided when our rudder jammed, and the *Indianapolis* rounded up onto a heading that would have put us at the intersection of Second and Main streets in the waterside town of Sausalito. I wasn't on the navigation bridge, of course, but I later talked with quartermasters who were. They said the Pig's face turned every shade of white and red there is. Captains in those days were harshly treated if they put their ships on the ground, and I suppose the Pig was seeing numbers flying off like startled gulls. If the Pig allowed the *Indianapolis* to touch bottom, he would be in deep trouble.

Fortunately, we didn't ground. The crew was at their special sea detail stations for entering port, and the engine room alert for orders from the bridge. All engines were put immediately into full emergency back. The ship rattled and trembled under the strain. I cannot be sure, this long later, but I think we let go the bow anchors as well. In the end, we came to a panting stop a hundred yards or so off the beach.

After the rudder fault was corrected, we got under way again, although at a more decorous speed, and made our way to Mare Island, where we arrived long after dark. Those who wanted to could go ashore if they didn't have the duty.

I did not get to go ashore because the chief, remembering, I suppose, my ineptitude at holystoning, gave me a midnight to four o'clock fire watch. This, called the middle watch, or more simply the mid, was the least popular of all Navy watches. It meant you did not get much sleep, and it was commonly used as a punishment. This chief was a strong believer in the traditional Navy chief's motto: "Maybe I can't make you do that, son, but I can sure as hell make you wish you had." By four o'clock the next morning I wished very much I had paid more attention to my holystoning.

The fire watch, incidentally, was stood in central station, a small compartment far below the waterline, where, in battle, much of the ship's well-being was monitored. There were many dials and panels of colored lights. The man I relieved briefed me, very briefly, by saying, "See all those colored lights? Any of them green ones turn red, you take this phone, here, and tell the guy that answers the number of the light that's turned red. You got that?"

It didn't seem a hell of a lot to get, but I told him I understood, and he disappeared up the ladder and closed and dogged the hatch behind him with a large and disconcerting bang. I was sealed into a locked compartment, God knows how far below the water, with no idea what all the gadgets around me meant, or what would happen if I should happen to touch one of them. It had been emphasized, to a fault, how important my lonesome job was. The fate of the whole damned ship, and everyone in her, depended on me, it seemed. But, even then, I wondered why anyone as smart as the people who ran the Navy would leave a multimillion-dollar ship in the hands of a guy making thirty-six dollars a month.

We didn't have any fires that night. The only lasting lesson I learned from that watch was not to drink Navy coffee. Few duty stations in the Navy, either then or now, I understand, are without their own coffee gear. Central station was no exception. But, since there was only a skeleton crew—me—that night, no one had bothered to make fresh coffee in a long time. And it was cold down there. I had always heard that a good, hot cup of coffee had a warming effect, and I could sure as hell have used some warming effect. I could have turned on the electric pot, I suppose, but I was afraid to touch anything and fell back upon the hope that cold coffee would be better than nothing. It wasn't. God knows how long that poisonous brew had been sitting there, lying in ambush for me. All I know is that it tasted awful. I don't like coffee to this day.

The next day we spent alongside the Navy yard wharf, working to clean the ship after what the yard workmen had done to her. By evening, I thought we had done a pretty good job, but the division chief found a whole lot more to do. Luckily we could not very well work in the dark—probably to the chief's great disappointment—so liberty was granted. This time I was included.

Naturally, going to a movie in Rodman Center, the yard's recreation facility— even a civilian movie in Vallejo—was not enough. Sailorlike, we had to get onto a bus and go all the way to Oakland, twenty-five or thirty miles away. Being new to the drill, I went along with the rest. About all I remember of the ride is that the bus driver at one point drove us along the shores of Oakland's beautiful Lake Merritt on roads he said were a favorite lovers' lane. He said Lake Merritt was the only rubber-lined lake in the world.

This was obviously funny as hell, but my new shipmates had to explain it to me. They thought it was uproarious too that I had not yet made the acquaintance of condoms. The other guys were all older—and far more experienced—than I was. Once off the bus, they quickly moved into realms I knew little about: Oakland's famous-in-the-Navy Wonder Bar, for instance. The guys said it was the longest bar in the world, but in the years to come I ran into a number of bars that were the longest in the world. Whether it was or not, I never learned. They wouldn't let me in.

I was then too young to drink legally, although bartenders were not very fussy in those days—especially not for sailors. But I had always borne the curse of looking much younger than my age, and my Methodist mother's dire warnings about the perils of drink had left me afraid of the devilish places in the first place. I do remember there was a sizable lot of women and girls on the sidewalk outside the bar, all glamorous as hell to me in the garish light of neon beer signs. My shipmates quickly got through the bargaining phase and paired off to go inside.

A very young, very pretty dark-haired girl looked back over her shoulder to me. "Aren't you coming?" she said. I shook my head, too embarrassed to speak. Her name was Penelope. It is odd that I should remember her name after all this time, but I do. She stayed and talked with me on the sidewalk for a little while, and then, before she followed the others inside, she reached and kissed me lightly on my lips. It was a very nice shock to learn how soft and warm a girl's lips are, and how they taste of lipstick.

I never saw nor heard from Penelope again in my life, but I found my way back to the ship in a rosy glow of euphoria at this, my first wild sexual encounter as a sailor. On my way from the bus station to the Mare Island ferry in Vallejo, I walked down Virginia Street. We had gone up Georgia Street earlier that night, and I always liked to come and go by different routes in strange towns. You see more that way. Virginia Street, only one block from Georgia, was where the whorehouses were, but I didn't know that then.

They were old two-story wooden Victorian houses with high narrow windows. Each sat back from the street behind a little front yard with low wooden or bent wire fences and brick or concrete walks to the front door. They did not look well kept at all. The glass of their windows, for one thing, must all have been loose for, as I went by on the sidewalk, I could hear them rattling. I thought it strange because there was no wind that night. I later learned the rattling was caused by the girls' rapping their knuckles on the glass to get my attention. At least I had Penelope to remember.

The following morning we sailed early to rejoin the fleet in Long Beach. The yard period was over, and the ship had to get back to work. We slipped down the river as we had the morning of our yard trials. The *Cimarron* and some odds and ends of district small craft rendered us passing honors. Navy ships, in passing each other, sound "Attention" on bugle or whistle and everyone topside stands at attention facing the ship being passed. It is, like everything else in the Navy, tradition from many years ago. Merchant ships dip their flags to naval vessels for the same hoary reason. In any event, that was the last time I would see Mare Island while I was in the Navy. After the war I would come to live not far away.

It was a cold and wet passage south. The weather was bad until we were almost within sight of Point Hard-on.

During the trip I was discovered to be a school man and hustled up to the signal bridge. The chief signalman was a square-built man named Maxwell. He was, by character, equally square, in the modern sense. First rated in World War I, he had stayed in the Navy and, so far as I was ever to learn, never had another interest in his life. Navy regulations were his Bible, and admirals his college of cardinals. He was a stolid man, but fair and given, sometimes, to colorful figures of speech. I remember the first time he sent me aloft to repair something on the port yardarm, a height of maybe a hundred feet over the water—and forty to fifty above the bridge itself. "You drop anything up there, son," he said, "you be sure and turn loose of it."

Hawghead Barbour was the bridge first class. He was a southerner, chubbier than most sailors of the time, and the owner of a neck almost as wide as his head, hence the nickname. He too had been in the Navy a long time. Men did not then make first class or chief as quickly as we did in World War II.

As I recall now, there were three second-class signalmen. Mother Scott was one of them. He was a small, slightly built man with a very large nose. One of the flag signalmen once said Mother was the only man in the Navy who could smoke a cigar in the shower—a cruel but only slightly exaggerated comment. Mother got his name for his sweet tooth and his worrisome nature, which tended to take responsibility for others whether they wanted him to or not.

Jimmy Brower was another second class. He was a good-looking blond man who wore his hair as long as he could get away with. He pushed it up on the front of his head like a destroyer's bow wave. He loved swing music and was forever pounding out a syncopated beat with semaphore flag sticks on bridge railings, dodgers, or whatever else came to hand. He had the added distinction of being married, although he had not seen his wife in years. She lived somewhere on the East Coast, I believe. He and Hawghead were the only two married men on the bridge.

The third second class was Joe Wise, a tall, thin man with curly black hair and a crooked smile. He was one of the men then returning to the fleet from the China

Station. He was Asiatic as hell. "Asiatic" was not a complimentary term in the Navy then. Especially not with officers and senior petty officers. Asiatics cared little for discipline or regulations of any kind. They wore—when they could get away with it—fancy tailor-made uniforms with scarlet dragons embroidered in silk inside their cuffs and waistbands or anywhere else they could be put so they would not be seen by inspecting officers.

They seemed to go out of their way to bug officers. Joe's wash bucket, for instance, was the standard galvanized Navy bucket, but it had been chromed and polished to glittering brilliance. A Chinese dragon in red brass wound about it, and its handle was a mass of fancy decorative rope work. Joe's bucket made ours look like nail kegs in a jewelry store. But it had started life as a regulation Navy bucket, and no one could find a law against what Joe had done to it. Of course, that didn't stop the Pig from glaring at it every time he inspected our compartment. I looked up to Joe Wise as a junior grade god. In my young eyes, he was everything a sailor should be, but I knew better than to follow his example.

I get a little mixed up now in trying to recall the third-class signalmen. There was one named Boulware, I think, a taciturn man who professed to hate the Navy. He was from Colorado and returned there the minute his enlistment was up.

Frank Jordan was another. His nickname was Tackline, for the six-foot length of signal halyard used to separate flags in a hoist. When Jordan stood erect his silhouette was very much like that of a tackline. He was slender. He would die a lonely and unnoticed death in a submarine in the coming war.

Honk Taylor was a destroyer man from the Atlantic Fleet. His original home was Plattsmouth, Nebraska, and he was a tough cookie. No one referred to signal girls when Honk was around. He had the cocky good looks of a young Clark Gable, although his nose did stray a little off course as a souvenir from some forgotten disagreement. He wasn't tall, but he was catnip to women. His peculiar nickname came from a remarkably deep and resonant voice.

Honk and I would later be taken into Admiral Andrews' Flag and would serve together under four different admirals in ten different ships altogether. He used to correspond with my sister Zena Mae, but nothing ever came of that. He would die as a commissioned flight deck officer in the escort carrier *Liscombe Bay* off Tarawa.

Stinky Clark was a third class too, as I remember. He had a reputation on the bridge for having an aversion to bathing, a serious offense in the Navy. He was said to have suffered at one time the traditional cure of a scrub down by offended shipmates with hard canvas and harder deck sand, but I doubt that. His problem, I think, was skin that looked dirty even when it was clean and messy hair he seldom bothered to comb. He was close to a genius in mathematics, though, and introduced me to classical music with his windup phonograph and collection of records. The first time I heard Cotelby was on one of Stinky's records.

The rest of the signal gang included Bogeman, an Indianan who must have been close to the Navy's minimum height. His claim to fame was a rounded butt and a walk that was entrancing when seen from behind. Honk told him one time he should sue the Navy for building its decks too close to his ass. And Moffatt, a big, gangling, good-natured kid whose nickname was foreordained when we reached Honolulu, where there was a triple-decked night club named Wo Fat's. Our Moffatt became Mo Fat. And Fitch, an archetypal New Yorker from Poughkeepsie who quoted his father as telling him he wished he had used a rubber and flushed him down the toilet.

There were others whom I have forgotten. Some left and others came, but these were the original bridge gang as I remember them now. These are the men who, in a very real sense, became my family. Most of them had been in the Navy a long time and had long since lost touch with their real families—if they ever had had any. And we who were new came quickly to share some of their feelings. It was not that we loved our families less, but that we were so completely isolated from them and all normal contact. The contemptuous animosity we sensed on the part of civilians toward us and the studied impersonality of our relationships with our officers helped too, I suppose. We were driven to look inward and to rely on ourselves for the support normal people get from their families.

I arrived in Long Beach considering myself every bit a sailor. The ships we had seen anchored there on our way north in the *Cimarron* were still there, long rows and ranks of them, with ships' boats milling about them like water bugs on summer ponds. But we steamed blithely past them, rendering and acknowledging passing honors right and left.

This was where, and when, I learned that rank not only hath its privileges in the Navy, it hath the ability to invoke those privileges even when the holder of the rank is not present. Admiral Andrews was in a relief flagship somewhere in Hawaiian waters at the time, but the *Indianapolis* was his permanent flagship. Normally she secured to Buoy George, and to Buoy George we secured this time.

Buoy George was inside the inner breakwater in Long Beach, a brisk three- or four-minute motor launch ride from the Pico Street Fleet Landing. Ordinary mortals in their ordinary ships had a sometimes cold and wet thirty-minute to an hour ride out to their ships. In fog it could take a lot longer than that. When California's famous Santa Ana winds blew they sometimes could not get home at all, giving rise to what was known to sailors as Shanghai liberties. So, even though Admiral

Andrews basked in the warm Hawaiian sun, we basked in the warm glow of his reflected glory, swinging to Buoy George.

Long Beach in those days was to sailors the Pike. The Pike was an amusement park the likes of which I never saw anywhere else in the world. Two to three blocks deep at times, it ran along the beach for what seemed a very long way. Roller coasters, bumper cars, hoop throws—every entertaining ride, dodge, scam, and practice known to man was on the Pike. There were bars, hot dog stands, chili parlors, and ice cream joints. Some of us never got beyond the Pike on Long Beach liberties. Tourists and people from all over Southern California—especially teenagers and young adults—came to the Pike too. For girls, it was where the sailors were. For boys, it was where the girls were.

The only worry in it all was the zoot-suiters. There was virtually open warfare at the time between Navy sailors and the largely Hispanic gangs known as zoot-suiters. The zoot-suiters had their own uniforms: low-crowned, broad-brimmed hats, long-skirted coats nipped in at the waist and extravagantly padded in the shoulders, peg-top pants, and a metal keychain so long it hung below their knees. And knives. Few sailors dared go ashore alone when the zoot-suiters were out. There were casualties on both sides, but the *Indianapolis* was not there long enough for any of us to get into serious trouble.

The liberty I remember most vividly during that brief visit was when Mo Fat invited me to visit his sister with him. She was some years older than Mo Fat and lived in a pretty little stucco bungalow on Las Feliz Boulevard in a nice residential area of Los Angeles. We took a big red Pacific Electric interurban streetcar from Long Beach to Los Angeles through what seemed long miles of orange groves. From downtown Los Angeles, we took an ordinary streetcar out past Pershing Square.

Residential Los Angeles in those long ago and smog-free days was an extremely tidy place of tended lawns, tall palm trees, incredible flower beds, and geraniums, geraniums, geraniums. Mo Fat's sister lived in a house much like all the others on Las Feliz, far better than anything I ever had lived in or even visited. But, young sailors that we were, neither sister nor her nice house was what we had in mind for what would be one of our last liberties in the States—Hawaii was then a territory. After paying our respects, we hurried back to the Pike's more sophisticated and uplifting environment.

We sailed for Hawaii only two or three days after arriving in Long Beach. The *Indianapolis*, by that time, was immaculate in preparation for receiving Admiral Andrews and his Flag. Her decks were as white as sand, saltwater, and sailor sweat could make them. So white, in fact, that we were not allowed to sit down on deck without taking off our shoes. Our rubber heels might leave black marks, you see.

That brings to mind the interesting question of where sailors did sit. Except for the mess benches—and a half-dozen chrome and plastic chairs—the kind furniture stores sell as dinette sets—in the tiny ship's library nothing was provided for the purpose. If we wanted to sit down, we sat on deck—and took off our shoes.

At any rate, we sailed one afternoon. Except for a couple of glancing blows of a few hours at San Diego and San Francisco—and one two-week leave in 1940—I would not see the United States again for four years. I didn't care. I had come into the Navy to go to sea. When my dreams of Annapolis collapsed, the land no longer held much charm for me. I watched America sink beneath the horizon astern with a kind of elation. The passages, north and south, along the California coast had found us never out of sight of land. But now—now the world had become all water and sky, with only the horizon to mark the difference.

That evening, when we took our planes aboard some hundred miles or more to sea, the *Indianapolis* was finally complete and an operating unit of the American Navy's Pacific Fleet. I was where I wanted to be. And since happiness is something best known in retrospect, I think I was happy.

Our heavy cruisers in those days did carry airplanes, four each of the hallowed SOC Curtis biplanes, which remained operational throughout World War II. We fired them off catapults and retrieved them from water landings alongside—to the great admiration of a British officer we had on board one time as an observer. Similar British ships, he said, carried but one old Walrus pusher flying boat, which also was launched by catapult. But it was retrieved by landing it in the open sea and mooring it to a buoy on a sea anchor. The ship then would maneuver to recover its airplane. Once all that was done, there was the buoy to be recovered. The operation took a long time. It could not be done in rough water.

We, on the other hand, landed our planes in the slick formed under the quarter of a turning ship. Ships change course by skewing their sterns to one side or the other, until their bows are pointed in the direction they want to go. In doing so, their skidding sterns flatten the water, forming a relatively smooth area off their inside quarters in which an airplane can safely land. It can then taxi forward and hook onto a trailing net that holds it in position under a hoisting crane.

While the first plane to land is being secured on its catapult carriage, the ship swings the other way and the second plane lands in the slick created on that side, repeating the process until all four airplanes are safely on board and lashed down. The system made possible air operations in all but very bad weather. And it was remarkably fast. When the flag was embarked, we sometimes carried five airplanes. There were times when all of them were recovered in ten to fifteen minutes.

When sitting on their catapults the airplanes were only a few feet from the signal bridge. I had a whole new focus of interest. I wanted to be a dungaree pilot, you remember.

With planes secured on board, bunkers full of fuel, storerooms stowed with provisions, and—in the Navy's traditional phrase—ready in all respects for sea, we steamed west into the night.

5

A Sailor at Last

THE PERIOD THAT STARTED with our sailing from Long Beach was, in some ways, the most idyllic of my entire life. It has always seemed to me that happiness for men is something seldom recognized except in retrospect. Rarely do we know we are happy in the moment. That is what made the coming months and years so remarkable for me, I think now. I knew at the time I was happy. I was young, healthy, in one of the Navy's best ships, steaming in tropical seas, eating regularly—and blessed with absolutely no responsibility other than that of my two four-hour watches per day, drills that became so routine they required little thought at all, and cleaning stations that were largely idiot work.

Signalmen, along with radiomen and quartermasters, were what then were known as watchstanders. Except for our cleaning stations and drills, we had no routine duties. We were also treated more gently than other sailors. We were called later in the mornings, for one thing. Those having the mid watch were given night rations at sea, thick slabs of meat or cheese on hunks of the Navy's hand-sliced bread. When in port, if we didn't have the duty, we were given liberty at one o'clock in the afternoon. The common folks had to wait until four or five o'clock. We didn't even have to serve our own meals. Men from deck divisions were assigned to our mess for that purpose. As may well be imagined, little of this endeared us to less fortunate types.

Watches in the Navy, starting at eight o'clock in the morning, were typically four hours each, though the afternoon watch from four to eight was cut in half so that men would not stand the same watch every day. This practice of splitting the watch was called "dogging the watch," and the resulting two two-hour watches, from four to six and six to eight, were the dog watches. For most of the day we were on watch four hours and off for eight.

That was not too bad, except for the fact our eight hours off were frequently broken into by drills and inspections and the like. Those of us who did our laundry had to find time for that, as well as for bathing ourselves. Whatever time was left we could use for sleeping. As watchstanders, none of us ever had a full night's sleep at sea.

Bathing and doing laundry were entirely new experiences at sea. In the first place, the ship was put on water hours the minute we got under way from Long Beach, meaning all taps, except those for drinking, ran for only limited times during the day. Freshwater was made in ships by evaporating seawater. Evaporating seawater required burning fuel oil, and Navy captains were judged on how economical they could be with fuel oil. The Pig clearly was not going to spend any more fuel making water than he had to.

We enlisted men were allowed one bucket of freshwater per day for washing both ourselves and our clothes. We drew the water in one or the other of the ship's two washrooms, large, white-tiled compartments with showers at one end, urinals and a stainless steel trough running with a continuous stream of seawater for a toilet along one bulkhead, and a bank of sinks and shaving mirrors along another. The showers, of course, were never used at sea. We bathed ourselves from our buckets and washed our clothes in what was left. We drew our water from a tap and heated it by holding it under a jet of live steam, which, with a shattering blast of noise, brought the water to a boil almost instantly.

Since the great part of the washrooms was nothing but open space, we squatted by our buckets to wash ourselves first, then got down on hands and knees to scrub our clothes on the tiled deck, using the same water for both jobs. This would not have been all that bad had we been alone in the washroom. But usually—especially when liberty parties were getting ready to go ashore—the washrooms were so crowded that, in the Navy's hackneyed expression, we had to scrub, on average, three asses before we could be sure we had scrubbed our own.

There were two drying rooms for wet laundry built alongside the furnace uptakes for the number two stack, where temperatures were well above a hundred degrees. We were never allowed to hang wet laundry in living compartments; it made for too much of what the British called "fug," a wonderfully apt term for unhealthy dankness where we slept.

Signalmen, radiomen, and yeomen—the communications rates—all lived in the C Division compartment two decks below the main deck and just at the waterline. Before the war we actually had glass portholes in our compartment that could be opened to admit fresh air when the ship was moored in calm waters. Some of the guys used to lie in their bunks and fish from these ports, until Hawghead explained their remarkably good luck by pointing out that the outfall from the heads was just below.

Of course, the ports had to be closed and dogged down tight anytime we were under way, for sometimes they would be rolled ten or fifteen feet underwater, even in relatively calm seas. But the effect at those times was spectacular. In daytime, the ports would frame beautiful pastel green circles whose glow lighted everything in the compartment with a weird, unearthly shimmer of color. At night, the effect could be even more impressive, for the water outside was usually alive with phosphorescence in electric shades of blue and green. Sometimes I would lie at night and watch it for hours, pondering the mysteries of the sea. And all the while I'd be listening to the homey clinking of our wash buckets as they shifted idly in their racks with the motion of the ship.

We were rarely in our compartment, however, except to sleep and to take care of our gear. The bunks were triced up close to their stanchions during working hours. It was possible to crawl into the space between two paired bunks and to sleep in the narrow *V* they made, but it was a punishable offense to be caught doing so. We might come down to retrieve something from our lockers sometimes, but generally we were expected to stay clear of our sleeping compartments during the day.

The signalmen's real home was the bridge anyway. This was a roughly triangular deck, three decks above the main deck and one deck below the navigation bridge, the place from which the ship was controlled while under way. The bridge was also the Flag bridge, for here the admiral had his plotting station and held sway with his staff of officers and allowance of enlisted men. It was a curious convention in the Navy that admirals had no direct control over their flagships. They were considered passengers and made their wishes known to the ship's captain on the navigation (nav) bridge above through the formal chain of command. That flagship's captain then would issue the necessary orders to his officer of the deck.

Physically, the signal bridge was anchored by a lightly (two or three inches) armored conning tower at its forward end. This conning tower was fitted with narrow observation slits and was meant for the use of senior officers during battle, but I never saw anyone in the thing. There was also a narrow outdoor catwalk forward of the conning tower, but I never saw anyone use that either, except for sailors who sometimes slept there when we sailed into hot weather down around the equator.

Just aft of the conning tower was a room—the admiral's plotting station, commonly called Flag plot. The whole starboard side of this compartment was taken up by a waist-high, green-topped chart table, with shallow drawers holding corrected charts for all the world's navigable waters. There were deeper drawers and fitted racks for sextants, stadimeters, star finders, and chronometers—all the gear for navigating the ship wherever she might be ordered to go. At the after end of the table there was even a mechanical dead-reckoning tracer that printed a continuous record of the ship's movements. All this was the realm of the Flag chief quartermaster, who would come aboard with the admiral when we reached Pearl Harbor.

The forward bulkhead held a powerful Hallicrafter radio and other communications gear that would seem primitive now to modern sailors. On the port side, except for the one entry door and its light lock, a comfortable leather settee stretched the full length of the compartment. The whole thing made an admirable signalmen's club when the admiral was not on board. Sometimes on the Hallicrafter we could pick up Bob Wills and his Texas Playboys from Tulsa's radio station KVOO. A blanket spread on the always clean deck made a good spot for shooting craps.

Outside, on the port side, there was a comfortable chair behind glass windows for the admiral's pleasure. This too found good use by enlisted asses when the admiral's exalted buttocks were not present. At the outside after end of Flag plot there was a hooded log desk with a clock and a lanyard for striking the bells. A shallow drawer held pencils, logbooks, and message blank forms. The bell itself was mounted high on the mast, but signalmen were responsible for striking it every thirty minutes in a time-honored system, stemming probably from the ancient use of half hour sand glasses—except during the night hours when our sleep might be disturbed. We did not strike bells after taps.

Here too was a landing with ladders leading down to the communications deck below and to the navigation bridge above. The radio room was on the communications deck. At this point, the signal bridge extended the full width of the ship before the war and was carpeted with black rubber mats made of wafers of automobile tires strung on brass rods by convicts in California's San Quentin Prison. Snowy white coco-fiber runners outlined traffic lanes.

The entire forward part of the bridge was fronted and protected by glass windows that could be rolled down. We had to roll them down when firing or they would be broken by the muzzle blasts of the six big 8-inch guns forward. The slanting legs of the ship's tripod mast—and the vertical supports for fire control directors to either side pierced the signal bridge. Outboard of them were the semaphore platforms, one to either side, where men could stand to be seen when sending messages by that means. There too were the big 36-inch searchlights whose bluish beams could be bounced off clouds to signal for miles beyond the horizon at night.

In the wings of the bridge to either side were the keys to operate yardarm blinkers—small lights set at the end of the yardarms on both masts, used most often for administrative work in harbor, but sometimes for maneuvering ships in peacetime. I don't remember them ever being used during the war. Here too were the 12-inch searchlights used for routine work and mortar tubes for firing signal rockets and flares. A counterbalanced 45X telescope was mounted to either side as well for spotting flag hoists.

Across the after end of the bridge were the flag bags, where the ship's two complete sets of signal flags—both international and Navy—hung from varnished wooden racks over deep sheet metal bins called, by tradition, bags. Two heavy brassbound wooden benches with red linoleum tops backed against the forward face of the flag bags. These ostensibly were for the use of Flag staff officers wanting to take a load off their feet. But when moved to the railed area aft of the flag bags, they made excellent balcony seats from which signalmen could view the movies shown against the forward bulkhead of the airplane hangars amidships. Protected from the presence of lesser types, we could smoke and sip coffee with our movies in a state superior even to that of the officers on the quarterdeck below.

That was our shop. It was home and club to us. Spotlessly clean, comfortably carpeted, light and airy, and off limits to the common herd, the signal bridge was ours to enjoy in port. Even at sea the starboard side was our sanctuary so long as we did not interfere with the watch. A low metal pyrotechnics locker—for signal rockets and flares—made a table for our coffee gear. A standard wash bucket of water was stowage for the community cups. There was no admiral's chair on this side of the bridge, but we made do. Officers rarely intruded and kept decently to their own side.

The one aggravating flaw—and it was a minor one—on the *Indy*'s signal bridge was that the ship's whistle and siren were mounted on the forward edge of the number one stack, which loomed over the bridge's after end. When they were sounded after having been idle for a time they spewed scalding water over us. Before getting under way the whistle had to be tested, of course. It was the quartermasters' job to do that. I know damned well they waited sometimes until a signalman was in range before pulling the whistle cord.

Altogether the *Indy*, for signalmen, was what was known in the Navy then as "a home and a feeder"—meaning good duty, although we did drill our butts off on that leisurely passage to Hawaii. The new men had to be fitted in and made capable of doing their work, you see. The old-timers had become rusty during the long inactivity of the yard period as well and had to be brought back up to snuff before the Flag returned on board. We steamed alone on that passage. This is usually a signalman's dream because it means no signal work must be done, except in the case of the odd merchant ship that might or might not bother to call us. Still Chief

Maxwell did not let anything as simple as that slow him down. He organized us into port and starboard teams and pitted us against each other in endless drills to see which team would become the fastest and most accurate.

Flag hoist signaling—the kind in which strings of pretty flags are hauled up to the yardarms—was the most critical. Flag hoist was used then almost exclusively in maneuvering formations of ships at sea during daylight. The Navy used the standard international code flags and pennants, but it had its own numeral flags and a number of special purpose flags as well.

The signal gang was organized into spotters, benders-on, hoisters, and stowers. As a flagship we would be originating most of the tactical signals. The Flag lieutenant would give the Flag chief the signal to be made. The Flag chief would call out the flags, and the benders-on would hook them onto a halyard and yell "Hit it!" to the hoisters.

In the *Indianapolis* the flag bags where the flags were stowed were reversed from the way of most ships. Our benders-on faced forward in the *Indy*—as I already had come to call her. They could see the hoisters and could guide the flags from their bags. This was a much better arrangement than was looking aft and having the hoist dragged across your face, as was done in most other ships.

Each halyard had two hoisters. They faced each other with the halyard between them. When the bender-on was ready and cried, "Hit it!" one hoister would grasp the halyard as high up as he could and jerk his hands down to his knee level. In the meantime, the other man was reaching as high as he could reach and pulling down while the first man was reaching high again. In that way two trained men could run up a hoist smoothly and with surprising speed.

The *Indy* did have one unfortunate problem from a flag hoist point of view. On the deck above the navigation bridge, two decks above the signal bridge, she had fire control directors for her 5-inch guns, one to either side. At high speed they created eddies of wind in their lee, which had a fiendish tendency to wrap flags around their halyards so that they could not be read. It became the job of benders-on to flick the downhaul at just the right moment—and in the right direction—so that the flags would make it past the hazard and fly free. It was tricky, though. I never became expert at it.

While we signaled, the receiving ships would hoist identical flags to their yardarms. But they would not two-block-run them all the way up until the signal was understood and the ship was ready to execute whatever action was ordered. And no ship would be ready to execute until all other ships more distant than themselves from the flagship were ready, with hoists two-blocked. Thus, when the receiving ship replied, the admiral—or other officer in tactical command—

knew that his signal was understood by everybody. Our spotters in the *Indy* were responsible for seeing that the flags were repeated correctly in the nearest ships.

Then, when all was ready, the Flag lieutenant would cry, "Execute!" and we would haul down the hoist. All the other ships addressed would do the same, and the ordered action would begin. The stowers would have to get busy and have the flags all back in their proper slots, ready for the next signal.

This, in the telling, sounds complicated, but in practice it was quite simple and one of the most reliable and efficient ways of maneuvering ships in formation ever developed. Its great drawback, of course, was its uselessness at night or in fog or rain. Even sun glare and stack gases could make a hoist unreadable sometimes. It was not easy, either, to read a hoist when directly ahead of or behind a ship. The flags tended then to look like a trembling black line against the sky. We tried, in those conditions, to spot the flags as they came free of their bags, hoping to read them before they became twisted and entangled about their halyards.

Hoisting and stowing were jobs saved for the most junior men on the bridge. I got a lot of bending and stretching exercise this way. The chief kept us at flag hoist drill until we were ready to drop. But we were not the only ones suffering. We could hear the 5-inch loading machines banging for hours on end. The big 8-inch guns trained from side to side and pointed up and down in the same unending practice to make perfect. And those guys—the deck divisions—had the additional blessing of ridding the ship of the last vestiges of her yard trauma lest the admiral, when he came aboard, suspect she ever had been soiled at all.

I suppose the Black Gang was going through the same hassle, but we could not see them. The Black Gang was what we called the engineering divisions. They were the men who made the ship go. They had been called Black Gang since Navy ships burned coal for power and the men in the engine spaces often were literally black with coal dust. It was strange in a way, I suppose, but I never gave any thought to what went on in the engineering spaces. The *Indy* was a forced draft ship—her fire rooms were under positive pressure so that her fires burned hotter and her steam was super heated. For that reason, entry to the engineering spaces was by means of airlocks. In all the time I was in the Navy, I never stepped through one of those airlocks. I never saw an engine room. The ship moved. That was enough for me.

For the whole 2,500-mile passage, the *Indianapolis* was like a Big Ten football team being readied for the Rose Bowl or some other big game. We drilled until responses became unthinking reflexes. The most important of the drills, of course, was general quarters—battle stations. But we had collision drills, fire drills, fire and rescue, flight quarters, and probably more I have forgotten.

I remember thinking it odd that the bugle call for flight quarters—meaning stations for flying our planes off or on—was the old horse cavalry's "Boots and

Saddles." Upon hearing it for the first time, I thought it sounded familiar. I had heard it once before while on Third Army maneuvers with the Oklahoma National Guard. A horse cavalry troop bivouacked one night by a little creek at Camp Travis just north of San Antonio, not far from where my field artillery outfit was camped. Small world.

As a rite of passage when coming aboard any Navy ship, every sailor was given a place on the ship's watch, quarter, and station bill. This assigned him to a watch, told him where to fall in at quarters for muster, routine announcements, and ceremonies, and assigned him his proper station for all the drills and evolutions mentioned above. Even his bunk location was given so that he might be called for night watches. Theoretically, no matter what happened, a sailor could look at the watch, quarter, and station bill and know where he was supposed to go and what he was supposed to do when he got there.

The new guys fitted in quickly on the signal bridge. My cleaning station—everyone in the Navy has to have a cleaning station—was the ship's bell and the little catwalk outside the conning tower. The bell was mounted on the mast some twenty to thirty feet above the signal bridge. Signalmen struck the bells that told the time in ships by means of a lanyard led through fairleads to the signal log desk. My job was to keep the bell brightly shined on the outside and painted red on the inside. Since it was about two feet in diameter and not much more in height, it was not a burdensome responsibility.

Neither was the catwalk. It was about thirty inches wide and maybe fifteen or twenty feet long, all sheltered behind a sheet metal dodger shaped to deflect wind over the heads of any observing admirals during battle. I never saw an admiral—or any other kind of officer for that matter—on my catwalk in all the time I was in the *Indy*. The conning tower was lightly armored, as I have mentioned, but the catwalk dodger was sheet metal. It would stop not much more than the spray that sometimes rattled against it in rough weather.

As did most peacetime Navy sailors, I quickly learned that it is easier to put on new paint than to scrub old paint. My catwalk, as well as several other places on the ship, had no hard corners. They were all rounded under thick coats of paint, which made them burn remarkably well once we got into the shooting kind of war.

Contrary to Navy custom—and I have sometimes wondered if maybe the naval architect who designed her might not have gotten himself into some trouble for the fact—the port side of the *Indy*'s signal bridge was officer country. Traditionally, starboard is the side of honor.

Whatever the reason, the starboard side of the *Indy*'s signal bridge belonged to us. That is where the coffeepot was. Every duty station had to have its coffeepot and its associated gear. The junior man of every watch was required to stop by the galley on his way to the bridge and pick up coffee, condensed milk, sugar, and water. Collectively these items were known as the coffee gear. If he were unusually conscientious, the man might even change the filthy water in the cup bucket, but that was expecting a good deal.

When a man finished his coffee—sometimes even before he had finished it— he would drop his cup in a bucket of water kept on the bridge for that purpose. After a while, the water became raunchy, to use a sailor word. Sometimes it got so raunchy that you had to fish around with your hand for a while to find a cup. The doctor used to worry about the utter lack of sanitation of the bucket, but so far as I know, no one ever got sick. I suppose the mess itself was so powerful that no germ could live in it long enough to infect anyone.

It was the institution of the coffee gear that got me into my first disciplinary trouble on the bridge. Since I didn't drink coffee—something that made me suspect in the eyes of the old-timers in the first place—I didn't care how dirty things became. And they did get dirty. Sugar was scattered about, and coffee spilled onto it to make a sticky goo on top of the pyrotechnics locker. The condensed milk can was often a disgusting sight—especially in fly country. I objected to having to carry up the damned coffee gear at all. If I didn't drink it, I didn't see why I had to do the idiot work of carrying up its makings.

This logic failed entirely to impress the more senior people on the bridge, so I took a more direct course. One night I brought up saltwater for the pot. I still don't know whether using saltwater to brew coffee makes any difference in the product, but I assume it does because the chief gave me another telling demonstration of the old admonition: "Maybe I can't make you do that, son, but I can sure as hell make you wish you had." I certainly wished I had not brought up saltwater. And I never did it again. Memories of the six cold and wet hours I spent high up on the director platform one stormy night saw to that.

Drinking coffee incidentally was a time-honored tradition in the Navy. God knows how many names sailors had for coffee. Joe, jamoke, java, paint remover, battery acid, and horse piss were just a few. The criterion for strength was that it be able to hold the spoon upright without its touching the sides of the cup. Sailors not only drank it by the gallons at mealtimes, they spent much of the day and night sipping the stuff. It was said that when some of the old chiefs died their cups had to be cut out of their hands before they could be buried. I have always questioned reports of coffee as a threat to health. Hell, if coffee were harmful, there would not have been a living sailor in the American Navy.

Actually, life aboard a Navy ship of that time was about as healthful as any place could be. All of us were diligently screened for health problems before we were accepted into the club in the first place. Doctors and hospital corpsmen—medical attendants—kept their eyes on us with sometimes embarrassing intensity. This was especially true for the first nine days or so after leaving a liberty port. Nine days is the incubation period for the dread gonococcus bug, and we were regularly lined up and told to drop our pants and "milk it down" in what we called short arm inspections.

This was before the time of penicillin and all the other wonder drugs available now. The Navy took a puritanical view of venereal disease, to the point that time lost in its treatment was called "bad time." It had to be made up at the end of the poor patient's enlistment. We were constantly exhorted to remain pure and to trust in nothing other than the only two sure-fire drugs we did have then: Sulfadenial and Noassatol.

The Navy was not so naive as to believe even these drugs would always be used in the heat of alcohol and young passions. Pro stations (prophylactic stations) were set up at strategic locations in liberty ports, and sailors could find after-the-fact preventive treatment there. Corpsmen would do the honors for those still in need after returning on board. The sailors' endearing term for corpsmen, in fact, was "chancre mechanic," for their role in the treatment of chancroid and chancres.

Still, social diseases did find their way on board. Doctors tried every way they knew to learn the names of the infectors, but sailors usually stubbornly refused, out of some misguided sense of honor, I suppose, to rat on the women. Certainly, the woman would never be reported as a prostitute or other seasoned campaigner. Our force medical officer told me one night, over a cup of signal bridge coffee, that every case of clap he ever treated was contracted from a Long Beach virgin.

Old sailors professed to consider venereal disease lightly anyway. No worse than a bad cold, they would say. But they all lived in dread of deep irrigations. One of the effects of gonorrhea is the development of strictures inside the patient's penis: strictures put an effective end to peeing. The Navy's treatment for this condition was deep irrigation, a procedure in which an instrument with four folded blades in its end was inserted in the patient's penis. The folded blades were then opened and the instrument withdrawn—all without benefit of anesthesia. It was meant to hurt. And, by all reports, it did. Grown men were known to cry out.

If all this makes it seem venereal diseases were rife in the Navy, I have overstated. I never knowingly saw a case of syphilis and few of gonorrhea before the war. After we began operating in the Hawaiian islands and beyond, the problem all but disappeared. Honolulu whorehouse staffs were subject to regular health inspections—and they represented just about the only exposure available to enlisted sailors. It was only when we touched at stateside ports that sailors displayed the results of loving not wisely but too well.

I don't remember anyone in the signal gang ever becoming infected during that period. The hairier rates—boatswain's mates, gunners, and the like—would say that was because we were not man enough to get laid in the first place. These more primitive types liked to make fun of us, calling us signal girls. This was possibly out of envy for the privileges we were given. A boatswain's mate of the watch one time in Long Beach passed the word that "a boat will be leaving in five minutes for the Pico Street landing and will take any yeomen or seafaring men desiring to go." Throughout the ship, a yeoman's bath was said to be a handful of talcum powder thrown into each armpit. Signalmen, quartermasters, and storekeepers were commonly grouped with yeomen as the "effeminate rates."

Another reason for our good health was Navy chow. It was not always good, but it was always wholesome. And there was always plenty of it. The signalmen's mess in the *Indianapolis*, for instance, was two tables set in a recess on the port side forward in number two mess hall. This allowed us to be set off from the main body of slurpers and grunters, and we had two nice big portholes that could be left open in good weather to let in pleasant light and air.

Each division's mess was ruled by its senior petty officer. This man determined the character of conversation and the general demeanor of the mess. Some of them were strict, others not. The tables and benches were set up and the food brought from the galley by men known as mess cooks. They were not cooks at all but did the work of the waiters and busboys in shoreside restaurants.

It was another sign of signalmen's privileged status as watchstanders that deck divisions provided our mess cook. Ours was from Third Division—my old alma mater of holystoning memory. He was a pro. He had been in the Navy a long time and didn't want to be anything but a mess cook. I don't remember ever meeting a more contented man. I no longer remember his name, but he was said to be married and to have children somewhere in Appalachia. Mess cooks were paid a little extra for the work, and no one could be a mess cook if he were rated higher than seaman second class. Our mess cook was content to remain on that lowly rung. For one thing, he said, he couldn't afford to be promoted.

Every payday a soup bowl was placed in the middle of each mess table, and men put in money according to their rates. Since our mess cook was very good, he did well in the matter of these tips. Somehow, he got the choicest bits from the galley for us. He delivered the food hot to the table, and he set it out for us in metal tureens so that we could help ourselves. Often there were extras, as well. Once we reached Hawaii, for instance, every morning found a large bowl of freshly cut pineapple on our two tables. Our holiday tables always had hard candies, dried fruits, and other delicacies. Human nature being what it is, I suppose our guy greased a few palms in the galley, but it certainly made for a pleasant signalmen's mess.

This old mess cook, however, unwittingly first planted the seeds of doubt in my otherwise perfect faith in the Navy. I say "old" because he was much older than the rest of us; probably close to forty, I would guess. One day in Pearl Harbor he was on the dock alongside, white apron tucked up about his waist while he did some chore for the ship's cooks, when a pink-cheeked young ensign reported for duty on board, complete with a sizable pile of luggage, including one large bag of golf clubs. The officer of the deck ordered our old mess cook to drop what he was doing and carry this character's baggage on board for him. It was a minor thing, I suppose, but it didn't seem right. It stuck in my mind.

For the most part, though, my faith in the Navy continued unblemished, even though, as junior man on the bridge, I got some good-natured hazing and drew, as a matter of course, the dirty jobs. Except for the few all-hands evolutions, signalmen rarely were called on for working parties, but if ever we were, the honor would be mine. That was the nature of the beast. I accepted it.

I always drew the boat duty, for instance. Every boat that left a Navy ship at sea had to carry a signalman with semaphore flags. Most guys hated the job, but I loved it. At man overboard drills, for example, the pulling whaleboat—just like Ahab's, with steering oar and everything—was lowered to recover Oscar, the man-sized dummy that was thrown overboard from time to time. This was always done with as little notice as possible in order to simulate the real thing. The Navy's special five flag, kept ready at the foremast head, was broken and run down to the dip—ten feet or so below the top of the mast—and the whistle was blown to draw attention to the flag. The boat's crew would run to its stations. A man would be sent aloft to keep Oscar in sight—a man in the sea is extraordinarily hard to find if ever lost to view. The ship would be maneuvered accordingly, and the directional flags bent on, ready to direct the boat: right, left, toward, or away from the ship. It could be exciting because until the boat was in the water and drawing near to the dummy, we could never be sure it was not the real thing. Those of us going in the boat would run to our stations and pile into the boat. Holding to knotted lines to reduce strain on the boat and its falls, we were lowered away at the run.

It is an odd illusion, being in a small boat alongside a ship in rough seas. The boat seems to be steady, while the ship pumps deep into and out of the water. The underbody of the ship is seen to be ragged with green sea growth and there is a great washing and sloshing of water along the great gray cliff of her side.

Riding a small boat in rough seas is, in itself, a glad experience. I came to a whole new appreciation of Melville's descriptions of whale boats. Our boat was not so pure in design as Ahab's had been, but it was close enough. In boot camp I had pulled number seven oar in our company boat, but that had been in the calm waters of San Diego Bay. I never handled an oar in the open sea, but I saw enough to learn that it was not easy. At one time the blade of an oar might be five feet in the air, then, in an instant, buried six feet deep in the water.

The hairiest part was in coming back to the ship. Navy whaleboats, though stout, were not designed to be crashed against the sides of big, hard, old ships. The principal concern was that the boat might be hooked onto her falls, bows first. Since the ship likely would be moving at least slightly forward, to hook onto the after fall first would be disastrous. Once hooked on the boat was hoisted aboard. We held again to the knotted lines and stepped out onto the deck, Oscar dripping and sodden, but saved again. It was always an exciting exercise, and I sometimes volunteered to go even when it might not have been necessary. The day always seemed brighter after a man overboard drill.

In this way, our slow passage to Hawaii was used to bring the ship up to operating level. We all wanted her to be in what the British call top form when the admiral returned on board. There were some cynics among us, I suppose, but most of us wanted the *Indy* to show and do well. And when, one day just after morning twilight, we raised the island of Oahu over the horizon on the starboard bow, the ship was as ready to take her place in the fleet as we could make her.

6

The Islands

IF HEAVEN HAS A COUNTERPART anywhere on this earth for sailors, it must lie somewhere in the trade wind belts of the world's oceans. When, four or five days out of Long Beach, we changed into white uniforms, it signaled our entry into one of those blessed regions. Even Southern California in January can be gray and raw with winds and cold rains, but the world into which we steamed was one of eternal spring—lashed though it might be from time to time by great storms from the south—in which water never froze. Nor did the air ever become heavy and oppressive with damp as happened in equatorial latitudes farther south. The days remained ever fresh, scrubbed clean by winds, and the nights sparkled with stars.

I never outgrew my fascination with what I saw—and still see—as the minor miracle of making an intended landfall when and where expected. Even when I later learned how to navigate myself, I remained respectful—not so much for modern navigators, with all their tables and instruments developed by someone else, but rather for the ancient Arabs and Chinese who first noticed order in the movement of stars and learned to use them to guide caravans and ships about deserts and oceans around the world.

This fascination was never greater than it was the morning, just after morning twilight, when we raised the Hawaiian island of Oahu over the horizon off our starboard bow. It was the first tropical landfall of the many I would come to know, and, as such, I remember it still with greater clarity than any of the others. In the first place, we did not see the island itself for some time. It remained a murky mass of shadow under a massive heaping of clouds over inland mountains. The heaving sea itself was still dark in the early morning light, and our decks still wet with night damp. At first sighting, the land did not look like land at all, but, through our telescopes, we could see the slow white bursting of surf on a shore of black rocks and knew the island was there.

Our landfall was made on Makapuu Point, and we steamed on at our decorous ten knots past Koko and Diamond Heads, the steadily growing light returning color to the world and revealing more and more details of the land. After a time, we could see the modest houses of Honolulu's Kaimuki District, and the mansions of the rich along white beaches hemmed in by humped boulders of black lava. Once around Diamond Head, we could see the then modest buildings of downtown Honolulu and Waikiki: Aloha Tower, Royal Hawaiian Hotel, Barbers Point—all the landmarks whose bearings would become so familiar in the coming months and years.

I missed breakfast that morning to watch this, my first arrival at a Pacific island. The pink of the Royal Hawaiian Hotel and the white mass of the old wooden Moana Hotel were the most visible of Waikiki's few buildings. The only other beach hotel at the time was the Halekulani, but it was a low building hidden in coconut palms and other tropical foliage. The notorious Waikiki Tavern was completely invisible somewhere behind the Moana.

Competition for the starboard 45X long glass on the bridge was fierce and was decided, as was almost everything else in the Navy, on the basis of rank and seniority. I was surprised at how many of the old-timers had never been to Hawaii.

We were on our way to Pearl Harbor, some eight or nine miles to the west. Even off Honolulu, we could see Barbers Point Light. In another hour or so, we could see the Pearl signal tower, though the harbor itself could not be seen from the sea. The quartermasters, one in each wing of the navigation bridge, then began their chanting of bearings for Signal Tower, Aloha Tower, Royal Hawaiian, Barbers Point Light, Oahu right tangent, bearings the navigator would use for a running plot of our position as we felt our way for Pearl Harbor's narrow entry channel, dredged as it was, through Oahu's bordering coral reefs. We would hear this chanting many times in the years to come.

Pearl Harbor, for all its importance, is small in area. Only recently dredged, at the time of our arrival, to take large ships, it consisted of a central basin—with the airfield of Ford Island in its middle—and a number of branching arms called, oddly, by the Scottish name of lochs. The entrance channel itself is tight. Small breakers splash close aboard to either side as ships come and go through the beautiful pastels of tropical shallows.

Ships round Hospital Point—named, logically, for the hospital then situated there—to starboard and proceed on to berths at the few docks and mooring dolphins alongside or secure to buoys in the stream. There is not room enough for ships to swing at anchor in the normal way. The overall effect is more that of lakes and rivers than of ocean harbors.

For our part, we swung wide on the Ford Island side of the central basin and came alongside Ten-Ten Dock, just outside the base's one permanent dry dock, which was then empty and with its gate open. There was a floating dry dock off to the right, but it was empty too. The destroyer *Shaw* would be blown up in that dry dock when the Japanese attacked Pearl Harbor sometime later. A small marine railway, where ships as large as destroyers sometimes hauled out, and a clutter of shops, foundries, and other such structures flanked the dock area, all backed by a grassy tree-lined parade ground and a neat gathering of administration buildings and officers' residences.

Except for some tugs and small Bird-class minesweepers, no other ships were present when we arrived. The clang and clatter of machinery that we would later come to associate with Pearl Harbor was absent when we arrived. There was not even any activity on Ford Island, where we could see airplanes parked but nothing flying. The whole place seemed nothing more than what it appeared to be, a sleepy tropical port with sugarcane fields, like green mats laid over the slopes of foothills to the Koolau and Waianae mountain ranges, and the sounds of mynah birds in algaroba trees.

The only obvious signs of life were on Ten-Ten Dock itself, where a small group of yard officers waited to greet us with a rather self-conscious Hawaiian band of ukuleles and guitars and three or four plump hula dancers making cellophane grass skirts do interesting things in the eyes of the deprived young males in the ship.

The only untoward incident was our dismantling of a mast at the end of the dock. It was there—fitted with three vertical red lights—to warn away PBY patrol planes, which often practiced night takeoffs and landings in the crowded harbor. The port anchor, housed as it was in our outflaring bow, engaged and neatly removed the mast to some embarrassment on the part of the Pig and satisfaction on the part of the men who took pleasure in anything that embarrassed their burly captain.

Dismantling that mast with its warning lights incidentally became such a regular event that, one time, we arrived to find a yard officer waiting with his arms folded alongside a pickup truck filled with materials and men for repairing it. The Pig was not amused.

We did not know it then, but we had come home.

Only three or four days after our arrival in Pearl, the rest of the ships of the Hawaiian Detachment (HAWDET) entered harbor. They had been away on maneuvers when we arrived. They were eight heavy cruisers—the Fifth and Sixth divisions: *Chicago, Northampton, Louisville, Chester, Minneapolis, New Orleans, Astoria,* and *Portland.* Named for American cities, come to the mid-Pacific in defense of the nation's aims and ends, the ships read like poetry to me. These, plus an attendant squadron of destroyers, with its leader, had been sent to Pearl Harbor in September 1939, with the *Indianapolis* as their flagship. Vice Adm. Adolphus Andrews was embarked in one of the other cruisers that served him as relief flagship only while the *Indianapolis* was undergoing yard overhaul.

It was a moving spectacle to see the ships filing into the harbor, flags flying and immaculate white-clad crews standing at quarters, bugles sounding passing honors, right and left, as they came.

There were few berths alongside in Pearl then. Most ships had to secure to mooring buoys in the stream—their crews had to suffer the inconvenience of riding liberty boats as they came and went. The poor destroyers—my first uninformed love—always had to moor out, usually nested together in the most remote parts of any harbor at which they called.

But there lay the good old *Indy*, all snug at Ten-Ten Dock, where the big eight-passenger taxis from Honolulu could pick us up and deliver us to the foot of the gangway. As we had learned in Long Beach, rank doth indeed have its privileges.

I believe it was the *Louisville* that had then been relief flagship—I know she served us later in that role. Regardless, within minutes of the ships' entering harbor, a little flotilla of small boats approached the *Indianapolis*. One, painted a glossy black and trimmed with all manner of polished metal and decorative rope and canvas work, was the admiral's barge itself. Another was an officers' motorboat bringing his staff officers. A third was an ordinary open motor launch carrying the enlisted men of the Flag with their own and the officers' baggage.

It may be well here to explain that a naval ship's small boats were not simply boats. Boats assigned to admirals were painted black and called barges. A boat assigned to a ship's commanding officer was a gig. Boats for officers' use were called officers' motorboats, of all things. All three of these were of identical design and construction, although finished and decorated in varying degrees of opulence according to the ranks of their passengers. Some of them were works of art, decorated by crews who sometimes had little else to do for long periods. Heavy white canvas would be frayed, then painstakingly rewoven in intricate patterns called McNamara's lace, for curtains. Cushions were upholstered in snowy white canvas, and any paint and metalwork kept glistening.

Boats for enlisted men were called motor launches. They were open to the sky, whatever its mood, and their passengers sat on bare wooden thwarts whose hardness was softened by nothing thicker than varnish, a coating whose gloss was preserved by the jealous concern of the crews, who would not let foot fall on the gleaming wood. Metal plates were provided along the outboard ends of the thwarts as stepping places. God help the man who stepped anywhere else.

This little fleet approached us with our Flag, and we made preparations for its proper reception. Admirals, then as now, were provided with staffs of officers and allowances of enlisted men to assist in the performance of their duties. Depending on his rank and command, an admiral might have a staff and allowance of twenty or more people who followed after him wherever he went.

Admiral Andrews, for instance, as Commander, Scouting Force, and Commander, Hawaiian Detachment (COMHAWDET), had a four-stripe captain as his chief of operations, in charge of seven or eight staff officers, as I recall. Then he had his own signalmen, radiomen, yeomen, a Flag chief quartermaster, his barge crew, his own steward, and a pilot and rear seat man for his personal airplane. There may have been more, but these are all I remember now. Collectively, staff officers and men alike were known as the Flag.

The *Indianapolis* was designed and built to be a flagship. This meant staterooms were provided in officers' country for staff officers and a comfortable suite was provided for the admiral himself. Flag enlisted men were merged with their opposite numbers in the ship's company and operated with them in their various specialties. In effect, the signal and radio gangs were simply made larger while the admiral was embarked to handle the extra communications he generated.

I leaned that morning on the signal bridge railing aft and looked down at these men about whom I had been hearing so much ever since joining the *Indianapolis*. In appearance, they seemed no different from other sailors, except, possibly, for the fact they were all older and more experienced and carried themselves with a greater assurance. They also carried their own lashed hammocks and seabags. From my high vantage point, they looked like ants trying to salvage their larvae from a flooded hill. From above, they seemed much alike, although differing, naturally, in size. But, I noticed, there wasn't a wash bucket in the lot of them.

I don't remember any special ceremony when Admiral Andrews came aboard. I suppose there were side boys at the gangway for him, but I don't recall any music or honor guard. Chief Maxwell already had sent men aft with a blue three-starred admiral's flag made up for breaking. On his signal, the flag was broken and we were a flagship. At the same instant Admiral Andrews' flag was hauled down in the *Louisville*, and she wasn't a flagship anymore.

When a flag is "broken" in a ship, that is, in a sense, what happens. The flag is tightly rolled and bundled and bound with sail twine in such a way that, when it is hauled to a masthead, a tug on the downhaul causes the sail twine to break and the flag to fly free. From a distance, the flag seems to appear at its masthead as though by magic.

The only other instance I know of a flag being made up for breaking is in the case of the Navy's five flag's being so prepared and hoisted to the foremast head.

(An admiral's flag is worn at the main.) The five flag is the signal a ship makes upon suffering a steering failure or other mechanical problem leaving her out of control. It is broken at such times—and the whistle sounded to call attention to the fact—to let nearby ships know instantly of the danger. The same signal is made for a man overboard—except that the flag is then lowered to the dip in that case. It was an evening ritual on the signal bridge each night at sea to haul down the five flag and make it up with fresh twine so that it might not break on its own owing to rotted lashings and cause all kinds of consternation in close high-speed formations.

Admiral Andrews was not the first admiral I had ever seen, but he came close. He was not a very tall man but impressive in his dog-collar whites with their golden shoulder boards and a cap that must have weighed two or three pounds. The Pig greeted him with a good deal more effusiveness than he might have used for an ensign, I suppose, and they all—admiral, captain, executive officer, and a mixed bag of ship's and Flag officers—went below for whatever it is officers go below for.

In the meantime, the Flag enlisted men were coming aboard their own gangway, and laying below to our sleeping compartment, where they immediately laid claim to choice bunks and lockers, regardless of who might have taken them over in the Flag's absence. This was one reason Flags were not welcomed in ships assigned as relief flagships. Flag men were apt to step on the toes of ship's company men who might not agree with them on the rights and privileges due. Spirited exchanges sometimes resulted, but the *Indianapolis* was designed as a flagship, and her crew was used to the problem.

Unfortunately, I no longer remember the names of all the Flag signalmen who came aboard that day. Probably some of the men I named earlier as members of the ship's company were Flag men. I do remember one man most vividly: Edward Sanderson, signalman first class, known to everyone on the bridge, including the admiral, as Sandy.

Sandy, although senior signalman on a three-star admiral's Flag—and doing the work of a Flag chief signalman—was not a chief petty officer at all. But he took immediate charge of our signal bridge. The ship's own chief signalman was relegated to housekeeping in port and to nav bridge liaison at sea. His station was on the navigation bridge and his duty was to report signals made on the Flag bridge below at sea—and to keep the bridge clean when in port. We were immediately aware that something had changed in our lives.

Sandy was not very tall, but he had a commanding presence. His hair was a color in keeping with his name, and he was a tough sailor. He and Honk got along perfectly—if warily. Sandy was the smartest man I ever knew in the Navy. In the ship's folklore—all ships have a folklore—he had been a professional hockey player in his native Boston, a claim he boosted a bit by saying he was the only goalie in the league who could skate upright in the cage. As I said, he was not very tall.

When war did come, and he was still a first-class petty officer, he was commissioned at once as a full lieutenant and made a lecturer on naval tactics at Duke University. The last I heard he was commanding officer of the fleet tug *Papago*. When he was detached from the *Indianapolis* he promised me he would stop in Tulsa and see my family on his way to the East Coast, but he didn't.

The Flag officer who made the greatest impression on me was Lt. Cdr. Frederick J. Bell, Flag lieutenant to Admiral Andrews—who called him "Freddie" to the commander's obvious embarrassment. Commander Bell was an Annapolis man, slightly built and with fine and aristocratic facial features. It was easy to imagine him in cape and plumed hat. He was of an old Baltimore family with a tradition of service in the Navy. He had already at that time written at least one book—*Room to Swing a Cat*—a study of old Navy customs.

In port a Flag lieutenant's duties were many and varied, I learned, consisting primarily of making the admiral's life as easy and pleasant as possible. This seemed to apply especially to social affairs. Admiral Andrews was married to a woman who became active in island society on both the outer islands and Oahu. I remember her coming aboard for dinner in the ship with parties of plantation people from Maui, Hawaii, or Kauai when we sometimes anchored off those islands. She must have gone to those places in the little interisland steamers that then served the islands in order to be there when the *Indianapolis* arrived. (There was no regular air service between the islands in those days.) There were also parties in the Andrews' big house on Oahu when we were in Pearl. One memorable time, a detachment of the ship's Marines was detailed to park guests' cars—with disastrous results when the resentful sea soldiers got into the party liquors.

At sea, however, the Flag lieutenant was in charge of the signal bridge during tactical maneuvers. The bridge was under the admiral's direction, I suppose, but Commander Bell—with Sandy—ran the show when the big cruisers were twisting and turning in high speed evolutions. The two, Commander Bell and Signalman First Class Sanderson, had a beautiful working relationship. Under the two of them, the bridge became a taut but happy place to work.

The Navy then had a regulation that enlisted signalmen were not to memorize signals. The theory was if the signalmen ever were captured by an enemy, they could be made to reveal secrets under torture. But the idea that we would not memorize signals was as impractical as it was silly. Men cannot work with simple one-, two-, and three-letter signals for years on end without memorizing at least some of them. Sandy memorized a lot of them. I saw him and Commander Bell handle a formation for hours at a time and never glance at the signal book.

They were an odd pair—cultured aristocratic officer and rough, tough, hard-drinking sailor—but I always had the impression they were good friends. They talked easily together on the bridge. Their mutual respect was obvious, yet each was careful to stay on his side of the officer–enlisted man divide. It was as though they each recognized the basic silliness of the rule, but accepted it as a part of a game they had agreed to play.

At any rate, we began almost at once a strenuous schedule of drills, inspections, and practice aimed at reaching the highest possible stage of readiness by the time the entire fleet arrived in April for the annual fleet problem.

Ships then operated on a four-tier training regime. Some things—damage control and engineering problems, for example—could be done by individual ships. Other things were done in cooperation with other ships of the same type—cruisers with cruisers and destroyers with destroyers, for instance. Tactical maneuvering at sea was that kind of thing. And still other things were done by entire forces. The Navy then was organized into three forces—Battle Force, Scouting Force, and Mine Force. Every ship, according to her design and function, would be part of one of these forces. Auxiliaries, such as tankers, tenders, ammunition ships, and the like were in an organization of their own, called, for some obscure reason, "the train."

The big exercise, the one toward which all the others were pointed, was the annual fleet problem in which all branches took part. In 1940 this exercise was named Fleet Problem XXI, as I recall. Like the Super Bowls to come, they were designated in Roman numerals, and this one would pit the Hawaiian Detachment as a defending force for Pearl Harbor against the West Coast battleships, light cruisers, carriers, submarines, and their own destroyers as an attacking force. For the months leading up to the great event everything we did was with the fleet problem in the backs of our minds.

The Hawaiian Islands remained for me, during this time, a wonderland. I was then little more than six months out of Depression- and Dust Bowl–era Oklahoma. The memories of its cold winters and harsh summers must still have been fresh in my memory, I suppose. The endless spring of Hawaii was beyond anything I ever had imagined, and I could hardly accept the exotic flowers and trees as real. Even my readings of Joseph Conrad, W. Somerset Maugham, and other great writers of the tropics had not prepared me for the fact. But it was the time at sea I most loved.

Heavy cruisers of that time were fast and powerful ships, but with an agile grace that made them nearly as beautiful as they were strong. Sweetly curved clipper bows and raked masts lent them an air of grace all but totally missing in modern ships of war with their boxy lines and flat sterns, which make them look as though they have backed into something hard. The sight of our nine ships racing through the improbably blue trade wind sea, sugar white wakes streaming, flat and wide, all the way to the horizon astern, multicolored flags snapping and trembling in the wind of the ships' speed, white spray flying at their bows and curling over the forward guns in pretty aerodynamic curves—all of this is a spectacle that will never again be seen. It remains, to this day, still bright in my memory.

We operated then at high speeds—saving fuel was no longer the measure of a good captain, it seemed. And we operated at very close quarters in order to concentrate the maximum number of our guns on an enemy in the shortest possible time. Much of this, to the ignorant—as I certainly was at the time—seemed pointless and an unnecessary risking of ships, for near collisions convinced even the greenest of us of the dangers involved. One night, two of our destroyers did collide, and we saw upon returning to Pearl the damage done. We also saw the dead man—fortunately only one—hauled off for burial ashore.

Mister Bell used to lecture his signalmen before an operation, telling us the purpose of what we would be doing. (As a lieutenant commander, he rated the title of commander, but he was always addressed and referred to as Mister Bell on our bridge.) After the operation, he would call us together again and point out what happened and why certain things were done. He called these meetings critiques. He was the only officer I ever knew who bothered to give his men such feedback.

The ship's only reason for being, Mister Bell pointed out, were her guns. Her hull was designed and built for the one purpose of floating those guns within range of an enemy. (Or to get us the hell out of the way if the enemy proved to be stronger than we were, Sandy muttered later.) All else—the signalmen, storekeepers, yeomen, radiomen, and the like—were merely support. But that support was vital, Mister Bell said. The signalmen, by binding together individual ships, made effective units of what would otherwise be nothing but a bunch of ships, each going her own way.

I had never thought of our work that way, and I came to have a greater appreciation for what we were doing in our endless maneuvering of ships and the running up and down of colored flags. Someday the skills our ship handlers were learning would prove invaluable. Just as the imperfection of those skills would prove disastrous in the bloody night battles off Guadalcanal—things then far from our minds.

Every ship in those days had a number of different firing practices—day battle, night battle, air defense, for example. My experience with the old French 75s in my Oklahoma National Guard unit did little to prepare me for the violence of the

Navy's big guns. Every broadside from our nine 8-inchers meant the more or less controlled explosion of several hundred pounds of powder—and the sending away from the ship of several hundred pounds of shells at a very high rate of speed. The laws of physics being what they are, this meant an equal force pushing the other way in the form of recoil.

The power of these forces is reflected in the fact that before every firing, electricians went about the ship screwing out lightbulbs and securing other sensitive gear against the shock. On the bridge we rolled down our glass windows and latched all drawers and locker doors to keep them from flying about. One time I was on one of the 45X long glasses during an 8-inch firing. I came away with a beautiful shiner from having my face slammed against its eyepiece with every salvo.

We on the signal bridge took a special beating when the six forward guns were fired over the shoulder—that is, fired at a target abaft the beam. This put the muzzles of those six big guns not far away from us when they were fired. We were knocked about pretty good. The concussion and nose-pinching fumes made it hard to breathe for a while. That part of Navy life was not especially pleasant.

In fact it killed a man from the Third Division—my old alma mater of holy-stoning memory. Each shell had a soft metal band circling it near its base. This was called a rotating band. It was meant to engage the rifling inside the gun, causing the shell to spin as it was forced out the barrel and, thus, to fly more accurately as a result of the gyroscopic effect induced. The fatal accident occurred when one of these bands failed and detached from its shell. It went whirling off into space as a shower of jagged metal fragments. Since the guns were trained well aft at the time, one of the fragments whipped across the ship's own stern. It hit a man standing there and killed him.

Oddly, the sound itself of the big guns was never so intimidating. Their blast was more like a blunt instrument. The sharper crack of the eight 5-inchers was more painful to our ears. Sailors on smaller ships, armed with their nasty little 3-inchers, said those guns were even worse in that regard.

One of the more exotic parts of gunnery exercises was enjoyed by the target repair parties. Targets were large canvas sheets, lashed to metal frames and towed on special barges behind oceangoing tugs. Since jobs like these fell to the most junior men on the bridge, I got a lot of them. We used one of our own motor launches, loaded with men and materials for repairing holes in the unlikely case one of our guns made a direct hit.

After each firing run we dropped back in our boat and inspected for damage, repairing any we found. Then we would return to the safety of the towing tug for the next run. There we would drink tugboat coffee and watch officers on the tug's rounded fantail observing the fall of shot—a phrase going back to sailing ship days. They used something called a rake, a long wooden board with vertical wire teeth at intervals, much like a comb. Each ship's shells were dyed a different color so that, when more than one ship fired at a time, the spray kicked up could be identified. It was interesting as hell for me. But, before long, it got even more interesting.

The cruisers' 8-inch firing range then was in the waters between the islands of Hawaii and Maui. Now, the weather and waters of tourist Hawaii may seem all nice and well behaved. But, where the trade winds are funneled between islands, they can often be neither. The seas can build to impressive heights and even more impressive steepness. Navy motor launches were not good sea boats in the first place. They were designed for doing the ship's work while in harbors and other protected waters. Their bottoms were virtually flat to facilitate nesting and storage on board ship for one thing. But they were all we had for the target repair parties, and we used them. One time, on a target repair party, I was in a motor launch steaming hard to catch up with the tug. It was a particularly rough day, and the coxswain warned us to hold onto something solid. As we dropped off the backsides of waves, the boat would sometimes drop so fast that a man could be left hanging in midair for a moment. By the time he dropped back onto his thwart, the boat would be coming up again. The effect could be jarring. This particular time it was more than jarring—it broke a man's leg. The snapping of his femur could be heard over the commotion of the small boat in rough seas. The experience the poor man suffered until we got him on board something more stable could not possibly have been pleasant.

Night battle was always more spectacular for me than daytime firing. You did not get to see the great gouts of brown smoke, but the muzzle flashes were enough to blind us sometimes. The Japanese were said to have flashless powder, but we sure as hell didn't. Not in 1939 we didn't. I still don't understand how the fire-controlmen in their directors high up above the bridge could see what they were doing. I guess they were far enough away from the muzzles not to be affected as much as we were. Maybe they had special glasses or filters or other gear.

The big shells—the 8-inchers—were fitted with tracer charges so we could follow their flight. It was fascinating to watch them at night. They seemed to move ever so slowly, until finally they dipped into the black and invisible sea—and skipped off in wild ricochets before blinking out. Sometimes they would bounce two or three times, like flat stones skipped off a pond back home. The concussion of the guns seemed more violent at night too.

Antiaircraft firing could be even more exciting sometimes. Once we fired at—and shot down—real airplanes. The Army had some obsolescent old F4B biplane fighters that it rigged with radio controls and flew over us as targets. The exercise didn't really prove anything since the planes came over relatively low and slow and took no evasive action as a real enemy would have done. Still, we dutifully shot them all down, and they made a satisfying splash in the sea.

That was the first time, I think, that I realized the wastefulness of war. An airplane's engine alone is a marvel of engineering and craftsmanship. God knows how many hours and how much skill went into making those airplanes we had so blithely destroyed. And we sent them to the bottom of the sea, so that they lost even their scrap value. Oh well. We would see worse in a few years.

If all this makes it seem we were constantly busy, it is not all that far from the truth. The fleet problem was drawing steadily nearer, and we had a lot of catching up to do. Still, there were times of great peace and serene beauty. Especially so at night when—unless there was a specific night exercise—we would throttle back and dawdle through the night hours at an easy fuel-saving speed.

As I have said before, if there is a heavenly counterpart on earth, it must lie somewhere in the world's trade wind oceans. This felt especially true on the nights when the water was warm, the winds soft, and the clouds unhurried in their passage across starred skies. These clouds, amorphous and glowing faintly in nothing more than starlight, were like none others in the world and flew so low—and at such uniform heights that they echoed the earth's curvature, dipping down at the horizon and vanishing as though the earth disappeared beneath them and they followed after.

And, although we were a small town of six hundred men, encased in a metal hull shaped to move fast through the sea, and dedicated to the killing of other men, there were times when I felt myself to be alone with wind and water and whatever gods there may be. Sometimes, in such nights, I would feel tears gather in my eyes and a lump form in my throat with the sheer beauty of it all.

I don't know if others felt any of that, but I suspect they did. At least sometimes I think they did. I remember one night we were far off to the south, somewhere down around the Line Islands, and had put in a hard day. But, as night fell—and night falls suddenly in the tropics—we pulled away from the other ships on some mission of our own and slowed to our usual nighttime pace. The engines grew quiet, and the sounds of wind were no more than a sleepy hum about the masts and stacks. Even the ever-present whir and bump of blowers and auxiliary motors seemed stilled for a time. The sea rose and fell in low swells that were little more than the breathing of the world, and the clouds passed over us in their never-ending squadrons.

It was hot below decks that far south, and, after the evening meal, almost the entire crew not on watch would come on deck and find places where they could lie down, sometimes in a jackstraw formation in which one would lie with his head resting on another, with still another's head resting on him, in a kind of repeating pattern extending over much of the open decks. Everything would be still then, and we would watch the masts moving about among the stars like fingers feeling for some particular place that would be abandoned as soon as it was found.

Some critics who are less familiar with the sea may question the intimacy of sailors lying in such a way, but I recently came across a photograph in a book that shows sailors doing exactly that.

I remember one such night when we lay like that. I don't know exactly how long it was, but it seemed a long—and peaceful—time. Our lives felt suspended without feeling and without motion. Then someone began to sing. It was an old song, probably a Steven Foster song with a simple melody and words most of us knew. And, slowly, one by one, others joined in until we were all singing. I would later serve in a British ship in which the crew often sang together like that at night, but I never heard—either before or since—the men of an American ship sing in such a way.

The singing, too, went on for what seemed a long time as we followed one song with another. Several of the tunes were old church songs. Shy and inhibited as I always had been, I had never been able to join in group singing in school, or even in my one brief stay in a Boy Scout camp in Oklahoma. But that night, down by the Line Islands, I found that I could. The words seemed to come of their own accord and to find a kind of musical tuning I had never achieved before. I sensed the strange warm feeling of being in harmony with something larger than myself. It was something like the feeling I had known in boot camp when marching in formation. But nicer.

The feeling was strange to me. I found myself singing with a greater abandon than I had ever known before in doing anything. But, as at so many other times in my life when I found something enjoyable, I did not join in the singing until it was almost over. I felt a great disappointment when the men, one by one, stopped singing and went below to their bunks. That is one time I think others were moved by the beauty of the sea as much as I was, for, as they got to their feet to go below, they were strangely quiet and seemingly subdued, much as though they too were aware that something special had happened.

We in the *Indianapolis* got more of this kind of detached duty, I think, than the other ships did. It may be the admiral simply wanted to familiarize himself with the area, but we made a number of such independent sorties into remote places. We went one time to Midway, and two or three times to French Frigate Shoals, a strange array of reefs that are said to disappear from time to time only to reappear later. When we saw them they hardly broke the surface of the sea. We saw them more as the white spray of breakers than as solid land.

We visited Johnston and Palmyra islands too. These were low coral atolls of blinding white coral sand where coconut palms leaned out over their lagoons from a rich green bed of pandanus and ironwood and other tropical foliage. We never went ashore in these places, but we came in close and, with our powerful long glasses, we could see into their vastnesses. One time I even made out land crabs scurrying about.

It was very much like exploring. The islands could not have been much different from what they had been when first seen by white men. Only on Johnston Island and Midway was there any sign of human presence. Midway was a stop for Pan American Airways' China Clippers on their way to Asia. Construction of what would become an airfield had just then begun on Johnston Island. I would, during the coming war, be evacuated on a hospital plane that landed for refueling on that airfield. For a young dreamer, this was all good duty.

What was not such good duty was our practice then of boarding sampans. Although not the real sampans of the Far East, the commercial fishing boats working the waters off Hawaii then were called sampans. They were stout wooden vessels with squarish lines, very high bows, and extreme sheer from fore to aft. They were good sea boats. We saw them out in all weathers. We found them, in fact, just about everywhere we went.

That was the problem. Many of the fishermen were of Japanese ancestry. It was common knowledge throughout the Navy that all Japanese fishermen were really lieutenant commanders in the Imperial Japanese Navy, posing as fishermen to spy on us. I don't know why they were always lieutenant commanders. I guess that was a rank conveniently high enough to be taken seriously, yet not so high as to be improbable.

I know I went along on the boarding of a lot of sampans. There had to be a signalman in the boat, you see. We were looking for cameras, but all I ever saw were scared fishermen with weathered faces and hands scarred from years of handling hooks and lines. I never saw an American lieutenant commander with hands like those in my life. But it made a welcome break in routine and gave us some useful practice in small boat handling at sea.

There was another duty too that did not really delight me. When I packed my leggings on leaving boot camp, I had assumed my marching days were over, but it turned out that ships in those days had something called landing forces. These were units designated and trained to go ashore and fight as infantry for the protection of American lives and property in foreign lands.

Since the only thing sailors hated more than calisthenics was landing force; that job too fell to the most junior men. In this case, it fell to Bogeman—a very short signalman from Indiana who was blessed with remarkably rounded, almost feminine buttocks—and me. We got to go ashore and drill and march in parades and do all the stupid soldier stuff.

We also found ourselves one day in motor launches off the target island of Kahoolawe. Kahoolawe was a small, uninhabited island used by the Navy as a gunnery and bombing range. It lay between the islands of Maui and Lanai, as I recall now, and the gods who decide such things for sailors decided it would be good if our landing force landed and took the godforsaken place.

There were a number of problems with that idea. For one thing, we did not have landing craft in those days. And, like many coral sand beaches, this one shelved steeply. Because motor launches have deep forefeet, when their bows took the sand their sterns were still floating in six to ten feet of salty water.

Also, since motor launches did not have bow ramps, we belly flopped over the side from wherever we happened to be sitting. Instead of striding dramatically ashore as Gen. Douglas MacArthur later did for the cameras, those of us sitting toward the stern in the boat found ourselves scrabbling about on the bottom under seven or eight feet of saltwater, held down by packs and rifles we dared not drop and the old dishpan steel helmets of World War I. This was especially upsetting for those of us who—like me—could not swim.

Eventually, I was dragged, coughing and sputtering, onto dry land and set out with all the dignity I could muster to conquer the island for God and country. It was a small island, but it was almost a thousand feet high, and hellishly steep and bristling with hard rocks, sharp cactus spines, and a lot of rusty bomb and shell fragments from previous exercises, all of which shredded first our shoes and clothing then our precious flesh. Even worse, we were wearing our regulation black shipboard shoes. At the time of our dunking and being dragged through the surf, these low-cut shoes, although we were wearing leggings, managed to take on a full load of coarse coral sand, which, as we charged up the island slope, sandpapered our feet to what felt like the bone.

Add to this mix a good, hot tropical sun and some notion of the subject and character of our conversation can be had once we reached the top of the island and were informed that we could then go back down again. A couple of young ensigns commanded this famous assault—the lieutenant in overall charge had had the good sense to stay in the motor launch. The ensigns were wise enough to stay some distance apart from us, lest they be forced to punish us for the opinions being aired.

To make the whole thing worse, when we returned to the ship and climbed up to the quarterdeck, I was so tired and uncomfortable that I forgot my training, shifted my rifle to my left hand, and saluted the colors and the officer of the deck with my right hand in the usual way.

A Marine captain named Van Ness had the deck. (Marine officers did sometimes qualify and stand deck watches in Navy ships.) He motioned me out of the line and had me stand as nearly as I could at attention while the whole damned landing force filed on board and lay below to get their nice showers and their wounds dressed. I, for my part, was tired, sticky with dried saltwater and coral sand and bleeding from an assortment of cuts and scratches.

Captain Van Ness must have, in the end, taken pity on my sorry state. All he said was, "Were you taught the rifle salute in boot camp, son?" When I confessed that that had indeed been the case, he let me go below and listen to the gunners' mates in the armory comment on the condition of the rifle I returned to them in something less than the state it had been in when I had received it that morning.

We had a similar experience with rifles and coral sand, though not so damp, sometime later when we went to fire on the Army's range out near Barbers Point. We rode the Army's narrow gauge railroad—built to carry ammunition for coast artillery batteries then in place there. The whole area was flat by Hawaiian standards. It was also hot and dusty in dense groves of algaroba trees, which, under those conditions, reminded us of mesquite trees in Texas.

Everything was fine until it came time for prone firing. We belly flopped onto the sand, our old Springfields supported by our elbows as we aimed. We were in skivvy shirts and shorts—and the old World War I steel helmets. This meant bare elbows on the sand. Every time we fired, the Springfield's sturdy recoil jolted us back, bringing our helmets down over our faces and stripping skin off our elbows as it did. When some of us suggested a canvas strip might be spread over the sand to protect our limbs, we were told there would be no time for such niceties in a real operation.

As you might expect, the result was not pleasant the first time we fired. When we fired again—and after our elbows were already raw—the effect was impressive. We also got our pretty black, low-cut shoes full of sand again, with the same predictable result of abraded skin on our feet.

Fortunately, we were getting a lot of new men in the ships at that time. Bogeman and I eventually seniored out of these less desirable duties. Our last assignment was the competition parade for all the HAWDET cruiser landing forces. We would be judged on our performance against the other ships in a final big review on the grassy Navy yard parade ground, and we wanted to do as well as we could.

I remember it most for the strategy Sandy suggested as a distraction for the other ships' units.

Sandy knew, since we were senior ship, that we would be first in line while passing in review. "Hell, all you got to do," he said, "is put Bogeman in the rear rank where he can be seen by the following units. There's not a man in the Navy that can watch Bogeman's ass and keep his mind on what he is doing."

That was the extent of my landing force experience. I never marched under arms again for the remainder of my time in the Navy.

On the whole, we in the *Indianapolis* continued to lead a privileged life. As I have said, Admiral Andrews' wife was in the islands. According to scuttlebutt, she was a social lady and curious about the outer islands. One of her favorite locations was the Kona coast of the island of Hawaii. That was an isolated area in those days where communication was largely by means of potty little interisland steamers that looked much like the old steam schooners of the Pacific Coast of America.

The Parker Ranch—oddly for such a place—was one of the world's largest, we were told. Its *paniolos* used to drive cattle down to the beach there for loading into steamers anchored off. (Paniolos, Hawaiian patois for "cowboys," is a derivation of *espanoles,* the Spanish word for the first Mexican ranch hands brought to the island.) They rode their horses right into the ocean, driving the cows before them to the ships, where the cattle were hoisted in canvas slings, kicking and bawling, on board. I had seen nothing like that on any Oklahoma ranch.

Often at night, when we were anchored off like that, laughing parties of plantation people came off in boats to share dinner and the movies with us. But that was all officer gear. We had no part in any of it, except to man the boats and set up the chairs and benches for the movies—which were often delayed while the wardroom dallied over its dinner. The people from the beach had two standard ways of regarding enlisted men. Usually, they looked through us as though we were no more than inanimate objects that, by some trick, could be made to move and carry out orders. Or they would look at us with unconcealed curiosity. I didn't much appreciate either approach.

Even in Pearl there was a lot of social activity—on the officer level. The Pig had our shipfitters build a sheet metal fountain, which, for parties on board, was set up under the three 8-inch guns of number one mount. Once banked with island flowers and tropical foliage—and its tinkle of water turned on—it made a spectacular backdrop. The forecastle deck would be scrubbed and holystoned to glowing whiteness, made even whiter, it seemed, by the black striping of tarred seams. Brass work, including the brass stars in the guns muzzle tampions (pronounced "tompkins"), was polished to jewelry store brilliance. A white awning was rigged over the entire forecastle deck, and signal flags, selected for their appropriate colors, were placed at intervals along the lifelines for effect. The ship's band played dance music.

There was a narrow gap where the awning was lashed to jackstays at its after end. We peons on the bridge could sometimes grab titillating glimpses of bare shoulders and shining female hair. One time I even saw an anonymous commissioned hand doing something saucy to a guest who backed up against it with what must have been a gratifying readiness. But that was all officer gear too. We could listen to the music, though. That much was allowed to us.

From one of the berths we used in Pearl we could see the outdoor dance floor of an officers' club. Through our powerful long glasses we could see just about everything there was to see. Sometimes we saw things that even the people at the parties did not see. There were bushes, you see. When couples got behind those bushes and knew they could not be seen from the other side, they logically—but mistakenly—assumed that they could not be seen at all.

All of that, being vicarious, however, soon palled. People look awfully silly when they are dancing and the watcher can't hear the music they are dancing to. Besides, it was too strong a reminder, I suppose, for those of us who had had some social experience before they joined the Navy of what we were missing.

The island society open then to enlisted men was extremely limited. Even if we had been found acceptable, our pay scales did not allow much in the way of dining and dancing. The only time I remember being given any opportunity at all to meet good girls ended in disaster.

I've always thought Mister Bell was involved, but it may have been his wife—Mrs. Bell was in the islands by that time. At any rate, some group in Honolulu—I suspect now it was the Junior League or a similar well-intentioned organization—arranged a dance for the flag enlisted men at a club in Honolulu. Mister Bell extended the invitation on behalf of our would-be hostesses, but none of us would go. I suspect some of the younger men might have done so, until they heard Sandy say, "Hell, no. I ain't going to blow a liberty on a bunch of society broads that wouldn't give me a piece of ass to save my life." Sandy often affected rough language, though he could talk as well as anyone when he wanted to. His crude pronouncement set the mood, and none of the rest of us would go either.

Mister Bell was livid. He probably already had accepted, and when we would not go, he was embarrassed. He ended by sending men from the duty section, ship's company and Flag alike, and making those of us who would have had liberty stand their watches. Nobody was happy for a while on the bridge.

That was the only time I ever saw Sandy and Mister Bell at odds. But the feeling that prompted Sandy to do what he did was not uncommon among Navy enlisted men then. We knew that, if we went to the dance, it would be the first and last time we would ever see the inside of the club where it was held. And we knew damned well that if we chanced to run into a girl on the street or at the beach who had danced with us, she would cut us dead. None of us needed that.

We were not invited to any more dances.

7
Honolulu

HONOLULU IS ONLY ABOUT seven or eight miles from Pearl Harbor. As such it was necessarily the center of any social life a sailor might have. As a watchstander, I was free when we were in port to go ashore every other day at one o'clock in the afternoon and to stay away until eight the next morning if I wanted to. With special permission we could even get forty-eights sometimes on weekends—and on rare occasions, even seventy-twos. This meant two or three days away from the ship, but I never requested anything like that.

There was bus service between Pearl and Honolulu, but most of us used the big eight-passenger Honolulu taxis that picked us up at the foot of the ship's gangway and delivered us to the Army-Navy YMCA on Hotel Street in downtown Honolulu. The fare was a ruinous twenty-five cents—which put a significant dent in our budgets—but the service was so much better most of us went that way.

At any rate, watchstanders had plenty of time in which to become familiar with the island and its people—if only they had wanted to become familiar with us. Most of them did not, and the sailors reacted much as they did everywhere else by giving civilians what we called a good letting alone. We rarely met anyone other than bartenders, prostitutes, and taxi drivers, most of whom treated us with a grudging acceptance that disappeared at about the same time our money did. This was little different from what we were used to in the States—Hawaii was still a territory then and residents and sailors alike referred to the mainland as the States—but Hawaii was worse because Oahu was so small and options so limited. Disillusioned sailors came to call it "the Rock" and did their best to get off.

Although I felt it best to hide the fact from my shipmates, I liked the islands. My long fascination with sea stories had given me a good grounding, I suppose, in tropical islands—from the fiction writer's point of view anyway. The primitive color photography of *National Geographic* and early Technicolor movies had given me an idea of what I could expect visually as well. But nothing had prepared me for the islands' smells. Not that they were all unpleasant—we sometimes could smell island flowers far offshore. But the old Oahu Market down by the Nuuanu River was something else. Fueled by old and dead fish and rotting vegetable leavings in the hot sun, the market's stench was not pleasant at all. The stink was damned near visible sometimes.

Honolulu then was a small town, but unlike any small town I had ever seen before. Much of downtown was low two- and three-story wooden buildings with little in the way of doors and windows. The buildings had all been painted at one time or another, I suppose, but the paint had been deadened long before we arrived to drab browns and greens by the moist tropical air. Most of the ground floors were given over to small open-air shops, crammed full of merchandise, much of which we did not recognize. The streets were narrow, and sidewalks even more narrow, and all so well shaded by rusted metal awnings they rarely felt the sun.

There were dozens of *saimin* (noodle) joints with breast-high counters, where diners ate standing up. And, strange to my eyes at least, the barbers were women, most of them Japanese. There were not many tattoo parlors when we first got there, but they followed soon after. And many of the open-front shops and stores became open-front bars where sailors could be efficiently separated from their money. None of this was noteworthy, of course; it could be found in any Navy town. But there was one thing special to Honolulu—photography studios with phony grass shacks and bored hula girls in cellophane grass skirts that were artfully parted when the camera was snapped to show some leg. Sailors could have their pictures made with these island maidens to be sent home to impress friends and families. These enterprises lined Hotel Street, Honolulu's main entry route from Pearl Harbor and the Army's Schofield Barracks.

There were some solid masonry buildings of five or six floors in the downtown area: the Alexander Young and Blaisdell hotels, for instance, and some modern office buildings along Fort Street. The Army-Navy YMCA on Hotel Street was one of the most impressive buildings in town at the time.

The Y was the heart of Honolulu for us. It sat behind a U-shaped drive, in a parklike setting of palm trees, flowers, and tropical foliage. There were several floors of rooms upstairs in the Y, where soldiers and sailors could take a break away from duty stations. I never got beyond the big tile floored lobby with its wide entry doors, which never closed. They never closed because there were no doors to close, just a wide entryway. There was a nice dining room off to the left, where I was introduced to island papayas and mangos and avocados for the first time in my life. Fresh pineapple—diced, sliced, mashed, and prepared in every other imaginable way—was epidemic. The Honolulu pineapple cannery—with its water tank in the shape of a giant pineapple—was a local landmark we could see from sea. It had fountains in its lobby that ran fresh pineapple juice for the taking. There were rooms in the Y, too, for reading and writing letters. The Y tried, I suppose, to create a home-away-from-home atmosphere for us—with varying success.

Before the battleships came out in May 1941, Honolulu seldom was crowded —not even on Army paydays—and most of us, after we had been in the islands a while, got civilian clothes to give an illusion of freedom from naval identification. We couldn't keep such clothes on the ship, of course, but there were institutions in Navy towns then that were known as locker clubs. Mine was owned by a gentleman named Battleship Max Cohen. He had a club in Long Beach too and probably more in other Navy towns. The one in Honolulu was on the second floor of one of the town's common wooden buildings and belonged to the shed school of architecture.

There was a splintery pine floor that had apparently never been painted or covered in any other way. Rugs or carpets would have been a complete anomaly. Dirt equaled in effect, if not in charm, curtains at the few windows in the front wall of the place. Furniture consisted of metal lockers smaller than those we had in the ship, and wooden benches we could sit on to change our shoes. Unshaded bulbs, made a more or less uniform height by knots tied in the wires from which they hung, provided light. There were supposed to be showers and heads beyond some paint-chipped swinging doors at the back, but I was never brave enough—or desperate enough—to try them.

My complete wardrobe of civilian clothes consisted of a pair of white cotton pants and an Aloha shirt so full of glue size it became cheesecloth after one washing. A pair of what we called go-ahead sandals completed the lot. It was not much, but it was enough to get me out of uniform for a while.

Of course, we didn't fool anyone in the streets or on the beaches. There might be some confusion as to whether we were Army or Navy, but no one was dumb enough to think we were civilians. The haircuts, if nothing else, gave us away. And most of us were a head or two taller than the islanders. One of the first things we noticed in walking the streets of Honolulu was whether the locals had their hair parted straight or not. Even the shore patrol and military police knew us for what we were and hassled us just as much as if we had been in uniform. The only thing they could not hang on us was wearing our hats crooked.

No, I am not kidding. The only time I was ever stopped by the shore patrol in Honolulu was one night when I came out of the Beretania (the Hawaiians' pronunciation of Britannia) movie theater with my hat on the back of my head. A shore patrol struck like lightning. They did not arrest us for wearing our hats crooked, but they took our liberty cards and we had to explain to the officer of the deck, when we returned to our ships, why we didn't have them. Subtle as hell, I suppose, but effective. At least it didn't cut short our liberty. Not that one anyway.

I did not really want civilian clothes when we first arrived in Honolulu. I was still inordinately proud of my uniform. But I was already suspect in the eyes of my shipmates for my gung-ho attitude and thought it would be a good idea to be one of the boys. Later, I came to like the imagined freedom my civilian clothes gave me.

Most of the time in those early days I went ashore by myself. I never tired of walking the narrow streets, running as they were with endless streams of small brown and yellow people—mostly Asian, but with the occasional Hawaiian. I loved the incomprehensible clatter of their jabbering talk, which was unintelligible to me even when they were speaking what they called English. The colors, smells, sights, sounds, and touch of things, all lent Honolulu a wonderful feeling of adventure, which seemed entirely lost on my shipmates, who were becoming more and more disenchanted with the islands.

I quickly learned not to mention any pleasure I found in the islands. Not even to Sandy. And, most especially, not to the men we were beginning to get from the China Station. To them, all native peoples were "slopes" or "gooks" or even less flattering terms. Since I grew up in Oklahoma and had lived all my life with prejudice against American Indians and blacks, this should not have bothered me, I suppose, but it did.

I also learned during this time that nothing so sets a man apart from his shipmates as simply wanting to be alone. Because I had so much wanted to be accepted, this hurt. At first I continued to make my liberties alone for the most part. But eventually I decided to compromise: I'd make my afternoon liberties alone and join the others in the bars when they came ashore later.

One fascinating result of this compromise was my discovery of the Bishop Museum and Library. About the only pleasant memories I brought away from my year in college were those of the upstairs reading room in TU's McFarlin Library. When I found the Bishop Library, I found a depth to Honolulu and the islands I had not even suspected.

The early days of the sandalwood trade and the whalers at Lahaina came alive for me as we sailed the same waters in our big modern cruiser. Even more interesting, the ways of the ancient Hawaiians—their awful cruelty to each other and their convoluted social systems of land tenure and taboos—came alive for me. I spent many pleasant afternoons in that library. The kindly middle-aged women there came to know me and led me ever deeper into island history.

Now, all these years later, I still remember facts I read there during that time. One anecdote was about how Hawaiian children learned to read from the missionaries at a time when there were few books in the islands. The teacher would sit in the center of a ring of eager young students and point out in his book the various letters of the alphabet and give them names. It was said that grown Hawaiians, many years later, held their books upside down when reading or at varying angles depending on where they had sat in the circle when learning their letters.

I began in Honolulu a practice I would follow in strange towns wherever the Navy took me. I would take buses and streetcars to the ends of their lines, then walk to the end of another line for the ride back to town. You can see a lot of a city that way. Honolulu's streetcars, incidentally, were like none I had ever seen before. Made of highly varnished wood, they were open for their full length. Running boards allowed passengers to board at any point along the length of the cars they liked and to sit on wooden benches fitted lengthwise in the car. They were something like San Francisco's cable cars, except they were considerably bigger and had no closed section at all. They were like San Francisco's cable cars, too, in that they were often just as crowded, with passengers hanging on wherever they could get foot- and hand-holds.

Honolulu's trolley buses were also new to me. They were rubber tired buses, powered by a wheel on a pole moving along an overhead wire like streetcars. They later became popular in some mainland cities, but Honolulu's were the first I ever saw.

Even though I did enjoy the streets of Honolulu, I came to like the little plantation towns of the countryside even more. They were company towns in the same sense that the oil field camps among which I grew up in Oklahoma and the coal mining towns of Appalachia were company towns. And their inhabitants were probably exploited in the same way. But the towns in Hawaii did not have the same depressing air of stateside oil and lumber and mining camp company towns. Maybe because the tropical growth in which they were all but buried, hid, in part, the fact that the houses were actually shacks.

The streets were the unpaved red earth of the island itself, lined with little board-and-batten wooden houses, all painted much the same bilious green color and raised on posts against the threats of rot and termites. Roofs were rusted corrugated iron, and the spaces under the raised houses were closed off behind a latticework of crisscrossed wooden slats. All were fitted with covered front porches. I never saw a closed window or door.

Each house had its own rickety outhouse, and a tangled growth of papayas, bananas, and other fruits and vegetables for family consumption—with maybe a little left over for sale in the old Oahu Market in Honolulu. Children ran loose, much as did a remarkable lot of dogs and pigs and various kinds of poultry. The kids wore little more clothing than the livestock.

The plantations provided a general store and minimal other services. There was even a rudimentary movie theater in most of the towns. But the gentle climate asked little help in the way of creature comforts, and the people seemed happy.

Most of the people on the plantations when I was there were Filipinos. The preceding waves of Chinese and Japanese already had left the fields for the greater rewards and comforts of Honolulu. Oddly, perhaps, the plantation Filipinos were seldom seen in Honolulu. Their rendezvous in town was Aala Park, where Hotel Street crossed the Nuuanu River. It was a leafy, neat enough area that became very dark at night. The only light then was that which spilled from the open fronts of shops lining the surrounding streets. There was usually a delicious scent of broiling meat, mingled with pale blue wood smoke among the trees.

The Pearl Harbor buses and taxis entered Honolulu along Hotel Street and passed Aala Park, but I never saw a sailor get off there. It was reputed in the ships to be a dangerous place for sailors. The men there were all believed to carry knives—and to be very jealous of their small but beautiful women. This, interestingly, was the same warning given us about Mexican men when we passed through El Paso as recruits.

I don't know if all this was true of Aala Park or not. All I know is that the Filipinos I met in the plantation towns were the friendliest of all the few people I met in the islands. They were surprised sometimes, I think, to see a Navy sailor walking their poor streets, but they never failed to smile and say something in Tagalog, their native language. Their kids were like kids everywhere and tagged along after me. Maybe that is why I liked the plantation towns. The contrast between them and Honolulu's unfeeling streets was warming to one grown used to rebuffs.

All of this is not to say the Navy didn't provide for sailors' recreation. Each ship had a chaplain and a ship's service officer who organized group activities such as picnics, swimming parties, and athletic events. The *Indianapolis* even had a dance band that sometimes played on deck for our entertainment during the noon hours. There were smokers and amateur entertainments on board as well. I remember once in the *Indianapolis* we even had a spelling bee. And all ships had athletic teams that competed not only with other ships but also with Army and civilian teams on the beach. These things were financed by profits from the ships' geedunk stands.

A geedunk stand sold "geedunks"—usually ice cream and candy and all forms of tobacco. It was a tradition—yes, the Navy has traditions—that a man bought cigars for his messmates when he was promoted—much as new fathers will buy cigars for friends to celebrate the birth of babies. Sometimes geedunks were given instead.

Swede Nielson, for instance, always gave geedunks. Swede's former nickname had been Dog, a name given then throughout the Navy to men who are especially vigorous in the more raunchy aspects of liberty. Swede, by all accounts, earned the name. But, one time, as the ship passed through the Panama Canal, Swede, drunk, paused to listen to a Salvation Army band on the streets of Panama City. He was never the same again. He got religion and hurried back to the ship to throw away all his smokes and other bad ways. He would not buy cigars for us when he was promoted because he didn't want to contribute to our delinquency. He bought us ice cream and candy instead. Later, along with some like-minded sailors, he held prayer meetings in the after signal station at the foot of the mainmast.

This brings to mind what the Navy called divine services. In boot camp we had been required to attend church services, but in the ships we were not. Except for Swede, I don't remember any of the signal gang ever doing so. But it was the signalmen's duty to rig for divine services. If in port, this consisted of a couple of us grabbing armfuls of signal flags and displaying them from the awning jackstays on the fantail or after deck, where the chaplain and his assistant would already have set up their workbench, with candles and bells and all the other tools of their holy trade, under the muzzles of the three big 8-inch guns we had there.

Usually a white awning would be rigged overhead, and the signal flags around the edges gave a kind of poor man's stained glass effect when the sun shined through them. That is about as close as we came to any kind of relationship with God—except for frequent irreverent references to Him in times of stress. After the service, we would retrieve our flags and that would be the end of the business for another week.

The most elaborate of official functions provided for us were ship's parties. For these, a band, beer, and food were furnished, as I recall. The parties were usually held in nice places we didn't see at any other time. They were also subject to the same prejudices, on the part of old-timers, that had foiled Mister Bell's attempt to have us entertained by the Junior League. One difference was that ship's parties were for all hands—that is, the entire ship's company not in the duty section. Even officers attended.

I remember three ship's parties in the *Indianapolis*—but I attended only two of them. I had duty once when the dance was held in the Sky Room of the Alexander Young Hotel in downtown Honolulu. I guess that one went off all right, but both of the parties I attended were disasters.

One was at the House in the Garden, a fancy nightclub set in the woods of Nuuanu Valley, not far from the Royal Mausoleum and well out of town. It was a nice place, virtually buried in tropical growth and beautifully furnished inside. Unfortunately one of the signalmen—I think now it was Joe Wise—drank, not wisely, but definitely too well. Joe was Asiatic enough to have done it. I don't remember the specific outrage he committed, but the chaplain suggested he leave. The other signalmen took this to be an intolerable professional slight, and we all left. I, and a couple of the others, had not drunk anything at all and were sober as could be. We were smart enough, though, to troop along with the others. These were our messmates, and we owed them our fealty. We knew they would stick by us if the tables ever were turned.

As it happened, it turned into one of the wildest liberties I remember. I still don't know if there was an ice-skating rink then on one of Honolulu's commercial piers, but I have a vivid memory that there was. I have a further vivid memory that we rented the little motor scooters that were just then becoming popular in the islands and invaded that ice rink—with results easily imagined.

The second ship's party I attended was in the seaside Banyan Court of the old white wood-frame Ala Moana Hotel, which still survives on Waikiki Beach, though it is now so engulfed in tall modern hotels as to be hard to find in photographs. This, too, was a handsome setting, with a dance floor and tables and chairs, all set outdoors under the enormous banyan tree for which that part of the hotel was named.

The most remarkable amenity provided by the hotel was a large cut-glass punch bowl. Waiters and busboys brought the bowl down to a special table near the trunk of the banyan and filled it with a pretty punch of some kind, complete with a large cake of ice and lots of tropical fruit. That was what got us into trouble.

I think Sandy himself was the ringleader this time. The Banyan Court extended then almost to the water's edge, where there was a stone retaining wall, if I remember correctly. We, as watchstanders, arrived early and lugged the beautiful bowl to the seawall, where we poured off all the liquid it held, saving only the ice and fruits. Back on its nice linen covered table, the bowl was refilled and set among its glittering cups as though nothing had happened.

But something had happened. The innocent punch the bowl had held was replaced with straight rum. I still don't know where the guys got all that rum. It took several bottles to fill the bowl. And the results were spectacular. I suppose there was enough residue of the original punch to make the rum drinkable, but there was enough rum to get the party off to a good start. Sandy, Joe, and the other smokers stirred their punch with their cigars and sat back to admire the pretty blue flames that then flared up when the cigars were lit.

That night marked my first—and for a long time, my last—experience with both tobacco and alcohol. I did try one of the loaded cigars—and became so sick I still do not know how I got back to the ship that night.

The most common form of unofficial recreation was plain and fancy drinking in sailors' bars. Each ship had its own headquarters ashore—a favorite bar. You always knew where to find help or support or just plain company on the beach. The *Indianapolis'* bar in Honolulu was called the Log Cabin, I believe. It was in a little bit of an alley just off Fort Street. It was very much like the bar James Jones described in *From Here to Eternity*, the one where Fatso and Pruitt had their knife fight.

The architect who invented the phrase "form follows function" could have had the Log Cabin in mind. There was a horizontal surface to hold the glasses and bottles on active duty, as well as a back bar for reserves. But no one had been foolish enough to put in a mirror. Most customers stood to do their business, but there were some much scarred tables and badly crippled chairs about the place. The floor was done in spilled beer, with odds and ends of cigarette butts, broken glass, and pieces of naval uniforms. The walls, leprous with old paint and splitting boards, served only two apparent purposes: one, to hold up the ceiling, and two, to keep customers from drifting away without paying. A garish neon-lit jukebox was the only touch of class in the joint. Sandy used to say you could tell time by "the goddamned juke box in the Log Cabin"—loud, blaring swing early on, becoming increasingly maudlin with sticky romantic ballads as the drunken night wore on.

But it was home to the *Indianapolis* signalmen. It, and others like it around the world, was about the only home some of us ever knew. Even the bartenders came to know our faces—if not our names—and we got at least a semblance of the pleasure normal people take for granted in being recognized. I never saw a woman in the place. And few soldiers or civilians.

All of which brings to mind the whorehouses. The New Congress Rooms seemed to be the house of choice for our ship. I was never in it—or any other—but the merchandise in the New Congress was often talked about in the ship. The military—with the active cooperation of municipal authorities—kept the girls on a tight rein and inspected them regularly for disease. It was said that no one ever got a dose of clap in a regular house. It was the "goddamned amateurs you got to watch out for." The price, as I recall, was two dollars.

Although I was never brave enough to stand in one of them, I often saw, after the battleships came out and thousands of new soldiers were brought to the islands, the long waiting lines stretching down the stairs and out onto the sidewalks in front of whorehouses. The guys were no more self-conscious than they would have been had they been waiting in line for a haircut or a shoeshine. Civilians in the streets paid them no attention at all. They did not turn their eyes away; they simply didn't look.

These lines, incidentally, and the pressure of time they represented, led to the institution of rain checks in the industry. If a guy could not make himself ready in all respects for action when he reached the head of the line, he was given a rain check, just as baseball fans were given rain checks if games were canceled owing to weather. Rain checks were good for another visit when the sailor might be in a more operable condition of readiness.

I first saw rain checks in the crap games that frequently took place in Flag plot when we were in port and the admiral and his staff officers were not there. They were common currency and fully acceptable at face value, usually with a detailed discussion of the new talent arrived on the latest Matson liner.

The subject of sex was treated with a bland, if never-ending, matter-of-factness that fascinated me. I had grown up on farms and ranches and had hung around small town feed stores enough to know the mechanics involved, but I had absolutely no personal experience in the field—a fact I kept as a close-held secret. My mother's good Methodist tutelage had been strong enough to keep me from participating in sex—maybe—but it had done damned little to keep me from being interested in it, young gonads being what they are. Although I would have died before admitting it, I left the islands eventually as pure, sexually, as I had been when I arrived.

That is not to say that romance didn't enter my life in Honolulu. One mysterious letter home of the time talks of a family I met. The father was an officer in a trust company, I wrote, and the mother a bank teller. You can't get much more respectable than that. In the words of my letter, they had "two very attractive daughters." Oddly now, I remember neither their names nor how I came to meet them. It would have been highly unlikely for a sailor of the time to meet such a family. I suspect now that the kindly ladies at the Bishop Museum were probably to blame.

Equally oddly, though, once prompted by my old letter, I do clearly remember the family home. It was on Magazine Street, in the hills overlooking the roofs of Honolulu and the harbor and the sea beyond. It was not a very big house, but a bright and breezy one with wide overhanging eaves, cool varnished wooden floors, and white rattan furniture with floral print cushions.

I no longer remember when or why I stopped going there. I am sure now the people were nice and well-meaning, but I was coming more and more to identify with my shipmates. I could not have been comfortable, or much at ease, in such a home.

Then, more seriously, there was Ilse. Honolulu's fanciest moving picture theater then was the Waikiki, across Kapiolani Boulevard from the Royal Hawaiian Hotel. It sat well back off the street, behind a large entryway and lobby. Its proscenium arch was painted as a rainbow, and its interior side walls were flanked by long planter boxes of artificial palm trees and other tropical foliage to give the impression of a garden. An organist named Sawtelle played at intermissions and before the featured film. If you could request a number he could not play, you were given two free tickets. Stinky Clark was the only one I ever knew to stump Sawtelle.

In those days, theaters had crews of usherettes who used flashlights to show patrons to their seats. In the Waikiki, the usherettes were all dark-skinned—either naturally or from long exposure to the Hawaiian sun—and they wore fetching white satin blouses and bell-bottomed slacks, with a wide red sash at the waist. The combination was deadly. I soon fell victim to a piquant little brunette with laughing eyes. Ilse.

Given my utter shyness with girls, it probably would have gone no further than my ardent but silent adoration in the darkened theater—and her complete ignorance of what was going on in my breast. But one day the *Advertiser*, Honolulu's leading newspaper, ran a feature story on the Waikiki usherettes, and there was my beloved in a group picture with her mates. She was the most beautiful of them all, naturally. And there was her name: Ilse, with some German surname I no longer remember. It was a strange name for the islands. It turned out her father had been a German seaman who jumped ship in Honolulu and married an island woman.

My next time ashore, I called on my vast newshound experience at the Tulsa *Tribune* and ran the poor girl to ground in the city directory. She lived in a small wooden house on Hotel Street, not far from Thomas Square. I used to walk by her house—without stopping, of course. I never saw her there, but I felt a little thrill in knowing that that was where she lived. Freddy Eynsford-Hill would later sing the same sentiment in the musical *My Fair Lady*.

All right. I had her name and knew where she lived, but I didn't have the first notion as to what to do next. She was beautiful, small, and delicately built when compared with her more robust island colleagues, and her rich brown hair was closer to her head and more glossy than the others' frizzled mops.

Fortunately, I had the good sense not to tell any of the guys on the ship. Ilse was far too precious a pearl to be thrown before that lot. What I most feared was that they would discover my secret and brand me for the damned fool I was for not knowing what to do. They would have known what to do.

Characteristically, I fell back upon pencil and paper. I wrote her a letter. And she answered it! Then I was in a bind. And again, characteristically, I wrote her another letter. Thus began the strangest correspondence I have ever had. I tried mightily to keep my eager puppy love out of what I wrote, but I suppose she read between the lines and knew what was going on. I later learned girls are good at sensing things like that.

Mostly I wrote about the beauty of the night sea and of the islands we visited to the west of Hawaii. Sometimes I told her about Oklahoma and the horse and hunting dog I had had there as a boy. Eventually she even wrote to one of my sisters in Oklahoma, I think. Ilse's answering letters were treasures to me. I guarded them with my life. But Sandy picked up the mail one day on his way to the bridge and noted that one of them was in a feminine hand and that it had been mailed in Honolulu. He lifted his eyebrows and teased me a little, but he never told any of the other guys. I had always admired Sandy, but after that, I damned near loved him.

There are many things in a Navy warship, but privacy is not one of them. I had to sneak away to read my letters from Ilse without being seen. Finally, I took to keeping them in the envelopes of the letters my family wrote to me from Oklahoma.

I have many times since thought that Ilse must have been a remarkable young woman. There was nothing of the pen pal in her letters to me. She wrote of what she knew, the islands and their life—and she wrote well. She was interested, too, in Oklahoma, especially in its Indians. She urged me to make myself known.

I continued going to the Waikiki, of course. Hell, wild horses could not have kept me away. I always sat in the back, in an aisle seat—on whichever side Ilse was working. But I never identified myself, and there were usually lots of sailors in the audience. I could see her studying the men—and died a thousand deaths when some sailor more bold than I would notice her interest and make his move.

I would have expected her to confide in her friends and to have them join in the hunt for her bashful admirer—with a lot of giggling and finger pointing—but she never did. It apparently didn't occur to her either that I might be a dangerous sexual deviant. She just went on studying the sailors who came in, saying nothing.

Gone With the Wind finally blew my cover. The theater held it over for what must have been a month or two. Ordinarily, if a man goes to see a new movie, there is nothing remarkable in the fact. But, when he comes week after week to see the same movie, it is apt to be noticed. And I did go every week, although it was not to see the movie. One night when I was sitting on the aisle as usual, and Ilse was standing beside me, she put her hand on my shoulder. When I looked up to her, she smiled.

After that, we did talk sometimes, although we never actually dated in the conventional sense. I don't know if she would have gone out with me had I asked, but I never asked. She would come early to work sometimes, and we might have a

Coke or an ice cream, but never anything more formal. Sometimes, after the show, she would talk with me for a while until her bus came. She was never so comfortable, though, at those times. It would be night, and good girls were not to be seen with sailors. Especially not at night.

One of the thorns sticking deepest into the flesh of girl-starved sailors in Honolulu at the time was the sight of the old open touring cars with canvas tops that we saw so often in the islands piled high with laughing young people strumming ukuleles and singing at the tops of their voices. For most of us, I suppose, it called up memories of hay rides and summer picnics with girls back home. For me, who had no such memories, I felt merely a vague aching of something missing from my life.

One time when I was waiting to cross a street, a car like that careened around the corner so close I had to jump back onto the curb to keep from being hit. Ilse was in the car. She was laughing up into the face of a good-looking young man who had his arm around her in a way that suggested it had been there before.

Ilse had not seen me, but I did not talk with her anymore after that. I wasn't angry with her. I don't think I was even jealous. There was nothing I could do for her, but I was in love with her for a long time. And, God, I missed seeing her.

I tried going ashore more often with the other guys. The swimming at Waikiki was all right. The ship's doctors prescribed it sometimes as a treatment for a rash we occasionally got on our feet. We called it in those politically incorrect days "spick itch," but it was probably some form of athlete's foot. Although I still could not swim, I found that I could float in saltwater. An afternoon of sun, saltwater, and rough coral sand would clear up our foot conditions for a while.

I couldn't hack the Log Cabin on a regular basis. The noise and the confusion and the deadening sameness of it every time was too much. I think now my spirits were beginning to flag. Failing to get into the Academy was, I suspect, a harder blow than I would let myself admit. I had been in the Navy long enough for the novelty to be growing thin, I suppose. My life did not appear much different from what it had been in Oklahoma. I was eating better—and certainly more regularly—but, for the rest, I was just sitting under palm trees instead of Osage County's blackjack oaks.

Sometimes I would stay in the ship for three or four weeks at a time without going ashore at all. Even the Bishop Library palled. The only place I found any peace at all was Trader Vic's, a restaurant owned by a one-legged man named Vic Bergeron. His restaurant in Honolulu was a branch of his original place on San Pablo Avenue across the bay from San Francisco, but he spent a lot of his time, apparently, in Honolulu. Unlikely as it seems now, we got to know each other.

Trader Vic's was in a low, scattered out, thatched roof building in a grove of coconut palms at King and Ward streets, about halfway between downtown Honolulu and Waikiki, as I recall. It was furnished in tourist-Polynesian style, with fish spears, giant clam shells, dugout canoes, poi bowls, and the glass balls Japanese fishermen use as floats for their nets. It was pretty corny, I suppose, by modern standards, but it was effective with me. And the food was good.

I stumbled on the place one early afternoon and wandered in to nurse one of Vic's exotic rum-and-fruit drinks for what turned out to be a long time. After that first time, I came often. They were tall drinks. I could make one last a long time. No one ever hassled me. If the place became busy—which it almost never did in the daytime—I would leave. I almost never saw a sailor there—unless he was in civilian clothes, as I almost always was when I went to Vic's.

There was one table—set in a corner—from which I could see the crushed shell walkways winding their ways among the trunks of palm trees. I always tried for that table. The tropical sun was muted and diffused by the palms' interlocking fronds, lending a greenish tint to the air. It was blessedly quiet, and I could be alone for as long as I liked.

I seldom had money for dinner—Vic's prices were not low—but, when I did, Vic's is where I went. Hidden speakers played soft island music, and when it rained, water ran off the ragged edge of the thatched roof by my open window in streams of diamonds silvered by the bar lights. Big toads would hop from cover and sit in the rain facing the light, their white throats shining and their eyes blinking stupidly when hit by raindrops. If someone had set out to design the absolute opposite of the Log Cabin, he would probably have come up with something like Trader Vic's.

It was a place I could go and be alone, even after the battleship sailors came out and overran the town. It was a place I always wanted to bring Ilse, but I never did.

8
Fleet Problem

THE SORTIE OF WARSHIPS from a harbor is a stirring sight at any time, even for veterans. I've seen men with twenty or more years of service stop what they are doing to watch ships getting under way. Even senior officers might forget their dignity long enough sometimes to pause and watch.

There is all the pageantry of flags and pennants and flashing lights, and the sounds of bands and bugles and whistles blowing as passing honors are rendered and returned. The ships themselves seem conscious of the picture they make, their crews all standing at quarters for getting under way and small boats coming and going on last minute errands.

The destroyers go first to sweep the waters offshore for possible enemy submarines. Airplanes circle overhead on the same precautionary assignment. The cruisers follow, with the force flagship bringing up the rear. Finally, the harbor is left strangely silent and empty. There is nothing so empty as a busy harbor from which the ships have gone.

It was all like that one morning in early April 1940, when we sortied from Pearl for Fleet Problem XXI, in which we would defend the Hawaiian Islands against the battle force even then steaming westward from California to meet us in simulated battle.

I had heard about Fleet Problem XXI even before leaving boot camp. In a way, it would be my confirmation as a Navy sailor. For most of the year in the Navy of that time, ships operated as types—destroyers with destroyers, cruisers with cruisers, and so on. Less frequently, they operated as forces—all ships of the scouting force, for instance, or of the battle force. But, once each year, usually in the spring, they came together for a fleet problem in which all units, regardless of type or force, took part. That was what Fleet Problem XXI was for the year of 1940.

There were certain nuts-and-bolts arrangements to be made for the handling of large numbers of ships in company at sea. The ships cannot be allowed simply

111

to go their own ways and to hope for the best, no more than the men of an army on the march can be allowed to do so. For this purpose, the Navy had a number of prearranged formations called cruising dispositions. The disposition chosen depended on conditions at the time, and those to be expected. Usually the disposition would be signaled to all ships present, and specific orders given for its formation along with course and speed.

Courses were ordered in degrees, and speed in knots. The speed signal would specify a standard speed on which all subsequent speed orders would be based. If, for instance, standard speed were established as fifteen knots, one-third speed would be five knots and two-thirds ten. Full speed was understood as being five knots above standard, and flank speed five above that. Speed signals were made using a red pennant with the appropriate numeral flags. (Oddly, this same red pennant was used at anchor when the crew was at meals and thus excused from certain obligations, such as rendering honors. When used in this way, it was called the bean rag.)

One of the first of these organizing signals would designate one ship as guide, the vessel on which all the others would base their stations and movements. Individual ships' stations would be expressed as a distance and bearing from the guide. At the same, or nearly the same, time signals would be made establishing fleet course and axis. Course was simply the direction to be steered, and axis was an imaginary line, expressed in degrees, that controlled positioning of ships within the formation. This can be confusing for laymen, but it may be more easily understood if it is remembered that, except for speed changes, there are but two basic maneuvers in the handling of ships in formation.

The first is column movements in which ships in column turn in succession, each ship turning in the same water as that in which its preceding ship turned. This maneuver changes both course and axis. It is signaled with a long red pennant with two white circles that is called Corpen. Either two or three numeral flags specify the amount of the course change in tens of degrees or the new true course to be steered. On completion of the maneuver, the ships in formation will hold their same relative bearings from the guide, but their compass bearings will have changed.

The second basic movement is called turns together. In this exercise, ships literally turn together, that is, all at the same time. On completion, their relative bearings from the guide will have changed, but their compass bearings will not. Fleet axis remains unchanged. This evolution is signaled with another special Navy flag, a long pennant with vertical blue and white stripes, along with the appropriate numeral flags.

This description, of course, is a gross simplification and probably best skipped over by the casual reader. The fact remains, however, that ship tactics are intrinsically easy—but their execution is tricky as hell, depending as it does on endless practice, intimate knowledge of the characteristics of ships—both of one's own ship and of others in the formation—and, to some extent the character and tendencies of other commanders. For this reason, the Navy had predetermined procedures called doctrines for each type and force. These doctrines tried to anticipate all conceivable situations, the goal being that commanding officers would react in predictable ways. This proved a disastrous disadvantage in the later fighting of World War II, especially so in the night fighting off Guadalcanal—when strange ships and commanders were often required by circumstances to operate together without mutual familiarity.

At any rate, this brief summary may enable you to understand that, for the first few hours after leaving Pearl, the *Indy*'s signal bridge was a busy place. Flag hoists hurried, one after another, up and down the halyards. Sandy stood in the middle of the bridge calling out the signals to be made. Mister Bell stood, usually by the admiral, in the port side of the bridge, relaying his plain English orders to Sandy who would interpret them as they were in the *General Signal Book*—a thick brown canvas-covered book that was weighted to ensure its sinking if capture ever became imminent. From time to time, searchlights would flash the admiral's displeasure to ships that did not find their positions in formation fast enough or goofed in repeating a flag hoist signal.

Using plotting sheets called maneuvering boards, the ship's navigators solved the problem of a mystifying little deal called the relative movement line, which enabled them to reach their assigned positions by the most direct courses possible for given speeds. But this indeed is too complicated for easy explanation to laymen. It is enough to know that, for some time, the formation was a scene of considerable dramatic confusion—with significant risk of collision as ships competed to be first in position. Cruisers, depending on the disposition chosen, were likely to be in their positions, or nearly so, as they cleared the channel mouth, but the destroyers, deployed as they had been in their screening for submarines, were all over the ocean for a while. There was a good deal of dashing about.

But, in a surprisingly short time, the group was steaming in sedate formation, each ship in its designated position, planes aloft on close-in antisubmarine patrol and more distant scouting assignments. It all must sound complicated to the uninitiated, but it was actually simple. A chief told me one time that if he were given a couple of weeks and enough bananas, he could teach a monkey to do it. For example, if you wanted all ships to change course, at the same time, ninety degrees to the right, you would hoist the Turn Pennant *over* the Numeral Flag Nine. Easy?

If you wanted your ships to turn together ninety degrees to the left, you would hoist the Turn Pennant *under* the Numeral Flag Nine. And, when all your ships had repeated the complicated signal correctly, you would haul down your hoist, and all your little ships would obediently turn the way you wanted them to go. See?

Using another even more exotic system called the International Code of Signals, Navy ships, either visually with flags and lights or by radio, could talk with merchant ships and naval vessels of all the principal maritime nations of the world. For the first time since the Tower of Babel, men speaking different languages could talk together. At least their sailors could. But I don't remember ever using the international code even once in my time as a Navy signalman.

For purposes of fleet problems, conditions were made as nearly as possible what they would be in a real war. We steamed at darkened ship, for instance, meaning we showed no lights at night and never slowed below fifteen knots or so, as a presumed protection against submarine attack. Crews were kept, if not at general quarters—that is, at battle stations ready for immediate action—at one, two, or three conditions of readiness. Fleet problems were not restful times for sailors.

Because before you could shoot an enemy you had to find him, the first part of a fleet problem—as it would be in real war—was to search for and find your opponent. Of course, for purposes of getting the show on the road, it would serve equally well if the enemy found us. But there are definite advantages in being the finder rather than the findee. Ships that get in the first licks in a sea fight, especially at night, are apt to be the winners.

So, our first few days were spent in searching. The Pacific is a large ocean. In the old days, scouting lines of cruisers were used for tracking down an enemy, but by 1940 airplanes had largely taken over the task—in daytime. We had no radar then, so planes were less effective at night, but they could search hundreds of miles in the last hours of daylight and give a certain sense of security in the hours of darkness—at least in the first few hours of darkness. I don't remember our ever forming a formal scouting line of ships. We had come to depend almost exclusively on airplanes for searches.

The attacking force approaching from the eastward was using carrier aircraft to find us. We, the defending force, had our cruiser float planes and, more important, the long-range PBY flying boats operating out of Pearl Harbor. Theoretically, the two forces were, therefore, about equal in search capability. And, as it turned out, about equally ineffective.

Contact, when it did come between the two opposing forces, came in a way no one expected. There were well over a hundred ships involved in the combined attacking and defending forces, steaming toward each other at probably fifteen knots, giving a closing speed of thirty knots. They came together, virtually head-on, with no warning at all, in the small dark hours of an early morning.

We had no radar then, as I have said, and it had been several hours since the last aerial patrols had returned. The first indication we had of enemy vessels anywhere about came when we saw the phosphorescent flash of wakes and bow waves and the dark loom of unlighted hulls against the night horizon. There had been no plan for this. Instant confusion took hold, including some panic—probably—as the ships raced past each other. In this regard, at least, we had succeeded admirably in simulating real war conditions.

Some commanders tried to improvise countermeasures, as they would have had to do in actual combat, but most reverted to the simple imperative of avoiding collision. Collision at sea can be equally as fatal as enemy gunfire. And naval captains then were sensitive to the inevitable censure and loss of numbers that would follow collision with a friendly ship.

I remember enemy destroyers dashing past us to either side. Then the dim shape of a light cruiser appeared and disappeared so quickly that it seemed almost not to have been there at all. The range of vision in the unlighted night was so short that relative speeds were exaggerated impressively. The atmosphere on our Flag bridge was a mingling of natural concern and anger that such a thing could have happened in the first place.

Finally, when the fortlike shapes of the battleships began to appear around us, the order was given by radio to turn on running lights. It was deemed better to surrender simulation than to lose ships to collision. Admiral Andrews was made officer in tactical command (OTC) for the whole mess and directed to sort it out before somebody got hurt, a process that took us well into the next day. Even with running lights burning, the confusion was little reduced. The night sea was a milling mass of red, green, and white lights that, by that time, had spread over several square miles of ocean.

Radio had been adequate for getting the lights on and solving the immediate problem, but it was virtually useless for getting the ships into any kind of order. No one knew which ship was guide or where she was. And individual ships cannot be identified by their running lights alone.

Sandy and Mister Bell finally managed the job by training our two big 36-inch signal searchlights up at forty-five degrees to either side. The huge resulting blue-white V could be seen for fifty miles or more, and when signalmen used them, in synchronized dots and dashes, to send out tactical orders, order slowly came from chaos. Enough, at least, to get the various types of ships separated into cruising dispositions in which all were going in the same direction at the same speed. Fine-tuning could come after daylight.

Those big searchlights, incidentally, were a bane of the signalmen's lives. They were arc lights. Adjustable pure carbon rods protruded from rounded ceramic heads so that there was a gap between them. A powerful electrical current, arcing across that gap, caused the rods to burn with a flickering blue flame that, when focused by polished 36-inch mirrors, created an intense blue-white beam. If the rods were not kept properly adjusted, however, the ceramic heads would be burned, and the poor signalman who let it happen would pay, for some time and with considerable discomfort, for his carelessness. After all, the damned heads probably cost fifty cents or so. We hated the big lights for that reason and used them only if absolutely necessary. They were slow and clumsy to use in the first place. But they saved our bacon that night in Fleet Problem XXI.

After more than a half century I remember that night. No one slept. The entire Flag, officers and men together, was on the bridge, all bathed in the eerie blue glow leaking from behind searchlight shutters. Mister Bell and Sandy stood in the middle of the bridge aft, calling out the signals to be made, both of them as calm as though at a drill.

They could hardly have had a more distinguished audience. In addition to Admiral Andrews, Secretary of the Navy Frank Knox, Wild Bill Donovan of World War I and OSS fame to come, and *Life* magazine photographer Carl Mydans were all on board the *Indianapolis* for the fleet problem and spent most of their time on the Flag bridge with us.

Knox was a large, fleshy man with white hair who seemed always in a good humor. Donovan was surprisingly short for the reputation he had. He was, by that time in his life, roly-poly and pink faced. He would have made an excellent Santa Clause for the Christmas parties Navy ships held for orphans in those days. Mydans was also short, but he had lank dark hair and an air of birdlike watchfulness. Had he fallen over the side, we would never have been able to save him. He was a walking display rack for what seemed to be a dozen or more heavy cameras and lenses.

We gave them a good show that night. And, before the entire problem was completed, we took them back to Pearl in the *Indianapolis*, in a dashing high-speed run before rejoining the fleet for the remainder of the exercise.

Once daylight came after that first wild night of accidental meeting, we reverted to flag hoist signaling, and the fleet came to steam in orderly array, except for the occasional errant destroyer racing up to gain his assigned station. The plan for the problem was adjusted and carried out from that point on as though nothing unusual had happened. Oh, the Navy could be adaptable when it had to be.

So well had Mister Bell and Sandy brought order out of chaos, official notice was taken. All the signalmen had commendations entered into their service records, specifying the length of time we had spent on the bridge without relief. Sandwiches and coffee were brought to us, and buckets provided for the necessary exercise of natural bodily functions.

As it turned out, Fleet Problem XXI was the last of the Navy's great peacetime gatherings of ships, all glistening in their prewar light gray paint, scrubbed teak, and polished brass. And they were operating in a trade wind ocean, of all seas the most beautiful. Deep blue water, flashing white wakes and bow waves, and skies filled with endless drifting fleets and squadrons of cotton ball clouds.

I can remember yet the thrill of standing on an *Indianapolis* semaphore platform, fifty to sixty feet above the water racing alongside the ship, the wind of our thirty-knot speed tearing at my body and tugging at the little flags in my hands. I was supported only by intersecting loops of welded tubing that came no higher than my knees. Sometimes, under the stress of a full rudder turn, the ship would heel far over, and I could feel the sea reaching up for me. It was like nothing else I ever knew. For a young man of excessively romantic bent, it was the best of all possible worlds. I forgot for a time my disappointment at having failed to get to Annapolis.

As I recall now, we did no firing in that fleet problem, but we did everything else. There were mock carrier aircraft attacks and simulated submarine torpedo firings. And night destroyer torpedo attacks on the battle line. This last was the hairiest part of the whole show. The attacking destroyers had to thread their way, at very high speed, through and around screening cruisers and destroyers to get at the battleships. And all with neither radar nor running lights.

It was much like the melee that followed the first meeting of the two forces, but this time we were expecting it and everyone knew what was supposed to happen. Even so, two of the destroyers did collide. The *Farragut* drove her bow halfway through the *Aylwin*, killing a reserve chief petty officer who had just been recalled to active duty. Talk in the fleet was that he had been in his bunk at general quarters—a cardinal sin—and that he probably never knew what hit him.

We could see from our bridge the dull orange flare of ruptured electrical circuits in the two ships and called away our fire-and-rescue party as we headed for the scene to be of whatever help we could. As it happened, the poor reserve chief was the only serious casualty, and both destroyers managed to control their damage to the point they were in no immediate danger of sinking. With their out-of-control lights burning, they pulled out of formation and headed for Pearl Harbor on their own,

The bad luck did not end there. The next day, as the carrier *Yorktown* was launching her air group, we lost two airplanes and six more men. The fighters and dive-bombers already were clear and orbiting the carrier. The torpedo planes— called torpeckers by their crews—being heavier and needing longer deck runs, were the last off. They all became safely airborne; only when the last plane was sliding into its wing position in formation did disaster strike.

Given my interest in flying, I was, as usual, watching the operation through binoculars. The last plane cleared the *Yorktown*'s flight deck and climbed, cutting corners on his squadron, which was circling at probably five or six thousand feet. But he came in at too great an angle and skidded into the next inboard airplane. He was in virtually a vertical bank when he hit the other plane. Their wingtips seemed barely to brush together.

A bit of debris flew back from the impact, and both airplanes stumbled on for an instant or two. Then both nosed over as though on purpose and plunged, nose first, into the sea. Neither spun or floundered about. And no one jumped. The planes made a surprisingly small white flash in the blue sea: they simply disappeared. There was no fire.

We were the nearest surface ship and steamed onto the scene within minutes, but the airplanes already were gone. The two pilots' bodies were floating face down in their life jackets. We recovered them, but the four enlisted men had gone down with their airplanes.

This accident, coupled with the destroyer collision, sobered us all, but the exercise went on. Coincidentally, it also resulted in the only formal disciplinary punishment I would ever receive in the Navy. I was so moved by the tragedies that I wrote of the experience in a letter to Roger Devlin, my old boss on the *Tribune*. He was then no longer wire editor, as he had been when I worked for him, but had started writing a daily column called "The Rambler." He printed my letter in his column.

I had forgotten all about it when, two or three months later, I was called to the executive officer's cabin. The executive officer in a Navy ship is second in command and handles the nuts and bolts of the ship's administration for the captain. I suspected nothing wrong. I had passed my final flight physical examination a few days before and assumed I was being summoned to receive the glad news of my orders to Pensacola. Well, like hell I was.

Commander C. T. Joy was the exec. He would later be an admiral and, I believe, head the United Nations delegation to the Panmunjom truce negotiations

Floyd Beaver's second childhood home just outside Tulsa, Oklahoma. The outside water tap was an improvement over his first home, where water had to be hauled in from a distant spring.

The author (second from right) in 1928.

The author (on right) in 1934.

Graduating from Navy boot camp in San Diego in 1939.

Waikiki Beach in 1940.

The Army-Navy YMCA in Honolulu in 1940.

Floyd Beaver's first ship, USS Indianapolis.

The author taking part in a man overboard recovery drill in 1940.

Crew of HMNS Moa *in Tulagi Harbor. Five of these men were killed when the ship was sunk several weeks later. Author is at the extreme right rear.*

Floyd Beaver as a chief petty officer.

at the end of the Korean War. He would also have a destroyer named for him. He did not look happy. He passed me a clipping of my old boss' column. "Have you seen this?" he said. I looked at the clipping and said that I had not seen it. "Did you write it?" he said then with some impatience.

I read some of the column and admitted that I had. But, I protested, I had written it as a personal letter not meant for publication. I didn't see any problem even if I had written it for publication. But I could tell from Commander Joy's manner that I had not particularly pleased the Navy. He explained at some length that I had embarrassed the Navy and exposed it to criticism. Beyond that, I had given aid and comfort to the enemy. That sounded ominous as hell. I realized then, I suppose, that I was in trouble. I responded by hyperventilating and fainting, an unfortunate weakness that has plagued me all my life. It must certainly have upset Commander Joy. He had lost his audience at the height of his tirade.

It turned out that a recruiting chief in Oklahoma City—apparently Oklahoma had a recruiting station by that time—happened to see the column and had reported it to the Navy as a breach of security. Military public relations was in its infancy then in comparison to what it is now, but the Navy's brass, even then, did not like boo-boos revealed. I could not help thinking later, though, that if it took the Navy that long to act against someone like me, it would be in big trouble with a real spy, a suspicion that the Pollards and Walkers of later years have justified.

A second, and more poignant, result of the incident was that the mother of one of the dead pilots saw the column too. She lived in Norman, Oklahoma, and wrote me a moving letter. She got my address through the *Tribune* and sent me presents of cakes and cookies throughout the coming war. She wasn't mad at me at all.

At any rate, once I had recovered from my less than heroic fainting spell, I had to report to captain's mast, a judicial proceeding in the Navy, where punishments were meted out to sinners. I was given a warning for my crime. This is the least of Navy punishments and is expunged from your record after six months, if you have committed no further wrongs.

The remainder of the fleet problem went off without further trouble, and we came in the end to anchor off what was then the hamlet of Lahaina on the island of Maui. All 150 of our ships! And liberty was granted!

At one time, during the heyday of whaling, Lahaina had rivaled Honolulu in size and importance, but that time was long past in 1940. There were a few poor shops, some hastily erected souvenir stands under enormous banyan trees—and the famous Whalers' Inn Hotel. There was one small stone boat landing, at which the liberty boats of the entire American Pacific Fleet were expected to land a huge number of sailors. There was no real harbor at all, just an open roadstead in the lee of Haleakala and a couple of off-lying islands.

I never saw such a mess in my life. Boats could land only one at a time. Even so, they managed to land the sailors ashore without too much trouble. They did so over a period of hours. But after a little while on a shore, where there was nothing to do, and oiled as they were with rum, beer, and the islands' own potent *okolehao*, all baked under a hot tropical sun, the sailors wanted to come home. And they wanted to come home all at the same time. Boats milled about in a crazy melee of bells and cussing and gunned motors that went on well into the next day. Irritable remarks were common. There were even fist fights. It was the worst liberty I ever spent.

When Fleet Problem XXI ended, the entire fleet—battleships, carriers, cruisers, destroyers, and submarines—crowded into Pearl at the same time. Pearl is not a big harbor. Putting that many ships in it at one time created a problem for signalmen who were responsible for keeping track of ships present, a job that became virtually impossible. The only comfort we of the Hawaiian Detachment found lay in the belief that the crowd was temporary. The invaders were supposed to return to the mainland after giving their crews a shot at liberty in Honolulu. We of the Hawaiian Detachment could then return to our former comfortable torpor.

Well, like hell we did that. The word came down that our guests were going to be with us indefinitely, a decision that was controversial at the time and became more so later.

Even aside from what all this did for our quality of life in Pearl, it completely destroyed the fun of liberty in Honolulu. Hotel Street ran wall-to-wall with sailors. The Army, too, was sending out thousands of new men. And every arriving ship dumped even more thousands of civilian workers with their union wages on the island's limited resources. For a while we Hawaiian Detachment sailors survived under a typical Navy preferential system, but we knew it could not last.

Under the Navy's bureaucratic system, Pearl had been designated our home port sometime before. This was a formal naval declaration that made it possible for married men—not many of us were married then—to bring their families to the islands at government expense. There were other minor provisions as well, but the most significant for us was that we would continue to get overnight liberty, while the battleship sailors had to be back on board before dark.

In theory, that was not a bad arrangement for us. The battleship sailors could go ashore early and get the girls all warmed up, and we could come ashore and move in with a minimum investment in time and booze. In practice, it didn't work worth a damn. First, there were no girls. Second, Honolulu prices went through the roof. We were not happy at all.

This homeporting, incidentally, and the coming of families to Hawaii caused my first problem with Mister Bell. He had a wife and a young daughter, as I recall. He rented a big old wood-frame house in Nuuanu Valley and detailed a working party of signalmen to move his furniture into the house. Given my admiration for him, I would gladly have helped him move, but I resented being ordered to do it. I know some of the others did too. It reminded me too much of the goddamned Safeway store manager in Tulsa who made me load waste vegetables in a truck for the hogs he kept on a farm outside of town. It was too much like being a servant.

It *was* interesting to see the interior of such a house, though. And the rich furnishings we moved into it. Ship's scuttlebutt had it that Mister Bell had money. I don't doubt it. Even officers were not paid much in the Navy then, and that house would have been a stretch for a lieutenant commander's pay. But the richness of the house and its furnishing was a stinging reminder, too, that I would never have such a house. And it was galling to realize that Mister Bell took our services for granted, as something that was his due and not to be thought about. I never really felt about Mister Bell again as I had before.

Despite such petty irritations, we came, that summer, for the first time, to believe there might be trouble in the wind for us. One by one, the steps were taken that would put us on a full wartime footing. We steamed always then at darkened ship and never dropped below a good maneuvering speed. We no longer anchored among the out islands, the experience I had always enjoyed so much. Our beautiful light horizon gray, almost white, paint was covered over with a grim gray so dark it looked to be black. Even the teak decks generations of deck apes had sweated their lives away to keep white were painted over. An unpainted teak deck, wet with spray or night damp, could, when a ship rolled in moonlight, flash a reflection of light that might be seen miles away.

It was sometime during this period too that an antisubmarine gate was installed in the entrance channel to Pearl. A net, made of interlocking steel rings, was suspended from floats across the channel in such a way that a tender could open and close it to allow the coming and going of friendly vessels while keeping out strangers.

And we stripped ship. Navy ships were made ready for battle in two steps. The first, stripping, required putting everything ashore that was not essential to the fighting of the ship or that would present a special hazard. Everything wooden, for example—including the boats. Except for two whaleboats carried in davits to either side as lifeboats, rafts took the place of boats. The ornate wardroom silver service given to the ship by the city of Indianapolis at the time of her commissioning was put in safe storage on the beach. So were all the trophies the ship's athletic teams had won over the years. Clearly, someone expected something to happen. Unless, of course, it was just some more look-see pidgin.

The ships were all degaussed too. This meant adding a cable around their hulls through which an electrical current was passed to neutralize their magnetic fields and, thus, prevent the triggering of the magnetic mines then coming into use by the countries already at war. The neutral merchant ships we sometimes saw at sea were painted with large national flags of their countries.

As it turned out, in all this grim preparation for war, one backward step was taken. Someone in the ranks of Navy brass decided our uniform-of-the-day should be skivvy shirts and shorts. The skivvy shirts were simply our regular short-sleeved undershirts. But our Navy, unlike the British, had no shorts in stock. No problem. The legs were cut off our regular white pants. Instant shorts.

An interesting sidelight revealed—literally—Navy shins that had not seen the light of day in years and a remarkable array of scrapes, bruises, and scar tissue. Stairways in the Navy were called ladders. Their rungs were hard-edged metal. High coamings at hatches and watertight doors were other hazards. Together, they left their marks on lower legs that had bounced off them for years. Collectively, these mementos were called ladder chancres.

I always suspected the brass who ordered this fiasco had been impressed with the smart appearance of British officers with their stylish flared shorts and high white socks. But our shorts were not stylish at all. They looked like white pants with their legs cut off. And our black socks rode in embarrassing wrinkles about our ankles. The most tragic result of this order, though, was the horrible flash burns suffered later in the Japanese attack on Pearl Harbor. It was found then that even the lightest clothing offered some protection from the searing flash of bursting bombs.

Construction in the Navy yard and the fuel storage area on a hill overlooking the harbor went on night and day. The rattle of jackhammers and bang of pile drivers never ended. At night, the sputtering blue light of welding torches burst everywhere, each with its pretty rain of sparks. One by one, the landmarks of the old yard disappeared, buried under the raw mass of new construction.

Our operational schedule was made even heavier too and was frequently complicated in the practice areas by the presence of all the new ships. Often at night when we were at sea, we would see the orange-red flicker of gunfire over the horizon and, some time later, hear the hollow rumbling of great guns. This was reminiscent of distant summer lightning and the rolling of thunder over Oklahoma prairies.

We seldom anymore drew the independent operations I had enjoyed so much, but sometimes we did. I remember once when we struck so far north we shifted into blues and broke out our long-idle wool sweaters and pea coats. There we ran one night into a wild black storm like nothing I ever had seen before. Normally, we came and went to the signal bridge along the outer weather decks. But the weather that night was so rough we were permitted to pass through the hallowed protected passageways of officers' country—a part of the ship we were not otherwise permitted to enter unless summoned.

Of all that storm experience, I remember most the noise: the screaming, almost living, howl of the wind, and the crashing clamor of waters collapsing on themselves or slamming against the ship's steel sides with force enough to shiver the full 10,000 tons of her. I had not realized that things as soft and giving as winds and waters were neither soft nor giving at all. In one shrieking squall, we lost two of our airplanes, swept off their catapult cradles by wind and boarding seas, over the side. Those catapults were forty or fifty feet above the water, I would guess—giving some idea of the sea's height. In the end, even our powerful ship had to slow her engines to prevent further damage.

Such storms and cold winds were new to the Hawaiian Detachment. We usually kept well inside the balmy tropics. Mister Bell lectured us one time on the subject. The Japanese, he said, would have an advantage over us in any future war because they routinely trained in the far northern Pacific, where weather alone tested their ships to the limit and men frequently were lost over the side. American mothers would not put up with that, Mister Bell said. They would write their congressmen, who would call the Navy's brass, who would see that we were kept down where everything was nice and warm.

I didn't know about that, but I do know that one trip north did much to satisfy my appetite for cold. The only good that came of the run north was that, instead of returning directly to Pearl, we ducked into San Francisco and anchored off Treasure Island, where the World's Fair was in full swing. With our telescopes, we could see everything that was not behind something else. The lights at night were spectacular for their time, but our experience of them was both fleeting and from afar.

We came in well after dark and sailed before dawn. In the meantime, tugs brought an ammunition barge alongside, and we took on board a hundred or so shells for battleship guns. I think now they were 16-inchers. They were stood on end in the after starboard corner of number one mess hall and lashed in place with a good deal of care.

I could not help recalling the famous French story in which an old-fashioned carriage gun had gone adrift in a ship at sea and battered the wooden vessel to destruction with its weight. Each of the shells in our mess hall weighed a ton or so.

It took little imagination to picture what would happen if they should break free of their lashings. Even if they didn't explode—which was unlikely because they were neither fused nor armed—their weight would batter the ship in an undesirable way. It would be the devil's own job to tie them down again.

I never heard why we were given that assignment in the first place. The Navy had ships even then designed and built to handle ammunition and crews trained for the job. Appropriately, these ammunition ships were named for volcanoes. But all ships during that period were often given odd and unusual missions. Just as their crews were given hard and messy jobs to do.

Nowadays, for instance, I understand yard workmen handle the gooey job of dry-docking ships and cleaning their bottoms. In 1940 the ship's own hands did the work. And it was an all hands operation, just as coaling ship had been in an even older Navy. There were no exceptions. Even the watchstanders, those privileged prima donnas, were allowed to participate. Chiefs took over the watches throughout the ship. Everyone else went over the side—in the oldest clothes he had.

Each division was assigned a portion of the ship's length and stages were rigged over the side. As the water level dropped in the dock, those stages were lowered with it, and we stood on the stages and scraped away the noxious growth of barnacles and other marine organisms that would otherwise reduce our speed and increase fuel consumption. We used tools very much like ordinary garden hoes with straightened blades. Their wooden handles were about six to eight feet long, with blades maybe six to eight inches wide. For a ship six hundred feet long, that meant a lot of thrusting strokes.

And it was hot. We were well down in the narrow space between steel hull and concrete dock wall. When the tropical sun hit down into that space, the effect was impressive. We had been ordered—in the interest of health, I suppose—not to touch the dock water. But no one had ordered us not to fall into it. Pretty soon the dock waters were a splashing playground as men fell off and clambered back onto the stages.

Since the water was nearly as hot as the air, any benefit was temporary at best and largely psychological. The water was so foul with the disgusting stuff we had scraped off the ship's bottom it was nearly stiff. Swimming lost its appeal, and we sweated and suffered in silence, working simply to get the job done as soon as we could. (For the sake of modern environmentalists concerned about toxic pollution, I remember not one word about the dangers of swimming in and spitting out mouthfuls of the foul slop. Nor do I remember anyone's getting sick from the fact.)

And the smell! Some fish were always stranded when the dock gates were closed. As they died, cooking for a few minutes in the sun and the ripe marine growth piling up to a depth of a foot or so in the dock's bottom, they made a scent that I still remember. The stench was damned near visible as it rose out of the dock and seeped into every corner of the ship.

To make things even more interesting, when we reached the bottom of the ship, its plates bent inward. The steel plates became horizontal, and we found ourselves working over our heads—taking a rain of rapidly decaying marine plant and animal life that left us drenched and reeking.

Then, once that exercise was completed, we were hoisted on our stages back to the waterline, to work our way down again with a poisonous anticorrosion paint that left us with stinging hands and faces. Once done with that, we were hoisted again to the waterline and lowered to coat the huge hull with anti-fouling paint that was even more toxic. Once we had cleaned and three times painted it—with increasingly poisonous paint—it is a wonder any of us lived. Modern OSHA bureaucrats would blow all kinds of gaskets, I suppose.

I don't remember how long all that took, but it was easily long enough. For those of us not used to hard physical work, it was tiring. Especially so when it is considered that when we were at last hoisted inboard, we had the interesting task of cleaning both ourselves and the decks we fouled simply by our passage over them.

We earned our money that day. And we had bitter thoughts on the subject a few days later when Navy working parties were called away to unload one of the few merchant ships that ever entered Pearl Harbor. Most merchant ships called at Honolulu. Navy men were used to unload this one because her civilian crew was on some kind of strike and would not turn to. They were being paid a damned sight more than we were, but they sat on their asses and watched a bunch of swabbies do their work for them. That left a foul taste.

During this period I shed my first blood in the Navy. Navy crews were so healthy then and so closely watched, that our medical people rarely had anything to do beyond routine short arm inspections and giving pros to returning liberty parties. The corpsmen were apt to get a little rusty. We had one doctor—Old Foreskin, we called him—who took the initiative in looking for things to fix, whether they were broken or not. One of the things he most often found to fix was, as indicated by his nickname, foreskins. In the tropics, they tended to get various uncomfortable conditions under them, and he saw the problem as a dandy way to give his corpsmen some practice and training in surgery.

That is how I came to shed some blood. I had been warned not to go to sick-bay, but I did. The damned doctor's eyes glistened when he saw what I had brought him, and he immediately set me up for the major surgery of circumcision, handling the procedure as he would have handled something really serious. Sandy commented that the old rabbis used to remove foreskins with their thumbnails, but this doctor shot the works on me.

I don't remember the operation itself as being much, but I do remember the thoughtfulness of my shipmates. They came down to sit with me that night in sickbay, bringing all the pornographic pictures and erotic conversation they could gather for the occasion, including highly clinical discussions of the newest girls in the New Congress Rooms and their various ingenious specialties.

If you've ever tried not to think about some specific thing, you know what happens. And my dear shipmates damned well meant for it to happen. Old Foreskin had warned me against the discomfort of erections so long as I had stitches where I had stitches. But by the time my shipmates were finished with their presentations, stitches were popping on all sides. It hurt. I sure as hell remember that.

At any rate, Fleet Problem XXI in many ways represented both the high point and the end of my good times in the Navy. It was the last time, so far as I know, that the fleet operated as a whole in the old, time-hallowed certainties of battle line tactics. For the last time, we acted in unquestioning confidence in what we had been taught—except for that one hairy night when the two forces came together unexpectedly. All that followed up to and through the first months of the war itself was improvisation and feeling our way.

I remember even then a feeling of sadness at what was happening, for, though the coming of the battleships and their supporting vessels had disrupted our largely pleasant time in the islands, what happened in the *Indianapolis* was even worse.

9

The Rock

FROM THE VERY BEGINNING some Hawaiian Detachment sailors hated duty in the islands. Especially so those who had family and friends or shack jobs in Long Beach. These men called Oahu "the Rock." They considered the island much as a prison and lived for the time when we would all be returned to stateside ports.

After the battleships came to foul our formerly comfortable nest, the feeling became all but universal. Honolulu's limited facilities were overwhelmed by masses of new men, Army, Navy, and civilian workers alike. Simply getting to town and back became an ordeal, and prices for everything rose drastically. Even those of us who had enjoyed the islands became resentful.

Life in our ships themselves became less and less comfortable as well as the vessels were readied for war. We could not escape the new frustrations even by staying on board. Morale went to hell. Virtually all of us began to refer to Oahu as the Rock.

Therefore, when, sometime in the summer of 1940, the *Indianapolis* was called back to the States for yard overhaul there was general elation among the sailors. Going in the yard meant only one thing to us: leave! Even I, who had liked island duty, was excited at the thought. I had had leave only six months or so before, but conditions had become so unpleasant in the islands that the thought of getting away for a time was appealing. I had been away long enough to think of my family with a new appreciation, I suppose. I looked forward to seeing them again. And to getting away from the Rock.

I knew that Flags did not go with flagships into the yard. Our own Flag, for instance, had been in another ship at the time I joined the *Indianapolis* in Vallejo. But I did not see how that would make any difference to me. I was ship's company. Sandy quickly explained how it could make a difference.

When the word came for the Flag to move to a relief flagship—the *Chester*, in this case, a Fifth Division heavy cruiser a bit older than the *Indianapolis* but otherwise similar—the word also came that Honk and I would be going with it. We had been taken into the Flag. From that time on, it was "whither thou goeth, there will we go," as far as Admiral Andrews and Honk and I were concerned.

It was supposed to be an honor to be chosen for the Flag, but the honor was dampened a good deal for us by the knowledge we would be getting no leave. Honor be damned! Honk and I saw it only as being screwed out of a leave.

But, as happened to me several times in the Navy, neither Honk nor I was given a voice in the matter, and we followed the rest of the Flag into the *Chester*, where we went through the, for me, new drill of kicking *Chester* men out of their bunks and lockers to make room for us. This, somehow, fell well short of endearing us to the *Chester*'s men and led to a certain frostiness in relations, a frostiness that occasionally deteriorated into discord.

It was not just in living arrangements that trouble arose. The Flag's coming on board meant a good deal of dislocation and interruption of working relationships and pecking orders on the signal bridge. The *Chester*'s chief signalman, for instance, was actually a chief and did not take kindly to the idea of serving under a first-class petty officer, which was Sandy's rate at the time. Chief Maxwell in the *Indianapolis* had long since become used to the fact, but the *Chester*'s chief had to be broken to harness.

Honk and I were both given watches over senior ship's company men as well. It may have been true—certainly it was true of me—that the *Chester*'s men had more experience in the Navy and probably were better signalmen, but they knew nothing of Flag operations, and Sandy was not at all patient about training someone new when he had Flag-trained men ready at hand. Oh, there were some interesting times, but things were eventually sorted out.

During this time we came to know an instant response to any kind of bitching that came up. Honk had had his nose out of joint about some hang-up with the Navy. "Goddamned Navy—" he began. Sandy growled back, "You wasn't drafted." Ever after, when any of us complained about anything we got a rousing chorus of "You wasn't drafted!" We were all volunteers. As the British put it, we had taken the king's shilling. We had asked for anything we got.

Another rude, but completely accurate, saying in the same vein was that while God might well own our souls, the Navy sure as hell owned our asses. If there was one universal lesson the Navy taught us, it was adaptability. We adjusted for the one overriding reason that we had no other option.

One obvious result of the *Chester* men's resentment of us was that we, as Flag men, drew more and more close as shipmates and friends. This probably accounts for the solidarity so often found in any minority in its relations with its majority community. In self-defense, if nothing else, I suppose, our ties to each other grew stronger each time we moved into a new ship. This became even more remarkably true as the war came closer and our ranks were raided for manning new ships under construction and for instructors in stateside schools and training stations. The older hands became clannish and defensive in regard to replacements.

Honk and I, for instance, in the following three or four years served in the Flags of four admirals in eight ships through five battles. Although the number of Flag men was maintained through replacements, Honk and I sometimes felt as though we were alone together in the company of strangers. We had come to know one another.

The physical layout of the *Chester* was much like that of the *Indianapolis*. Both were heavy cruisers and had the same nine 8-inch guns. But there were some nagging differences. The *Chester* already had been converted to cafeteria-style feeding, for instance. None of us liked that worth a damn. Instead of clean tables, set and waiting for us when we came off watch, we had to stand in line for our meals and to eat them off cold aluminum trays with table mates we might or might not know. We even had to carry our own trays to the scullery, for Christ's sake. Cafeteria-style undoubtedly was more efficient in getting food into sailors' stomachs, but it was a damned poor way for a man to eat.

There were other things too. The *Chester*'s bunks already had been made four high. More lockers were fitted wherever they could be crowded in. The glass ports in the sides of the ship, which made such pretty lights when rolled under the water, were sealed with welded steel. It is best not even to mention, either, what the always crowded heads and washrooms had become as more and more men, most of them hardly trained, were packed into the ships.

We did not realize it at the time, but these unpleasant alterations were being made to all the Navy's ships during that period as they were prepared for war. They were being made to the *Indianapolis* in Vallejo at the very time we were bitching about them in the *Chester* for that matter. It was sad to lose the few amenities Navy sailors had.

Working conditions became worse too. The *Chester*'s signal bridge did not meet the *Indianapolis* standards to which we were accustomed. It was considerably smaller, for one thing, and the guy bending on faced aft. This meant the hoists were dragged across his face when the hoisters were told to "Hit it!" The only improvements were that the goddamned whistle didn't spew hot water over us, and the 5-inch gun directors, for some strange reason, did not create the irksome eddies we had suffered in the *Indianapolis*. Thank God for small favors.

Our operations continued much as they had before. We continued to steam as the fifth ship in the Sixth Division, which included the *Minneapolis*, *New Orleans*,

San Francisco, and *Astoria*. These ships, along with the Fifth Cruiser Division and our escorting destroyers, were the ships of the Hawaiian Detachment, but we seldom operated as such after the battleships came to stay. We became more like regular elements of the fleet as a whole. We operated as ships of a common type for the most part.

In fact, it was at about this time that the task forces built around carriers were formed. Each carrier, along with whatever cruisers and destroyers were available at the time, was put under the command of an admiral and operated very much as a self-contained body. Task forces were made up of task groups, which were made up of task units. It was a most flexible organization, and a strong argument against those who accuse the Navy's senior officers of being hidebound and resistant to change.

Our admiral—Wilson Brown, by that time—was given Task Force 11, with the *Lexington* as his carrier, but we remained in cruiser flagships until the beginning of the war. Admiral Halsey got the *Enterprise*. I don't remember who got the other carriers, but from that time on, we operated almost altogether in that format. The old division and type tactics were seldom practiced. Maneuvers and cruising dispositions were simplified. Almost always—especially in daylight—we steamed in antiaircraft dispositions in which supporting cruisers and destroyers, deployed in rings about the carrier, were expected to stay close enough to their carrier to support her with their guns—while, at the same time, staying far enough away so as not to be run down by the bigger ship as she maneuvered to evade bombing and torpedo attacks.

Fortunately, we were beginning to get radar in the ships by that time, though few had that wonderful invention in them when the war broke out. In our force, for instance, the *Lexington* had radar. It was a primitive set by later standards, but it was a comfort nevertheless. Its antenna was a large rectangular affair that looked very much like king-size bedsprings. It is not pleasant, even now, to think what the coming carrier war would have been like without radar. God knows it was bad enough with radar.

In the *Chester*, as relief flagship, of course, we retained the privileges of rank. When Admiral Andrews' pretty three-star blue flag was hauled down in the *Indianapolis* and broken in the *Chester* the whole Flag rigmarole moved with it. Often, when approaching Pearl after an operation, for instance, we would run up the three-flag signal Tare Queen Yoke, which meant, as I recall, "Disregard movements of this vessel."

Then, while the rest of the formation steamed on at its stodgy ten knots, we would haul out from our usual station at the rear of the column and dash past them at a lively eighteen or twenty knots. Our liberty party would be on its way ashore before the other ships rounded Hospital Point. *Chester* sailors didn't complain too much about that part of being a flagship.

They did not complain about the berth we got in Pearl either. After the battleships came to stay, the *Pennsylvania*, as fleet flagship, ranked us out of our old berth at Ten-Ten Dock. But we got an even better one at Magazine Island. Magazine Island had not been much developed then. It was joined to the mainland of Oahu by a causeway, but there were none of the installations that now cover the area. Our new berth lay at the end of a narrow road winding through a grove of algaroba trees extending all the way to the ship. That was the first—and only—time I ever woke up in a Navy bunk to the sounds of birds outside. The big Honolulu taxis still came to the foot of our gangway.

A few months later, when submarines were transferred from the Battle Force to the Scouting Force for administrative purposes, we got an even better berth. Admiral Andrews was still COMSCOFOR and he promptly asserted his right, as commander of submarines, to a berth at the submarine base in Pearl.

Submarine sailors, owing to the rigors of their branch, were always well treated in the Navy. Our new berth was one of flower beds and tennis courts and swimming pools. There was even a two-lane bowling alley. All were just across the pier and available to us anytime we were not on watch. The *Chester* sailors found these amenities acceptable too.

Since I had been with the Flag signalmen in the *Indianapolis* for several months, we knew each other, and I felt little loneliness. But I did miss what had been my first ship and the friends I had made in her. For the first time, I was discontented in the Navy. It was traditional for sailors to be unhappy with the ships in which they found themselves. The saying was that there were only two good ships in the Navy: the one you had just left, and the one you were going to next. A man's current ship was a miserable bucket of bolts to be escaped as soon as, and in whatever manner, possible.

Tackline Jordan—the thin one—was a Flag signalman who came with us in the *Chester*. He and I agreed one day that there must be a better way to live. I already had passed my flight physical and met all the other requirements for flight training, but before I was called, an ALNAV (a message addressed to all naval ships and stations) came out putting an end to the taking of men from the fleet for pilot training on the reasonable, if frustrating, grounds that replacements for us would have to be trained; the Navy could get college boys to drive its airplanes. Tack had applied for flight training as well and was also rejected, for the same reason. We felt trapped. Neither of us was in a good mood.

We decided then to put in for submarine duty. I did not especially want submarine duty, but I did want to go to the Asiatic Fleet. Surface sailors on the China Station had it so good they wouldn't come home. The old submarines out there were so bad, though, that their sailors would even return to the States to get out of them. The only way to get to China was to go in submarines. Well, what the hell. I wanted to go to China.

It all became academic, for me at any rate, because I was rejected. As a matter of policy, the Navy did not explain why men were rejected for submarine duty. You were simply told that you had been found unacceptable.

Tack was accepted, though, and left for New London two or three weeks later. New London, Connecticut, was the location of the Navy's sub school. Another of our little Flag family was gone. I never saw Tack again. He went missing in the coming war.

I think I was signalman second class by that time. With the Navy expanding as it was, promotions came fast and often. And, as a result, they did not mean as much as they once had, when someone like Sandy never did make chief. We still had to do the work and take the responsibility the older guys had not had to shoulder until they were much more experienced.

This was the time, too, when men from the Fleet Reserve were coming back into the ships. These were men who had left the Navy but who were coming back to help man all the new ships being built. Some were all right, but others were more hindrance than help. Old Mac McCrorey, for instance, was a fine man. He had been in the Navy in World War I and had been in the Siberian Expeditionary Force following the end of that war. He must have been a least forty years old, but he was still healthy and vigorous. He was a born storyteller and held us all in his hand through slow night watches as he told stories of the strange things that had happened in China and Manchuria after World War I.

We had another little guy who was never of much use. He had been a professional prizefighter on the outside. Given his size, he could not have been much more than a flyweight or bantamweight. He was a rated signalman, but I always suspected he had been promoted more for his boxing prowess than for any signaling skills. That may not be fair because when he came back into the Navy he was punch-drunk as hell. It was an act of mercy to warn him when we were going to strike the bells. Otherwise he would drop into a fighting crouch and strike out at anything near.

As we acquired these new men, we were losing old hands. They were being taken as cadres for new crews and as instructors in training stations and schools. Inevitably, efficiency fell. I remember once, while I was on a target repair party, the *Northampton* opened fire at 27,000 yards—well over the horizon—and hit the target with her first salvo. That was luck, of course, but the old veteran gunners and fire controlmen we had before the war were rarely far off the mark. Later, it was said, in the Komandorski Islands during World War II, the *Salt Lake City* exchanged salvos with a Japanese cruiser for more than two hours and scored only one or two hits. Happily, the Japanese didn't do much better. Maybe they had expansion problems too.

At any rate, about the only memorable thing that happened while we were in the *Chester* was a flying trip stateside. I no longer remember the circumstances, but we had a couple of days in San Diego and another two or three in San Francisco. It was startling to see how much San Diego had changed in the few months since I had been there. The training station I had known was all but hidden by new buildings, with still more going up. Downtown streets were crowded, and bars and nightclubs jammed at night. I remember a place Honk took me called Sherman's. It struck me as the ultimate in sophistication. Its dance floor was set in a border of glass bricks in which colored lights were embedded. Now that was living.

San Francisco too, when we got there, was booming. Wars, and the getting ready for wars, are good for business. But there were not as many sailors and Marines in San Francisco, which made the place a better liberty town. In sailors' eyes, towns were rated in inverse ratio to the number of sailors present. The ideal, I suppose, would be to be the only sailor in a town of one million girls.

It was my first time ashore in San Francisco. We had not gotten liberty the night we loaded battleship ammunition off Treasure Island in the *Indianapolis*. I was hoping to go ashore with Honk. He had been there before. Honk had been everywhere before. But he had other plans. He had met a model on our brief visit to San Diego, and she was coming north to meet him in San Francisco. And, in his words, he didn't want "any dirty-assed sailors slowing him down."

San Francisco was a dream liberty port in those days. Even the civilians were friendly to us—and God knows how many bars and nightclubs there were in the town. Most of them still followed an enlightened policy of serving every third or fourth drink on the house. The Bal Tabarin, Bimbo's 365 Club, the Dawn Club, and dozens of workingmen's bars opened their arms to us—and our cash. But at least San Francisco gave us a run for our money, which was more than most sailor towns did in those days.

The Barbary Coast, for instance, was two or three blocks of Broadway and Pacific streets, which were home to nothing but bars, restaurants, and nightclubs. It had grown out of San Francisco's glory days as a shipping port. Its tradition was more that of merchant seamen, but it welcomed us gladly. Although possibly squalid in a sophisticate's eyes, to a country boy it was a fairyland of glamour and excitement and adventure. I could picture Jack London characters at every foggy, neon-lighted street corner and alleyway.

I never learned where Honk went that night with his model. He had wangled a forty-eight-hour liberty—after getting me to take his watch—but he came back to the ship long before his liberty was up. He looked awful. He would have looked worse in whites—blood does not show so starkly on blues—but he looked bad enough. Somebody had worked him over good. He was not in a talkative mood. I don't think even Sandy ever found out what had happened. I know I never did. And none of us was brave enough to ask. Honk was a tough cookie, and his manner made it clear he did not want to discuss the matter. We let the subject drop.

As it happened, we were not given time enough to tire of the *Chester*. Once back in Pearl, she was ordered in for yard overhaul herself, and the Flag shifted into the *Louisville*, another Fifth Division heavy cruiser virtually identical with the *Chester*—though, thankfully, she had not yet been altered.

Oh, we had to go through the usual unpleasant business of displacing unappreciative people from their bunks and lockers. But the ship herself was a home and a feeder, in the Navy's traditional top rating for a vessel. Her bunks still were only three high, and she fed in the old division mess system, where we sat at our own tables and had our food brought to us. Ports in her living compartments could still be opened in port for light and air. And the *Louisville* served the best chow, especially salads, I had in the Navy before I made chief.

The only problem we had in the *Louisville*, in fact, was with her chicken-dropping officers. Usually, only the enlisted men in a relief flagship resented a Flag's coming aboard. In the *Louisville*, it was the bloody officers too. Maybe some of them had been kicked out of favorite cabins by Flag officers.

First they tried to cut off the traditional night rations served to mid-watch standers in exposed positions. The *Louisville* officers argued that, because the signal bridge had glass windows at its forward end, it was not an exposed position. Well, that could be argued, I suppose, but it was still a chicken-trick thing to do. The Navy was feeding its sailors then on about thirty-four cents a day per man. Two more slices of dry bread and a slab or meat or cheese was not going to break the taxpayers' rice bowl, for Christ's sake.

The second hassle came the first time we appeared on the quarterdeck to go ashore on liberty. All of us, by that time, had tailor-made whites. Some of the old Asiatic Fleet guys had beautiful white silk shark skins. The boxy, squared-off sack style of regulation uniforms had always been a sore point with sailors. The more radical of them claimed the goddamned officers made the uniforms that way so they would look better in comparison with us.

The *Louisville* officer of the deck wouldn't let us off the ship in nonregulation uniforms. Well, one thing led to another. Sandy got hold of Mister Bell. Mister Bell got hold of the ship's executive officer. The executive officer got hold of the captain, I suppose. Officially Flag officers had no direct authority over flagship operations, but as in any other bureaucracy, there are ways. In the end, the officer of the deck gave in, but his final resentful words to Mister Bell were, "Their hair's not cut right either."

So long as the Flag was embarked we were all right, but I would not have wanted to be Sandy if he were ever assigned to the *Louisville* as ship's company. The officers' behavior goes pretty far along the road of showing how petty grown men can be sometimes. I remember once when Chief Maxwell rode Jimmy Brower, who was very vain about his beautiful blond hair, to get a regulation haircut, pointing out that haircuts were not all that important. "If they're not important," Jimmy said, "how come the Navy makes such a big frigging deal out of it?"

We spent the whole summer steaming and shooting in one ship or another until sometime in September. The battleships had been with us then for four or five months, and morale continued to plummet on Oahu. In response, the Navy set up a program of stateside leaves. Men were allowed to ride as passengers in whatever ship might be going back to the States, take their leave there, then hitch a ride back to Pearl on some returning vessel. And, wonder of wonders, Flag men were included in this plan.

That's how I came to get my first ride in a battleship. The *New Mexico* was a Third Division ship, originally commissioned in 1917. She and her sister ships *Mississippi* and *Idaho* had been extensively modernized since. One of the improvements was the moving of the signal bridge aft to the mainmast. I don't know what the powers thought they were doing, but the arrangement was a disaster for signalmen. Not only did it separate the ship's navigation and signal bridges—two nerve centers a normal person might think better kept together—it also subjected watchstanders to all those nice gases from the stack immediately forward. These same stack gases also kept signal halyards—and everything else on the bridge—coated in a nice, greasy black goo that completely ruined white uniforms. But, again, I was given no voice in the matter.

As passengers, the leave party was expected to work, of course. And, since there were not bunks enough even for all the ship's company—many battleship sailors slept on wood-and-canvas folding cots—we slept in our hammocks. These we slung in the spaces once used for casemate guns in the old battleships. Casemate guns are those set into the sides of ships. They could fire only to one side. To increase their limited field of fire, the hulls were indented, forming odd-shaped compartments closed off from the weather outside by demountable shields fitted around the barrels of the guns. It was in these odd-shaped compartments that we slung our hammocks from hooks in the overhead.

Although I had slept in hammocks in boot camp, this was my first experience with them at sea. It was great! Battleships had a stately motion at sea in the first place. They were so heavy it took a sizable sea to give them even a ponderous pitching up and down motion. But they did roll—remarkably. It was a slow and deliberate roll, but even in apparently calm seas, the broad decks heaved up, first one side, then the other.

In our hammocks, of course, we hung suspended, all but motionless, while the great mass of the old ship moved about us. It was an odd sensation. Seen from below by men not yet mounted, the hammocks formed a bulbous, down-sagging ceiling, swaying in unison from side to side to give an entirely different, but equally odd sensation.

Sleeping in hammocks was no great problem, but rigging the damned things and stowing them for the day was. Sheet metal bins called nettings were installed along mess hall bulkheads for the stowing of hammocks. They were called nettings because, in the old sailing ship Navy, hammocks were stowed in topside nets along the bulwarks, as splinter shields. Things change slowly in the Navy. Especially so in the battleship Navy. Tradition was all.

When "Hammocks!" was piped at night, for instance, you did not simply go to the nettings and get your sack—usually referred to irreverently as your fart sack. Oh, no. You went to the nettings and stood there at attention, facing aft—in the direction of the colors—and waited in reverential silence. It was a ceremony meant to honor all the dead sailors who had gone before. It was only on a given signal that you pulled out your hammock and rigged it for the night. It was impressive, in a way, but I was glad I did not live in battleships.

No exercises at all were carried out on the passage to the West Coast, as I recall now. We simply plodded along, with majestic gait and slow speed of advance, to come in due time to Long Beach, where we anchored off the outer breakwater and the leave party was put ashore.

It is a curious lapse in my letters home of this time that there is no mention at all of this leave period. I remember very little of it now. In my nearly seven years in the Navy, I had only four leaves—and one of those was but a delay in reporting. One might reasonably expect that each would have been memorable, but this one apparently was not. I do remember riding the shiny Santa Fe Streamliner, going and coming, but I remember no problems such as I had known before with the football players and the civilian whose brother-in-law had been ruined by the Navy.

My family by that time had moved to town and lived in still another rented house I had never seen before. All of them—except for Zena Mae, who was still in school—had jobs. Oklahoma's long dormant economy had come alive under the influence of what had come to be called "defense spending." The heightened activity was something new to me. I felt ill at ease and unfitted to life in Tulsa. Even a visit to the *Tribune* newsroom to see the people I had known there proved uncomfortable. Honk, Sandy, and Tackline Jordan were often in my thoughts. Once again, I returned to the Navy with a sense of relief.

The *New Mexico* was no longer in Long Beach when I returned there after my leave. No problem—I hitched a ride in the *Oklahoma*—another old battleship from World War I. Although less radically modernized than the *New Mexico*, she had the same stately motion and stodgy pace. And we again had to sleep in hammocks, but I don't remember the formal hammocks ceremony I recall in the *New Mexico*. Still, the more rigid discipline and stricter observance of regulations in battleships were unpleasant for cruiser sailors.

At any rate, we did get back to Pearl. The most memorable part of the passage for me, in fact, was its ending. The *Indianapolis* was back from the yard by that time, but she was not in Pearl when we arrived. She was operating somewhere off Hawaii's Kona Coast. We were put aboard the *Portland*—a heavy cruiser identical to the *Indianapolis*, except for the fact she did not have Flag quarters for admirals and their staff officers—for transfer to our own ship.

There had been, shortly before, a liberty boat accident in Norfolk, Virginia, in which a number of sailors had been lost. This was much in my mind as we came up with the *Indianapolis* in the midst of a black night and with a heavy sea running. There must have been twenty-five or thirty of us in the boat. With our seabags and hammocks, we made a heavy load. Navy launches were not good sea boats in the first place. They were designed for use as ships' work boats in harbor.

I don't think I was the only one scared that night. Our freeboard was down to inches. Water splashed over the side too often to be reassuring. And none of us wore life jackets—the Navy then was not so solicitous of its sailors as I understand it is now. The big danger was that the boat's gunwale might be caught under the landing stage of the port gangway—which, as enlisted men, we were required to use. If that were to happen, the boat would immediately be capsized and all of us thrown into the heaving black nothingness that was the ocean that night.

The boat was rising and falling eight to ten feet with the passing of every sea along the towering black cliff of the ship's side. We had to time our leaps carefully. Timing leaps carefully is not too hard for a young and active man, but when a young and active man is asked to do it with the awkward burden of a lashed seabag and hammock on his shoulders, it becomes more daunting.

In time, we all got safely on board. It was good to be back in the *Indianapolis*. Although I had been in her less than a full year, she already had become home to me, an impression heightened by our experiences in the *Chester* and *Louisville*, to say nothing of the potty old battleships.

But if I had expected the *Indy* to be as she had been before, I was quickly disabused of the notion. The opening ports in our compartment, for instance, had been sealed shut with welded steel, making it a dark and oppressive place into which the light of day never again reached, even in daytime. The bunks, like those in the *Chester*, had been made four high, and more lockers were added. Even worse, the *Indy* had been converted to cafeteria-style feeding, and the various gangs in the ship split apart so that no one specialty all slept in the same compartment.

This was rationalized on the grounds that a single bomb or torpedo hit might not destroy an entire specialty. Signalmen lived with machinists, deck apes, electricians, or whatever other odd life forms might surface at the moment. The effect of this policy was to destroy the old family identification of men who lived and worked and ate together. It was all logical and efficient and rational, I suppose, but it was the end of the one thing I had found most satisfying and enjoyable in the Navy.

As a result, we signalmen—and other rates, as well—spent more of our time at our duty stations. In our case, in Flag plot and around the starboard side joe pot on the signal bridge. We tended to go to our assigned compartments only to sleep and to take care of personal chores.

This was not too bad in port, but many stations were closed off to hangers-on when at sea. The Flag plot, for instance, would be full of staff officers at sea, and only a handful of men could be accommodated around the joe pot because the signal bridge itself had been made smaller. Where before the wings had spread the full width of the ship, afterward they were trimmed to allow wider fields of fire for the new antiaircraft guns that had been added.

Altogether it was depressing. But, as with so many other things during that time, we accepted it because there was no alternative. We still had the same drills and exercises to go through, and there was always something new to be learned if a man wanted to take the trouble. Willkie, the Flag chief quartermaster, for instance, taught me celestial navigation, a subject that had always fascinated me. I had learned in comm school the idiot work of taking times, calculating sunrise and sunset, correcting charts, and plotting bearings, but Willkie showed me how to take the sights themselves and to work out the ship's position. There were always extra sextants around, and Willkie was glad to teach anyone who wanted to learn.

Willkie was a fine-featured, slightly built man who was always immaculate in his uniforms. There was a character actor in Hollywood at the time who played the roles of drunks—usually in full dress. Willkie looked just like that actor, though I never saw him take a drink. The hundreds of charts in Flag plot, the dead-reckoning tracer, and other navigation gear and instruments were all his responsibility. The Flag officers treated him with obvious respect, and he carried himself with impressive dignity. I liked Willkie.

Navigation, using modern methods of precalculated tables and simplified forms, proved to be surprisingly easy to learn, but I never became expert at it because I never used it in actual practice. Nevertheless, the lessons made a welcome break in routine.

God knows there were few enough such breaks then. Weeks and months ran together. We almost never got the old independent missions to the outer islands that once had been such fun. Sometimes when we were operating close inshore to Oahu, we would anchor for the night off Waikiki; this was about as close as we came to the old missions. When we anchored off Waikiki we escaped the congestion and confusion of Pearl Harbor. Our liberty boats landed us at Pier Five in downtown Honolulu.

One time when we were going ashore like that, a big white Matson liner barely missed running us over. It was raining hard—unusual weather in Hawaii—and the boat's crew huddled under ponchos, staring straight ahead. Soaking wet, the rest of us endured our misery as best we could. Our first notice was the slight bubbling of the slowly moving ship's bow wave, but our own boat's motor pretty well deadened the sound of that. The towering silent white mass of the ship came upon us, unnoticed, from astern. We escaped by nothing more than the depth of a couple of coats of paint. Such encounters were unusual, and the risk was more than made up for by the convenience of landing in town. We also saved fifty cents in taxi fare, a significant sum for men being paid one or two dollars a day.

One of my most vivid memories is that of our eight or nine heavy cruisers anchored in a line off Waikiki. Their riding lights could be clearly seen from the rooms and terraces of beachfront hotels. From time to time, people onshore could hear the heavy bumping of depth charges where some poor whale was catching hell from a destroyer whose soundmen were so ill-trained they couldn't tell the difference between marine mammals and submarines.

Those depth-charge bumpings were an odd feature of Waikiki liberties then. People could sit at nightclub tables, drinking fine drinks and eating fine food, and feel the heavy concussions. Ilse asked me one time what they were, but I don't think either of us realized what they truly were: audible portents of the horrors to come.

It seems strange now, but as the signs of impending trouble grew ever clearer, my realization of what was coming grew ever more uncertain. It must be that even a sense of danger is dulled over time. Perversely, the more we drilled and practiced and anticipated, the less menacing the thought of war became. I don't know now how anyone could have seen the sometimes near frantic pace of construction and military buildup then going on in the islands and not realize war was coming, but we did. We sailors did not take the Japanese Navy seriously. It had for too long been caricatured and derided, I guess.

We slipped into a more or less monotonous routine in which I came to think about getting out of the Navy. There were less than two years left of my enlistment, and I had been frustrated in everything I had tried to do: Annapolis. Flight training. China. Submarines. In looking at Sandy, who was far smarter and a much more effective leader of men than I would ever be, I could not see much future for a man like me in the Navy. But I had not lost my fascination for the sea. I began to consider the Merchant Marine, where standards were not so rigid nor procedures so hidebound.

Liberty in Honolulu had become impossible. Even the Bishop Museum and Library palled because of the hassle of getting to town and back. In my frustration I came more and more to identify with the older career sailors in the ship. They did not seem to need liberties. Why should I bother? I don't mean to imply that these older men were not intelligent; rather they had come to a more realistic appraisal of the world than I could find in my romantic fantasies. They seemed to have found a contentment that I had not—and never would, for that matter. I came to feel, I suppose, that maybe they were right.

Sometimes I would stay on board for three or four weeks at a time. When I did go ashore, it was more apt to be with the other guys, and we would go to the Log Cabin. I still did not drink in any serious way, but it was comforting to be with my own kind. The various noises and stenches and the profanity of it all seemed somehow appropriate.

I did not go to the Waikiki Theater during that time. I both wanted and did not want to see Ilse. I could see no point in it. About the only times I was alone were my increasingly infrequent visits to Trader Vic's, where I watched the toads in the rain. Then I would wish Ilse were with me.

But, even when a man did find some quiet oasis of calm, there was still the problem of getting back to the ship. We Flag signalmen were still getting our one o'clock watchstanders' liberty and could get to town reasonably well, but getting a taxi back was a hassle, even if you came back early. Hundreds of sailors, soldiers, and Marines formed often brawling lines in the big forecourt gardens of the YMCA. All were tired and frustrated and lonesome in a strange place. Some were drunk. And sometimes it rained in the soft Hawaiian way that soaked a man through before he ever felt a drop. Patience was uncommon, but fights were not.

The Shore Patrol and Army MP's did what they could. The Navy and the Army had different policies in that regard. The Navy's shore patrolmen were simply men off the ships, temporarily assigned to the duty. The Army had professional career military police. It always seemed to me that the Shore Patrol was far more understanding of sailor foibles and did their best to get us back to our ships without serious charges. The MPs, on the other hand, were more ready to run a man in. It was their job. We stayed clear of them as much as we could.

The big, brown-uniformed Hawaiian cops were the worst of the lot. They seemed to enjoy their work with sailors and watched us as though daring us to get out of line. They would finger their clubs and grin at us. We didn't like them worth a damn.

Altogether, liberty wasn't worth the trouble. Sometimes, when the battleships were out and there were only a few ships left in the harbor, a guy might make a decent liberty. But we were the goddamned Flag. If anybody were out, we would be out. It was easier just to stay on board.

About the only thing that happened during that time was Admiral Andrews' relief. Vice Admiral Wilson Brown, whose last assignment had been as superintendent of the Naval Academy, became COMSCOFOR and COMHAWDET. That was around February 1, 1941, if memory serves. Commander in Chief, Pacific Fleet (CINCPAC) and Commander, Battle Force (COMBATFOR)—and probably some I have forgotten—were all relieved on that same day. And, for convenience, I suppose, all the ceremonies were staged on the *Indianapolis*' quarterdeck at Ten-Ten Dock.

I didn't know there was that much gold in the world. Husband E. Kimmel, Claude C. Bloch, Adolphus Andrews, and Wilson Brown all had at least three stars. God knows how many two-star division commanders and the like were running around. And we, as Flag signalmen, were right in the big middle of it. We had to report the approach of every barge and sedan so the officer of the deck could lay on the proper honors. Side boys. Marine guard. Bugler. Band. Ruffles and flourishes. Sword salutes. The works.

Despite my then-jaundiced view of the world, it was interesting. It was only long after that I learned the significance of the changes in command. The controversy over keeping the battleships at Pearl still makes work for historians and analysts. Had the old ships been kept on the West Coast, the Japanese might not have attacked. To me, at the time, the ceremony was just a show, just as so much in the Navy in those days was show—or, in the white hats' words, look-see pidgin.

None of what went on made much apparent difference to us on the bridge once all the hullabaloo was over. I didn't give a damn whether Andrews stayed or went. He had always been even more aloof with us than most senior officers were. The only one of us who ever scored anything on him, that I recall, was Mother Scott.

Mother, in addition to his big nose, had a sweet tooth. He was forever stashing candies and cookies in hiding places about the bridge. Oreos were his favorites. We used to steal Mother's goodies and hide them from him, but we never ate anything of his. It was just a game with us. But someone was stealing Mother's Oreos and, apparently, eating them.

After a while, Mother laid a trap. He scraped the cream filling from some Oreos and replaced it with saltwater soap mashed to a paste. Saltwater soap was a particularly harsh soap we used for washing things in seawater. It is strong. It probably doesn't taste very good either. Mother took his loaded cookies and stashed them out of sight on the lip of an overhead angle iron—and got his man.

Sometime late in the eight-to-twelve watch, Old Andrews came, spitting and sputtering, around the corner by the signal log desk and asked for a cup of coffee. I had never known him to ask for our coffee before, and he offered no explanation for why he wanted it that time. But Mother never lost anymore Oreos.

The Pig left us at about the same time Admiral Andrews did, as I recall. None of us was sorry to see him go. I never heard of him again until after the war started. I read then that he had been made rear admiral and given a force of three or four obsolescent four-piper light cruisers in the Southeast Pacific. I guess that was as far from the war—and as safe from foul-ups—as he could be put.

Oddly, our new captain, E. W. Hanson, was as good as the Pig had been bad. He was an excellent ship handler, for one thing. One time he put the *Indianapolis* into her tight—very tight—submarine base berth in Pearl without tugs—and with all those nice, tender submarines so close all around. He had been military governor of Guam before coming to us and had served a long time on the China Station. Scuttlebutt had it that he had married a white Russian woman out there against the Navy's wishes. If he had never done another thing in his life, that alone would have endeared our new captain to us. But the truth was that part of the story was highly unlikely. No officer in much disfavor would have been given command of a ship like the *Indianapolis*. Especially not when she was a force flagship.

Mister Bell left us around this time as well. The Flag was going to hell. We did regret Mister Bell's leaving. We had the carpenters build a beautiful mahogany box, lined with velvet, in which we put a pair of silk semaphore flags for him. He had been good to us—except that time he forced us to move his goddamned furniture. I don't know where he went, but he later got command of the destroyer *Grayson* and wrote a book called *Condition Red* about her adventures in the Solomons. He retired after the war as a rear admiral.

The really crushing blow, though, came when Sandy got his orders. Everyone in the signal gang who was not on watch stood about to watch him pack his gear and lash his hammock. No one said very much, but I think we all realized what we were losing. When he was finished, we walked with him to the boat. The Navy had no prescribed ceremony for bidding enlisted men good-bye. A goddamned shame it was too.

Things were never the same after Sandy left. Honk and I did the best we could, but everything had turned sour for us. I remember one night we were on the bridge in Pearl. Neither of us had the watch, but both of us were on the bridge. Honk was having a cup of joe, and I was just hanging out, in the vernacular of a later age. The plantations were burning cane fields back of Aiea, and the fires lay like slowly moving strings of ruby beads over the black hills. In the morning, there would be black ash from the fires all over the ship. It had been several weeks since Sandy left, but when Honk said softly, "You ever miss him?" I knew who he meant. "Yeah, I miss him," I said. "I'm going to turn in. We're sailing in the morning."

The date was December 5, 1941.

10

War: The Early Raids

AT EIGHT O'CLOCK HONOLULU TIME on Sunday morning, December 7, 1941, the USS *Indianapolis* (CA-35) was lying to off Johnston Island—some seven hundred–plus miles southwest of Pearl Harbor—in company with four old World War I four-piper destroyers that had been converted to fast troop carriers for hit-and-run raiding. They were loaded that morning with Marines who would stay on the island as a defense garrison, but we were putting them ashore in the form of a landing exercise. Why a flagship, with its task force, including its carrier, several hundred miles away, should have been assigned a mission like that I don't know.

For the few months before the war the Navy had been operating in new tactical organizations called task forces. Each of our carriers was given an escort of whatever cruisers and destroyers were available at the moment and placed under the command of an admiral who might or might not be embarked in the carrier itself. These task forces were made up of task groups, which were made up of task units to form an extremely flexible organization for carrying out largely independent operations quite apart from the traditional structure of battle lines and scouting forces.

Vice Adm. Wilson Brown, peacetime commander of both the Scouting Force and the Hawaiian Detachment, for instance, was made commander of Task Force 11, with the *Lexington* as his carrier, but he and his Flag remained in the *Indianapolis*. The *Lexington* and her other supporting vessels were on a different mission far to the north of us the morning the war came at last to change our lives forever.

It had been a splendid two-day run from Pearl for us, much like the old excursions we had once made in the more relaxed times before the battleships came to Pearl to stay. The trade wind weather, as usual, was perfect, and there had been little need for signaling on the passage. Once clear of the harbor we had simply put the old destroyers in a column formation behind us and steamed to Johnston Island. Except for daily noon position and fuel reports, we signalmen hardly

144

raised a flag or touched a light. And the island itself, once we got there, seemed much as we had seen it from time to time before, except for an amount of work that had been done in our absence to make the island into an airfield. There were some new buildings, and the facilities seemed ready to receive ships, although we did not enter the lagoon that day.

After breakfast I had gone to the bridge to relieve the four-to-eight watch. Only a few minutes after I arrived an officer with a radio message form in his hand ran onto the bridge. In those days no one ran on a ship's bridge in the U.S. Navy. Admiral Brown and his staff were all there, observing the landing operations already under way. The admiral glowered his disapproval of the radio officer's unseemly haste. Admiral Brown was good at glowering disapproval.

His disapproval turned quickly to something else, though, as he read the message thrust into his hand. I no longer remember his words, but in minutes the entire ship knew we were at war. The alarm gong bonged for what seemed a long time, and the bugler sounded general quarters. The crew ran to their battle stations and looked at each other, puzzled. There was nothing to shoot at.

The morning continued on as physically beautiful as before. The sun still shone, and the trade wind clouds, in their endless fleets and squadrons, sailed on in their gentle passage above our masts. Our little destroyer transports continued to put their landing craft over the side, and the island itself lay calm and unchanged before us as though nothing at all had happened.

But, suddenly, everything was changed. The day had become dark and menacing. The time for getting ready was past. Everything we had done, everything we had learned, however adequate or inadequate, would now have to be enough.

The first thing that crossed my mind as I stood that morning on the signal bridge trying to make sense of what was happening was the fact of where we were. In Mister Bell's lectures to us before the war, he always had assumed that any Japanese attack on us would come from their bases in the Marshal and Gilbert islands, and we were lying, that morning, approximately halfway between those bases and Pearl Harbor.

Since Pearl had been attacked, the attacking force, according to conventional wisdom, must have passed very close to us in its approach. And, even more troubling, it would pass not far from us in its withdrawal. And we were virtually alone. The old destroyers would not be of much use in a fight—their fire rooms had been cut back to make room for troops. They would not be able to make the speed necessary to keep up with us in any serious steaming. For all practical purposes, we were alone in the sea.

Our first job, of course, was to get back with the *Lexington* and the rest of Task Force 11. After all, Admiral Brown was the task force commander. It would be nice if he were with his task force. We immediately, as I have said, went to general quarters—ready for immediate action. The transports were ordered to put all their Marines ashore and to follow after us as best they could. Before our signal searchlights had completed the messaged orders, we were off. We built up to thirty knots and headed away on a northerly course, our starboard hangar still stacked high with crated oranges meant for the Marines on Johnston Island. We ate a lot of oranges in the *Indianapolis* in those first few days of the war.

I don't remember it now, but we must certainly have launched our planes, for the bland tropical sea horizon suddenly had become threatening. We needed to know what was over it. With our planes up, we might have at least some warning of what was there. Since we had no destroyer escort, we also required an overhead antisubmarine watch.

At the speed we were then making a destroyer escort would have been of dubious value regardless. The noise ships make at high speeds makes sonar largely ineffective. And the relatively low speed of submerged submarines meant an attacker would have to be extremely lucky to get off a shot on a fast ship. England's great passenger liners made that point when they sailed as troop transports without escort throughout the war. Ironically, and tragically, the *Indianapolis* herself would prove the possibility of trouble when, near the end of the war, she was sunk by submarine attack while steaming alone. She both began and ended her war steaming all alone in the sea.

All this time communications out of Pearl offered nothing but confusion. We knew only that there had been a Japanese air attack. We did not know by how many or what types of planes. We didn't know what damage had been done or where the attacking force had come from—or, more important in our circumstances, where it was. We knew only that we needed to rejoin our task force. We piled on to the north, running for the comfort of friendly company in an ocean grown suddenly cold and menacing.

The confusion was heightened even more late that afternoon when we were ordered back to Johnston Island. A Japanese submarine was reported to be shelling the place. I don't know what a heavy cruiser could have done about submarines. We carried neither sound gear nor depth charges. Maybe, if the submarine commander were considerate enough to stay on the surface, we could shoot him with our 8-inch guns.

Altering course while our aircraft were away posed a special problem. All ships with planes airborne used a procedure called point option. This was an arbitrary point that moved at a given speed on a given course. Returning planes would navigate to intersect that point, and their mother ships were under obligation to be somewhere within visual range of it. Naturally, radio could not be used to advise pilots of changes in point option. If it must be altered, either as to course or speed, the planes and their crews ran the risk of returning to an empty sea.

I don't remember now how we solved the problem that day. Probably, since the orders to reverse course came late in the day, our search planes already had returned. But the matter remained a problem throughout the war, especially for the carriers. Sometimes a plane would be sent to orbit point option and to advise returning aircraft of any changes.

Nevertheless, orders are orders. Around we came, and back we went. Right into one of the scariest situations I met in the entire war. And that on the very first night.

Two or three hours after the brief tropical twilight, when the night was as black as it would ever be, strange ships were reported fine on the port bow and closing fast. My first reaction was, "Oh, Christ! Here we go." The war had hardly begun, and there we were, all by ourselves and up against what might be the entire Japanese navy.

We were already at general quarters, with all guns manned and ready. I could hear the low whirring sound of the forward 8-inch mounts training round to the reported bearing. I knew the port 5-inchers would be training out as well. By all indications, it would not be long before there was an awful lot of noise.

So far as we knew, there was not another American ship closer than two hundred miles. I wasn't happy at all when the admiral ordered us to challenge the approaching strangers. In a night surface action, the ship that gets in the first licks is usually the ship that continues to float. And the ship that goes around in the night challenging other ships is not likely to get in the first licks. A ship that gets a strange challenge is likely to open fire. And the signal light making the challenge is likely to be its point of aim.

I was signalman second class then and my battle station was the port side of the bridge. Chief Signalman Maxwell handed me a blinker tube and told me to make the challenge. A blinker tube is a metal pipe, four or five inches in diameter and about thirty inches long. It is mounted on a wooden stock like that of a rifle or a shotgun. At the after end of the tube, there is a very small flashlight bulb activated by a trigger. The bulb is so dim that the operator cannot tell by sight alone if it is working or not. An audible buzzer is fitted to let the operator know when the light is on.

Light challenges in those days were made in the form of an eight-letter word. The word that night was "masthead." The challenging vessel would send the first two letters, "ma," and the challenged vessel would reply with the next two, "st." Then the sequence would be repeated in reverse, with the challenged vessel sending "he" and the challenging vessel replying with "ad." If this happened, you knew you were among friends. If it didn't happen, you probably would not know a whole lot of anything at all for much longer.

I don't think I was ever more scared, then or since, than I was when I squeezed out that first "ma." The chief and I could feel everyone else on the port side of the bridge shifting over to the starboard side. There they would have at least the protection of the Flag plot bulkheads against the avalanche of fire I think we all expected to explode out of the night against us at any minute.

We felt little relief when the strange ships did not answer our challenge. Blinker tubes are not easy to see, even on dark nights. And we were closing rapidly with the strange targets. I heard the gunnery officer request permission to open fire.

The *Indianapolis*' captain leaned over the nav bridge rail and called down an order for us to give it another try. And, that time, a dim yellow light did blink back a hesitant "st" to us.

The strange ships were the little destroyer transports we had left that morning off Johnston Island. True to the ancient military dictum that there is always some dumb son of a bitch who doesn't get the word, they had not gotten the order to countermarch and had continued on to the north—to meet us almost head-on in the dark, to *my* consternation at least.

Shortly after the hubbub died down, our orders were again countermanded, and we headed again to the north at best speed. I don't know where the little transports went. We never saw them again.

This became the pattern of events for the next several days and weeks. We were supposed to be looking for the Pearl Harbor striking force. Thank God we didn't find it. If we had, it is unlikely you would be reading this particular account right now.

Even after we joined with the *Lexington* and her escorting ships, the confusion continued. One of our heavy cruisers was bombed by an American PBY flying boat that reported her as Japanese because she had rising suns painted in red on her bows. What she had was the gray-black paint knocked off her bows by high-speed steaming, exposing the red lead undercoating. Happily, the bombs missed.

At another time, we launched the *Lexington*'s entire air group against what was reported as a Japanese aircraft carrier that, oddly, had no escorting vessels or combat air patrol. Hell, it didn't even have a bow wave or leave a wake. None of this is puzzling when one realizes that the Japanese carrier was a barge, cut adrift by its towing tug so as not to hamper the tug's speed of escape.

Our attack planes, when they arrived on the scene, recognized the barge for what it was, of course. But there they were, sitting with their bombs and torpedoes still on board and facing flight deck landings with all that extra weight. In the interests of safety, the bombs were jettisoned immediately. But, we were told, the *Lexington* had only two torpedoes for each airplane, and since the war was so new, there was a good chance we might need them later. The torpedo planes, therefore, were ordered to land with torpedoes on board—not a recommended procedure.

American aerial torpedoes at that time weighed about two thousand pounds. Carrier airplanes are under marginal control on landing, even without an extra ton of weight on board. We did not even know if the mechanisms holding the torpedoes to the planes would stand the shock of an arrested landing. There was only one way at the time to find out.

Torpedoes in those old TBDs were carried nose down and half exposed, much like a male dog's penis. From our signal bridge in the *Indianapolis*, we could see the burdened airplanes swimming in anxious circles while the fighters and bombers came in to land. The TBDs were burning as much fuel as possible so that their weight would be lessened by at least that much. But, eventually, they too had to land.

There were eighteen airplanes in carrier squadrons in those days. Miraculously, all but two of the torpedo planes landed without big trouble. One lost its torpedo as it was jerked to a hard stop by arresting wires. The airplane stopped, but its torpedo skittered down the flight deck on its own, props spinning. Once those propellers turn a preset number of times, the warhead is armed and will explode with any relatively mild impact. Somehow, the flight deck crewmen managed to stop the torpedo without serious damage to anything but nerves.

The other loss was a TBD that stalled over the after end of the flight deck. It pancaked in so that the torpedo itself struck the curved after end of the deck, leaving a neat twenty-one-inch dent in the metal. The impact was great enough to snap the airplane into two pieces. The forward part, including the pilot and radioman, rolled up onto the flight deck and was saved. The after part, with the gunner, fell back into the ship's wake and was lost.

We were told this story when we shifted to the *Lexington* a few weeks later. It had become part of the ship's lore, which grows up in all vessels as they live out their lives.

For the first few days of the war, these events were typical. We were chased all over the ocean by often contradictory orders from Pearl on one wild goose chase after another. Not even Admiral Brown yet knew the truth about the damage inflicted at Pearl. A destroyer that had been there during the attack joined us one morning some three or four days afterward and signaled to us the dismaying count of lost and damaged ships.

In a completely unnecessary exercise in something or the other, the admiral ordered all signalmen to the other side of the bridge while we were taking the message. Because I had been taking the message and Chief Maxwell had been writing it down, we were sworn to secrecy. What the smart admiral apparently did not realize was that there were off-watch signalmen all over the ship who could read the destroyer's light as well as I could. There were even more radiomen and quartermasters in the ship who could do the same. Some of the old battleships even had Marines standing signal watches sometimes.

Hell, the word was in the compartments before I had rogered for the signal. And why not? We were all in the same Navy, for Christ's sake. We took it as one more indication of how some officers regarded the men they were, supposedly, leading. We were not to be trusted, you see. Even had some of us been spies, who the hell could we have told out there? We would learn the truth anyway when we returned to Pearl, as we had to sooner or later for fuel and provisions. The whole population of the island of Oahu, military and civilian alike, already knew the truth.

There was still no word on where the Japanese were. We were supposed to be hunting them, but after the war we learned they already were back in Japan by that time. I think now the Navy brass was just keeping us out of Pearl, where we would have been vulnerable to the same kind of attack that had done in the battleships. But we could not stay out forever.

After about a week we came in for fuel. We ran up fast one late evening behind a screen of destroyers and under an umbrella of airplanes. The quick Hawaiian twilight turned soon to night, but not before we saw what had happened in Pearl Harbor. The destruction could not be hidden any longer.

In the shallows to the right of the channel an *Enterprise* SBD dive-bomber lay half awash, a large hole in its fuselage from the American shell that had brought it down. Our own guns, that first nervous night of war, had shot down a number of *Enterprise* planes as they tried to come home to Ford Island. From the bridge we could see the ruined hangars of the Army's Hickam Field, scraps of sheet metal skin still hanging from their blackened skeletons. Beyond Hospital Point we could see the *Nevada* with her nose in a grove of algaroba trees. She had been the only battleship to get under way and had come under such concentrated attack that she was beached to prevent her sinking and blocking the channel.

After that, it was one dismaying spectacle after another. The long double row of battleships, with the wreck of the *Arizona* at the far end and the *Oklahoma*'s upturned bottom pinning in one of the cage mast battleships. The wreckage of the destroyer *Shaw* still lay in the floating dry dock where she had been caught. Some sailor's laundry flapped from its nearly intact stern section, one of the few signs left of continuing life in the darkening harbor. A light cruiser and the old mine-layer *Oglala* lay in our old berth at Ten-Ten Dock, with the *Pennsylvania* and two burned destroyers in the big stone dry dock ahead of them.

The most distressing thing of all to me was the harbor water itself. It lay black and dead under what must have been six to eight inches of fuel oil from sunken and damaged ships. Sailors come to think of water as something alive and moving, but the water of Pearl Harbor was neither alive nor moving that night. Even the wakes and bow waves of small craft moving about without lights stirred the water only briefly, lifting it in sullen little folds that fell back at once into the overall black melancholy. Here and there wreckage and flotsam, on one kind or another protruded from the oil like winter objects frozen in some obscene black ice.

And the sounds. If any one thing could be said to be characteristic of Pearl Harbor in previous months, it was the never-ending clang and bang of machinery, the hoot and shrill of whistles and horns, and the busy calling back and forth of men. But, that night, there was no sound at all.

We moved quickly to a dock and commenced fueling at once, intent on completing and being clear of the harbor before daylight. Stores were hurried aboard. New men came aboard from the sunken and disabled ships all around us. Few of them had hammocks and seabags at all. None of us got much sleep that night.

Honk and I were given the bridge watch while the more junior men were off on various working parties. But there was little to do in the strict blackout then in effect. The only lights anywhere were the blue-slitted headlights of official cars and trucks and, here and there, the muffled blue glow of a welder doing some emergency job behind canvas screens. The plantation towns beyond Aiea and Pearl City were black as well, and for all that could be seen of Honolulu, it might not have been there at all. The scattering of jewel-like lights that once had reached up along the spines of the island hills was gone. Every now and then, a nervous sentry let go with a rifle shot that snapped the silence like a slap.

I don't remember that Honk and I said anything profound. It was all too much for us, I suspect. Until we returned to Pearl, I don't think any of us realized how bad the attack had been. Mostly, I think, we were chagrined that the "little yellow bastards" had dared attack the mighty U.S. Navy. We were moved then to a more or less good-humored determination to give the Japanese a lesson in proper manners. But, once we actually saw what had happened, a cold and bitter anger took hold in us.

From our Magazine Island berth we could see the dim and shadowy shapes of our wrecked battleships lying in formation much as we had seen them so many times steaming in column at sea, with the *Arizona* at the end of the line, her foremast bowed over her forecastle as though in mourning for the hundreds of her dead sailors still awash in her flooded compartments. Those men had been our figurative shipmates, and we stirred to a primitive urge to see them avenged.

A more ill-defined anger was directed at those who had let it happen. Death seemed much more to be resented if it came by surprise, with its victims given no chance to defend themselves, and as a result of slackness on the part of those with a power to prevent it.

Nevertheless, the battle was joined. Those of us in the regular Navy stood to our stations as best we could. We had taken the king's shilling. As we had been told when we complained of anything before the war: we wasn't drafted. We retreated, I suspect, into the enlisted man's one sure sanctuary of taking responsibility for his own watch quarters and station bill duties and leaving cosmic concerns to those more qualified—and better paid—than we.

I went down to the galley and got us some sandwiches, and we took turns napping on the flag bridge bench for the rest of the night, getting what rest we could against a predawn sortie. Sleep came hard, but it eventually came—until the setting of the Special Sea Detail for getting under way woke us all.

In another display of great thoughtfulness we had been kept—when not actually at general quarters—in readiness condition II ever since the war began. That meant we were on watch four hours and off four. Four on and four off may not sound like much for healthy young men, but we seldom got our four hours off. Sub scares, meals, some kind of bathing and laundering—all cut into our off hours. We were dead tired. I came to a real appreciation for the men in the old sailing ships who stood such watches as a matter of course for months on end. They must have been better men than we.

At any rate, once back to sea, we maintained a schedule of what seemed endless—and pointless—patrolling. We entered Pearl only for fuel and provisions. Our planes made regular mail runs if we were anywhere near Hawaii, so we did have some contact with the world. But it was a frustrating time. We wanted to do something.

Finally, after what seemed a very long time, we were ordered to attack Japanese bases in the Marshall Islands. We had the *Lexington* and some heavy cruisers and destroyers. Morale zoomed—only to fall lower than ever when, the afternoon before our run-in for the next morning's attack, Admiral Brown ordered a practice firing of 5-inch antiaircraft guns. It was to be burst firing.

In burst firing, one ship would fire a 5-inch shell timed to burst in the air. All the other ships would then fire at the smoke of that bursting. It was a meaningless practice since the smoke was a stationary target, but it did give green crews a familiarity with the shock and violence of gunfire, I guess. Except that, this time, it did not even do that. The target shell—the one whose burst everyone else was to shoot at—did not burst. Neither did the next two or three we tried.

From that, we concluded that something was wrong with our ammunition. We had recently replenished from the Naval Ammunition Depot at Lualualei on Oahu. Rumors of sabotage immediately flew. I don't know if they were true or not, but our planned raid was called off, and we returned to Pearl more morose than ever.

During this time, on one of our flying visits to Pearl, we were granted a few hours of daylight-only liberty to wind up our affairs in Honolulu. Except for our meager civilian wardrobes of flimsy slacks and aloha shirts, Honk and I didn't have any affairs to wind up, but we did go ashore, and not for our civilian clothes. So far as I know, mine are still in Battleship Max Cohen's locker club off Hotel Street. As evidence we were indeed at war, we had to carry gas masks on liberty in Honolulu.

I think Honk had it in mind to do a little boozing and, in his words, dip his wick. But both ambitions were thwarted by strictures the military governor had placed on Honolulu. Various of the well connected, civilian and military alike, had cornered all the booze, and the cat houses were closed.

For the first time—and about the only time—I was able to do something for Honk in exchange for all he had done for me: I took him to Trader Vic's. He had never been there in all his time in the islands. It was far enough off the beaten track to be free of the hordes of soldiers and sailors then swamping downtown Honolulu. There were no other customers in the place at all the day I took Honk there. It may even have been closed, I think now, but since I was known there for my modest, though faithful, patronage, the maitre d' let us in and found for us some splits, or miniature bottles, of champagne. It was all he had to offer, he said.

We sat there for the rest of the time we had, drinking the little bottles of champagne in the hot tropical afternoon. It was so pleasant that I regretted the toads were not out. But our first liberty after the start of the war would end before dark. The toads would have to wait. As it happened, I never saw them again.

When it was time to go, the house provided us each with a fog cutter, powerful rum-and-fruit juice drinks in tall glasses about the size of a 37-millimeter shell. Things really did get pleasant then. Things got so pleasant I puked in the cab taking us back to the ship.

I thought that afternoon about calling Ilse, but I didn't. I had even less to offer her than before. Nothing would be served by calling her. Honk and I made our difficult way back to the ship. I would not be ashore again in Honolulu until 1945.

Back at sea, conditions became no more satisfying. We were ordered once to raid Wake Island, which, by that time, had fallen. But our tanker, the *Neches*, was torpedoed. Since refueling at sea would have been necessary, we had no choice but to turn back. Another debilitating dud.

None of this should be taken as meaning we were bloodthirsty. Certainly, I wasn't. It was just that we wanted to get the damned thing over with. I don't think any of us expected the war to last as long as it did. Even after seeing what the Japanese had done to us at Pearl Harbor, we were not overly impressed with them. We rationalized their success there as a lucky sucker punch. They had hit our guys while they were not looking. It would be different when we met them on even terms.

One thing that came out of all this early floundering around was that the Flag shifted to the *Lexington*. We had found that most of our signals were to and from the carrier. It would simplify things, especially at night, if the admiral could just yell down to Capt. Frederick C. Sherman and tell him what he wanted. (The *Lexington*'s Flag bridge was above her navigation bridge, the reverse of the setup in the *Indianapolis*.)

My time in cruisers was ended. Except for a brief stay in the *Portland* after the *Lexington* was sunk in the Battle of the Coral Sea and a full-power run to San Diego and return to Pearl in the *Chester*, I never sailed in one again.

Sensible or not, the move to the *Lexington* meant another adjustment on our part. Life in carriers, we quickly discovered, was much different from that in a cruiser. Aside from the fact all those noisy airplanes were around, living conditions were radically different. There was no room for Flag signalmen for one thing. I ended up living in the ship's library under the flight deck aft. I slept on a long leather-upholstered sofa, with an eight-volume set of Prescott's *History of Mexico* within arm's reach. Although long enamored of books, this was the only time I ever lived so completely surrounded by them.

The heavy thumps of airplanes landing on the deck above our heads and the scratching rattle of arresting wires returning to battery took some getting used to, but the library actually became a comfortable arrangement, even though I did not have a locker and had to live out of my seabag. And the geedunk stand was just across a passageway from us.

The proximity of the geedunk stand became important, we realized, when we used the *Lexington* mess halls. They were less satisfactory even than the cafeteria-style feeding arrangements in cruisers. A carrier's crew is much larger than a cruiser's, in the first place, and more of its men do hard and dirty work with, sometimes, no time to wash up before meals. The *Lexington*'s mess hall was noisier, more crowded, and dirtier than anything we had known before. Some of us virtually lived on geedunks.

And the washrooms themselves were a jolt. Carrier sailors apparently had never heard of water hours. We could take showers any time we liked. The washroom decks were often ankle deep in soapy oil-and-dirt-streaked water that rushed from side to side with the rolling of the ship and sometimes slopped over into the passageways outside.

The signal bridge of a carrier, too, lacked the amenities we had become used to in the *Indianapolis*. Forget overheads and glass windows and wind-diverting dodgers. The *Lexington*'s signal bridge was simply the top of her wheelhouse. There was nothing between us and heaven but the ship's mast with a kind of platform at its top. (Honk and I would later have a close relationship with that platform.) There were welded pipe railings around the edges to keep us from falling off but absolutely no protection against wind and sun. Some of us were so sunburned we had to go to sickbay. We used gobs of white zinc oxide and made little cardboard shields for our noses, but nothing worked perfectly. We just had to get used to it. As does everything else, it all became normal after a while.

Only a week or so following our aborted sortie against Wake, we were ordered west for what turned out to be our first meeting with the Japanese navy. Out around Barbers Point we steamed on a long, arcing great circle course that found us, sometime in February 1942, only three hundred miles or so east of the recently captured Japanese port of Rabaul.

In what had become standard operating procedure, we arrived at the point at a prudent, fuel-conscious speed; the final high-speed run-in would be made during the night hours for a dawn attack. It was the way the Japanese had made their attack on Pearl Harbor and was intended to minimize the chance of premature detection.

Unfortunately, the Japanese at Rabaul proved to be more watchful than our people had been at Pearl Harbor. In the afternoon of the day before our planned attack, we were snooped by three different four-engine flying boats. Our fighters shot down two of them, but the third escaped. The Japanese knew we were coming. Worse, they knew where we were.

Sometime around four o'clock that afternoon, they came after us. Eighteen high-level bombers came in two flights of nine planes each, all in perfect formation and very high. After two full months of war, it was my first sight of the enemy.

Happily, the *Lexington*'s primitive radar had given us a few minutes' warning, and our combat air patrol of two F4F-3 Wildcats was vectored out to meet the enemy bombers. Equally happily, a man named Butch O'Hare was flying one of them. His wingman's guns jammed, but O'Hare himself shot down five of the attacking planes. His F4F-3 Wildcat mounted only four .50-caliber machine guns—

later models mounted six. O'Hare's efficiency per gun was remarkable—so remarkable that he was awarded the Congressional Medal of Honor. Now one of the country's biggest airports—in Chicago—is named for him.

Most of the fight took place in full view of the carrier. We had been landing aircraft at the time of first warning. In the days before canted flight decks, that meant we had a lot of airplanes parked on the bow, which, in turn, meant we could not launch any more fighters until the bow was cleared.

The approaching Japanese bombers were a powerful incentive for the fastest respotting I ever saw. All hands not on watch were ordered to the flight deck to push airplanes. We didn't have tractors then. The flight deck became a stepped-on anthill of activity as yeomen, storekeepers, electricians, and cooks with white aprons tucked up about their waists rushed to push the parked airplanes aft.

All this time, the first flight of bombers was coming, seeming to crawl slowly across the sky, with the smaller dot of O'Hare's Wildcat climbing and diving through their formation. The first casualties already were falling toward the sea, followed by long twisting trails of black smoke.

Bombs, when they are dropped from an airplane, do not fall straight down from the point of release. They move forward, instead, at the speed of the bomber for a time and fall in a long predictable arc. A ship's captain, if he can estimate the airplane's speed and altitude, can calculate the point at which the airplane must drop his bombs to score a hit. If the captain then puts his ship into a hard turn to either side, he stands a good chance of escaping high-altitude bombing.

That is what the *Lexington*'s Captain Sherman did. And, unwieldy as the huge old ship was, her ponderous turn was enough to get her out of the bombs' path before they hit the water.

That was the first time I had heard bombs explode so close at hand. I had expected a sharp clap of sound, like thunder, but instead, I heard an odd ripping kind of a crash. Tall gouts of white water sprang like fountains from the sea precisely where we would have been had the ship not turned. We had not been touched. The bomb spouts lingered in the air for what seemed a long time, light and misty in the sun like slowly dying spirits.

Other fighters had by that time joined O'Hare, and the second flight of bombers were no more successful against us than the first had been. It was reckoned we got sixteen of the attacking eighteen, with the remaining two as doubtful survivors.

The scene on board was like that of a rooting section at a college football game. Our initial nervousness at the sight of the approaching enemy airplanes evaporated into shouting, yelling, and back-thumping elation as we stood and watched the Japanese airplanes fall, burning, into the sea. Hell, war wasn't all that bad!

This euphoria did suffer a momentary lapse, however, when one of the falling bombers, far out on our starboard quarter, suddenly pulled out of its spin and lined up for a run straight at us. Every gun that would bear, both in the *Lexington* and in her supporting vessels, opened fire, but on the airplane came. Finally, even the .50-caliber machine-gun battery on our big flat slab of a stack opened up. Bits of wreckage could be seen flying off the bomber, but still on it came. It crashed so close alongside that water was said to have been thrown onto the flight deck.

This all brought an abrupt end to the cheering. We had just seen a number of Japanese aviators die in a display of barbaric fanaticism—or incredible bravery, depending on one's point of view. We had seen how close death can come—and how fast. Although we did not realize it at the time, we had also seen a chilling preview of the deadly kamikazes to come later in the war.

(I never saw the second bomber, which tried to crash into our port side at the same time!)

At any rate, we held our westward course until after dark to mislead any possible snoopers, then we reversed course and got the hell out of there. For several hours that night we heard strange gonging sounds over our radios. The sound was like that of temple bells in a B adventure movie. We never knew what they were but assumed them to be some kind of homing device the Japanese were using to help their fallen planes find their way home.

Back in Pearl, after the long haul home, we were greeted with inappropriate applause. We hoisted a broom to the masthead, the traditional symbol of a clean sweep, but we had actually failed again in our efforts to hit a Japanese base. We had destroyed some Japanese airplanes, but it was generally conceded we were lucky to get away with what had been an unwise use of a single carrier in such a deep penetration of enemy-held waters. Any one of the bombs that fell so close around us, had it hit the flight deck, could have wiped out our air cover and, thus, have left us exposed to anything the Japanese wanted to throw at us. We would never again attack with a single carrier.

Also, while in Pearl that time, the eight big 8-inch guns the *Lexington* mounted were removed and replaced with dual-purpose 5-inch 38s that could be used against airplanes. The 8-inchers could be fired only to starboard in the first place. Their muzzle blasts would damage the flight deck if they were fired to port. More important, they were useless against airplanes.

After this work was done and after fueling and provisioning, we sortied on an even more distant venture. The Japanese had just landed at Lae and Salamaua on the north shore of the big South Pacific island of New Guinea. It was decided that we would attack them from the Gulf of Papua on the south coast of the big island, flying our planes over the island's lofty Owen Stanley Mountains to do so.

It was a more distant raid than even the Rabaul effort had been, but at least we had two carriers. The *Yorktown* went with us. If either carrier were disabled; the other could provide what already was considered essential in naval warfare—air cover. The second carrier, if undamaged, might even recover some of the damaged carrier's airplanes that, otherwise, would be lost.

As it happened, we carried out the raid with little loss at all, either to ourselves or to the Japanese. We in the ships saw nothing at all of the enemy and had what amounted to a pleasant day's excursion in a beautiful big bay of blue water and high green flanking mountains. During that part of the war we deliberately kept out of sight from land whenever possible. The sight of green growth beyond leaping white surf was refreshing after long unbroken weeks at sea.

The only excitement came when the heavy cruiser *Pensacola* rammed a whale. We maneuvered all that day at high speed against the possibility of enemy submarines, and the *Pensacola* cut a hapless whale virtually in half. We first took the flash of white water under her bows for a torpedo or a mine explosion, but a growing pink stain, lashed into foam by feeding sharks, told what really had happened.

A second incident came at daybreak of the second day of our withdrawal. As usual, all the ships were at dawn general quarters. A screening destroyer reported a strange vessel on the horizon ahead on the port bow. The carriers immediately turned away. Carriers of all nations are sensitive to the presence of enemy surface ships. Our cruisers deployed for surface action.

But it was all for nothing. The reported vessel was one of our own cruiser float planes that had become lost on the run-in, and its pilot had simply landed in the sea to await developments, in an interesting display of the problems sometimes arising with point option. As it happened this time, our retiring course led us straight to him. He started his engine, taxied alongside his home cruiser and was hoisted on board no worse for wear in time for breakfast.

In the end, we got no credit at all for this long raid. Although we had spent most of a day in plain view of New Guinea, so far as we knew, the Japanese had not spotted us. To keep them from knowing American carriers were in the area, it was reported the attack came from Army planes. This subterfuge involved the unlikely assumption that the Japanese would not know Army airplanes from carrier types.

After getting clear, in any event, we proceeded to the rendezvous where we were to be relieved by our sister ship, the *Saratoga*. Unfortunately, the poor *Saratoga* took a submarine torpedo en route and had had to retire for repairs. This meant we would have to stay on station several weeks longer than had been planned. And, since we continued to eat, we ran out of provisions. Tankers could, and did, come to refuel us, but we did not then have the Navy's later ability to re-provision ships at sea.

After only a few extra weeks, we began to run into shortages. One of the most pressing was that of starter cartridges for the fighters. F4Fs then were started with cartridges that looked like ordinary 12-gauge shotgun shells. When inserted and fired, they kicked the engines over. When we ran out of starter cartridges, we could not start fighter engines. And, if we could not start fighter engines, we could be in big, big trouble in an area where enemy aircraft might appear at any minute.

The problem was solved by flight deck boatswain's mates who rigged a system of shock cord and four-part tackles. With one end of the tackle engaged in the notched bronze tie-down slots in the deck and the other end attached to a leather cup fitted over the end of a propeller blade, tension could be set up that, when released, would turn over the engine. Although necessarily slower than cartridges, the jury-rig did work and we could operate our fighters.

Ironically, one of the men who devised the system was killed by it. The flight deck tie-down strips were made of soft metal. During one starting operation, the lower block pulled out and struck the man standing ready to trip the apparatus. Even on the bridge, it was said, the slap of the heavy block against the man's head could be heard.

We also ran out of food. Since it was deemed essential for our carriers to remain in the Coral Sea at the time, we simply had to tighten our belts and grin as much as we could. The destroyers, owing to their limited storage space, suffered first and most. We used to call them alongside and give them anything we could spare. But, eventually, even the *Lexington*'s cavernous storerooms were empty.

Navy ships in formation at sea make regular position and fuel-on-hand reports to the Flag every day at noon. Remaining fuel on board is a constant obsession of naval commanders. During the period in question we also took average weight-loss-per-man reports. It was the only time in the Navy that I remember being really hungry.

Once relieved, we returned to Pearl toward the end of March with a good deal more speed than usual. And, once there, our storerooms were crammed with mountains of provisions—most of which would soon lie at the bottom of the Coral Sea, uneaten unless by fish.

11
Lexington in the Coral Sea

THE WAR WAS FEWER THAN FIVE MONTHS old when we, with our supporting ships, took departure off Oahu's Barbers Point and set out on our third deep penetration of the South Pacific. We already had settled into a routine that made bearable the world of tension and threat into which we had been plunged by Japan's attack on Pearl Harbor. It may well be true that primeval man's natural state was one of eternal wariness and constant readiness to defend himself, but for modern man we found the practice exhausting.

The routine of watch-and-watch keeping we had followed in the first days of the war had long since been abandoned. Except for routine general quarters at both morning and evening twilight, we maintained what was known as condition of readiness III. This meant only a portion of our guns were kept ready for immediate action and the ships' watertight integrity—watertight doors and hatches—was eased enough to permit performance of their operation and maintenance.

Twilight held the greatest unexpected danger because its characteristic dim light reduced visibility. Morning twilight was considered the time of greatest risk because the preceding hours of darkness were without benefit of aerial patrols. It was always possible that we might have been closing on an enemy all night without knowing it at all until the return of daylight showed him already within range. For this reason we manned our battle stations, ready for immediate action, from one hour before sunrise until full daylight. And from sunset until one hour later. At other times, unless under actual attack or imminent threat, we steamed much as we had done before the war.

Ironically, the wayward cruiser float plane we had spotted while at dawn general quarters during our retirement from New Guinea, was the only such sighting I remember during either morning or evening general quarters during the entire war. But we continued the practice.

Oddly, the hours of twilight general quarters, both morning and evening, became somewhat social occasions when the men, who might not see each other at other times during the day, came together at their battle stations, but with nothing actually to do. A good deal of catching up was done, and words were passed in the waiting. People not on exposed weather decks could smoke and drink coffee. These times of what might be presumed to be greatest readiness were in fact filled with relaxation and shooting the bull. Early on they became routine and brought a semblance of normality to what was in truth a highly unnatural way for men to live.

Honk and I sailed this time under still another admiral. Shortly after our return from the New Guinea raids Admiral Brown was relieved by Rear Adm. Aubrey Fitch. This meant we lost a star in the blue flag flying at the masthead, but that was of little importance since we seldom flew personal flags during the war anyway. There was none of the ceremonial peacetime change of command at all. Fitch came aboard, and Brown went ashore. For Honk and me, the world continued on much as it had before. (Later we learned Admiral Brown was named naval aide to President Roosevelt, a job he held until Roosevelt's death.)

Admiral Fitch was an unusually short man for a naval officer. He had a brisk, no-nonsense manner and an impressive nose. He was what was then a comparative rarity in naval flag ranks: a brown-shoe aviation admiral. (Aviation officers wore brown shoes; surface officers wore black shoes.) He fitted into the *Lexington* in a way Brown never had.

Brown had not been a warm man on the bridge in the first place. He must then have been near to sixty years old and looked older. He had an unusually pale face and a skin condition that made him look even paler. I remember he sat through the whole bombing off Rabaul in a white wicker armchair planted in the middle of the signal bridge, seemingly uninterested in what was going on. But I remember him most clearly for something that happened while we were still in the *Indianapolis*.

In making his way out of the black-painted canvas light lock rigged in the door of Flag plot one night, he stumbled over the coaming and would have fallen had I not caught him.

I didn't expect any medals for what was no more than an instinctive gesture of help from one man to another. But I didn't expect the chewing out I got either, for daring to put my enlisted hand on his three-starred arm. Fortunately, I was too surprised to speak the thoughts that sprang to mind a bit later. But my admiration for naval officers was eroded some more, and I mourned the chance I had lost to let him fall on his three-starred ass. I realize now the man had a weight of responsibility I could not even imagine, but I didn't realize it at the time. Even now I don't see how reaming me out could have made his responsibilities any less burdensome.

At any rate, there was none of the fuss and feathers we had staged for change of command ceremonies before the war. There was just a different set of buttocks in the admiral's chair on the port side of the bridge. I remember no changes in the staff at all. Honk and I went on as we had before.

Our time in Pearl was much what had come to be routine when we were home from sea. Yard workmen swarmed over the ship adding new guns and electronic equipment and installing new bunks and lockers for the men who would man the new guns. The ship was becoming more and more crowded, but we did not complain about the new radar equipment that was put on board. So far as I was concerned they could put all the radar they wanted on the ship.

We had come to have a great affection for radar. Everyone topside kept a wary eye on the big bedspring antenna rotating at the top of the foremast. Anytime it stopped turning and backed up to stare at some particular bearing on the horizon, we got edgy. We knew radar could see things we couldn't see. As I have mentioned before, it is scary even now to think about what the carrier war would have been like without radar.

As usual fueling and provisioning were seen to first when we arrived in Pearl, all against the possibility of an emergency sortie. Given our hunger on our last cruise, we gave special attention to groceries this time. The deck force worked round the clock getting stores aboard. I don't remember going ashore at all, and in a week or two, we sailed again on the then-familiar long haul to the southwest.

We kept well to the south of the Japanese bases in the Marshall and Gilbert islands and saw no land. Since the waters in that part of the world are much alike, the illusion was that we had not moved at all. One day's horizon was much like the last—and the next. When, one April day, we rendezvoused with the carrier *Yorktown* in the Coral Sea, there was nothing obvious to say we were not still in Hawaiian waters, except that the trades blew out of the southeast rather than the northeast.

For several days we backed and filled in the same general area, fueling frequently to keep bunkers topped off in case of need. Winds are apt to be light down around the line, and carrier planes needed thirty or so knots of wind across the flight decks for them to take off in those days. We had no catapults. In a calm the ship had to make that wind with her engines, using enormous amounts of fuel in the process.

I remember once, on a day when there was no wind, a large silken swell lifted and fell as the residue of some distant storm. We were launching combat air patrol and steaming at probably thirty knots directly into the swell to get the benefit of what little wind there was. The bow was clear, but planes were parked from abreast the island all the way to the stern.

Gradually, the *Lexington*'s nine hundred–plus feet became synchronized with the swells and the ship's bows began to pump up and down ominously. Captain Sherman saw what was happening and hit the flight deck alarm horn. Flight deck crewmen were trained to react to that horn without thinking. Usually, it meant an imminent crash on deck, with the possibility of messy results. Everyone dived as a reflex motion into the safety nets rigged below and outward for the flight deck's entire length on both sides.

This time, in one great convulsive movement, the *Lexington* heaved her bow out of the sea. She seemed then to hesitate for a long moment before bringing it down on the next advancing swell with a force that shuddered the whole ship and caused her masts to jiggle nervously. Water exploded out from under her bow in huge white fans that for a moment blocked our view from the bridge of the horizon ahead.

Incredibly, water was scooped up and over the bow and raced aft at a depth of several feet. The wind barrier consisted of strong wooden slats that were raised to protect parked airplanes in storm conditions. Usually they rested in recessed slots in the flight deck so that airplanes could move freely over them. They were stout wooden staves, seven or eight feet long, designed and built strong enough to stand against the power of storm winds and seas, but the water we shipped that day whipped them erect and on over to flat again on the after side as though they were made of paper.

The water drained off to either side of the flight deck as it raced aft, but not before it had wrecked several airplanes. A good many of the men who had dived into the safety nets suffered injuries from the weight of water poured down on them. One lasting result was that the *Lexington*'s bow was warped upward from the blow for what would be the brief remainder of her life, sometimes giving pilots a cheap thrill as they bumped over the rise at the critical moment of takeoff.

That was one of the freakiest accidents I ever saw in the Navy. There was not a breath of wind that day, and the sky was marked by nothing more than drifting trade wind clouds that continued on their way as though nothing had happened. And the *Lexington* herself, once she had regained her footing, sailed on as before.

Once joined with the *Yorktown* and her supporting cruisers and destroyers, we fell quickly into a routine of morning searches and twenty-four-hour alerts. We were in dangerous waters, and we had seen in Pearl the penalty for unreadiness.

I have said that, after our lucky escape off Rabaul, we never attacked again in the *Lexington* with a single carrier. We didn't. But the *Yorktown* did. One day, while the *Lexington* was once more fueling from the tanker *Neosho*, Adm. Frank Jack Fletcher took the *Yorktown*'s force north for an attack against Japanese forces then landing at Tulagi, one of the Solomon Islands not far from the more famous island of Guadalcanal.

At the same time, a combined force of American and Australian cruisers and destroyers was detached to the west to counter a reported Japanese invasion force headed for Port Moresby in New Guinea. Our enemy was busy. We were left, poking along at fueling speed, highly vulnerable and completely unable to support either the *Yorktown* force or the surface ships then disappearing over the western horizon.

This was all at a time when the Japanese were moving south against Australia, New Caledonia, and the Fijis. We knew that an enemy force of fast carriers was cruising somewhere to the northeast of us and that the invasion force to the west had with it a small carrier and several surface warships. All this plus the forces landing in the Solomons was easily enough to make us nervous. Our first job was to find the fast carriers. Then we had to try as best we could to stop—or at least slow—the Japanese advance.

The *Yorktown* rejoined with exuberant—and exaggerated—reports of damage done off Tulagi. Then, after she and her force had refueled, we detached the *Neosho*, with the destroyer *Sims* as escort, to stand off to the southeast, where she would wait for us in what we thought would be relative safety until needed. We were as ready then as we could make ourselves and headed northwest into the Coral Sea to be in position to move against any of the opposing enemy forces we might find.

As it happened, we were under cloudy skies that day with black rain squalls prowling about to offer pleasing natural cover and make us hard to find. Search planes from the enemy's fast carriers in fact did not find us at all that day, but they did find the poor *Neosho* and *Sims*. These two hapless vessels were massacred by the full air group attack the Japanese sent against them—which obviously had been meant for us, had we been found.

Our own scouts, after some stumbling around of their own, did find the enemy's light carrier *Shoho* and her group off the southeast tip of New Guinea. The little *Shoho* suffered the same fate as the *Neosho* and *Sims*, providing one of the most memorable early quotes of the war: "Scratch one flattop!" One of our returning pilots shouted this into his radio.

We in the *Lexington* had spent much of the day in what had become a familiar, though never comfortable, nervous waiting for our planes to return, knowing that they provided our own best hope for survival. It was already recognized that the best defense against enemy carrier attack was to sink or disable the enemy's carriers before they could launch their own attack against us. But, then, nothing is perfect.

One of the first things that surprised me on boarding the *Lexington* was her flight deck crewmen's habit of playing an old children's game called mumblety-peg while waiting for our planes to return. I had often seen it played by boys in Oklahoma. The game is played with two-bladed pocket knives. One blade is opened only halfway, the second all the way, forming a right angle in which one blade projects straight out and the other straight down. The lower blade was struck lightly into the teak flight deck, then the knife's handle was flipped quickly upward so the knife was sent spinning two or three feet into the air. Scoring depended on how the knife blades stuck in the wood on landing. Some places in the deck were chewed up pretty good, but I never saw any attempt to stop the game. It helped ease the tension of waiting. Still, I could not help wondering how fast those old battleship and cruiser boatswain's mates, who had spent their lives in almost religious service to the sanctity of teak decks, would be spinning in their graves if they knew.

The weather continued thick for us into the evening hours. Radar several times showed enemy aircraft in our vicinity. Once we even launched fighters against them, but contact was uncertain and recovery hard in the conditions then prevailing. Carriers did not routinely operate at night in those days. For obvious reasons, we were reluctant to show lights with enemy airplanes around.

We didn't realize how near they were until some of them got into the *Yorktown*'s landing circle in what must have been one of the most bizarre incidents of the whole war. A respectable fireworks display resulted when our fighters opened fire on the confused Japanese airplanes. All of them then, friends and foes alike, disappeared upward into the clouds.

Even after everything settled down and the night was again unbroken black, there was a good deal of uneasiness on the bridge. We signalmen did not know what was going on beyond what we could see, of course, but Admiral Fitch and his staff officers were debating something. Enlisted men become sensitive to the actions of senior officers in situations like that. We knew that any decisions made would, in all likelihood, affect our own lives.

One thing we gathered from what we overheard was the possibility of a night surface action. Even the greenest of us knew that carriers, in a night surface action with enemy cruisers and possibly battleships was not a healthful exercise. Things were tense on the *Lexington*'s bridge that night.

At one point, our radar showed enemy aircraft orbiting in what appeared to be a carrier's landing circle only a few miles to the east of us. But neither we nor the Japanese attempted to close for a surface action, settling instead for the virtual certainty of a carrier battle the next day. It made for an uneasy night.

We were not overly concerned, though. The war to that point had been relatively easy for us. We had shot down sixteen of the eighteen planes that attacked us off Rabaul. We had bombed and torpedoed Japanese ships off Salamaua and Lae without so much as being spotted by the enemy. And that day we had sunk a Japanese carrier, small though she might have been. Things had not gone badly for the *Lexington*. So far. Still—

The next morning found us out in bright sunlight under clear skies with no place to hide. We got off our dawn searches and settled down to our usual waiting. But this time the wait was not so long as usual. Two of our search planes found the Japanese fast carriers, and we swung into the wind to launch our own attack of dive-bombers and torpedo planes against them. Unfortunately, the Japanese had found us as well and sent their airplanes winging against us. The two attacking forces actually saw each other as they passed on their opposite courses.

It was sometime around eleven o'clock in the morning when our radar picked up the incoming attack and we built to full speed. Carriers in those days carried few fighters. One squadron of eighteen in each ship, as I recall, with a few spares hung from the hangar deck overhead. We tried to make up the deficit by launching returned SBD search planes to act as fighters against torpedo planes. SBDs carried two forward-firing .50-caliber machine guns and a twin mount of .30-calibers in the backseat. But they were too slow and unmaneuverable to be truly effective against Japanese airplanes.

Other than the excited squawking of our pilots' voices on the radio, the first sign we on the ship had of the oncoming enemy was the sight of wriggly black plumes of smoke, seeming slow in the distance, moving down from sky to sea. Whether they were our planes or the enemy's dying before our eyes we did not know.

Then we could see the little clusters of black dots that were the Japanese airplanes. As they came ever closer we could see they were flying in neat formations. Distance made them seem to crawl slowly across the sky.

While still at high altitude the torpedo planes broke off from the others and came at us in long shallow dives. They dropped their torpedoes from much higher altitudes than American pilots did. Our planes tended to level off only a few feet off the water, but the Japanese dropped their torpedoes from what looked to be three or four hundred feet. In another difference, American aerial torpedoes were relatively short and stubby. The Japanese fish were long and thin. They looked like telephone poles to my staring eyes. One tumbled end over end and probably broke up on hitting the sea, but all the others entered the water cleanly and raced, unseen, toward us.

Soon after the dive-bombers reached their diving points at probably 12,000 or 13,000 feet. One by one, they pushed over and hurtled down at us. They seemed awfully small—each but a black dot against the bright blue sky, with the straight lines of its wings jutting out to either side. But they rapidly grew bigger.

The torpedo planes by that time were trying to get away. We had largely forgotten them in our awful concentration on the dive-bombers, which were then nearing their release altitude. We could see the disks of their propellers. We could see the color of the planes. And, finally, we could see the terrible black dots of the bombs themselves as they pulled away and plunged down at us.

Every gun we had that would bear—along with those of our supporting ships—was firing. The sky became blotched with dirty brown and gray bursts of smoke from exploding 5-inch shells—and streaked with the twisting light gray smoke of 20-millimeter tracers.

I never knew how many airplanes attacked us that day. It seemed they came down at us in a long, nearly vertical stream for a long time. Some wobbled and smoked and plunged on into the sea, but most dropped their bombs and made their escapes in the erratic mode pilots call jinking.

As I recall, we took two bomb hits. Other bombs exploded in the water alongside, sending up tall graceful plumes of white water that hung in the air for some time as ghostly mists, drifting off downwind. None was far away. Some were close enough to do damage from the mining effect of close underwater explosions. These bombs exploded with the same r-r-ripping crashes we had heard off Rabaul. Bombs that actually hit the ship exploded in hard, cracking bangs that jarred us.

While the bombs were still exploding on, in, and around us, the torpedoes struck home. All this time Captain Sherman had been trying to maneuver the unwieldy *Lexington* to comb the torpedoes swimming against her—that is, to turn the ship head on to them and, thus, to present a smaller target. But the old ship was too clumsy, and there were too many torpedoes in the water against us. At least two torpedoes took us in the port side. To me it seemed like more than two.

Unlike the sharp clamor of bombs, torpedoes exploded with a muffled jolt that, incredibly, seemed to lift the ship's entire bulk right out of the water and let it fall back into the sea in a series of up-and-down bounces that had the masts staggering and the rigging jingling. Bits of old paint and the dust of fourteen years was jarred from the ship's secret cracks and crannies.

The *Lexington*'s whistle was on the leading side of her great vertical slab of a stack. It was activated by a metal rod leading across the space between stack and bridge to a handle in the wheelhouse. During the attack something—we assumed it was a bomb—passed through the narrow space and hit that rod a glancing blow that bent it so that the whistle was left blowing at full decibels. It is not pleasant to think, even now, of what would have happened on the signal bridge had the bomb hit squarely enough to explode.

During the latter stages of the attack, the whistle was blaring, our guns were banging away, bombs were bursting, torpedoes were shaking the ship with muffled thunder, and airplane engines were screaming. It made for a noisy time, but, oddly, we found that we could hear ourselves talking—or yelling.

Once it was over, the silence was dismaying—except for the whistle that continued to blare until someone disconnected the bent rod so that it too fell silent. There were no more explosions of bombs and torpedoes. Enemy airplanes were disappearing black spots over the horizon. Our guns had fallen silent, except for the occasional one being unloaded through the muzzle. This happened sometimes when the order to cease fire left a shell in a gun somewhere. As a safety measure, the gun was fired rather than unloaded through its breach. There were almost always a few like that after an attack.

The silence was so intense that we could actually hear the bubbling sound of 20-millimeter gun barrels as they cooled. Guns, even those as small as rifles, get hot when fired for very long. Twenty-millimeter guns had extra barrels that for that reason could be exchanged after prolonged firing. Tubes of oil were fitted near the gun mounts. Hot barrels were put in these tubes to cool. We could hear the boiling sound as they cooled sometimes.

We could hear the snapping of signal flags above our heads as well. We hoisted an informational signal at the beginning of air attacks in those days that meant conform to movements of this vessel. This left the carrier free to maneuver as she liked. The other ships were under obligation not to get in the way, while yet staying close enough to provide supporting fire with their guns. It made for a grand picture: ships twisting and turning in a blue sea, guns firing, planes diving, colored flags snapping in thirty knots of wind. It made a grand picture, that is, if only one could be certain he would not be blown to bits at any moment.

And, even after all the noisy part was over, we still couldn't relax a whole lot. We remembered those god-awful torpedo explosions, and the way the huge ship had bounced in the water. We could smell, too, the sick stench of burning paint from somewhere below decks. The ship was taking a definite list to port. We were not out of the woods.

While all this was going on with us, the poor *Yorktown* was undergoing her own brand of hell. She was skillful—or lucky—enough to evade the torpedoes launched against her, but she did take some bomb hits and near-miss damage. Still, she was steaming well off our starboard side with no apparent serious harm done.

Nor, for that matter, did the *Lexington* show much outward sign of damage. Steel plates, carried for the purpose, patched bomb damage in the flight deck, and when, in only a few minutes, our own planes returned from their attack on the Japanese carriers, we took them aboard with little problem. The port list following the torpedo hits had been corrected. We had power enough for twenty knots or so, easily enough to operate aircraft in the brisk trade wind then blowing.

In fact we not only recovered our returning aircraft, we launched aircraft as well. It was not until around two o'clock that an ominous explosion from somewhere deep down in the ship caused her to shiver for a moment—and us to look at each other uneasily. We did not know it at the time, but a chain of events had been put in motion that would change everything.

We, even after that ominous explosion, continued to operate aircraft, but not for much longer. One after another, explosions shuddered deep in the ship. The pipes carrying aviation fuel, it was later concluded, had been ruptured by torpedo hits, and their fumes, collected in sealed-off compartments, had been ignited by a random spark to set off the first explosion.

After that the fire in one compartment heated its steel bulkheads to such high temperatures that paint on the other side ignited. Thus even though watertight doors remained closed and hatches sealed, the fires moved compartment by compartment through the big ship. Finally, around four o'clock that afternoon, engineering personnel were driven from their stations, and the ship coasted to a halt.

Ships without power tend to drift beams onto wind and sea. The *Lexington* skewed round and drifted sidewise before the wind driven by the great sail area of her hull and stack. She sank ever deeper in the water as her pumps failed one after another. The original list we had corrected returned and increased. She rose ever more slowly to the lift of the sea and took on a sluggish feel beneath our feet.

Admiral Fitch was still on board, but as the fires increased and smoke boiled from under the flight deck, it was harder and harder for him to maintain communications with his other ships—especially the *Yorktown*, which already had taken on board those *Lexington* airplanes still airborne when we went dead in the water.

The loss of electrical power silenced our signal lights, and the smothering smoke at signal bridge level made semaphore unusable. Flag hoist was unsuitable for the job at hand. Finally, Honk and I were sent aloft with semaphore flags to the platform high at the top of the foremast. There was a sound-powered phone there that did not require electricity and with which we could communicate with the bridge. We were high enough on the platform to be above most of the smoke and, thus, visible to surrounding ships, and there we stayed for the remainder of the *Lexington*'s life, the two of us her last link with the living world.

As the sun settled lower it became clearer and clearer that the *Lexington* was dying. A destroyer came alongside to help fight her fires, but the effort was far too little to make much difference. Admiral Fitch is said to have called down to Captain Sherman to get the men off before any more were killed in futile efforts to save the ship.

There was a saying in the Navy that there is always some dumb son of a bitch who does not get the word. In this case there were two dumb sons of bitches—

Honk and me! We wondered after a time why our telephone was so quiet and why no one answered from the bridge when we called. Then, from out of the smoke engulfing the bridge below us, two identical informational flag hoists rose, one to either side. Being signalmen we knew what the flags said: the *Lexington* was being abandoned. Everybody was leaving the goddamned ship, and there we were sitting up on top of the mast like a couple of big stupid-assed birds.

By that time flames were beginning to appear at the bottom of what was a very large leaning tower of black smoke. Honk and I decided it was time for some independent action. We couldn't raise anyone on the bridge by telephone. When we got to that level on our way down, we saw why: there was no one there. The bridge deck was littered with scraps of paper, some abandoned steel helmets and a litter of debris shaken loose by the great explosions that had wracked the ship—but there was not a soul to be seen, living or dead.

The flight deck, by the time we reached it, already had begun to burn. Little licking tongues of flame raced in erratic patterns across the wooden expanse, only to die out and to be replaced moments later by others. We could see nothing aft but fire and smoke. The bow was still clear, but the tar caulking between deck planks was beginning to bubble up. We could feel the heat on our faces.

There were still men on board. We saw some of them bent over and running about in the smoke on mysterious errands. I remembered I had almost a hundred dollars in my seabag in the ship's library, but one look aft talked me out of trying to get it. It was time to go. Honk and I took a knotted line and lowered ourselves over the starboard side forward, not far from the burned and twisted wreckage of a 5-inch battery that had taken a direct hit.

The water was warm. It was running in an appreciable swell that created the same optical illusion I had noticed before when coming alongside a ship in small boats. The sea seemed to hold level, while the ship rose high and sank deep in the water. We could hear the working of water along the base of the great gray cliff that was the dying *Lexington*'s hull.

Somehow, Honk and I became separated in the water. It was getting dark by that time, and the *Lexington*, driven by the wind, had drifted far away from the life rafts thrown over in the beginning. Everyone was on his own, suspended in a gray kapok life jacket over a wet abyss of several thousand feet. Some of us held hands and tried to keep together in order to be more easily seen, but I found myself alone.

The *Lexington* was a fearsome sight. From the water she looked to be far bigger even than she was. She listed heavily and burned with dirty red flames that blossomed from time to time as bombs in the parked airplanes—and the airplanes themselves—exploded on her flight deck. The darkening waters reflected the fire's light in a way that made the scene seem even more terrible than it was.

A motor whaleboat from the destroyer *Anderson* came in the end and dragged me from the water like a netted fish. She had fifteen or twenty other bedraggled men in her, and she moved at once to let us off before continuing her search for still more survivors.

The *Anderson* and our other supporting ships had let cargo nets down their sides to ease our climbing aboard from the sea, but I had no strength for the job. We couldn't have been in the water much more than thirty minutes. The sea was warm and not really rough at all, but we were so weak the destroyer men had to climb halfway down the nets and help us up. The emotional stress of the day must have drained us.

The quick tropical twilight was fully spent by that time, and as the unlit rescue ships disappeared in the murk, the burning *Lexington* was the only thing to be seen. The great smoke coming off of her could no longer be seen, but the darkness accentuated the lurid flames themselves. Even her metal hull glowed red in places.

When it was concluded that everyone who was going to be saved had been saved, we set off to the south at high speed. The *Anderson* by that time had more than three hundred *Lexington* survivors on board. There was not room enough below for all of us. Hundreds had to stay topside on the destroyer's narrow weather decks, where we were kept wet all night long by the spray of our speed, spray that, when it dried, left us stiff and gray with sea salt. My spot of deck happened to be over a fire room. The steel plates were so hot I could not lie still for long at a time. All night long I turned from time to time like roasting meat on a spit.

Whether by accident or by design to break up the oil slick being left by the damaged *Yorktown*, the *Anderson* was stationed in her wake. As a result, still more oil was added to that already soiling our dear bodies. After a time I posed absolutely no threat to the Imperial Japanese Navy. I wanted to cry out the traditional "King's Ex" children use when they don't want to play anymore. I sure as hell didn't want to play anymore. Not just then anyway.

When what was, I believe, the second night of our flight overtook us, we were still steaming south at high speed. For all we knew, the Japanese were in hot pursuit just over the horizon astern. No one bothered to tell us anything. We were lucky to get a drink of water now and then and a dry Navy sandwich.

Then, a still more pressing problem arose. Destroyers, when steaming fast, burn lots of fuel. And fuel is carried in tanks near the bottom of the ship, their weight acting as ballast. As fuel is burned a ship, especially a small ship like a destroyer, tends to become top-heavy. This becomes an even greater problem when the ship is laboring under a deck load of several hundred survivors. Already the *Anderson* was beginning to roll disturbingly.

Since fueling was out of the question, it was decided to shift the survivors into larger and more stable ships. I was sent to the *Portland*, the same heavy cruiser that had delivered me from Pearl to the *Indianapolis* following my stateside leave the previous year. So, during that long black night, the *Anderson* came alongside the *Portland*'s starboard side, and we were passed across in what were called coal bags—heavy canvas sacks with roped seams. The name came from the time when ships burned coal that was brought on board sometimes in just such bags. How we came to have them aboard during a time when ships burned oil, I don't know. Maybe the boatswain's mates made them for the purpose. They seemed new.

At any rate, a line was passed from the destroyer's bow to the cruiser's quarterdeck, and a second from the destroyer's fantail to the *Portland*'s main deck aft. There were two of us to a bag; we were hauled from the small ship to the big one.

The wind had come up in the night, and we were still steaming at a good speed. As a result, the sea, compressed as it was between the two hulls, became tumultuous, leaping and dashing from one to the other and working itself into a turmoil of crashing water between the two.

Those of us in the coal bags had all the best of it. We could see nothing but white water and black hulls. When the ships rolled apart we were snapped high in the air, suspended from a trembling line that might or might not snap. When the ships rolled toward each other the line sagged sickeningly down into a maelstrom of churning water. Sometimes the bags actually touched the water and were dragged skipping along over its troubled surface.

In the end, I thumped heavily onto the *Portland*'s blessed quarterdeck, in the lee of a catapult silo. As quickly as we were landed on board, we were hustled below for a rudimentary washup and something warm to eat and drink. It was the first time I had been below decks since the night before the *Lexington* sank. It was the first time I had been out of my life jacket as well. It was a wrench when that beautiful item of flotation was taken from me. Since I could not swim I had become fonder of my life jacket than had those who could, but it was taken away and thrown onto a sodden heap of others on the quarterdeck.

The *Portland* had been stripped for war since I had last been in her. The rich red—and flammable—linoleum was gone from her mess decks, for instance, leaving nothing but bare metal. Mess tables and benches were stacked and lashed down in a corner out of the way. Sailors squatted on the hard metal decks holding trays on their folded knees to eat. The only light was that of eerie blue battle lanterns, which turned our faces, dulled as they were by fuel oil and dried sea salt, into horror masks. But at least the *Portland*'s contours were familiar—she was a sister ship of the *Indianapolis*. I found a place where no one would step on me and went to sleep, the sailor's one sure refuge when all else fails.

I don't know how long I slept, but when I woke the ship had slowed. She no longer pounded with the hard vibrations of high speed, and when I went on deck I found the whole force had turned east and was steaming easily in a loose cruising disposition. The previous night's wind had died, and we were in bright sunlight. None of the ships seemed much damaged. Even the *Yorktown* steamed on as though nothing had happened, although she still leaked fuel oil.

We were by that time beyond reach of the Japanese, and life returned somewhat to normal. The *Portland* was crowded, of course. Eating and sleeping were problems, but it was for only a short time and we made do. In a day or so the entire force anchored in the harbor of Nuku'alofa, on the island of Tongatabu, to sort things out.

Nuku'alofa was the capital of the then-British Tongan group of islands. There was but one small stone pier—too small to be used by any of our ships—but there was room enough for us all in the anchorage. Shoreside was neat and gardenlike: broad green lawns under tall trees with white-washed trunks where, it was said, a giant tortoise lived, its shell carved with the initials of Captain Cook, who had given it to the island king as a present.

We were not allowed ashore, but we could see from the ship the big white Victorian-style wood-frame palace that was the home and seat of government of the Tongan kings. (When we were there *he* was a queen.) Tonga was far enough south to be clear of the oppressive heat and humidity of the equatorial zone. The day was bright and clear.

In looking on the sun-dancing waters and the green things ashore, it was hard to recall the Coral Sea's darkening waters of only three or four days before, all lit as they had been by the garish reflections of the dying *Lexington*'s fires. Human adaptability is remarkable. We laughed and joked and bargained with the Tongans who came out in their dugouts to trade with us. They seemed a happy and pleasant people. Our most popular items of trade in their eyes were skivvy shirts—our undershirts—which they called singlets. They offered in return coconuts, oranges, lemons, and whole stalks of the biggest bananas I ever saw in my life.

But we were not there for fun. Even before anchors were let go, ships' boats were in the water and threading their ways from ship to ship. *Lexington* survivors had been picked up by the nearest ship without regard to anything other than getting them out of the water and away from the closing Japanese. Some of the rescuing small boats had been recovered by ships other than their own. The *Anderson*'s motor whaleboat, for instance, had been picked up by another destroyer. There had been some confusion.

For the next few hours we were busy sorting all this out and preparing the ships for getting under way. The flag survivors, along with Admiral Fitch himself and some few ship's company survivors, were collected in the heavy cruiser *Chester*, which had served as our relief flagship only a few months before. Honk and I knew most of the signalmen in her and made ourselves at home. The *Chester* men were much better in that regard than the *Portland*'s had been. They gave up their bunks to us and saw that we were fed and had a chance to scrub the oil from our ears and noses.

Admiral Fitch went for a conference with Admiral Fletcher in the *Yorktown*, but he did not stay long. Once he was back in the *Chester*, the entire force got under way and was gone from Tonga as quickly as it had come. I could not help wondering what the effect the visitation had on the islanders. Maybe, given the re-silience of human nature, there was no effect at all. Regardless, once in open water, the *Yorktown* and all the other ships turned north to make rushed preparations for the coming Battle of Midway, but we signalmen knew nothing of that at the time.

The *Chester* peeled off to the east and built to her best sustainable speed for a long, solitary run to San Diego. The *Saratoga*, the *Lexington*'s big sister carrier— the one I had visited as a boot what seemed a long time ago—was working up and training pilots off the West Coast after a yard period to repair torpedo damage. Admiral Fitch was to go in her as his new flagship. Naturally, where Fitch went, Honk and I went. We were to join the *Saratoga* in San Diego.

The fast passage proved a vacation for us. With no other ships in company there was no signaling at all to be done. There were drills, of course. Even dur-ing the war we were drilled whenever opportunity offered because so many men were new. But Honk and I were excused from them. We were among friends, and we basked in the notoriety of being survivors. The weather was cool, even as we crossed the doldrums, owing to the wind of our speed, and we could sleep as long and as often as we liked. Our wake, white and straight as a paved highway, stretched to the horizon astern. We must have been doing better than 30 knots—720 miles a day.

The ship was crowded, but Honk and I were made welcome on the signal bridge and spent most of our time there, far above the madding throng. After only a week or ten days, we came up on the California coast in an opalescent dusk then characteristic of pre-smog Southern California. Point Loma grew out of the murk ahead, and we followed the channel to a berth at the foot of Broadway, the same berth in which I had first seen Navy ships—the nested Bird-class minesweepers. A fleet of gray Navy buses like those that had met my train to take me to boot camp met the ship and carried away any *Lexington* ship's company survivors. Fueling lines were taken on board immediately, and trucks filled with provisions lined up at the foot of the after gangway, where working parties turned to in what amounted to a controlled frenzy to get the stuff on board and struck below and the ship ready again for sea.

The *Lexington*'s loss had not yet been announced at that time, and we were threatened with dire punishments if we let the word slip out. We in the Flag were not even allowed to call home or to let our families know we were in the States. But there were a good many officers' wives on the dock when we landed. Obviously, officers' families were not as great a security risk as ours would have been. It made no difference to me—my family was in Oklahoma and could not have come to see me in any event—but some of us did have families in Southern California. They could have had a few hours together.

It was a wrench to see the *Lexington*'s ship's company survivors board their buses and drive away for their thirty days of survivor's leave. I don't know if it was a formal part of naval regulations or not, but survivors of sunken ships were usually given thirty days of leave during the war—unless they were in an admiral's Flag, we learned. In two or three days, the *Lexington* men would be back in their hometowns, in their families' bosoms. We in the Flag would be back in the *Chester* and, in Honk's words, "hauling ass for Pearl."

The *Saratoga*, faced with the Navy's desperate need for carriers at Midway, already had sailed when we reached San Diego. We would leave as soon as possible in hot pursuit. The *Chester* was abuzz with preparations for getting under way. She would sail first thing in the morning.

"You men might as well go ashore and have some fun," our new Flag lieutenant said to Honk and me. There wasn't anything we could do in the ship anyway. The *Chester* signalmen lent us some blues and black shoes and found us some money. I went ashore with Honk, but I wished later I hadn't.

I had had little experience with the fleshpots of San Diego when I was there before, but Honk knew the town well. Honk knew every town well. He took me to a place called Sherman's, a place I remember primarily for the fact that its dance floor was bordered with glass blocks in which colored lights were buried. That was the height of sophistication in my country-boy eyes.

With a directness that was impressive, Honk zeroed in on a fairly large brunette and worked with a speed based on his knowledge that we were sailing within a few hours. In a remarkably short time, he announced the twin facts that he and his new girlfriend were off to her apartment and she had a friend for me.

I was then twenty-two years old and still virginal, although I would have denied the fact to the death. I was not yet ready for Honk's pragmatic approach to sex. To his credit, Honk did not push me. When he and his girl shoved off, I went for a long walk through a residential neighborhood, where I played my old game of the window shades.

It was a place of modest homes, not far from downtown, as I recall. But the houses were beautifully kept behind trimmed lawns and shrubs whose green was tinged with yellow by street lights. Most were white stucco, with red-tiled roofs. I could picture the scenes being played out in comfortable living rooms, with smiling fathers and mothers and laughing children listening to radio shows. But, where in the past I had found comfort in the game, this time I found nothing but frustration and sadness. I made my way back to Sherman's expecting Honk to return there once his more immediate needs were seen to.

I ordered a Scotch and soda at the crowded bar—Scotch and sodas were what people in the movies ordered—and studied the scene before me. Loud, brassy, garishly lit, Sherman's was a factory designed for one purpose. The place was jammed full of sailors, Marines, and the women who preyed on them with a kind of frenzied intensity. The atmosphere of the bar lent the place a wild madness.

But, more than sailors and Marines, there were civilians too. Employees of shipyards and what were then known as defense plants. They laughed too loud and threw their money around. I remembered such men back in Oklahoma during the Depression. They had hitchhiked then and ridden freight trains all over the country in search of any kind of work. Now they were war workers dedicated to sacrificing themselves for the common good. At union wages, of course. I knew they were necessary. God knows we needed the stuff they produced. But, goddamn it, they didn't have to be so happy.

Somehow it was depressing, and I thought almost longingly of the dark waters of the Coral Sea with the fires of the *Lexington* reflected on them. I was glad when Honk did, after a while, show up. He was not in a good mood either. When I asked how it had gone, he ordered a drink and growled, "I could have had more fun with an old peacoat sleeve."

It was not a successful liberty for either of us. Under the circumstances, I couldn't think of any really convincing reason for not drinking. My mistake was in trying to match Honk drink for drink. When I woke up I was in a signalman's bunk in the *Chester*, and we were well out to sea on our way to Pearl.

12
The *Enterprise* at Santa Cruz
and Guadalcanal

SAN DIEGO LEFT A SOUR TASTE in my mouth, both literally and figuratively. I had not seen the home front side of war before. It had not occurred to me that people could make so much money and have so much fun during something so serious as a war. I could not see that the people I saw in San Diego, military or civilian, gave much of a damn about how the war was going; it had not occurred to me that anyone might view the war in any way other than the way we in the ships viewed it then. In Hawaii that early in the war, even the civilians took it seriously. I was shaken, I am afraid. So was Honk, who expressed our mood better than I could when he muttered into his drink, "The sons of bitches."

The literal sour taste in my mouth went away just about as fast as the hangover that brought it, but the figurative taste lingered for a long time. I was never again quite so gung ho as I had been before. Something had changed.

We did not catch the *Saratoga* before she reached Pearl Harbor. By that time even we had been let in on the fact there had been something of a battle off Midway Island. That approaching battle—and its very doubtful outcome—was why the *Saratoga* had not waited for us in San Diego. The Navy had wanted her as close as possible when all the stuff hit the fan off Midway. But, as it happened, she was too late for the fighting. She was in Pearl when we arrived. The Flag shifted into her as soon as we were secured alongside.

The battle had been decided by that time, but we did not know it. Except for the *Saratoga* and an escorting destroyer or two, the harbor was empty of combatants. Salvage work still was going on in the ships damaged in the December 7 raid that had put us in the war and new facilities were being built ashore. But the ships that had taken part in the Battle of Midway had not yet returned, and we entered a harbor of unnatural, almost eerie, silence.

This episode suggested something we white hats neither knew nor were ever told. How did the brass know those Japanese carriers were in the Coral Sea? And how did they know there was going to be a battle off Midway? How could they so confidently position their skimpy forces to meet the Japanese so neatly?

We on the Flag bridge knew there was an intelligence officer on board who brought a clipboard of messages to the admiral from time to time. But we did not know the messages were decoded orders from Tojo to his ships. We did not know until after the war that our decoders were reading Japanese orders to their ships almost as quickly as the Japanese were. We knew where they were going to hit. Thank God—and the decoders—we did. It would have been a far longer and more costly war had we not.

We discovered the *Saratoga*—when at last we caught up with her—was a virtually identical sister ship to the *Lexington*. Both had been started as battle cruisers during World War I and converted to carriers as a result of one of the arms limitations treaties negotiated after that war. Before our war, when both ships wore the Navy's light gray paint, they were so nearly alike that a horizontal black stripe was painted across the top of the *Lexington*'s great flat slab of a stack and a vertical stripe was painted on the *Saratoga*'s so they might be told apart. For Honk and me, it was like coming home to go in the *Saratoga*.

Only a day or two after we reached Pearl, the *Enterprise* and *Hornet* task forces did return from Midway. None of the returning ships showed much damage—but the *Yorktown* and destroyer *Hammann* were not with them. We saw the buses and the ambulances waiting on the dock to pick up the survivors and the wounded. Even the survivors did not show much sign of what they had been through. They were already in clean dungarees and their hands and faces had been scrubbed free of fuel oil. The Navy was now more adept in the handling of survivors than it had been when the *Lexington* was lost.

Once settled in the *Saratoga*, we fell into a strenuous if not dangerous pattern of training exercises for several weeks. Pilots flew until ready to drop. Gunners drilled until they saw shells and targets in their sleep. Below decks, damage control parties practiced the repair of any conceivable casualty. Only we on the signal bridge had little to do, other than the endless drills, of course.

We operated alone during that time, with seldom more than an antisubmarine screen of two or three destroyers and a plane guard destroyer tucked in on the starboard quarter to fish out aircrewmen who might find themselves in the water. Honk and I were excused from many of the drills. We did a little flag hoist drill, but most of the time we relaxed and enjoyed the fine Hawaiian weather. We knew it would not last. We would it enjoy it while we could.

Finally, deemed ready for action, the *Saratoga* was ordered south and west. But Admiral Fitch was ordered to a shore billet somewhere and his Flag afloat was disbanded. Honk and I were ordered to the *Hornet,* where we would be the nucleus of a signal flag allowance for Rear Adm. Thomas Kinkaid. We then, for another several weeks, continued in the *Hornet* what we had been doing in the *Saratoga*: training, training, training. It became monotonous as hell, but Honk pointed out the bright side: "There ain't nobody dropping nothing on us," he said.

We came into Pearl fairly frequently during that time, but I don't remember going ashore more than once or twice. Honk went fairly often to "dip his wick." Honolulu was not much fun for me anymore. I never called or saw Ilse after the war began. She probably thought I was dead. She knew how I felt about her.

I did take Allen Nations to Trader Vic's one time. But it was daytime and the toads were not out. Nations was a quiet-spoken man from Bisbee, Arizona, a desert mining town not far from the Mexican border. His middle name was misspelled Quarterman, in honor of the hero in a Haggard novel his mother read while pregnant with Allen. I don't know who made the spelling error.

Nations is the only man of the *Hornet*'s signal gang I remember now by name. We were in that ship only about a month, and Honk and I had been in so many ships the names have become confused in memory. I did not get to know even Nations very well, but we became friends in the quick way that sometimes happens between men and I do remember him now.

Then, toward the end of August, as I recall, the *Enterprise* returned to Pearl from the Battle of the Eastern Solomons. She was and had been since the war started—except for the Battle of Midway—Adm. William Halsey's flagship and enjoyed a reputation in the Navy for being both good and lucky. That was not a bad combination at all. Halsey was aggressive and little given to the chicken-effluent observance of regulations that made life more miserable than it had to be for sailors under some officers. He was popular with his men.

As it happened, about that time Halsey was made Commander, South Pacific Forces (COMSOPAC), with headquarters ashore in Nouméa, on the French island of New Caledonia. Admiral Kinkaid was given the *Enterprise,* and Honk and I went with him in her—our fourth ship in three months.

Once in the *Enterprise,* our days of training were over. She had a veteran crew, kept together more than most, I suspect, by Halsey's clout. Within days, we sortied from Pearl for the long haul to the Coral Sea. This had become a familiar road for us by that time. Frequently, we did not even fly searches in order to save wear and tear on planes and pilots.

In skirting the Japanese-held Gilbert and Marshal islands we sometimes were snooped by big four-engined flying boats and would send up fighters to knock them down. But, most of the time, we steamed in near peacetime-style, except that we did not show lights at night. Because we moved fast and kept up a close patrol of cruiser float planes, submarines were of little concern in daytime.

This all changed, however, when we arrived in the operating areas to the east of the Solomon Islands. Our Marines had landed in those islands in early August, but whether they would be able to hold them was still very much in doubt. Fortunately for us, throughout the Solomons campaign the Japanese made their counterattacks piecemeal. Had they brought down the full force of their carriers and battleships in one massive counterblow, it is hard to see, even now, how we could have held them off. It was sometimes a near thing as it was.

We rendezvoused with the *Hornet* on station and began active patrols and searches in support of the Marines ashore on Guadalcanal and Tulagi. One of the few advantages we had during that time was the presence of Henderson Field on Guadalcanal. In extremity, we could shuttle airplanes from carriers to Henderson to carriers. At worst, if our carriers were lost or disabled we could at least save their planes by flying them in to continue the fight from Henderson Field.

We were always handicapped in the South Pacific by our lack of good long-range reconnaissance and the communications that would have made it useful. Our PBYs, operating from tenders anchored in forward areas, did their best. They often discovered the enemy carriers and other ship movements, only to have their reports—gained at such great cost—be lost or so delayed as to be made of little value. Slow and poorly armed, the PBYs were dead meat if caught by virtually any of the Japanese aircraft, including their own lumbering patrol planes. The courage and dedication of the PBY crews were remarkable, but for most of the time we had to rely on our own carrier planes for searches. This added hours on both planes and flight crews and reduced the number of planes available for attack groups.

In a tactical sense, the Japanese seemed always to know where we were before we knew where they were. They had two kinds of four-engined flying boats of very long range that could operate from sheltered water just about anywhere. They once used even the marginal shelter of French Frigate Shoals—the low-lying atoll we had seen from the *Indianapolis* before the war—to make nuisance raids against Hawaii. They were faster and better armed than our PBYs as well.

At any rate, toward the end of October we got word that Japanese fast carriers were headed toward us as part of still another attempt to retake Guadalcanal. Intelligence reports listed four fast carriers, two battleships, and the usual supporting cruisers and destroyers—all on their way to meet our two carriers and their handful of cruisers and destroyers.

It is interesting now to note that the presence of battleships in the enemy force should not have so impressed us, but it did. Battleships were unlikely to be a threat, unless we should happen on them in the night, but the mere word won respect. I suppose we had been for too long conditioned to think of naval power in terms of battleships.

Actually, for this fight, for the first time, we had a battleship of our own with us. The new fast battleship *South Dakota* had joined us a few days before. She would be of little use against the enemy carriers but she did have a lot of nice antiaircraft guns that might well come in handy. We also had some of the new antiaircraft cruisers designed specifically to fight airplanes. Each carried sixteen 5-inch, .38-caliber dual purpose guns plus as many 20- and 40-mm guns as could be found places for. When those little ships opened fire with all their guns at the same time, they looked as though they were themselves on fire.

We were beginning to get some new tools. I came to have a little more respect for the home front, but I still was not comfortable with what I had seen in San Diego.

The new 40 mms we got about that time were especially welcome. To me they were the most effective gun we had against airplanes in the entire war. In quadruple mounts they fired explosive shells at almost machine-gun speed. And they filled the sky with satisfying visible bursts that, even if they didn't hit anything, made us feel a good deal better simply for seeing them. The mere sight of all that smoke and fire must have had a disconcerting effect on enemy pilots who had to fly through it.

After the usual preliminaries of fueling, searching, backing, and filling for position, we came together—we and the Japanese—on the morning of October 26, as I recall. Our search planes, in this case, found the enemy ships first, not far from the Santa Cruz Islands, a group of islands so virulently malarial that neither the Americans nor the Japanese bothered to take them.

In fact, the scouts who found the enemy ships managed to drop bombs on and set fire to one of the carriers, knocking her out of the fight. This evened the effective odds against us a bit but was of little immediate help. The Japanese carriers had already launched their attack groups against us. We were in for another close-in fight.

We were then steaming in company with the *Hornet* and her supporting ships. The *Enterprise* chanced to be in a blessedly dense local rain squall at the time of the first Japanese attack, while the *Hornet* was exposed in bright sunlight. Thus temporarily hidden we were spared the first heavy blows that fell instead on poor *Hornet*. We saw the attack on her. Dive-bombers plunged down on the writhing carrier, and torpedo planes seemed to crawl low over the water against her. Actually they were flying fast, but distance made everything seem slow and deliberate. Even the shells exploding over the *Hornet* seemed to explode slowly, their dark puffs seeming to appear out of nothing, like dropped ink on the pale blue cloth of the sky.

We saw it when the *Hornet* was hit. A flash of fire on the island structure, and a growing plume of dirty brown smoke trailing aft marked the death of Allen Quarterman Nations and virtually everyone else on the signal bridge that morning. Men Honk and I knew. Men with whom we had been shipmates only two or three weeks before. We knew them all, and they were dead.

A dive-bomber had crashed the signal bridge. Whether the attack was deliberate or the plane was out of control from battle damage, we didn't know. I couldn't see that it would make a hell of a lot of difference to Nations. The plane had hit the ship's mast first, apparently, rupturing its fuel tanks and drenching the bridge and everyone on it with burning gasoline. It must have been a horrible death, tempered only by the fact it was probably fast. I thought of the bomber off Rabaul that had tried to crash the *Lexington*'s bridge. What had happened to the *Hornet* could have happened to us.

The *Hornet* was torpedoed as well. She went dead in the water, still under heavy attack.

We were by that time under attack ourselves. The squall that had sheltered us dissipated. The clouds that had first protected us now turned against us by hiding the enemy airplanes lurking overhead. The dive-bombers reached their pushover points without being challenged either by fighters or ships' guns. They dived on us in twisting chains of individual attacks down long chutes and chasms of thunderstorm clouds. We could see them only after they were well into their dives and could do nothing but whale away at them with every gun we had.

Some people claim to know how many airplanes attacked that day, but I don't. All I know was that there were lots of them. Appreciably more than had attacked the *Lexington* in the battle of the Coral Sea. They seemed to come for a long time— and to dive to almost point-blank range before letting go their bombs. We could see the bombs clearly as they fell away, how they seemed to wriggle momentarily, as though finding their way, before boring straight for us with a terrible purpose. It is a characteristic of bombs that, whether you are standing on the bow or the stern of even a very long ship, the damned things always seem to be heading straight for you.

The water boiled around us and great gouts of white spray rose higher than our mast. The *Enterprise* twisted and turned like an animal in torment. But she could not escape forever. One bomb hit the flight deck on the port side forward. It pierced the flight deck at an angle, went through the overhang of the hull, and exploded outside the ship, sending fragments back into her. A second bomb hit more nearly amidships and penetrated down deep into the forward elevator well before exploding and putting the machinery there out of action. It also killed forty-five men, we learned later. A third bomb burst outside the ship aft, but so close that a number of plates were sprung, major damage was done to a main bearing, and some minor fragment damage was done to the hull above the waterline.

Even so, we were lucky to get off so lightly. The *Enterprise*'s veteran damage control parties were at work before the bombs stopped falling. The ship showed little effect from the blows she had taken. The smells of burning paint, though, were unsettling for those of us who had been in the *Lexington*, for it was the smell of burning paint that had signaled that ship's loss. But the *Enterprise*'s fires were quickly doused. Steel plates were fitted over holes in the flight deck, and flying operations continued on as before.

The most ominous damage was that to the forward elevator. Without it, our efficiency in handling aircraft on deck was cut more than in half. With it, we could strike planes below as they landed, service them in the hangar deck, push them aft, and send them up on the after elevator to be launched again. But without a forward elevator we had to wait until all airborne planes were landed. Then they would all have to be pushed aft on the flight deck to permit launching. Then all of them would have to be pushed forward to permit landings. It meant constant, slow, and tedious manipulations even to maintain the minimal combat air patrols of those days.

The first lieutenant, the ship's damage control officer, reported after a time that the forward elevator could be lowered, but he could not guarantee that it could be raised again. This was no help at all, since the elevator, when down, left a large hole in the launching area of the flight deck. We might be able to land airplanes, but we would not be able to launch anything.

Before all this could be digested, the attack on us was renewed by Japanese torpedo planes. Unlike those we had seen in the Coral Sea battle, these came in low and fast over the sea. By the official count, nine torpedoes were dropped against us. From the bridge we could actually see them sometimes swimming in the clear water alongside.

This was more torpedoes than were dropped against the *Lexington*. The difference lay in the *Enterprise*'s much greater maneuverability. Sailors on the hangar deck reported we actually shipped water in the hangar deck, the ship heeled so much in her frantic twisting and turning. I know it was scary on the bridge, she heeled so far.

The airplanes were dark green Kates, the same type used against the *Lexington*, but I remembered them in that battle as being a kind of mustard brown. And these attacked the *Enterprise* from both sides—that is, they tried to do that. But our rapid maneuvering left one group out of position astern. Rather than attack from that unfavorable position, they veered to the left and flew along, low over the water in a long line-ahead formation of eight or nine airplanes, trying to reach a position from which they could make a beam attack. That is when our new 40 mms proved their worth.

The enemy planes were strung out like tin ducks in a shooting gallery. The range looked to be from one to two or three thousand yards. But one by one, taking them in turn, the 40s downed four or five of the planes with seemingly no effort at all. The planes simply dipped into the sea and disappeared in a burst of white water. The rest either were handled by our escorting ships or aborted their attacks. I had never seen Japanese airplanes break off an attack before.

Thus, at the cost of virtually all their torpedo planes, the Japanese scored no hits at all on the *Enterprise*, although the *Portland* did report being hit by three duds. This was a satisfying bit of news for our side, since we—especially our submarines—had suffered so many torpedo failures early in the war.

This matter of our escorting ships knocking down torpedo planes brings up another problem. When ships fire at airplanes they must lead them, just as a duck hunter must lead the birds he shoots. This meant that when ships' gunners were firing—especially at torpedo planes—they are looking at the airplane, but they are shooting at a point some distance ahead of it. The idea was that shell and target airplane would arrive together at the same point. Sometimes we in the *Enterprise* were at that point. Our own escorting ships' 5-inch guns, 40- and 20-mm cannons, and .50-caliber machine guns sometimes shot into us, with interesting sounds and unsettling effect.

At any rate, we in the *Enterprise* suffered nothing that was not sustainable. The *South Dakota* reported a direct bomb hit on top of her number two turret—which the men inside were said not to have heard. (In view of the bangs made by bombs hitting anywhere in any ship I was ever on, I find that hard to believe.) The battleship's captain, however, at his station on the bridge, was wounded by a fragment from that bomb.

In one bizarre development, the destroyer *Smith*, on our starboard bow at the time, was crashed by a Japanese torpedo plane with its fish still on board. It is unlikely that a deliberate suicide attack would have been made on a destroyer when so many more important targets were at hand. Probably the plane was damaged or its pilot dead or badly wounded, and he crashed into the only target he could reach. I noticed he wavered up and down a couple of times before crashing into the poor *Smith*.

The entire forward part of the destroyer burst into flame, and smoke swept back over her full length in the wind of her speed. I still do not understand how anyone on the bridge could have survived, but some did. The captain, for one. He shifted control to the after steering station—all warships have an after steering station for just such emergencies—and managed to keep from being run over in what had become a confusion of racing ships. The *Smith*'s after guns never stopped firing.

The *Portland* too suffered a steering casualty in the melee and was steered from her after steering station as well, breakdown flag flying and whistle bellowing as she careened around, past, and between ships.

Aside from planes, the only loss in our force was the destroyer leader *Porter*. Destroyer leaders were a class of limited value in carrier warfare. They were slightly larger than ordinary destroyers, and although they were designed with eight 5-inch guns rather than the ordinary destroyers' four, their guns could not be elevated to fire at airplanes. They might conceivably be used against attacking torpedo planes, but they were useless again high-level or dive-bombers.

The *Porter* was stopped to rescue a downed air crewman when a sudden spout of white water shot up alongside her higher, then her mainmast. Right in the middle of a carrier task force under intense air attack, she had been torpedoed by a Japanese submarine. That's all we needed. It must have been upsetting for the aviators to find themselves torpedoed while in the process of being rescued.

It is not surprising that the submarine had not been detected. In the first place, antisubmarine sound gear is ineffective in ships moving at high speed. In the second place, the nearby exploding bombs and torpedoes were distracting, to say the least. I know submarines were the last thing in the world on my mind at the time. A destroyer was detailed to take off the *Porter*'s crew and to sink her when she was found to be unsalvageable. We had no time for salvage operations at the moment.

The action ended for us in a dwindling series of straggling attacks by single planes and small groups, but the main blows had been struck so far as we were concerned. We hauled out to the south, the blackened *Smith* showing the only apparent damage. The *Portland* had solved her steering problem.

By that time we could no longer see the *Hornet*, though we could see a smudge of smoke over the horizon astern where she was burning in her death throes. Sometimes, with our long glasses, we could see bursts of antiaircraft fire over her and knew her ordeal was not yet over. We would learn later that the *Hornet* survived even the shells and torpedoes put into her by our own destroyers. She was sunk in the end by the Japanese carrier force, which actually closed her burning hulk that night and used their own more effective destroyer torpedoes to finish her.

It was hard to leave one of our own, burning and helpless as she was, but it was the right thing to do. Of our six prewar carriers, four—*Lexington, Yorktown, Hornet,* and *Wasp*—already were gone. Although the *Saratoga* survived, she seemed forever to be in the yard with submarine torpedoes in her. The *Enterprise* was the only remaining American carrier operating in the South Pacific—and she had only one elevator working. It was essential that she be saved. Sentiment could be allowed to play little part in the decision.

The most pressing need was to return the *Enterprise*'s forward elevator to operation. There were no yards closer than Pearl or Sydney where a proper job could be made of it, and they were impossibly far away. We headed instead for Nouméa. There was no Navy yard there, but we did have the beginnings of an American forward base, including a detachment of Seabees, the Navy's new and super effective corps of civilian construction men taken into the Navy to ply their civilian trades largely free of the Navy's usual inhibiting bureaucratic interference.

New Caledonia was one of the most pleasant islands I ever knew in the South Pacific. Far enough south to be out of the enervating heat and humidity of equatorial waters, its fresh winds and moderate temperatures made it a therapeutic change from the sweat boxes the steel hulls of warships become in the tropics. In appearance it was much like Central California's coast, with grassy hills and wooded ravines leading up to a central spine of high purple-blue mountains.

Nouméa itself was built beside a roomy, if undeveloped, harbor, which was entered with some difficulty along a twisted channel through off-lying reefs and islands. A quartermaster told me one time that twenty-seven course changes were required. That it was not safe from submarine attack was evidenced by a liberty ship high on one of the reefs. There was a hole in its side big enough to drive a small landing craft through, a vivid reminder of the power of Japanese torpedoes.

The town was low and wooden and of much the same monotonous dirty green color throughout. Sidewalks were covered by overhanging metal awnings. It was an impressive place, complete with an ornate bandstand and a statue of an early governor in French army uniform. A stone cathedral, flanked by a statue of Joan of Arc, backed a scrub-jungled hill at the upper end of town. There was also the usual market found in towns without refrigeration, and a more varied population than any we had seen before.

The native Melanesians, male and female alike, were burly figures with coarse facial features and big feet, often swollen as high as their knees by elephantiasis. They wore the great bush of their hair trimmed flat across the top and dyed a dirty orange. Their mouths were discolored by the betel nut they chewed. The men wore whatever scraps of cloth they could find, usually some rudimentary shorts, which may have been laundered at some time long ago. The women wore Mother Hubbards—like the muumuus of Hawaii—that touched them only at their shoulders and in front hung on their massive breasts, dropping straight down to hang loosely about the rest of their bodies. Shoes were rarely worn.

In dramatic contrast, there were many petite, neatly turned out, and impeccably clean Annamese and Tonkinese brought down by the French from their colony in Indochina as indentured labor to work in the nickel mines and as servants in their homes. They were small and attractive people.

The French themselves were little in evidence. Like colonialists everywhere, I suppose, they seemed self-conscious and ill at ease around us. I remember once what appeared to be a family passing our anchored ship in a boat for what seemed to be on an outing to a nearby island. Though we waved and called out to them—there were women in light print dresses in the boat—they ignored us. The split between Petainists and DeGaullists was as strong there as it was in France itself, I suppose. A strong movement for independence following the fall of France did not add much to the serenity of the place.

There was a small garrison of French army troops in Nouméa and a small white sloop of the French navy. It had been summoned by the governor from its usual station in Tahiti in an effort to maintain order. We were told that one group was loyal to Vichy and the other to DeGaulle, but I don't remember which was which. A debate reportedly took place between them when the Americans showed up as to whether we would be welcomed or not. I presume the welcomers won, but neither force was notably friendly toward us in my experience.

Nouméa was most notable for its nickel works, a large smelter as dirty and rusty as anything ever seen in Pittsburgh. It was the only industrial installation I ever saw in the South Pacific, other than a rudimentary generating station once in a great while. But New Caledonia held—and still holds—some of the world's greatest deposits of nickel, iron, and a number of other important minerals.

We were given little time, though, on that first visit to appreciate much of what we saw. We came in with all our remaining ships—our own escorts as well as those of the sunken *Hornet*—and anchored out. A force of Seabees boarded us immediately with their gear and set to work on our damaged elevator. The other ships busied themselves with their own repairs, and the *Hornet's* and *Porter's* survivors were sorted out and put ashore for shipment home. The harbor bustled with boats shuttling from ship to ship and ship to shore. But the activity lasted for only three or four days, as I recall now.

Word came—again from our mysterious intelligence sources—that the Japanese were on the move again, advancing with heavy forces on Guadalcanal in what looked to be the most massive attempt yet at taking it back. Although still crippled, the *Enterprise* sortied at once, taking our toiling Seabees with us. These were brave men, but they demonstrated the strain people feel when facing danger in strange surroundings. They were uneasy.

Once again at sea, we turned north and took a station to the southwest of Guadalcanal where we would be far enough away to be out of range of shore-based Japanese airplanes, but close enough to strike with our airplanes at anything approaching the island. There we sawed back and forth, maintaining that precarious balance until the advancing enemy ships were located.

As I recall, there were no carriers with the Japanese main force. We must have hurt them more at the Battle of Santa Cruz Island than we realized at the time. But there were strong surface forces of battleships, cruisers, and destroyers—and a large number of troop-laden transports—all steaming under cover of land-based airplanes from Rabaul. The same Rabaul we had tried to strike from the *Lexington* in February, a time that seemed years in the past rather than the nine months it actually had been. Our airplanes, along with others from Henderson Field on Guadalcanal, struck the transports first. If they succeeded in landing such large numbers of troops, the battle for the Solomons could well be lost. The Japanese soldiers, our aircrews reported, were standing shoulder to shoulder on the open decks of their transports. It is awful to imagine what must have been the effect of thousand-pound bombs exploding in such concentrations of human flesh.

Our airplanes and those from Henderson Field flew all that day shuttling bombs to the virtually helpless transports. Japanese air cover had been destroyed or driven off. Our planes dropped their bombs and flew back for more. They dropped those too for as long as there was daylight to see, but the enemy ships came doggedly on, unwittingly decreasing with every mile the distance our airplanes would have to fly to hit them. I talked with some of our rear-seat guys who said they were made sick at their stomachs at seeing such slaughter.

As night drew near and it became clear that the Japanese were not going to turn back in spite of their terrible losses, we flew off what was left of our airplanes to Guadalcanal, where they would continue the fight from Henderson Field. We also detached our escorting ships for the desperate night surface fight off Guadalcanal we knew was coming.

The *South Dakota* was sent off to join with the *Washington*, another of the new battleships that had recently come to the area. Together they would cooperate that night to sink the Japanese battleship *Kirishima* in one of the few actions between battleships in the entire war. At the same time, our cruisers and destroyers would fight a much stronger Japanese force in the narrow waters off Guadalcanal.

Although suffering heavy damage themselves, they left a second battleship—the *Hiei*—so damaged that Henderson Field planes could finish her off the next day.

The *Enterprise* seemed strangely naked to us with our screen of cruisers and destroyers gone. She seemed empty too and strangely silent without her planes. Her air group people had little to do, and that is an uncomfortable situation for men exposed to danger. The Seabees at least had the distraction of their round-the-clock labor and were coming to be more comfortable with being at sea, I think. All of us wondered, I suspect, what was happening with our surface ships.

Our part in that battle was over, though. Taking only two destroyers for the necessary antisubmarine screen, we returned to Nouméa at high speed—our embarked Seabees still working their butts off to repair the forward elevator. We had to get that fixed and other repairs made to make ourselves ready to meet the next Japanese carrier thrust, a thrust we never doubted would come. It was always their carriers we feared most.

Nouméa's harbor was very quiet for the next few days. I suppose the admiral knew how our ships had made out in the fighting off Guadalcanal, but we didn't. Now, it may seem strange that Americans might have been apprehensive, but we were. We had seen our carriers dwindle from six to two cripples—one of which was not even in the area. We had seen whole squadrons of our airplanes lost. Our strength in heavy cruisers was down to almost nothing. And the Japanese always had bested us in destroyers. Yes, as we watched the empty harbor and peered out to sea, we were nervous.

Soon, though, our surviving ships began to return. Heavy though our losses had been, these scarred and battered ships proved by their presence that we were not yet whipped entirely.

As it turned out, they had handled the Japanese so roughly they would never again make such a determined effort to retake Guadalcanal. The two or three of their transports that did reach the embattled island were so damaged they were run aground and their troops had to swim ashore without arms or supplies. Thus, only more appetites and empty stomachs were added to an already starving garrison. We did not know it at the time, but the tide had turned in the Solomon Islands.

The tide had turned for Honk and me as well—in a different way. The *Enterprise* was to be sent back to Pearl—or maybe even to the States—for more permanent repairs. Honk and I were transferred to Admiral Halsey's Flag for administrative purposes. He then flew his flag in the old World War I transport *Argonne*, moored in Nouméa. Ordinarily there would have been a certain honor involved in being selected for Halsey's Flag. He was the closest thing the Navy had then to a hero. But we never went to sea with him. He lived ashore and flew his flag in the *Argonne*, I suspect now, only to qualify for sea pay. He didn't need signalmen.

We were billeted in a schoolhouse in Nouméa. Lessons in French grammar were still written on its blackboards, and books and papers littered its floors. We slept on those floors as well and washed where and when we could. Latrine facilities were both primitive and overwhelmed, leading one night to a dreadful run—no pun intended—of dysentery. The only good thing about the place was that there was a bakery around the corner, and I discovered the delights of croissants and French bread for the first time in my life.

It was pleasant walking through the little town in the cool of the evening. There were band concerts sometimes in the *place* (village square), and the people paraded in a scene that made the war seem far away. Flowers bloomed and birds sang. Even in town, with all its competing stinks, the scent of the island's ubiquitous *niaouli* trees, a kind of scrub eucalyptus, was heavy on the air. It was nice.

I even wandered into the *hôtel de ville* (city hall) one time before learning it was off limits to American sailors. It was a wooden building of vaguely Chinese design, set in a rank tropical garden behind a wrought-iron fence of fancy scalloped design, with ornate lamps on its gate posts.

I don't remember what Honk was put to doing, but I was sent to stand watch with French sailors in a small stone watchtower dating from the time when the island was a penal colony and a source of labor for blackbirders who took the natives to work on Australian plantations. The tower stood on a hill back of town. About all we did was report ship movements. I did not speak French, and the Frenchmen didn't speak English. My college Spanish, though, was still relatively fresh in my mind, and one of the Frenchmen did speak Spanish. He spoke it a lot better than I did. They reported to their bosses in French, and I to mine in English, what we had discovered together in Spanish.

It was not altogether unpleasant. I was high on a hill overlooking the harbor and its approaches. I used to watch the grass bend and wave before the wind exactly as it had done in what seemed a long ago Oklahoma. But it was boring as hell and did not seem to be doing much for the advancement of the war. Like a damned fool, I felt that I had been trained for something more. I felt as though I was not pulling my own weight.

Then one day, while I was sitting morosely on the stone steps before the tower's door busily watching the shadow of the French flag flop from one side of my feet to the other, Honk skidded to a stop in front of me. He was in a jeep, and he was wearing a starched khaki uniform with the crossed anchors of a warrant boatswain on his collars. "All right, sailor," he said. "On your feet and salute, you lousy bastard."

It turned out some officer with whom he had served a long time go remembered Honk and put him up for warrant boatswain. Honk hadn't known anything about it until his orders caught up with him in Nouméa. I was happy for him. I never knew a man better qualified. But, goddamn, it was going to be lonesome without him. He and I had been the last of the little family the Flag had become in the *Indianapolis*. We covered up the emotion I think we both felt with profanity and a refusal to be serious. Nothing lasts forever. Not even Honk, who would become a flight deck officer in the escort carrier *Liscombe Bay*—and die in her when she blew up and sank off Tarawa.

Not long afterward I saw a strange little fleet of four small ships coming up from the south. The leader looked like an excursion boat of some kind, except that it had a deep well deck forward and unusually heavy lifting tackle for so small a vessel. The other three were proper warships, though small. They were built with the square, boxy lines characteristic of British ships, and they flew the Royal Navy's white ensign.

I looked up their signal numbers in the French signal book and reported them as the converted New Zealand buoy tender *Matai* and three New Zealand corvettes: *Moa*, *Kiwi*, and *Tui*. All were named for New Zealand birds, I would learn later, except for the *Matai*, which was named for a kind of tree.

I watched the unfamiliar fleet make its way to an anchorage but paid them little further attention. The South Pacific was full then of strange ships. It did not occur to me that these four would have any significance for me at all. But they did.

13
HMNZS *Moa* at Guadalcanal

WITHIN TWO HOURS OF THE TIME the little New Zealand ships anchored in Nouméa, an American ensign named Thatcher skidded his jeep to a stop at the open entry door of the French signal tower overlooking the town. Again, I was sitting on the stone sill of the door not doing much more than watching the shadow of the French flag flop from one side of my feet to the other. It was very much a replay of Honk's final visit. I spent a lot of time watching that flag's shadow in those days, as I remember it now.

"Come on, Flags," the ensign said. "Let's go for a boat ride."

"I got the watch," I said without much enthusiasm. I had been on boat rides before.

I suspect the ensign had been promoted from the ranks. He looked older than the usual college boy found in the rank in those days. "Forget the goddamned watch," he said. "Get in."

On the way down the hill he explained that the four New Zealand ships I had just logged in were on their way to the Solomons. They were going to need American signalmen if they meant to operate with American ships. One American signalman was to be placed in each of them. Then he told me I had just volunteered.

I was used to that kind of volunteering, and I didn't argue the point. It didn't make a hell of a lot of difference to me. Since Honk was gone I didn't much give a damn where I went. As it happened, it was some of the most interesting duty I ever pulled.

We stopped at the schoolhouse only long enough to pick up my gear. I didn't have much to pick up. The seabag I had lost in the *Lexington* had been only partially replaced. I had no blues at all.

By then it was late afternoon. A jeep came with three other signalmen, and we nodded glumly to each other. "You volunteered too?" one said to me. None of them had much more gear than I did. I guess they were all survivors from sunken or damaged ships. We didn't discuss it. That didn't make a hell of a lot of difference either.

A *Matai* boat took us off. The ensign went with us. He would stay in the *Matai* and be in charge of our group. Although each of us would be subject to the orders of the commanding officers of our individual ships, we would still be in the American Navy and would answer to the ensign in matters of administration.

Since it was late, we all spent the night in the *Matai*, sleeping on folding cots the New Zealanders called camp stretchers. The next morning, after an exotic breakfast of dried fish and big mugs of tea—tea!—dimmed to a light shade of tan by condensed milk, we were assigned to our ships. I drew the *Moa*. A *Matai* boat delivered me to her at once.

Naturally my arrival in the little New Zealand ship stirred a good deal of curiosity—on both sides. The ship seemed stark and austere by American Navy standards. No cooled drinking water, for one thing, and one rudimentary washroom about the size of those found in Pullman cars in the States. There was a bathtub, I discovered, but it was officer gear and not for the likes of me. There was a lot more wood than in American ships too. The mess table of heavy wood was fixed permanently to the deck. The ladder going up to the weather decks was wood too. So were the berths.

My bunk in the *Moa* was a deep, coffinlike wooden box. It was fixed athwartship against the after bulkhead in what the British called their berth deck. That was bad because, when the little ship rolled, I was alternately feet or head down. It is much better to have bunks aligned fore and aft in a ship.

I was just as strange to the New Zealanders as they were to me, I suppose. They were particularly fascinated with the quality of the cloth in my uniforms, just as I had been on being outfitted when fresh from Depression-era Oklahoma. They stood about and watched with great interest as I unpacked and stowed my gear. They were more reserved than would have been a similar group of American sailors, but their friendship seemed real and we soon got on well enough. I was especially lucky in the *Moa* to find Jack Salter as the ship's leading signalman. He was a good man. We became friends and would meet again, fifty years on, at his home in Dunedin.

Lt. Cdr. Peter Phipps was commanding officer of the *Moa*. He was a short man—as were all the New Zealanders except Jack Salter—with a crisp Royal Navy manner. He had already served in escorts against the Germans in the English Channel during the early days of the war and had—in the American vernacular—been around. After the war he would rise to vice admiral and serve as New Zealand's first chief of naval staff. He would also win the American Navy Cross and be knighted by a grateful queen for his services. My wife and I would meet him fifty years later in his small, trophy-laden retirement flat in Picton, New Zealand.

We sailed the next morning and set our course north. The corvettes were powered with triple expansion reciprocating steam engines, which, though they were extremely dependable, were distressingly slow when it is considered that we were headed for waters in which Japanese cruisers and destroyers were capable of thirty to thirty-five knots. "We can do perhaps twelve knots," Captain Phipps said while briefing me on the little ship, "provided all the chaps will but dangle their feet over the stern and kick like mad."

The little ships were armed with single 4-inch bag guns on circular platforms forward. In bag guns, shells and powder were loaded separately, just as in our big 8- and 16-inch guns. It is a slow means of doing things and should not be necessary in guns so small. Shells, well rusted and completely exposed to weather, were stuck nose first into holes in a raised flange around the gun platform. That kept them ready-to-hand for loaders, but anything made of steel rusts beautifully in salty air. Especially so in tropical salty air.

Powder was kept in a closed, though not very substantial, locker. The whole thing looked a bit vulnerable to me. There were depth charges aft, both in racks and K-gun throwers. A couple of Hotchkiss .30-caliber machine guns were back there as well on mounts welded to the bulwarks. These were not all that formidable since their metal clips held only a couple dozen rounds and were spent in a sudden spurt of fire lasting not much longer than a respectable burp.

Twin mounts of World War I Lewis machine guns in each bridge wing were more practical. This was the machine gun I fired in boot camp, but these were pedestal mounted at shoulder height. Air-cooled and fed from round pancake magazines on top of the breech mechanism, they could be fired against either surface or aerial targets. More important, as I would later come to appreciate, they were mounted behind stout steel shields.

That completed our offensive armament, but the *Moa* had one good defensive arrangement I never saw in our Navy. In each bridge wing, there was a vertical shield of two steel plates fitted at right angles to each other, forming four secure niches into which men could duck away from strafing planes no matter the direction they came from. I thought that was nice.

Steaming to the north at our stately cruising speed of ten knots or so, we set off to strike terror into the hearts of the Japanese. The *Matai*, looking more than ever the excursion boat when seen from astern, led. I could only hope that the Japanese navy would be no more impressed with us than I was and would, thus, not be likely to waste much in the way of bombs and torpedoes on us. This hope, in the event, proved dramatically lacking.

As the only American on board, I was not entirely comfortable all the time. One time I remember was the second or third night of our passage north. I was summoned to the *Moa*'s stuffy little wardroom. Captain Phipps introduced me to all the ship's officers and explained in front of them that he wanted my stay with them to be as pleasant for me as he was sure it would be for them. It was a graceful little speech, but I got the impression that the subject of the Yank signalman had come up in after-dinner conversation and it was decided to have a look at him. Some genuine interest was shown, but there were some loaded questions too and a good deal of amused smiling at my answers.

One interesting thing, for me, was to see officers on board a naval vessel with drinks in their hands and bottles standing ready on the cloth-covered table. An American did not expect to see anything like that in a Navy ship, but it was the British way at the time. Officers had wines and spirits in their wardroom mess.

Rum was carried for enlisted men—what the British call ratings. It was carried in heavy glass jugs of five gallons or so, protected by woven brown wicker covers against breakage. It was blood red. All Royal Navy spirits, I was told, were dyed as a preventive against unauthorized sale on black markets. The Scotch I saw that night in the *Moa*'s wardroom, for instance, was a bright yellow.

Each morning, at around eleven o'clock or so, the coxswain piped up spirits, and the hands gathered in the mess around an oaken tub whose brass rings were inscribed with a toast to the king. The coxswain in a Royal Navy ship, so far as I could tell, has no counterpart in the American Navy. Chief master at arms would probably come closest. He was a senior petty officer who seemed to be responsible for many different things. Serving out the daily tot of rum was one of those things.

A copper dipper with a wooden handle was used for the purpose. It was called a tot and held about the equivalent of a double shot glass in a Honolulu sailors' bar. As a guest in the ship, I was graciously offered my tot, which I refused with equal grace, since I was not then a drinking man. If the ship's own men—in keeping with the Royal Navy custom they called themselves Moas—refused their tots, they were called TTs—for teetotaler—and had a small sum of money added to their pay in lieu.

In a variation of the ancient custom, the tots were served neat in the *Moa*. In proper Royal Navy ships, I was told, the rum was watered to make what was known as grog. This was done so that the hands could not save up their tots until they had enough to get seriously drunk. In the *Moa* no water was added for reasons of economics, I learned. In the Solomons at that time, anything alcoholic—even the fluid from torpedoes and our compass bowls—enjoyed a crazy seller's market. All a Moa had to do was pour his daily tot into anything that wouldn't leak and take it ashore on Guadalcanal for sale to the Yanks. He could name his own price.

We stopped only once on our way north—at Espiritu Santo, a then-French island that would be the last friendly base we would see before Guadalcanal itself. The harbor was beautiful, with green offshore islands and equally green mountains inland with their heads smothered in gloomy clouds like those of the Koolaus behind Honolulu. Opaque white mists hung here and there in the mountain valleys like phlegm in the throats of tuberculars. An airfield already was operational, and there was a lot of construction activity. There was little sign at all of any former structures that might have been there.

The harbor was as crowded as it was beautiful. Oilers. Transports. Store ships. Repair ships and tenders. Small craft buzzed about the larger ships in a scene of great and purposeful activity. The worn-looking combatants were there too, resting from the trials of farther north. The little New Zealand ships seemed hardly noticed in the general press. We did not stay long in any event. We paused long enough only to top off our bunker fuel. Ships moving north tried to go with tanks as full as possible to reduce demands on scarce supplies in the Solomons.

Once past Espiritu Santo, I felt again the old sense of being exposed. It is strange how an insignificant land mass, such as a small island group, can give an illusion of shelter—when you know damned well that it would not deter attacking ships and airplanes at all. But north of Espiritu Santo we all kept a little sharper watch on the horizon. We had no radar, you see, and radar is something to which sailors become quickly attached. You miss it terribly when it is no longer there.

We approached Guadalcanal from the southeast, coming up on the high island —some of its islands rise as high as eight thousand feet, we were told—early one morning. We could see the misty outline of Malaita far off on the starboard horizon and the low jungles of Florida Island rising over the bow beyond a scatter of islets and coral reefs that defined Lengo and Sealark channels, through which we had to pass.

Most of the surface actions off Guadalcanal took place in what later came to be called Ironbottom Sound for the number of sunken ships that came to lie on the seabed there. The area was bounded on the west by Guadalcanal itself, on the east by Florida and Tulagi islands, and to the north by Savo Island. The south was seemingly open, but cluttered with rocks and reefs, not all of which were properly charted.

Physically, it was a handsome body of water, clean and clear, except for floating debris left from the recurrent bloody battles of the past two or three months—

and the occasional brown snaking of fuel oil from sunken ships. Except for a gathering of landing craft and unloading transports and cargo ships off Lunga Point on Guadalcanal, and a patrolling F4F Wildcat or two, there was little to indicate a war was going on. Two or three miles west of Lunga the Japanese transports bombed by our planes in the recent big battle lay beached with their bows in the air. They were already rusting, but they looked peaceful enough. In looking at the bright, sunlit slopes of Guadalcanal itself, it was sobering to realize that the trees and high grasses hid armed and expert men who fervently wished me dead. The war seemed suddenly to have become a more personal affair than it had been in the carrier battles I had known. When we closed the landing beach to report our arrival we could see the awful clutter of war close up. The original landing on Guadalcanal had been unopposed, but the all but incessant bombing and shelling since had left their marks. The land was an area of coconut plantations, the tall trees planted in neat grid patterns, with ground cover beneath to hold down more rank native growths. There were thousands of the trees along the coastal plain, but few had escaped entirely the raking fingers of bomb and shell fragments or the shattering impact of direct hits.

One of the most remarkable things we saw upon closer approach was the mass of telephone wires strung in what was left of the trees. It looked like some great spiderweb and must have consisted of miles of copper wire. Wrecked landing craft littered the beach, as wrecked guns, vehicles, and airplanes littered the lands farther inland. Men, like feral animals fearing the light, had dug into the wet ground everywhere. Equally omnipresent, great mounds and piles of supplies rose as monuments to the waste of war. I remember one huge pile of Marine sand shoes—the ones with smooth side in, rough side out. They had simply been dumped on the ground, to wait for the first tropical rain to ruin them with wet and mildew. If a man wanted shoes, he found his size and helped himself.

We quickly learned that, though we controlled the sea around and the skies above Guadalcanal in the daytime, the Japanese controlled them at night. Cruisers and destroyers still came down from time to time—in what came to be called the Tokyo Express—and bombarded Henderson Field while trying at the same time to succor their own troops on the island.

When darkness came, everything stopped on the landing beaches. Airplanes were parked where they would be thought safest. The ships off Lunga either pulled out for sea or took refuge in Tulagi Harbor some twenty miles away. That was our first assignment in the *Moa*. As a matter of fact, shepherding cargo ships across to Tulagi was an exercise that would become routine for us. We would screen the landing beaches all day against enemy submarines, and then, as darkness came, we would escort the ships to Tulagi against the threat of Japanese cruisers and destroyers, which came in the night. Then, with the return of the sun, we would take them back to Lunga the next day.

But we in the *Moa* spent our first day in the Solomons simply nosing about to become familiar with the place. One place we nosed into was a narrow riverlike channel that split Florida Island into two parts. We followed its narrow passages all the way through to the east side of the island and returned by way of Sandfly Passage to the north.

That night, when we did enter Tulagi Harbor, we found it strewn with the wreckage of what had been, before the war, the capital of the Solomons. The flimsy wooden buildings of Chinese stores along the waterfront were flattened. The Burns Philp trading store—one of a chain with stores on virtually every island in the South Pacific—was on a small island in the harbor and had suffered less. A downed PBY lay half awash on the foreshore, one wing lifted high toward the sky that had failed it.

As it does throughout the world's tropical zones, darkness came quickly that night. And with it, shadows crept out from shoreside trees, creating an illusion of shrinking the width of the channel. Unbroken blackness covered everything, and a silence grew so profound we could hear the voices of men in casual conversation as they used the privies built on stilts over the water.

An ominous note was struck when we heard the PT (patrol torpedo) boats moving out on their nightly patrols. They would hide under overhanging trees in the Maliali River during the day, taking what comfort they could from their tender, the *Niagara*, a converted yacht that once had belonged to a famous millionaire. Painted as black as the night itself, the PTs moved out slowly, their engines muttering through silencers, their presence felt more than seen. Sometime after they were past, we would hear the little waves of their wakes slap against our hull. Then nothing until morning—unless it was the distant rumble and flash of guns during the night to tell that they had found work.

A lighter note early that night was a message from the Tulagi signal tower as we came in. The tower was a rickety structure of scrap lumber with a thatched sunshade over its platform. There was light enough for us to see the green flag flying from a small central mast—a signal that all was clear for the moment. A red flag would have meant an air raid was imminent. A black flag would have warned of an expected enemy landing. We would see the black flag only once during our time in the Solomons. The message from the tower invited us ashore for movies, an invitation we quickly accepted, with proper British courtesy.

The theater was open air, of course, with seating on improvised wooden benches set out on a cricket pitch on the island's north side. Tulagi had been a

British colonial capital before the war. The theater was reached through a narrow defile cut through the rocky spine of the island. It obviously had been cut by hand. The amount of labor needed for the job must have been impressive—especially in that climate.

We were the first British ships to show themselves inshore, and as such we attracted a good deal of attention. I, as the only American in the *Moa* crowd, attracted some as well. The picture that night—I remember it still—was *This Above All*, with Tyrone Power and Joan Fontaine.

The next morning we got at once into our assigned routine. Each ship would spend five days under way, then enjoy two days off—just like in the unions, although we were not paid overtime when we were stuck with extra duty. The first of our days off was usually spent in fueling, watering from the *Niagara*, or doing those bits of repair and maintenance we could not do while under way. The second day, however, was free for what, in a later war, would be called R&R.

The British, in my experience, were notably more casual about the war than the Americans were. They had been at it longer than we had for one thing, I suppose. They didn't make nearly as much fuss about formal discipline or—most especially—uniforms and haircuts as we did—sometimes to their significant cost.

I remember the picnics the *Moa* men used to have on their free day. The Americans held then only a relatively small perimeter around Henderson Field and the landing beaches on Guadalcanal. The rest of the big island was open to the Japanese wherever they wanted to go. But the crazy Moas would put something together for a lunch, man their clumsy wooden lapstrake boat, and go for what they called "a run ashore." Completely unarmed, as I recall, they foraged the abandoned plantations for limes, lemons, and wild pineapples. Had they bumped into a Japanese patrol, the lot of them would have been killed.

"Come on, Yank," they would call to me. "Let's have a go." But I almost always had something urgent that wanted doing on board.

That is what our life became: screening the landing beaches all day, herding the ships to shelter for the night in Tulagi, plodding the rest of the night on some boring antisubmarine patrol station, and returning at dawn to take the ships back to Guadalcanal. Even danger, it seemed, can become boring if long enough experienced.

Sometimes we did draw unusual and interesting assignments. Once we were sent to the out island of Malaita to pick up contract labor for the airfields on Guadalcanal. I learned later that prewar planters in the Solomons prized Malaita boys over other islanders because they were believed to be better workers than other islanders. They were reputed to be more fractious, though, and harder to handle.

We didn't have any trouble with the Malaitans we picked up. We lay to in a narrow bay at the mouth of a river where high cliffs came to the water's edge and even higher trees shaded the beach. The scene was like those old prints of Captain Cook's landings, when his *Endeavor* would be the center of a mass of canoes, and the foreshore crowded with curious natives.

Solomon Island canoes of that time were narrow dugouts made of some dark wood. Their sterns were built high and finished with carved fetishes, usually with inlaid mother-of-pearl picking out details of eyes and teeth. The workmanship was surprisingly good. Paddles were long, pointed, and spearlike.

Brassieres, of course, were unheard of, and we marveled at the islanders' pendant breasts. It was entirely possible for a woman to sit in a canoe and get wet, port and starboard at the same time, unless she took care to see that all was properly tucked inboard.

We must have taken two hundred men aboard. They were short, coarse-featured Melanesians with great masses of hair and betel-stained mouths. Each man carried a rolled grass mat for sleeping and a small cloth bag for his personal gear. A hollow section of bamboo, stuck into his waistband, held the lime and nut used in the betel ritual. That waistband, incidentally, holding a small sack of the man's most private parts was all he wore.

Curious, the islanders were soon all over the ship, peeking, prying, and grinning wide grins when they were caught doing something they shouldn't. It was several days after we landed them on Guadalcanal before the smell of them was entirely out of the ship. It was not an unpleasant smell—something like that of sheep or goats made wet by a rain.

I don't know what the legalities involved in securing native labor might have been. The South Seas have a lurid history of exploiting native labor for white men's mines and plantations. On this recruiting mission, for instance, we had a British civilian embarked who must have held some colonial post in the islands before the war. He was a very thin man, dressed always in starched and spotless uniform, and he held himself with a stiff dignity. He had a small launch I saw sometimes in Tulagi. It was fitted with a white sun awning and was manned by islanders in white lap-laps and bare feet. The Moas called him the "Jolly Old Majuh" and seemed to regard him with some amusement. The Jolly Old Major handled whatever needed handling, and we delivered the Malaitans to Guadalcanal, where they built airfields for us.

Another time, we were told off to tow a captured Japanese landing barge—the kind with high twin prows—out to the Russell Islands, some twenty-five miles beyond Guadalcanal. The barge was to carry a reconnaissance party of Fijian soldiers under command of a New Zealand army officer. This party was to be put ashore for several days for a thorough study of the Russells. The captured barge was used against the possibility of its being spotted by the Japanese. It was felt they would be less suspicious if they found one of their own barges pulled up on a beach than they would be if they saw one of ours. No one seemed bothered by the possibility that the Japanese might decide to take the found barge and use it themselves, leaving the poor Fijians marooned on an island with what might be a whole lot of Japanese soldiers.

We carried the Fijians in the *Moa* until close off the Russells and fed them a meal before casting them off in their Japanese barge. They were much bigger men than the local Melanesians and were reputed to be very good fighters. Their sergeant was an especially imposing man. Fortunately, he was also good-natured. He showed me a snapshot of his girlfriend in Suva. Unless the camera lied, she was easily as big as he was. From the looks of her, it would have been an interesting exercise in judgment to determine which of them would be the deadlier in a fight.

This night also brought Lukey into a new light on board. As was the British custom, we had taken two Solomon islanders on board to do the laundry and other menial chores. Ours were named Lukey and Benny. Benny proved fickle in that one day, during a torpedo plane attack on ships off the landing beaches, he thought of something to do ashore and dived over the side to see to it. Lukey, however, proved a brick and helped pilot us into the Russells that night. He had served in mission schooners and knew the waters.

I could not see how knowing the waters would help much when the night was so black we could not see the ship's bow from the bridge. But Lukey did the job. He stood quietly in the bridge wing, pointed this way and that, and gave his muted verbal directions as suggestions. Lukey knew his place; he knew that the next day he would be back with his laundry buckets. But with his help, we got in and out again without being spotted or going aground. It was as remarkable a show of seamanship as I ever saw.

Another interesting aspect of this little show was that there was an American intelligence officer along with the Fijians. Captain Phipps told me, with some excitement, the man was Gene Markey, a name that meant nothing to me until one of the Moas told me he had been a one-time husband of Hedy Lamarr. In bringing the *Moa* out from Scotland, Captain Phipps had called at the U.S. West Coast. He had been entertained at the Hollywood Canteen in California, where he met some Hollywood stars. He was left with a lively interest in anything having to do with American movies and was openly thrilled at having Markey aboard.

Aside from escapades like these, our duties became monotonous after a time. All day we would plod about off the landing beaches with the tiresome pinging of our sonar gear marking the time. The British called their sound gear Asdic, but I was told it was the same mechanism in both navies. In the late afternoon we would move the ships to Tulagi, then move out on whatever patrol station we were assigned for the night.

Sometimes we stayed in Tulagi Harbor. One night when we were there the destroyer *Grayson* came in and anchored not far away. I knew that Mister Bell, our Flag lieutenant in the *Indianapolis* before the war, had been her commanding officer. I borrowed the *Moa*'s punt—a small, squarish boat ships carry for working along the waterline in harbor—and sculled over to see if he still might be. I was lonesome for the sound of American voices, I suppose. The *Indianapolis*, and the men I had known in her, held a warm place in my heart. It seemed a long time ago that I had been in her.

As it happened Mister Bell was still in the *Grayson*. He saw me in his cabin and gave me a glass of cold orange juice. I was wearing ragged shorts and Marine sand shoes from the pile on Guadalcanal—and nothing else. It was presumptuous of me even to be there in the first place, but we talked easily for a few minutes about Sandy, Honk, Hawghead, and the other guys from the old Flag. I was not asked to sit down, but it was nice.

I often wondered later who the *Grayson*'s officer of the deck had thought the hairy, nearly naked stranger who called on his captain that night might have been. I did gain a bit of status in the *Moa*, though, when it was found I had called upon—and been entertained by—a destroyer captain.

The strong efforts of the Japanese to retake Guadalcanal had largely ended by that time, but their destroyers sometimes ran in under cover of darkness to throw over steel drums of rice and dried fish, which their troops would try to retrieve in small boats from the shore. It was a desperation tactic, but it was just as well we never ran into any of those speeding destroyers. They would have made short work of us.

When morning came we would steam among the floating drums and sink them with machine-gun fire. In the early days on the island, our Marines had eaten captured Japanese food, but by that time they had more than enough rations of their own. It must have been galling for the starving Japanese soldiers onshore to watch us deliberately destroy food they so desperately needed. But they never shot at us. I suppose they were afraid of return fire.

There was a road running along that part of the island shore, just inside the first rows of palms. Sometimes we could see Japanese soldiers, singly or in small groups, walking that road. And, sometimes, Captain Phipps would fire a round or two from our 4-incher at them. There was not much chance we would hit them, but it livened the day and showed how far along the road to savagery we had come to find entertainment in shooting at human beings.

Fleet destroyers, while waiting for their convoys to unload, would often do the same thing. They would steam slowly along the enemy coast and shoot at whatever caught their attention. The Japanese could not have led a very restful life those last few weeks of their occupation of Guadalcanal.

Then, too, there were accidents to brighten our days. I remember one time a PBY, in circling to land off the beach, banked too steeply and dug in a wing tip float. The big airplane cartwheeled violently in a great burst of white water and was torn in two just abaft its wing pylon. Our lifeboat was an old wooden pulling boat—meaning it was powered by oars—but we were closest to the scene and got there in time to retrieve the only man still afloat. He was still conscious and spoke to us. But, as we pulled him up across the boat's gunwale, we saw he was cut virtually in half. He was kept together only by his spine and his loin muscles. He died in the boat.

The nights were the scary times. There was always the chance that Japanese cruisers and destroyers might come down the slot and catch us. "The slot" was our name for a water route between islands of the Northern Solomons that the Japanese used for their surface runs against Guadalcanal. But, even when they did not appear, there was almost every night the dull red winking of antiaircraft bursts over Henderson Field.

The muzzle flashes of the guns made little lightning storms in the trees, throwing tons of shells high into the night sky—and, since almost everything that goes up is likely to come down, we tended to keep under cover when the antiaircraft guys were shooting. Often we could hear the little splutz of shell fragments hitting the water around us. Once in a while, there would be a loud clang as a fragment hit a steel deck somewhere.

These were not serious raids. The Japanese were just trying to keep the guys on the island from getting any sleep. There almost always was an enemy airplane over us at night—we called him Washing Machine Charlie for the tinny sound of his engine. Every now and then, he would drop a bomb. You never knew when it was coming. It was unsettling at first.

We in the little New Zealand ships had been in the Solomons more than two months before we got our tails caught in anything serious. The situation on Guadalcanal by that time had stabilized pretty well. Reinforcements and supplies were coming in greater and greater quantities. The Allies would win the island unless the Japanese made a major effort, and they showed little sign of doing that. The Japanese soldiers already on the island, by all indications, were in hard rows, but they showed little sign of giving up.

As a part of our efforts to keep the enemy deprived, the *Moa* and the *Kiwi* were assigned one night toward the end of January to a patrol station in Kamimbo Bay, just beyond Cape Esperance, to prevent landings there. Kamimbo was the closest sheltered water on Guadalcanal to the Russells, and we knew reinforcements and supplies had been landed there before from armed barges. In daylight, it was a pretty little bay, flanked by high green mountains and grassy slopes, but at night it became a dark and menacing place that belonged to the enemy.

That patrol started off much as had so many patrols before. It was not until about ten o'clock that anything out of the ordinary occurred. The *Kiwi* made a sound contact and depth charged to the surface a big Japanese submarine that had a large gun on its deck. What was either a very lucky or a very skillful round from the *Kiwi*'s 4-incher set something afire on the submarine's deck. A lively dance began in the dark and limited waters of Kamimbo Bay.

The *Kiwi*'s essential task was twofold. The submarine had that very large 5- or 6-inch gun on its deck. It was desirable, from the *Kiwi*'s point of view, that that gun not be allowed to fire. She therefore used her machine guns to sweep away the Japanese sailors who swarmed out on deck to man it. The range was that close.

The *Kiwi*'s second essential task was to prevent the submarine from lining her up for a torpedo shot. Round and round they went in the narrow waters, the *Kiwi* banging away as fast as she could with her 4-incher and rattling machine-gun fire off the submarine to keep her sailors under cover. The range was very close at times, which, oddly, made hitting the submarine difficult. Either the *Kiwi*'s rounds streaked harmlessly over the sub's low freeboard or they hit short and ricocheted away equally ineffectively. Muzzle flashes of the *Kiwi*'s gun blinded her gunners between rounds.

We in the *Moa* were interested spectators to all this, but we could not fire for fear of hitting the *Kiwi*. All we could see of her were the flashes of her guns, and she was very close to the submarine. We did fire star shells to illuminate the target and acted as Asdic vessel for the *Kiwi*, but we did not get seriously into the act until after Captain Bridson in the *Kiwi* announced by voice radio that he intended to ram.

He did too. But the result was other than planned. Damage to the *Kiwi*, as rammer, proved to be greater than that to the submarine as rammee. After a moment or two of silence, Captain Bridson rather sheepishly announced that he was retiring. He asked us to take over, and we did.

Fortunately, the fire continued to burn on the submarine's deck. It was the only aiming point we had. But we proved no more successful in hitting the damned thing than the *Kiwi* had been. It circled round and round. Either it had suffered a steering casualty or it was trying desperately to line us up for a torpedo shot.

Then, to our horror, the fire on the submarine began to die. Without that blessed fire, we would not be able to see the submarine at all. We fired faster and faster but did no apparent damage at all.

I don't know now how long that little party went on, but I do remember the near panic I felt when the fire on the submarine went out entirely. There we were, penned in what was a small bay, with a crippled but obviously still dangerous enemy who, owing to our higher silhouette, could see us a good deal better than we could see him. We were blind except for what our Asdic operator could tell us—which was not much under the circumstances.

It made for a long night. We never found the submarine again and were bitterly disappointed at having to accept the fact that it had apparently escaped. Our only consolation was that it had not found us either, at least not well enough to get off a torpedo.

But, when daylight came, we found the enemy submarine hung up on an inshore reef, its bows thrust so high into the air that we could see its diving planes. It was obviously dead, but we put in a few rounds of 4 inch just for the hell of it—an exercise the American intelligence people who dived on the submarine did not appreciate for the unnecessary destruction of what might have been valuable materials in an already sunken enemy vessel.

The shores of the bay were ominously quiet and deserted as we scanned them through our glasses. We did see what appeared to be a scattered litter of discarded gear and supplies, but there was no sign of life at all. We came within machine-gun range, but no one shot at us. It was spooky. The shoreline at that point is dense jungle. We knew slitted black eyes were watching our every move, but we could see nothing. After poking about a bit, we pulled out to return to our daytime patrol station off the landing beaches.

On the way, near the mouth of Kamimbo Bay, we came upon what we took at first to be a floating coconut. The waters down there were full of floating coconuts. But this coconut sank beneath passing swells, reappearing in the troughs. Coconuts do not normally do that. In fact it was the head of the submarine's gunnery officer. He had machine-gun bullets through his right thigh, but he had remained afloat and alive for almost ten hours after being hit. He had been trying to get to his deck gun when either ours or the *Kiwi*'s machine-gun fire had knocked him off into the sea.

He was a large man for a Japanese—six feet or more tall—and unnaturally pale, probably from having been in the water so long. Submarine service is not conducive to tanning, either, I suppose. He spoke good English and asked for a knife so that he might do the honorable thing. But the New Zealanders wrapped him in blankets and laid him in the waist. When we reached Lunga, we turned him over to the American Marines. Whether that was an act of mercy or not was questionable at that time and place. I have often wondered since what happened to him. He went to Japan and became a Protestant preacher, I suppose.

From what this prisoner said and what American intelligence people found in the wrecked submarine, we learned the Japanese were evacuating Guadalcanal. What we and the *Kiwi* had been trying to stop that night was a rescue attempt, not the reinforcement we had thought: In a neat demonstration of the confusions of war, we had been fighting to keep the Japanese out of Kamimbo Bay, and they had been fighting to get out of Kamimbo Bay. Ah, war!

I don't remember that I ever saw the *Kiwi* again. She had gone off to have her damaged bow seen to. We were left to bask in our newfound glory alone. We were quite full of ourselves and with becoming modesty accepted the messaged congratulations pouring in from high authority, American and New Zealand alike.

The British at that time had a commendable practice called "splicing the main brace." It was an obsolete phrase from the time of sailing ships that had come to mean serving extra rum rations on celebratory occasions. Sinking a large Japanese submarine (its surface displacement tonnage was more than twice that of our two little corvettes' combined) was deemed such an occasion, not only was extra rum served, but the wardroom also sent round a number of bottles of Royal Navy Scotch to the mess deck. You have never seen a main brace spliced so well in your life.

Fortunately, we were excused our daytime duties and rode out an alcoholic day at anchor off Lunga. Officers and hands alike appreciated the day off and considered it well earned. So well earned, in fact, that we expected the coming night off as well. But, as evening shadows stretched out from shore, a picket boat brought us our orders. The *Tui* would replace the damaged *Kiwi*, and we would return to Kamimbo Bay. There was a good deal of resentment expressed, but off we went like good little soldiers.

That night, too, began evenly. We didn't expect much to happen after the previous night's fireworks. This was not the first mistaken estimate in the history of naval warfare.

The *Moa* was not that night in the top hole of readiness, I am afraid. Splicing main braces can be wearing work. As I recall now, only Captain Phipps, the helmsman—a TT—and I were on the bridge. Again, near ten o'clock, we were plodding along on our patrol station when we saw something. The night was, if anything, darker than the one before. We could not be certain of what we saw. We could not even be certain that we had seen anything. Finding and identifying the enemy in night surface actions was always touchy. We were especially nervous about the American PT boats operating out of Tulagi. They were forever straying off their assigned stations and messing things up. One of them even fired a torpedo one night at the *Kiwi*. It missed.

When we did become certain that something was out there on our starboard bow, Captain Phipps ordered me, in the absence of any more able gunner at the moment, to put a shot across its bows with our Lewis guns.

It turned out that "something" was Japanese armed barges mounting at least one 37-mm antitank gun behind rice bags filled with sand. The soldiers in the barges must have been lying doggo, hoping we would not see them—but with their rifles cocked and trained on us if we did. The instant I let go with the Lewis guns, they let go with what seemed like every rifle in the world. And their aiming point was my muzzle flashes. And, since my muzzle flashes were not far from where I was at the time, anything fired at them came extremely close to me. Things became very noisy for a time.

Momentarily blinded by the flashes of my own guns, I was instantly the center of a great deal of activity. Bullets stirred the air all about me and clanged against the gun shield that I was ever so glad was there. Bits of metal from shattering bullets and chips of paint sprayed whatever part of me they could reach. I would find odd bits for years after when, in the shower, I would discover they had worked their way free of my skin. I was especially bothered by one nasty splinter that pierced my left eyelid and pinned it to the eyeball under it. I could feel blood on my face, and became convinced that my blindness was owing to the scratch rather than to the muzzle flashes. That was a bad moment.

In the meantime, the Japanese got off a round from their 37-mm gun. The shell pierced our 4-incher's gun shield, caromed off the breech block, and passed through a charge of cordite in a loader's hands. The powder exploded, taking the entire gun crew out of action. The Japanese shell itself then exploded somewhere between the gun mount and the wheelhouse, splattering fragments everywhere.

In one brief violent spasm, we were effectively out of the action. One of the enemy barges actually bumped alongside us, giving rise to the alarming word that Japanese soldiers had managed to get on board of us. That was unsettling too. It would not be nice to run into armed soldiers about the dark decks.

Fortunately, this proved to be untrue, and silence fell again over Kamimbo Bay. The Japanese seemed content to leave things as they were. We saw no more of them, but we spent the remainder of the night pretty much on edge. The effects of main brace splicing were totally gone.

Strangely, my memory of this action is totally at odds with the official report, which credited me with silencing the fire of one of the barges. Like hell I did. After the violent reaction to my initial burst of fire, I fired no more. I was crouched, blinded and bleeding, behind the Lewis gun shield. Maybe that is why I didn't see the action described in the official report.

A PT boat came alongside to take off our wounded. The long bundles were handed across, and the PT boat took them at better speed than we could manage to medical help. It was quickly determined in the mess deck that my wounds were superficial—"multiple minor gunshot wounds" in the official report. Since I was his only contact with American ships, Captain Phipps asked me to remain on board. Afterward, those of us who were left felt much diminished and severely chastened. It had all happened so fast.

After that night, little else happened for some time. With the *Kiwi* gone off for repairs, we operated with three ships rather than four, but there were so many new ships arriving off Guadalcanal by that time, the *Kiwi*'s loss was hardly felt. The departure of the Japanese from Guadalcanal made for a much more relaxed attitude on the island. There were still occasional daytime air raids, and Washing Machine Charlie was a nightly caller. But on the whole Guadalcanal became a secure base for operations farther north. Destroyers and cruisers based there—in Purvis Bay on Florida Island—and no longer had to return each time to Espiritu Santo for fuel and replenishment. The place was settling down.

About the most exciting thing that happened in the *Moa* during that period was the crisis that arose when our rum stores ran low. A good deal of discontent was voiced until we received new supplies from New Zealand. It was a near thing there for a while.

Given my developed dread of the nights in the *Moa*, it was ironic that her most severe trial came in broad daylight. And while moored in Tulagi Harbor, which we had come to regard as a safe haven. It was in April, as I recall; we had been in the Solomons almost six months. It was one of our replenishment days. We had watered that morning from the PT tender *Niagara* in the Maliali River at the head of Tulagi Harbor and had just dropped back down the river to fuel. An old sailing ship hulk with its masts removed had been anchored in Tulagi and filled with fuel oil. Small ships operating there simply came alongside and helped themselves.

We had just moored alongside, and Captain Phipps had gone below to see to paperwork or other captain's chores. I was still on the bridge when I was summoned to his room. He told me that I had been promoted to chief petty officer for my heroism while crouched behind the Lewis gun shield in the action against armed barges. I knew better than that. After my first burst, I fired no more. I couldn't see anything. I protested, but Captain Phipps would hear nothing of it.

I don't remember being especially elated at the news of my promotion. Promotions were so readily available during the war they had lost much of their meaning. I knew damned well I had neither the experience nor the leadership qualities to be a good chief—but it would mean ninety-nine dollars a months, plus sea pay. That was acceptable. And living conditions would be significantly better in chiefs' quarters.

So, as a brand new slick-arm chief, I went below to get my head down while we fueled. (A "slick-arm chief" is one who is promoted before he has been in the Navy long enough to have a hash mark on his sleeve.) I had been on the bridge all the prior night. Nothing was likely to happen anyway. I had noticed the condition red flag flying from the Tulagi signal tower as I left the bridge, but, hell, it flew a lot of the time. I went to sleep readily.

The next thing I knew was the thumping bang of the Army's big 90-mm antiaircraft guns on the beach. That was not all that unusual either. They were long-range guns. Anything they were shooting at was likely to be pretty high and a long way off. I continued on with what New Zealanders call my stretchout.

But not for long. The 40s on the beach opened up next. I swung my feet over the side of my bunk. When the 20s began firing, I made a serious move for the ladder to topside. Anything 20-mm guns were shooting at would not be far away at all.

Our little .30-caliber guns may have opened fire as well, but I don't remember it if they did. The next thing I knew, the poor *Moa* jumped right out of the water and fell back, already sinking. The mess deck was murky with smoke and old dust and bits of broken things. Through the hatch leading below I could see water already swirling over the lower deck and men fighting to get clear of it and the wreckage holding them down.

The heavy wooden ladder leading from our mess deck to the forecastle deck— the only avenue of escape at all—was broken and blocking the hatch. We scrambled out as best we could. My inability to swim was much on my mind at the time. I had left my life jacket on the bridge. But as I fought my way clear of the hatch and stood erect on the forecastle deck, there it was lying at my feet. It had been blown off the bridge by the blast, I suppose, but I asked no damn fool questions. At the rate the ship was going down, there seemed little point in going to the bridge. I tied on my lifejacket and moved aft for a more convenient departure point.

Captain Phipps was struggling to launch the starboard boat. He was bleeding from a head wound and making heavy work of the job. I am not proud of the fact, but my mind was full just then of thoughts of all those depth charges we had on board. I didn't know if they had been put on safe or not. I did not stop to help the captain. All my life since, I have regretted that. My only excuse—and a feeble one—is that the ship was going down so fast, I thought there was not time enough to get the boat away.

Since our destroyer *Hammann* was lost at Midway, we in the U.S. Navy had been indoctrinated with the need to get away from any sinking ship with depth charges on board as fast and as far as we could. It was her depth charges that had killed so many of the *Hammann*'s men. The charges had exploded under survivors in the water. The concussion was deadly. That is probably why I didn't stop to help the captain.

At any rate, the water was about my ankles by the time I stepped off the *Moa*'s main deck. According to the official report, she went down in less than three minutes. The cozy print curtains at the open wardroom ports in her plump stern fluttered a last farewell as they were blown out by air trapped in the sinking ship.

Tulagi is a small harbor, and we were never far from help. But a couple of strafing Zeros gave us some interesting sensations for a moment as they lashed the water about us with machine-gun and cannon fire. I learned you can feel bullets hit water around you. The Zeros were the only two airplanes I saw during the entire affair. The bomber that had sunk us was long gone by the time I reached the deck. One of the strafing planes was hit and crashed into the jungled hills at the head of the harbor. It was a small comfort.

It was to be the last major air raid the Japanese would mount against the southern Solomons, but the fact would have been of little comfort to us even had we known. Boats came out from the beach to pick us out of the water and put us on an island in the harbor. I believe it was Bungana. It was the island with the wrecked Burns Philp trading store on it.

As it happened, the Japanese were gone and they didn't come back, but we didn't know that at the time. It was the only time I saw the black flag flying from a signal tower in the Solomons. The unharmed among us and the walking wounded were given rifles and placed in defensive positions along the shore against the possibility of a Japanese landing during the night. I earnestly hoped there would not be one. The smug sense of security we had come to feel in recent weeks was pretty well shattered. It was a very long night. I understood much better, in fact, why the Seabees had been so nervous in the *Enterprise*. I was nervous on the beach. I concluded danger must be easier to bear in familiar surroundings.

We were kept on Bungana until things settled down enough for us to be transferred by PT boat to Guadalcanal to await evacuation. Before we left, however, the *Matai* came in one day, and we all went aboard her for a memorial service to our dead. (Five men were killed in the *Moa*'s sinking.) American sailors from the beach brought out jungle flowers they had gathered for the occasion. I was proud of them for doing that. The New Zealanders were much affected.

Our more seriously wounded—including Captain Phipps—had already gone, so there was but a small party of us left when we reached Guadalcanal. We were assigned a bomb shelter back of Lunga Point and ate wherever we could find a chow line. The shelter was nothing but a hole in the ground with coconut logs placed over it and dirt piled on top. It was dark and spooky and spidery. When bombs fell anywhere near, dirt was jarred down between the logs and muddied our sweating bodies. It was not pleasant.

Admiral Fitch, my old admiral in the *Lexington*, was commander of aircraft in the Solomon Islands (ComAirSols). He was well settled into a neat grouping of rounded Quonset huts joined by crushed shell walks and the beginnings of flower beds. I went there once, but no one was left of the Flag I had known.

We were several days on Guadalcanal before space was found for us in an R3D, the Navy's version of the famous DC3. There were about enough of us to make a good load, especially since a large part of the cabin was taken up by a huge auxiliary fuel tank made necessary by the long miles between Pacific destinations. The pilot had us jam ourselves as far forward as possible so that he could get his tail up and thereby build more quickly to flying speed.

Even so, we went off the seaward end of the runway alarmingly low and climbed out painfully slowly. This was my first ride in a big airplane, but my only concern was a sudden panicky fear that a stray Zero might come upon us. The plane's cabin windows were fitted with little rubber-stoppered ports, which, we were told by playful crewmen, were for firing through with rifles. That implied there might be something to shoot at. And, if there was something to shoot at, there was a very good chance that it might shoot back. I didn't relax until we were a hundred or so miles on our way and could no longer see Guadalcanal.

We made a brief fueling stop in Espiritu Santos before droning on to New Caledonia, where we landed at Tontouta, a rough tree-lined grass strip several miles from Nouméa. The most striking thing I remember about Tontouta is watching four or five Army P40s crash while landing. They had been brought offshore in a delivery carrier and had flown off to land ashore. P40s have a narrow landing gear. The rough field was hard on them. One after another of them hit, bounced, bounced again, and caromed off into the surrounding trees. I don't think any of the pilots were seriously injured, but I could not help thinking again about the terrible waste of war. All the time and materials gone into building those airplanes. All the trouble and hazard of getting them so far—and they broke themselves up without ever firing a useful shot.

The New Zealanders continued on in the same airplane to their homes, and I was left alone in a strange land. A Navy sailor, administratively, exists as three paper records. His service record lists promotions, ships, and any commendations or punishments. His health record lists illnesses, wounds, treatments, and the like. His pay record lists the moneys due him. Without these records a sailor does not exist officially. And I had none of them. Nor did I have any other form of identification, other than the two metal dog tags hung on a chain about my neck. I wore ragged shorts and a pair of Marine sand shoes still stiff from the saltwater of the *Moa*'s sinking. I could have disappeared at that moment into the mountains of New Caledonia and no one would ever have known what happened to me.

But that was a passing fancy. I hitched a ride to Nouméa and turned myself in to an office on the waterfront. I never saw my New Zealander shipmates again— other than Captain Phipps and Jack Salter, whom I saw on holiday visits to New Zealand some fifty years later.

14
Home Front

NOUMÉA HAD CHANGED DRAMATICALLY since I had last been there. The central part of the town was not all that much altered: the market, the *place*, the cathedral, the *hôtel de ville*, the school where Honk and I had bivouacked before. But harbor facilities, roads, and public services had all been improved. Whole towns of Quonset huts and other prefabricated structures had spread out into the surrounding countryside. Admiral Halsey's headquarters themselves made up what looked like a whole new village. Clearly, the Seabees had been busy.

The Melanesians, Javanese, and Tonkinese seemed to be having a fine time, though the French seemed more surly than ever. They drove their funny looking Peugeots and Citröens, fitted with big charcoal burners in back, with an air of disdain. They would not so much as acknowledge our existence. We must have been a trial for them, though they did deign to make and sell to us something we called Butterfly Brandy. It was villainous stuff and left some men blind.

The big, red-faced Frenchman who gave me a ride in from Tontouta was friendly enough, though, and dropped me off at the landing where I could get a boat out to the *Argonne*, where I assumed my records would be. That was the last ship to which I had been formally ordered.

I felt naked there on the dock. Dressed in ragged shorts and Marine sand shoes—and nothing else—the metal dog tags hanging from a chain about my neck were the only identification I had. As I mentioned earlier, every Navy sailor had three paper records that went with him through his naval life. I had none of them.

As it happened, a chief yeoman in the *Argonne* (yeomen are the Navy's doers of paperwork and keepers of records) established who I was and reintroduced me into the American Navy. He even got me some clean dungarees and underwear—one suit. He also got me a passage in the SS *Tabinta*, a Dutch merchant ship bound for San Francisco, a fact for which I would later retract a good deal of my gratitude to him.

The *Tabinta* was a larger than average freighter of, I believe, the Java Far East Line. She was clean and had a long superstructure, suggesting a large number of nice comfortable passenger cabins. This turned out to be true, but if I had had any illusions of getting my ass into one of them, I was badly mistaken—and soon set straight.

There were about fifteen or twenty of us, as I recall: soldiers, sailors, and Marines—all of whom had, in one way or another, become lost from our units. Casuals—as we were called—were handled fairly informally in the South Pacific in those days. We were simply scooped up without regard to service or enlisted rank and put in the first ship or plane headed for the States, where we would be reassigned to something useful. We wore whatever rags and remnants of uniforms we stood up in. In fact, I was dressed better than the others since I did have that one suit of clean dungarees—but the poor *Moa*'s fuel oil was still black under my nails and in my nose and ears.

The *Tabinta* was officered by Dutchmen—pink-faced, well-fed men in starched whites—but the crew was entirely Javanese, and thank God for that. I don't know what was eating the Dutch officers, but they did not like their ragged passengers in any way that showed. Instead of the empty passenger cabins, we were herded into a cargo hold where we slept without bunks or bedding, making do with whatever dunnage from old cargoes we could find. God forbid we be allowed to eat in the crew's mess, much less the officers' hallowed spaces. We ate on deck, from dishes brought to us by the Javanese. From all indications, the Dutchmen regarded us as nuisances, although someone was probably being damned well paid for our passages.

I never understood the Dutchmen's open animosity toward us. We were supposed to be on the same side in the war, for Christ's sake. Maybe it had something to do with their loss of the Dutch East Indies. I knew there had been recriminations at the time of the Japanese conquest of the Dutch East Indies by some who thought the United States had not done enough to prevent it. Maybe that was what was bothering the *Tabinta*'s officers, and they were taking out their spite on us.

We took whatever comfort we could from the fact that the passage would not last forever—although sometimes it seemed that it might do just that. The *Tabinta* was empty and riding high. Except for lying to for a few minutes off Nuku'alofa to pick up mail from boats sent out from the beach, we steamed without pause or hindrance for thirty-two days. Without escort, without even seeing another ship the entire way, we plodded across the empty ocean with our half-exposed propeller thumping comfortably astern like a dog's tail on thick carpet.

It was interesting to see Nuku'alofa again however briefly. As you may remember, that is where we had come to sort things out after the Coral Sea battle. That time the anchorage had been full of scarred and burned ships, with small boats dashing about among them. From the *Tabinta*, the island was what a South Seas island should be, clean and serene and totally detached from a war that already had passed it by. I felt a great urge to get the hell off the Dutch freighter and sit out the rest of the war right there. But I didn't, and we sailed on.

I guess it is fortunate I remember so little about the passage in the *Tabinta*. It would just make me feel worse if I remembered more. The next thing I recall clearly was our arrival off the California coast and the weather turning cold. It was then late May or early June, but as sailors can tell you, the California coast can be cold at any time of the year. Especially so to men who have been long in the tropics—and who are wearing nothing but shorts or thin dungarees. There was no heat in the hold. We suffered from the cold especially at night, when, without blankets or cover of any kind, we huddled in the great empty space. We generated a little heat by cussing the Dutchmen, but it was not nearly enough.

In the end, we did get to San Francisco. We tied up to a pier under the West Tower of the San Francisco–Oakland Bay Bridge—and saw the biggest craps game I ever saw in my life. There must have been thirty or forty men shooting dice on the water end of the pier where they could not be seen from shoreside. We supposed they were drawing union wages.

A Navy tugboat from Goat Island (the Navy's name for what people now call Yerba Buena) came and took the sailors and Marines of us to the small base on the island's east side. I don't know what happened to the soldiers. I was so glad to be free of the *Tabinta* I didn't ask any questions.

Everything was closed at the little base—it is a Coast Guard base now. We climbed up onto the dock, not sure where we were or what the hell we were supposed to do. The tug was no help. Once he had us ashore he took off, with a roar of diesel engines, for somewhere else. It was becoming dark, and we were getting cold all over again. I had just about decided to march us over to Treasure Island, where the World's Fair had been when we anchored off in the *Indianapolis* to load battleship ammunition what then seemed a very long time ago. I could see light and activity across the little bay, which once had been a base for Pan American's China Clipper flying boats. But, before we were well started, a four-stripe Navy captain pulled up in a jeep and wanted to know who we were and what we were doing.

I told him, and he became upset that survivors should be treated as we had been. He was a tall, well-built man with the unmistakable air of a senior officer about him. He strode to a telephone booth, and within a very few minutes, a number of things happened. Lights came on in the little concrete buildings where we were, and the doors opened to let us into what was a small-stores and uniform shop. "Small stores" is the name the Navy gives to underwear and socks and the like. Uniforms are outerwear. At any rate, a number of storekeepers had appeared from somewhere, and within only a few minutes more, the lot of us was fitted with new uniforms and on our way in a bus to mess halls on Treasure Island.

It was the first time I had worn a chief's uniform. It felt strange. I had to fumble for some time to get the necktie right. But there is some truth to the saying that "clothes make the man." Dressed as a chief, I was treated as a chief. That felt funny too—funny, but nice.

I never learned who that captain was, but I remember him still, all these years later. Once the others were fed and settled in, he took me aside and gave me ten dollars, a sizable sum of money in those days. "Here, Chief," he said. "Get your ass ashore and see what you can do with that."

I didn't know whether to go or not. There had been no visored caps in the storeroom. I was wearing one of the little blue fore-and-aft caps in the style the Army calls overseas caps. There hadn't been any chief signalman crows either, so my new brass-buttoned blues were unmarked with branch or rate. I didn't have a liberty card, but the captain would listen to no objections. He wrote me out a long-hand pass and drove me to the bus stop. As it turned out, I didn't need the pass. Everyone on the beach took me for a Canadian. Canadians wore little blue caps like the one I was wearing.

San Francisco was much different from what it had been when I had been there with Honk before the war. What I remembered as a blaze of lights on Treasure Island and in the city itself was all browned out. All unnecessary lights were turned off, and even the necessary ones were shielded so as not to show to seaward. Cars ran with their lights dimmed and most advertising signs were turned off.

But to me it was still a romantic and glamorous place. The narrow streets of the Barbary Coast and Chinatown were more mysterious than ever in the muted light and drifted with fog as they were that night. The doors of bar after bar and nightclub after nightclub opened onto the streets, all crowded to their push-and-shove limits with sailors and soldiers and war workers. There were lots of sailors in San Francisco then. The old battleships, after being rescued from Pearl Harbor, were kept out of the way in San Francisco until the carrier task forces made the waters safe enough for them to go west of Hawaii. Those of us in those task forces called the battleship sailors Market Street commandos for the city's main downtown street. You could start a fight pretty easy that way.

There was light and music and the exhilarating excitement of wartime, but I felt somehow out of place. I didn't know anyone in San Francisco. All the people I knew were still somewhere out there in the dark ocean to the west. I felt guilty for not being with them. As I usually did in a strange city, I started to walk the streets and came at last to Union Square with its tended gardens and tall monument to Admiral Dewey's victory in another war.

The atmosphere there was calmer than in the sailor streets, and I walked west out Geary, marveling at the iron fire escapes zigzagging up the fronts of what appeared to be one hotel after another. I had never seen fire escapes on the fronts of buildings before. The hotels all seemed to be about the same height—six or seven floors. The street ran between them like a steep walled ravine in desert country. At one place about three or four blocks west of Union Square, a steep alleyway entered Geary from the north. And a few feet up that alleyway a dimly lighted sign announced the Cock-and-Bull Room. By sheer accident, I had found my home in San Francisco.

The Cock-and-Bull was what was then called an "intimate" room. It was small and quiet. The dance floor was maybe ten feet on a side. Its lights were dim and its music soft. Even conversations were low voiced and laughter controlled. I liked the place at once. It opened off the lobby of the El Cortez Hotel and could be entered from that way as well as from the alleyway I had used. In sailor bars that would have been seen as an advantage, since it would offer an escape route in case of shore patrol raids, not that the shore patrol was likely to enter such a place.

I didn't know what to order at the bar. Always before I had been with other sailors in bars and had ordered whatever they ordered. My only guides were those dashing heroes in the movies. They always ordered scotch and sodas. So, I ordered a scotch and soda.

It tasted awful. I think now the maitre d' must have seen that he had a green one on his hands. I was twenty-three years old at that time, but looked much younger—something of no use at all for a newly made chief petty officer who wanted to look tough. But it was the unfortunate fact. The rest of the staff took their lead from the maitre d', and I became something of a pet in the place. Waiters, bartenders, busboys—all saw to it that I had a good time. And usually without spending any money at all. Civilians then were generous about buying drinks for sailors, especially in places like the Cock-and-Bull.

Best of all, though, was Suzanne. The singer in the Cock-and-Bull was a striking Italian girl name Suzanne Aiello. She used only her first name professionally and dreamed of becoming an opera singer. She would be a club singer only until she got her big break, she said. The first night I saw her she was wearing a clinging silver lamé dress, which, together with her jet black hair and olive skin, had me completely outmatched from the very beginning. I was in love.

When the maitre d' called Suzanne over, introduced me, and asked her to be good to me, I would not have changed places with Admiral Nimitz. There was nothing sexual in it. Hell, it never entered my mind that I might have a chance with a girl like Suzanne. But, oh, it was fun to have her sing to me in front of all those other people.

Casablanca was the current movie hit of the time, and "As Time Goes By" its big hit song. Suzanne had a rendering of it that could make men older than I cry. She would sing it, her lustrous Italian eyes fixed on me, and there just wasn't anything wrong in the world at all. Then she would sit at my table between numbers, and all those other men would watch us. If only Honk and Sandy could have seen me then!

I realize now that Suzanne was just following the maitre d's orders to be good to me, but I didn't realize it then. After she was through for the night, we would walk up Nob Hill to a place called the Zebra Room in the Huntington Hotel on California Street. If the Cock-and-Bull Room was several notches above the sailor dives downtown, the Zebra Room was several more notches above that. There was only a pianist, but Suzanne would sing along with him sometimes. She did it, she said, for exposure. Apparently many important people came to the Zebra Room. It gave Suzanne a chance to be seen and heard by people who might help her career.

Then, very late, I would take her home. I never even kissed her goodnight until the night before I was to leave. She teased me then for not knowing how to kiss and gave me a brief lab course in the art and science. The next day, before I caught my train, I took a dozen red roses to the Cock-and-Bull for her—with a large red apple for the teacher in the box. I never saw Suzanne again. I hope she made it in opera. She may have, but I would never have known given the circles in which I traveled for the next few years.

I was in San Francisco that time for only a few days. I bunked in the chiefs' quarters on Treasure Island while waiting for my orders. During the day I monitored chow lines and did other idiot work to keep busy. One day I was even given a working party of black sailors and sent to unload heavy timbers from railroad boxcars at the Oakland Army Base. But every night I was in the Cock-and-Bull Room with Suzanne. I got so I could drink scotch and soda without flinching too much for sophisticated effect.

I had always assumed that when my new orders came they would send me back to the South Pacific. That is what I was trained for, and I assumed that is where I would be needed. I only hoped there would be some leave first. I had not seen my family in a long time. But the orders, when they came, were for the USS *Florence Nightingale* in New York. And I was to have thirty days' delay in reporting, less travel time, which meant I could have two or three weeks at home.

Instant visions of clean white ships, with big red crosses on their sides and running lights on at night, danced in my head. Hospital ships did not get shot at!

And they had all those nice nurses running around on them. The war suddenly took on a new dimension for me.

I should have known better from the start. Rather than a hospital ship, the *Florence Nightingale* was an attack transport, actually a converted C3 freighter fitted with bunks in her holds and racks on deck for landing craft. Her role would be to take troops to assault beaches and to put them ashore with her boats. There was every chance in the world that she would be shot at. And, her name aside, it was extremely unlikely any nurses would ever be seen running about her decks. My life as a hospital ship sailor was, therefore, very brief.

The *Nightingale* was one of a four-ship division, all of the same type. The other ships were the *Elizabeth Stanton, Susan B. Anthony,* and *Dorothea Dix*—surely the least warlike names ever carried to sea by vessels of any navy, but so many ships had been added to the Navy by that time finding names for them had become a problem.

The only saving grace was the thirty-day delay in reporting. The *Florence Nightingale* was to be in New York, and I was to go in her. But I had thirty days in which to do so. Thirty days in which I could go anywhere and do anything I could afford. It was the longest leave I would ever have in the Navy. Technically, I suppose, I was entitled to thirty days of survivor's leave for both the *Lexington* and the *Moa*, but I didn't push the point. I quit while I was no further behind.

Saying good-bye to Suzanne was not so hard as I had feared. I suppose—dumb as I was—I realized, as I had with Ilse, that there was nothing there for me. I took a hotel room in San Francisco for a couple of days before leaving, but it was more as a tourist than as anything else. I slept alone in unaccustomed solitude, content simply to be away from the crowds of shipboard life. When it was time to go I went to the Ferry Building at the foot of Market Street to catch my train for New York with little regret.

I had never been in the Atlantic, nor seen New York. I looked forward to that. And I would have all that time to wander over the country in between, including going to Tulsa and seeing my family again. Things were going all right for a change.

San Francisco's eastbound railroad passengers in those days rode big steam ferries across the bay to the Oakland Mole, where they boarded their trains. It was night when I left. The bay's waters were black and made blacker by a summer fog. The city's dimmed lights glowed mysteriously, and the looming mass of the Bay Bridge under which we passed was only dimly seen. Local trains ran on the Bay Bridge then. We could hear the rumbling of their steel wheels as we passed below. Again, I was reminded of the rumbling of wheels on the Arkansas River Bridge at Tulsa.

I thought then the scene was much like the one pictured by Jack London for the opening of his novel *The Sea-Wolf.* The night was dark and foggy. I was in a ferry. Other ships and boats honked and hooted all around. Fog horns called to each other, and buoy bells clanged softly in the calm harbor waters. It was all nice and dangerous—and I became aware of a girl standing by the rail not far from me. She was looking back at San Francisco as it disappeared in the fog. She turned then and smiled at me.

We rode together all the way to Kansas City. It was remarkable how quickly— and how completely— Suzanne left my thoughts. The train's window shades were drawn until we were twenty to twenty-five miles inland. That seemed a bit of over-kill, but it gave me a chance to play the intrepid sailor standing by his girl in the face of danger. I had all my insignia by that time. My blues were resplendent with eight shiny brass buttons, silver-embroidered crow, scarlet chevrons, and hash mark—I was not quite four years in the Navy, but I had the hash mark sewn on anyway—and a fine array of pretty ribbons studded with battle stars. Oh, I was loaded for bear, and the girl on the ferry proved a ready target.

She was returning home to St. Louis after seeing off her new husband. He was in the Army and had shipped out from San Francisco's Fort Mason only the day before. I would never have guessed any of that from her actions on the trip.

Trains of the time were always jammed, but soldiers and sailors were allowed to board first. I could not keep back a wry smile at the thought of my treatment in the Santa Fe dining car on my first leave home. I have sometimes since considered that that circumstance might have explained my attractiveness to the girl. By boarding with me, she would get a good seat. But, if that were all it was, she was an extremely good actress.

The train made the long and labored climb of the High Sierra's western slopes in darkness, but at the higher elevations we could sometimes see the dim glow of snow beside the tracks. It must then have been mid-June, or later, but there were still scraps of dirty snow about. It made the train seem all the more warm and safe as we nestled together in what became an 1,800-mile lab course in exploratory human anatomy, male and female.

This activity slowed a bit during daylight hours. We were in a day coach, and some proprieties had to be observed. But the nights were instructive as hell for me. At twenty-three years of age, I was learning things I should have learned a long time before—when the errors and lapses would not have been so painful. But, I must admit, I had never found education to be so much fun before.

In a couple of days, we arrived in Kansas City, where I would change trains for Tulsa. I tried my best to talk the girl—I no longer remember her name—into getting off the train with me. We could have a couple of days together in a hotel room, and she could show me lots of other stuff. But she wouldn't do it.

It is interesting that she did not refuse my generous offer on its merits—newly married though she was. Her objection was that she already had wired her arrival time to her parents, and they would be expecting her. She didn't know how she could explain such a delay. This was a blow to my ideas of feminine fealty, and a lesson in what had happened to Middle American morality. Here was a very attractive young lady, newly married to what was probably a very attractive young man who, even then, was off to fight for his God and country—and his new bride. Yet she obviously was willing to share a bed with me—we already had shared virtually everything short of that on the train. The only thing that stopped her was her fear that her family might find out about it.

I was disillusioned—but not so disillusioned that I wouldn't have joined her, had she come with me. That made me just as much a hypocrite, I suppose, as I thought her then to be. I would have been betraying the poor Army bastard just as much as his new wife would have been, but that is the way things were during the war. At least, I hadn't sworn to love, honor, and obey the poor son of a bitch.

Keatha, one of Dad's sisters, lived in Kansas City, in a standard middle-class house out on Grand. She was a small, delicately feminine, and very pretty woman. She was married to Walt, a large and loud red-faced man who worked for an insurance company. He had sometimes visited us in Oklahoma during the Depression years, but I don't remember ever seeing Keatha before at all. Walt, in a cliché of the time, had never met a stranger in his life. He was always well dressed, drove new cars, and knew a ton of stories he loved to tell to anyone who would stand still for them. He was a lovable—though loud—man. Everybody liked Walt.

Peggy, their only child, was a Kansas City public school teacher who was slightly older than I. In another cliché of the time, she had had every advantage. Altogether, they were as Norman Rockwellish as living people could be, I suppose.

When I called their house from my hotel room, Walt rushed downtown and, completely without discussion, checked me out of my room and took me out to their big wood-frame house on its wide tree-shaded Middle American street. Protesting did very little good with Walt.

I did not know what to expect in their house, and being alone in a hotel room of my own offered interesting possibilities in what I already had come to know were the mores of the time. Nevertheless, willy-nilly, I found myself in a flowered chintz bedroom with my Aunt Keatha fussing over me and Peggy standing by to show me the fleshpots of Kansas City once it became dark.

I don't know what kind of money Walt made in his job, but he had a very nice house. The largest and best I ever had been in before. The family also had a

crotchety old cocker spaniel bitch and a car they called Camille because it was forever dying. I was not used to literary references in casual conversation. The house
on Grand was going to be all right.

I remember Walt was suffering with a bad attack of hay fever the brief time I
was there and sat in his living room easy chair with a roll of toilet paper at hand for
wiping his nose. Keatha was mortified.

He recovered long enough to take us all out for an Italian dinner—the first
of my life—in a restaurant made from a former residence. After dinner, Walt and
Keatha made a thoughtful withdrawal, and Peggy and I set out in Camille to see
what we could see.

Peggy had a girlfriend she called Bird for me. Together, the three of us had
a good time. We ended the evening in the Peanut, apparently the "in" place in
Kansas City at the time. It was not far from the house on Grand and was distinguished mostly by peanut shells ankle-deep on the floor. Unshelled peanuts were
given away at the bar, and people simply dropped the shells where they fell. In my
innocence, I thought that another heady height of sophistication—right up there
with the lighted glass bricks in San Diego's Sherman's.

Peggy and her friends were everything I had envied during my days at the
University of Tulsa. White flannels, tennis sweaters, buck shoes—they had it all.
But it was hard for me to relax with them. I'll admit it was probably my fault. I had
no civilian clothes, and I was self-conscious in my blues among such people. In
two days I was ready to move on to Tulsa and to see my family again. It had been
a long time.

Peggy and I had some drinks at the Westport Room in Kansas City's Union
Station while waiting for my train. We became good friends, I think, and maintained a remarkable, if brief, correspondence after I returned to the ships. In one
of her letters she included the lines from Tennyson's *Ulysses* in which the old Greek
sailor says, "I am a part of all that I have met." I still remember these lines, which,
for me, paint the truest picture of a man's life I ever have found.

Tulsa was as much changed by the war as any other place I had seen. Douglas had a plant there that was almost a mile long. It produced B24s and hired
hundreds of people. Everyone referred to it simply as the Bomber, and it entered
almost every conversation sooner or later. There were other defense plants too,
and unemployment was but a faded memory. Streets and stores were crowded, and
there was much the same fevered atmosphere and loosened morals I had found
everywhere I went in the States.

Even my family was changed. Dad had all the work he could handle, all of it
at good wages. Cora was working as a cook in a cafe. Flo had finished business
college and had a good (and getting better) job in an office. Zena Mae was finish-

ing high school and would soon have a job of her own. My sisters had become women while I was away. Very attractive women.

As I have mentioned before, my family had moved to town sometime before and were established with new friends I did not know. The days were long while everyone was off to work. I found myself becoming edgy and impatient. Home leave was not what I had thought it would be. I found myself thinking more and more often of the *Indianapolis* and Honk and Sandy and all the others I had known. I wondered where they were and what they were doing. They had, in a very real sense, become my family.

I visited the *Tribune*'s newsroom to see my old friends there, but many of them were gone. Jim Lucas, for instance, a quiet and mild-mannered man, was off as a combat correspondent with the Marines. He won prizes for his coverage of the bloody Tarawa landings and, later, a Pulitzer for his work covering the Korean War. Roger Devlin, my old boss on the wire desk, was there; so was Harmon Phillips, as city editor. And Jack Charvat was sports editor. Jack had a radio show on KTUL and asked if I would appear with him that night. Radio hosts are always on the hunt for guests. For want of anything better to do, I agreed.

Dad let me use his old Oldsmobile sedan, and Zena Mae went with me. Jack asked me a lot of stuff about sports in the Navy, but I didn't have much to tell. Many sports figures had joined the Navy for the war, but most of them became physical education instructors in training stations and other shore installations. Still, the interview filled time for Jack, I suppose.

Afterward, Zena and I walked around Tulsa's downtown streets in the warm summer night. It was after 10:30, and the streets virtually deserted. Even during wartime, Tulsa was not San Francisco. We were strolling along Fourth Street between Boston and Main when a shiny yellow Plymouth convertible with its black top down cruised slowly by. A blonde was driving it. A striking brunette was in the right-hand seat.

Zena and I paid little attention to the car. We were talking and simply enjoying being together after being for so long apart. Then the convertible came by again, very slowly. Then it came by again, and I waved. The convertible stopped. I let Zena take Dad's car home. I didn't know she had never driven before and didn't have a license. Off I went in the yellow car, and Tulsa wasn't boring anymore.

The blonde lived in Sand Springs, a small town about ten miles west of Tulsa on low hills overlooking the Arkansas River. The car was hers. The brunette was a friend who happened to be riding with her. I didn't see much more of the brunette after that night, but I saw a lot more of the blonde. My education, which had started with Ilse in Honolulu and Suzanne in San Francisco, then moved into the upper grades with the girl on the train, now moved into postgraduate work, complete with labs, with the blonde in the yellow convertible.

I had a lot of catching up to do. I had never known Oklahoma to be so beautiful. It was near midsummer by that time, and the days were hot—though not as hot as it had been down around the equator—but the nights were lovely. Grassy fields became almost white in moonlight, all bound in by black tree lines and covered over with skies turned pale by the moon. Often heat lightning flickered, pale blue and white, along the night horizon. I thought of the red flashes we had seen so often in the sky over Henderson Field when Washing Machine Charlie flew over. I had once compared them to heat lightning, but they were nothing at all alike.

I had driven a car very little in my life. I had never owned one. I didn't even have a driver's license. Certainly, I had never driven anything like that yellow convertible, which the pretty little blonde let me drive all I wanted. There was gasoline rationing for some people, I suppose, but it was never a problem for us. I don't know where she got the stuff. Her father owned several businesses. I suppose he got it for her through some black market connection. My new moral corruption took another dip into the morass, for it didn't occur to me that we were doing anything wrong. If she were burning black market gas, at least she was doing it in a good and patriotic cause: the great pleasure of a deserving sailor.

The girl lived in a big square redbrick house in Sand Springs, but her family was away a lot. I never met any of them. Her brunette friend lived in another, almost as big, house across the street. I often thought, during that period, of what Sandy and Honk would have said had they been able to see me then. I was in what they would have called hog heaven.

My leave, which had begun to drag for me, speeded up dramatically after I met the blonde with the convertible. Before I knew it, it was time for me to go back to the Navy. I had not spent much time with Dad and my family. I felt bad about that. I had been reported to them as being killed in the *Lexington*'s sinking. Flo said Dad was much affected. I suppose the error was made in the confusion arising from the Flag's separation from ship's company sailors after the battle.

Dad cried when I left to return to the war. Except for when my mother died, I had never seen him cry before. Still, I had to go. But, it seemed to me, he and I were always afterward closer than we had been before.

I stopped again in Kansas City for a couple of days. This time I saw Curtis, one of Dad's brothers who lived there. He was an archetypical salesman of the old hard-drinking, woman-chasing school. During the war, however, he had nothing to sell. His company went into what was called "war work" and made him an "expediter." Mostly what he expedited was what he called "booze and broads" for corporate parties and ceremonies. "Goddamned pimp, you want to know the truth," he said bitterly.

Curtis had been in the horse cavalry in World War I. He still considered himself a touch or two better than Dad, who had been only a foot soldier. He lived high and made—and spent—a lot of money. He lived in a fine apartment in the Country Club Plaza area of Kansas City. He was away much of the time, he said. But he was home when I was there that time. His company had been awarded an Army-Navy "E" flag, and he was busy with putting together the celebration. He invited me to the ceremony.

The Army-Navy "E" program was established to recognize and to honor those civilian companies that distinguished themselves in one way or another in production for the war effort. They were given a special flag to fly outside their plants, a flag with the letter "E" in a circle of stars. I did not want to go to the damned party, but I did. I had lived with Curtis for a while after my mother died. He had no children of his own and had tried to adopt me, but Dad would have none of that. I didn't want to hurt his feelings.

I had heard, of course, about how rough things were on the home front for those who had to ride out the war there, but I never realized what those poor souls had to put up with until I saw that party. I had never seen so much food and drink in my life, all set up in a big white tent on a green lawn outside the company headquarters. In Curtis' words, there was "hot and cold running ass all over the place."

Neither had I seen so much brass since the February 1940 change of command ceremony in the *Indianapolis*. There were admirals and generals, captains and colonels, most of them soft-looking men with pink faces and slack bellies. They seemed to have a lot in common with the equally sleek types in business suits who were urging food and booze—and the women Curtis had found—on their military guests. I knew, even then—and very much appreciated—the things like 40-mm antiaircraft guns that people like these produced for us, and I knew how important such men were. But that Kansas City party was disturbing in a way.

I was only a junior chief petty officer—and dressed in relatively drab khaki at that. I didn't belong there. I noticed some of the brass looking at me closely sometimes, but none of them said anything. I got away as soon as I could.

When I changed trains in St. Louis, I thought of calling my little train companion who had so warmed me on the long leg from San Francisco, but I didn't want to embarrass her with her family. Besides, I already had learned that women were not in short supply. And I was beginning to get antsy to get to New York. If these inland towns were as productive of women as they had turned out to be, God knew what I would find in New York.

Eastern railroads, I found, were not nearly so good during the war as the western ones. I rode the Pennsylvania RR from St. Louis to New York. The car in which I rode was actually wooden, with narrow vertical planking and windows you lifted with leather straps to close, and seats whose backs could be flipped over to face either forward or back. The seats probably once had been red plush, but they were then so engorged with black soot and coal dust the original red showed only along edges where the black had been rubbed off. The cars were so crowded that body heat alone was enough to make them stifling. Air conditioning was something remembered from another time, and windows, when they were opened in desperation, let in as much in the way of coal smoke, cinders, small stones, and birds' feathers as they did air.

It was not a pleasant ride, and I marveled at the young mothers with their babies who seemed to be on every train during that time. We always made room for them and tried to help them with their babies. The older soldiers and sailors especially enjoyed playing with the babies. I guess some of them had kids of their own somewhere. I admired the courage and stamina of the mothers, many of them little more than children themselves. Sometimes I envied the men they loved enough to go through such suffering simply to see them for what might be their last time—and to show them the babies they might never see again.

We used to see newsreel shots of refugee trains in those days as various parts of the world were overrun by warring armies. After riding that old Pennsylvania RR day coach from St. Louis to New York, I had a much better appreciation for the ordeal of refugee travel.

The eastern part of the United States failed to impress. The hills and open countryside, green as they were with early summer growth, were pleasant enough, but the towns and cities were depressing. Squarish, two-story wood-frame houses stood in ragged ranks to either side of mean and cluttered streets. Paint obviously was one commodity whose rationing was being faithfully observed. Everything was dulled with a deadening layer of dirt so that even objects of differing colors seemed all tinted with the same drab grays and blacks of soot and coal dust.

The factories and mills spewed black smoke into an only slightly less black sky. The factories and mills were largely black themselves and well rusted. Even nearby grass and trees were the same melancholy monotone of industry. America's towns and cities do not show their best sides to rail passengers in any event, but I had not realized how drab human habitations could be. Depression-dulled Oklahoma was almost bright in comparison.

That is how I came to New York's Pennsylvania Station in the summer of 1943. Unless you find dirty concrete walls exciting, there is not much of dramatic interest in approaching New York by rail. The way is all through tunnels. Passengers last see the upper world in the dreary flat reaches of New Jersey. They emerge full-blown in the grandeur of Penn Station and the streets of midtown Manhattan.

15
New York

ONCE I HAD ARRIVED IN NEW YORK, my leave was over. I was back in the Navy, but it was a navy, and a war, like none other I had ever seen. I reported at once to the receiving ship, which was not a ship at all. It was Pier 92 on the Hudson River side of Manhattan Island, within easy walking distance of Times Square and the raucous midtown amusement industry of the big city, whose roaring vibrancy I could hear and feel all about me.

Right off I learned the *Florence Nightingale* was away to sea, and I settled in with what must have been several hundred other men who waited there for their ships. No one seemed to know where the *Nightingale* was or when she would return. So, I found a bunk and put down my bag.

The quarters were primitive but adequate. Spaces for sleeping quarters, washrooms, mess halls, and the necessary offices and supply areas were simply partitioned off areas within the overall dimensions of the vast pier shed. The walls did not reach all the way to the shed's lofty ceilings. The effect of the arrangement was more that of pens than of rooms. I suspected it would be cold as hell in winter, but it was July when I arrived and the chiefs' quarters were reasonably comfortable. There were few if any watches to be stood, and liberty was both often and extended. I had found a home and a feeder.

New York's harbor was a busy place during the war, but the ships for the most part were merchant types. Some had been converted and taken over by the Navy, but they were still merchant types. I saw no carriers or cruisers at all and only a few destroyers, which came and went sometimes with the Atlantic convoys. Clearly, it was a different war from that of the Pacific's fast carrier task forces.

One disconcerting fact was the presence in the very next berth to Pier 92 of the sad spectacle of the beautiful French liner *Normandie* lying on her side and sunk in the dirty harbor waters. She had been under conversion for war service when a welder's torch was said to have started the fire that killed her. New York's

227

zealous fire department had pumped her so full of water in fighting the fire that she capsized and sank in her berth. She remained a sad sight for all the time I was in New York.

I'm sure Honk and Sandy would have felt themselves to be in sailor heaven at Pier 92, but my time in New York proved to be one of the lowest periods of my whole time in the Navy. I had been trained to duty in cruisers and fast carriers, and it was a blow to my always shaky ego to be assigned to a ship whose maximum speed was eighteen or so knots. I knew even then that I lacked the experience and leadership qualities—whatever those are—to hold down a chief's job in the big time of the carrier task forces, but I thought I could do better than a transport. Ah, vanity.

I should have been happy. Although I had not yet been to sea as a chief, I soon would be. I would have my own signal bridge in a ship at sea, and I already had begun to enjoy the improved living conditions and increased privileges of life as a chief. But, as it happened, New York proved to be a disaster for me.

At first, the duty was not all that bad. When it became clear that I would be in New York for some considerable time, the girl with the yellow convertible came up from Oklahoma to help me wait for the *Nightingale*'s return. She did not bring her pretty car, but she did take a room in the Hotel New Yorker on 34th Street, as I recall, just around the corner from Penn Station and within easy walking distance of Pier 92. It was almost as though I were still on leave. I had what the Navy calls an open gangway at the receiving ship and could come and go as I pleased, checking in only from time to time to see if my ship had arrived.

We went to the top of the Empire State Building and to the Statue of Liberty, the Bronx Zoo, and the Tavern on the Green in Central Park—all the tourist things. At night we did the nightclubs. We saw Ted Lewis do his famous "Me and My Shadow" number at the Latin Quarter, then one of the town's most popular spots. I had drawn virtually none of my pay between November 1941 and June 1943. I had plenty of money, and my little friend from Oklahoma never seemed to have any problems in that regard. We did the nightlife scene pretty good. Altogether it was much like it had been for us in Tulsa, except for the exhilarating surroundings of wartime New York.

But when, in the end, she went back to Oklahoma, and the *Nightingale* was still at sea, I went into a bad time. The men in the receiving ship were, as I was, waiting for ships. They came and went almost daily, and there was no time for the feeling of being shipmates to grow among us. I took to going ashore alone and drinking more than I ever had before. I had never liked the taste of whiskey, but under its numbing influence, the loneliness did not hurt so much.

There was a hotel somewhere in the West Forties—the Piccadilly, I believe—where I often went. In its small bar—instead of the conventional backbar of mirrors and shelves of bottles and glasses—there was a small stage. The Three Suns, a popular trio of the time, played there. They made smooth easy-to-take music with an accordion lead, as I recall now. I used to go almost every afternoon and nurse drinks until the after-work and evening crowds began to gather. The feeling was like that of the Cock-and-Bull Room in San Francisco, except it had no dance floor, however small. The group would even play "As Time Goes By" sometimes, but there was no Suzanne to sing the words to me.

When the crowds became too pressing, I would seek out a quiet bar farther away from Times Square and mope at myself in a backbar mirror, trying to look tragic and dramatic, but I never got very good at it.

I knew by that time, of course, that I would not be going to Annapolis, nor to Pensacola for flight training. There was always the chance of becoming a warrant officer or even of being commissioned from the ranks—what the Navy called a mustang officer. But all the mustangs I had ever seen had been in yard tugs and barges and other dirty and menial ships of the dungaree Navy. That did not appeal to me. Besides, it would take years, even if I had the talent for it. And probably would mean being reduced to my last permanent enlisted rating when the war was over.

That was what had happened after World War I. I presumed it would happen again after World War II. Ironically, I was a luncheon guest in the nuclear carrier *Enterprise* one time in San Francisco Bay many years later. Neither the captain of the huge ship nor his exec was an Academy man. So much for prescience! Of course, neither of them was a mustang in the classic sense. They were ROTC officers out of some college somewhere.

I suspect now that I came then, during that time in New York, to conclude that, if I were never going to be anything but an enlisted man, I would damned well live like one. In all the time I was in New York—after the girl from Oklahoma returned home—I never visited a museum or attended a concert or went to a theater. Hell, I never went even to a ballgame. I had come a long way from the teenager who once spent his liberties in Honolulu's Bishop Museum and Library. I suspect now, too, that there was a good dollop or two of self-pity stirred into the mix by that time.

At any rate, that is what I did. I am not proud of it. And, though I never really got good at barhopping and womanizing, I got good enough to wind up in the clap shack of the hospital the Navy had established at St. Albans on Long Island. It was the most embarrassing event of my life, either in or out of the Navy. I was a chief, for Christ's sake. I was supposed to know better.

The Navy had penicillin by then. My shameful disease could have been cured within hours, but the Navy would not use the wonder drug for venereal disease. It was too good for bad boys. We were treated the old-fashioned way, along with some faddy new treatments, none of which worked. One theorist, for instance, reckoned that a body temperature of 106 degrees would kill the gonococcus bug. I volunteered to try that treatment and spent several hours in a box that brought my body temperature to just short of fatal levels. All I got out of it was a mouth full of fever sores.

This was another demonstration to me of the Navy's faulty logic. A man in the clap shack was just as absent from his duty station as was a victim of a more honorable disease or injury. The war effort, presumably, would be helped as much by the return of one man to duty as by the other. But, as mentioned earlier, penicillin was not to be wasted on bad boys. Bad boys were to be punished—just as they had been punished before the war by the painful practice of deep irrigations—even if it did mean the loss of their services for longer than was necessary.

Time lost to the treatment of venereal disease, incidentally, was bad time. It had to be made up at the end of the victim's enlistment. At any rate, by the time I was again pristine enough to serve my country, the *Florence Nightingale* was back from wherever she had been. I was put in charge of twenty or thirty men in a Navy truck and told to take them to the ship, which, I was told, was in Brooklyn.

The driver of the truck said he knew the address I was given. He did too, but when we arrived there we found the ship had shifted berths sometime before. The officious dock officer—a full lieutenant, for Christ's sake—wouldn't tell me where she had gone. He actually reminded me, "There's a war on, Chief. Vessel locations are national security secrets." His idea of how to fight that war was for me to take that truck full of men all the way back to Pier 92 and let the proper authorities there tell me the *Nightingale*'s new berth.

After I pointed out at some length, and with some indignation, that we were all supposed to be on the same side in the goddamned war he said was going on, and that the goddamned war might conceivably be more efficiently fought if crews could get on board their goddamned ships, and after raising enough hell in general in the Yard Office, a commander overheard the row and came out from an inner office to tell me the *Florence Nightingale* was at a pier on Staten Island. Praise the Lord!

There was no Verrazzano Bridge then. I would have to get the truck on a ferry to Staten Island. God knows how long that would take. All told, it was well past ten o'clock that night when we finally found the ship snugged into a pier where she was taking on stores. None of us in the truck was in a good humor. We were tired and hungry and sick of the nonsense we had just endured. The fact that my first assignment as a chief had ended so poorly did not help at all. The Pacific, with all its faults at the time, looked pretty good to me that night.

Even after I got my sailors all on board and saw that they were fed and bedded down, my mood did not improve much. The ship was all I had feared she would be: high bows and superstructure. A maze of masts, king posts, and booms all tied together with a confusing crisscrossing of stays and running rigging aloft. Nested landing craft piled on the forward hatches reached almost as high as the wheelhouse windows. Remembering the clean lines of the *Indianapolis*, as I recalled seeing them upon my joining her in Vallejo, I could have cried.

The chiefs' quarters, however, were comfortable. The mess itself was on the main deck at the forward end of the superstructure. It was large and well, if simply, appointed, with a permanent table fitted with a soft rubber cloth and wooden fiddles to keep dishes from sliding off in rough weather. There were individual chairs for eating and leather upholstered benches along the bulkheads for lounging and off-watch socializing. Large opening ports in the forward bulkhead made it pleasantly light and airy in good weather, although we often were embarrassed by the curious soldier faces they so often framed, peering in to see what their betters were having for dinner.

What their betters were having was considerably better than the slop the soldiers were given in their crowded quarters below. The chief storekeeper and the two chief cooks saw to that. The storekeeper set aside for the chiefs' mess the best of what came aboard in the way of provisions. And the cooks saw to it that it was prepared properly. Hell, we could even make personal alterations in the menu if we wanted to. I had never had it so good. Not in that regard. The *Flossie*, as her men called her, was indeed a home and a feeder—no matter how little she looked like a naval vessel.

Heads, washrooms, and a roomy bunkroom adjoined the mess aft. The bunks were the thick sick bay kind, and bedding was provided. Assigned compartment cleaners kept the whole thing clean for us. They even made our beds for us and saw that our laundry was done.

The other chiefs, I found, were a good group, though a lot of them were reserves and some on their first sea duty. Living in chiefs' quarters represented a sharp change in the Navy for me. Always before, I had lived and worked only with signalmen. As a chief, I would still work with signalmen, but I would live with men from all the ship's disciplines: machinists, gunners, cooks, yeomen, storekeepers, pharmacists, and the lot. In recalling it now, it seems a big deal, but at the time I paid it little attention. If nothing else, the Navy teaches sailors to be adaptable.

But there was one development in the *Nightingale* that was disconcerting. She already had a chief signalman on board! Here was a ship that, in my sardonic view, did not need one chief signalman, and the all-knowing Navy had fitted her with two. It was a job any good prewar signalman second class could have handled in his sleep. Of course, all the good prewar signalmen seconds were chiefs by that time, I suppose.

This situation could have been more ludicrous only if the Navy did nothing to correct it. And that is exactly what it did. Nothing. Not for almost eighteen months anyway. My value was so low that the Navy could keep me virtually idle for a year and a half in the middle of what we were told was a serious war. That did not do one hell of a lot for my ego either. But, I settled in as best I could. It was, sure as hell, a different Navy from any I ever had known before.

The other chiefs were good men for the most part. The resident chief signalman was a ruddy faced Irishman from somewhere in Appalachia. He had a turned up nose and a mop of red hair. George McMahan was his name, but we never called him anything other than Mac. He had been a destroyer sailor—in the *Cummings*, as a matter of fact, at Pearl Harbor during the attack that started the war. He had also been an armed guard sailor in merchant ships at one time. He was a happy-go-lucky type. I never knew Mac to be bothered one hell of a lot by anything. In Navy parlance, he took a "very loose strain." His unfailing advice to me when I bitched about having nothing to do was to relax. After the war, Mac would own his own highly successful air conditioning business in Fresno, California.

The chief quartermaster was a small, slightly built man with sharp features and a precise manner. He would become a Manhattan lawyer after the war. His name was McNulty.

Jack Choner was the chief boatswain's mate. He was tough and highly efficient at handling cargo and the often awkward exercise of putting our landing craft on and off the ship. A Scottish Bobby broke a nightstick over Choner's head during a spirited discussion in Glasgow one night. Although he bled from his ears for some time afterward, he did not turn in to sick bay until two or three weeks later. There it was found he had a fractured skull. He would become a New York bus driver after the war.

Tommy Coats was the ship's chief yeoman. He drank a lot. He was a comparatively short man with heavy black hair. He looked remarkably like a small Clark Gable, except that his nose had been knocked off course in some forgotten dispute. He reminded me of Honk in that respect. He was an intelligent man who stayed in the Navy after the war and rose to be a warrant officer assigned to various embassies about the world. After the war, he would marry a pretty Washington secretary and have children with her before dying six weeks after being diagnosed with a cancer. Tommy was an old pro. I liked him.

John Kurkjian was one of our two chief storekeepers. (The ship had two chief storekeepers and two chief cooks, but this was justified by the hundreds of troops we carried. Unlike the situation with Mac and me, they had plenty of work to keep them busy.) John had been a paper buyer for a Boston book publisher before the war. He was older than most of us. After the war, he would open his own advertising agency in Boston.

Benny Newman and a man named Jones (Benny was short and fat; Jonesy was tall and almost cadaverous—they were like Mutt and Jeff in the comics) were both chief cooks. They were good men, although about as different from one another as two men can be. After I left the *Nightingale* I saw Benny one time in Honolulu, but I never saw Jonesy again. I don't know what happened to either of them after the war.

"Doc" Weldon was the ship's chief pharmacist's mate. He was the clown of the quarters and a born scrounger. He took a most irreverent view of the Navy and of the war in general. He could chord a piano and knew many thoroughly scatological parodies of popular songs of the time. He would become a medical doctor after the war.

There were other chiefs in the quarters whose names I am embarrassed to admit now I have forgotten. Most were older than I. Some were well into middle age and had sober habits I would have done well to have emulated. The fact that I have forgotten their names should be laid to the frailties of age rather than to any lack of respect I felt for them either then or now.

These men were of what the Navy called the artificer branch for the most part. They made the ship go. I had always had an inordinate respect and admiration for men with mechanical and engineering skills, fields in which I was so totally deficient. I got along well with those in the *Nightingale*, I think. We simply did not have much in common.

This was my new family. We would live together for the next year and a half. I had some good times with all of them, but it was Mac and Tommy Coats with whom I became closest and most always went ashore. We stood virtually no watches in the *Nightingale* while in port and were free to come and go pretty much as we liked so long as we were back by sailing time. Our ratio of sea to port time was such that we always had plenty of money. (My salary at the time was ninety-nine dollars per month, plus sea pay and longevity.) All in all, it was not a bad life for young men who professed, and actually had, little thought for the future.

It may seem strange to some now, but I don't remember thinking at the time of what would happen after the war. I suspect I took it for granted that I would remain in the Navy and revert to what already had become a thoroughly unrealistic remembrance of my prewar life in the *Indianapolis*. I knew even then that Honk, Tack, and Nations were dead. God knew where Sandy was. As it happened, even the *Indianapolis* herself would fail to survive the war. But there would be other ships and other men like those I had known before the war.

I suspect now that we did not think more about the future because so much of the time it did not seem the war would ever end. All we knew, of course, was what we read in newspapers and magazines when we were in harbor—and what we saw with our own eyes while at sea. Sometimes I think we were much like the group of blind men trying to describe an elephant while able only to feel with their hands one small part of the otherwise invisible beast. We had very little understanding of the war as a whole, I think now. I know it was never discussed in the quarters.

I did come, however, to a more cheerful view of life in the *Florence Nightingale*. I became more settled and accepting of the fact I had nothing to do in the ship, although I continued to be humiliated by what I took to be a slap at my abilities. But, as Tommy pointed out, that was all out of my control, and I might as well relax and go along for the ride. Then, too, the Tea Drinker helped.

The other chiefs in the quarters named the Tea Drinker for her habit of ordering hot tea—in cups—in the bars and nightclubs we visited. She was a nineteen-year-old blonde from Albany. She was stage struck and apparently on her way, for she was in the chorus of the then new musical *Oklahoma*. She thought it intriguing that I was from Oklahoma and she was in a show named for that state.

She lived in an artists' residence on the Upper West Side. It was called either the Three Arts Club or the Seven Arts Club. I don't remember the number of arts now. The place had been endowed by a wealthy old lady who had wanted young actresses and dancers to have a safe place to live in New York while following their dreams of glory. In my experience, it was certainly safe. Men were not allowed beyond the lobby even if invited.

It was a large redbrick building with an ornate entryway overlooking Riverside Drive and the Hudson River with the New Jersey shore rising in gray cliffs on the far side of the river. One interesting fringe benefit for its young residents, as the Tea Drinker told it to me, was that each resident was assigned to an established actress who would serve as guide and adviser. The Tea Drinker's mentor was a small, black-haired woman named Marsha Hunt, whose own promising career was effectively ended soon after the war when she became entangled in a bitter congressional probe sniffing out alleged Communist influence in Hollywood.

The Tea Drinker was not a classically beautiful girl, but she had the universal beauty of all youth and she had a disarming innocence about her that won over even the most hardened of us. She wore her blond hair long, but pulled back smooth along the sides of her head. And she dressed more like the co-eds I had seen at TU than like a showgirl.

We met on the subway one afternoon. Her residence club was having some kind of a celebratory party that evening, and she didn't have a date. I guess I looked safe enough for her. I had become leery of women after my experience with the malady of love and deliberately showed no interest when she openly smiled at me. Finally, she simply asked me if I would go with her.

I know it sounds crazy now, but things happened that way sometimes during the war. Anyway, I went to the party with her. Afterward, we saw each other as often as we could when my ship was in harbor. Her work in the show gave her most of the daylight hours to herself, and I was standing no watches at all while waiting for my ship's return. She neither smoked nor drank—other than for her tea. The other chiefs with whom we later double-dated sometimes teased her and laughed aloud when she blushed. She came as close as anyone ever would to teaching me to dance.

Oddly, after the way I had been behaving in New York for the past few weeks, I found the Tea Drinker fun to be with. Our being together was entirely platonic. More like the way Ilse and I had been before the war in Honolulu. She invited me to her home in Albany one time, but we never got around to going. She also got me a ticket to see *Oklahoma*—the hottest ticket in town at the time—but the *Nightingale* sailed before the show date. We simply had a good time together.

The Tea Drinker was a Catholic. She had three or four Christian names she explained to me one time, all of them the names of saints. I had never before known that Catholics gave their children multiple names like that. As my mother had been with her Methodism, the Tea Drinker was ardent in her beliefs, but she never tried to change my iconoclastic views on religion. Her own father, she said, was not religious. Her mother had trained her in the church, and she had done one hell of a good job of it.

Mac, the other chief signalman in the *Nightingale*, it turned out, had a pretty black-haired girl named Marj who came all the way from Nebraska to be with him while our ship was in New York. Given the conditions of travel on wartime trains, love can't get much truer than that. They would marry and have a family in California after the war. Mac's Marj and my Tea Drinker got along fine. The four of us double-dated whenever we could, although working in the chorus made evening dates sometimes hard to arrange for the Tea Drinker.

New York had become much more pleasant for me.

I don't know how all of this would have ended if the Tea Drinker had not told her priest about me. So far as I know that was the only time in my life that I starred in a confessional. The irony of it is that we hadn't done anything to confess. After my experience with the dread social disease, I had become inactive in the field. I don't know what the Tea Drinker told him, but the goddamned priest gave her a penance. I was the penance. She was not to see me anymore.

I would never have known anything about it at all, but one Sunday morning just after we had docked after an especially rough westward passage of the North Atlantic, I went to her residence club. She wasn't in. The matronly woman at the desk didn't say it in so many words, but she made it clear that there was no point in my waiting. I was puzzled, but it didn't occur to me that anything serious might have happened.

By chance, on my way back to the subway, I met the Tea Drinker in the street. She was on her way home from church. She was not very happy. She told me what had happened. It didn't leave me a hell of a lot to say. I knew by that time how important her church was to her. I went on back to the ship.

I saw the Tea Drinker only once after that. And that was several months later. It was probably just as well. I was becoming too fond of her, and the religion thing would never have worked for us. Besides, there was always the war. I did not want to become tied down while that was going on. Although I was in little danger in the *Florence Nightingale*, Honk and I had concluded very early in the war that we were not likely to survive it. My prayer was only that it be quick when it came.

So, I became a loner again. I realize that, in reciting these various adventures with women, I must sound like a rounder, but my experiences were tamer than most. If only a small fraction of the stories I heard in the quarters or on the bridge were true, I let the Navy side down badly in that regard, I am afraid.

If Marj were in town, I sometimes would go with her and Mac. But that was a mixed blessing. They would ask where the Tea Drinker was, which would remind me all over again of what had happened. I would lie and tell them she was away with a road show of *Oklahoma*, but I think they sensed the truth.

Sometimes Tommy or McNulty would go with us, and Marj would be squired by all four of us. I still have some old nightclub pictures of us together that way. It was not a perfect solution, but it was better than being alone. I had all but stopped drinking by that time. Moping around by myself got to be pretty depressing. When the time at last came, I was never in my life so glad to get away again to sea.

16
North Atlantic

MY FIRST PASSAGE in the *Florence Nightingale* was to Belfast in Northern Ireland. It must have been near the end of August. The weather was good for most of the eastbound crossing, although we did hit a little fog off Newfoundland. I was pleasantly surprised to find my new ship a good sea boat. She pounded some when light and rolled when heavily loaded, but on the whole, she rode the seas well. I suspect the weight of her deck-loaded boats made her a bit top-heavy.

The view forward from the bridge, through all that tangle of cargo handling rigging, took some getting used to, though. The combat ships in which I had served before were clear forward except for the clean silhouettes of guns. At any rate, we made a good passage. It was good to be to sea again.

Normally we sailed in what were known as fast convoys and were escorted by plenty of real destroyers. Our convoy speed was usually fifteen knots or so, but we zigzagged against the threat of submarines, making our speed of advance considerably less than that. Still, it was better than the eight-knot convoys we saw sometimes plodding their ways across the dangerous seas with only a couple of Flower-class corvettes—they looked like the *Moa*—for escort. We moved faster probably because we carried troops and the other ships carried freight for the most part.

By that time in 1943, the U-boat danger was largely past, although we didn't know that at the time. We continued to zigzag and to steam at darkened ship and to take all the other precautions that had been developed through hard experience to lessen the danger of submarines. I don't think we were ever attacked. We heard depth charges sometimes, and we were frequently routed around the reported locations of German wolfpacks. The British had developed a way to locate them fairly well by that time, and we were fast enough to scoot around reported danger. I doubt the Germans wanted to tangle with our strong escorts, anyway. The slower and more poorly defended convoys must have been more tempting for them.

Still, there was always the chance of being torpedoed, with all the interesting possibilities that entailed. In the cold waters of the North Atlantic, abandoning ship was all but certain death from exposure and hypothermia. In the Pacific, except for the stress of the event itself, abandoning ship was not bad at all with a good life jacket. But, as winter came down on us in the Atlantic we did not bother even to wear life jackets. There seemed little point in doing so. The choice between freezing to death and drowning was a narrow one.

Convoy sailings—like the sorties of Pacific task forces—had an excitement all their own. I had always been moved by the spectacle of ships leaving the safety of harbors for the hazards of sea and war, and the North Atlantic convoys proved no less dramatic as ships struck out into the dark ocean.

Several hours before sailing—and we almost always sailed in darkness—the commodore, usually an old retired ship's officer called back for war service, would hold his convoy meeting for the captains—merchant and Navy alike—and escort commanders. This would be in a hall somewhere on the beach and would cover details of signals, steaming and zigzag plans, and all the other foreseeable issues that might crop up during the coming passage.

Signals were always a problem when Navy and merchant ships operated together. A special simplified code, called MERSIGS, was developed during the war, but some of the older merchant ship masters could be bullheaded as the devil. No bloody naval chap was going to tell them what to do. They had spent their entire lives getting ships about the oceans of the world. They would damned well do what they wanted to. No one will ever know how many ships were lost to that mind-set, for collisions between ships in a convoy could be just as fatal as Hitler's torpedoes.

At its individually designated sailing time, each ship would back from its berth and move out into the black harbor waters, which, in the process, would become alive with red, green, and white running lights to a hoarse chorus of hoots and howls from ships' whistles and horns, all echoing off Manhattan's windowed cliffs. Once clear, each vessel would grope its way to the open waters off Ambrose Light. There, while still under a comforting umbrella of shore-based aircraft—blimps and planes alike—they formed themselves into columns.

In our case, a Navy ship, because it was more likely to be fitted with radar, was named leader for each column and was expected to exercise some control over its following ships, but overall command remained with the commodore. The escorts had their own commander. There were sometimes as many as ten to fifteen columns in our convoys, and ten to fifteen ships in each column. Since there was a half mile or more distance between ships and columns—and the escorts ranged even farther afield—it can be seen that a convoy could cover a sizable lot of ocean.

Changing course was not a simple matter for such large numbers of ships, most of which had differing turning circles and other maneuvering characteristics. Evolutions were kept as simple as possible, but zigzag plans did require turning, though not usually of very great amounts at any one time.

Most of the time we used either one- or two-hour zigzag plans. A one-hour plan moved the convoy on varying courses either to one side or the other of a base course, so as to put the ships back on that base course at the end of one hour. A two-hour plan returned the ships to their base course after two hours. Remarkable, isn't it?

In good weather, without fog, the trip usually went fairly smoothly. There was only the occasional steering casualty to worry about. Of course, in that case, there would be a certain amount of consternation as a ship went careening off out of control across the bows of oncoming vessels, all with a great hooting of horns and screaming of sirens.

Other times ships might suffer engine breakdowns. In those cases, the affected ship would simply sheer out of column and drop astern. An escort might—or might not—be detached to stand by her, and the convoy would steam sedately on over the horizon. In the bad submarine times it must have been a horrible feeling to have one's ship go dead in the water and to be forced to watch all the other vessels going on their seemingly uncaring ways. In those early days, there were times when there were no escorts to be spared at all, and the stricken ship would be left to the mercies of the sea and the Germans. At least I missed that character-building experience.

We made a safe passage of our first crossing of the Atlantic. Early one morning we came to be off the green coast of Ireland. For some unannounced reason, our division of four ships peeled off and made for Belfast. The main body of the convoy continued on to the Clyde ports.

This is the first time I crossed swords with our captain in the *Nightingale*. Since Mac and I constituted twice as many chief signalmen as were needed in the ship, at times the job did not get done at all. For instance, neither of us was on the bridge for our landfall in Ireland. It wouldn't have made a difference, but still one of us should have been on the bridge.

The *Florence Nightingale*'s captain was named Nelson. He already had been nicknamed Chain Gang before I came on board. He was, and he was fully aware of the fact, a full four-stripe captain in the U.S. Navy, but ship's scuttlebutt had it that he had not been to sea since his midshipman cruise of 1924. He had been a meteorologist, much of the time at Coco Solo in the Panama Canal Zone. I don't know if that was true or not, but our crew firmly believed it was. Nevertheless, captains had to have had command of ships at sea before they could be named admirals. So Chain Gang was given command of a suitably inoffensive transport and told to put in his time if he ever wanted a flag of his own. Unfortunately, in the tradition of the Pig in the *Indianapolis*, Nelson was not a good seaman.

To make matters worse, the executive officer, Commander Gregson, was. He had been master of the ship when she was a merchant vessel, before the Navy took her over. He had even been present throughout her construction in San Francisco and had sailed her for a number of years. Although not as socially polished as a naval officer, Gregson was a good practical seaman who fumed a good deal under the command of a captain who didn't know what the hell he was doing.

Naturally, Gregson knew nothing about the Navy's inevitable paperwork. Neither did Nelson, for that matter. They both came to rely on the ship's excellent chief yeoman, Tommy Coats, who soon was virtually running the ship administratively. Tommy was a conscientious and intelligent man who accepted the situation as just another of the Navy's mysteries. His reading of his two superior officers was that while Gregson might fart in the wardroom sometimes, he could take the ship anywhere in the world and bring her back. Nelson, however, would keep his napkin ring polished, while running the goddamned ship aground.

We came, that time, upon the Irish coast in a misted dawn, with a wan sun burning a hole no larger than itself through a film of cloud. A wide, flat bog area to port faded off into nothing, with only free-form silver discs reflecting the sun's low angled light to say there was land there at all. The discs were bomb craters, we were told, blown in the bog by German bombs and since filled with water. I had not known the German air force had ranged so far.

To starboard there were green hills, misted gray and fading off into a dim blue distance. Ahead lay the grimy town itself. Well-blackened brick buildings with tall brick stacks spewing sullen smoke to add still more black to a town already black.

It could not be said to be a pretty town, coal-burning industrial center that it was, but it had a dramatic simplicity of form that was interesting. As my first foreign port—I do not count the Pacific islands—it had that charm as well. The streets, though grimy, held little clutter at all. Long rows of connected houses flanked the streets, cheek by jowl, with never a tree or sprig of green to break the melancholy of brick and stone and gray slate roofs turned shiny by the morning damp.

My father had always said his people had been Scotch-Irish. It was possible, I supposed, that some of my relatives had lived in that place. Some of their descendants might live there yet. I looked at the town with a new, but short-lived, interest. It was still a drab and gloomy place where we stopped only long enough to off-load. We did try the local pubs, however.

They were mean places as compared to American bars, and the locals eyed us with disapproval—it was the only place in Britain where we met with that reaction. We knew there was political ill feeling toward the Irish Free Staters because they stayed out of the war against Hitler, but the North Irish were supposed to be on our side. Maybe, in our ignorance, we had drifted into a Catholic bar.

But, as Weldon put it, if their friendship was no better than their lousy Guinness beer they could damned well keep both. We gave them a good old-fashioned letting alone and returned early back to the ship. My clearest memory of the evening is of Irishmen matching coins as a pastime. All Irish coins had a harp on one side and a chicken or other farm animal of some kind on the other. Instead of heads or tails, they called meat or music.

From Belfast we returned to New York for what we from the Pacific appreciated as a remarkably short cruise. We were used to being at sea for months on end, but my first round voyage in the *Nightingale* used only a little more than four weeks or so. Even so, it put our return passage well into September—and closer to the North Atlantic's famous winter weather. It was a bumpy ride, with one howling gale after another bashing us on the snout. Sometimes we had to slow down to avoid damage to the ship. Several times we suspended zigzagging on the grounds that the U-boats, in such weather, would be just as uncomfortable as we were. The Pacific's warm waters and balmy breezes became fond memories, to be called up when the weather was especially bad.

Upon arrival off New York, in what had become by that time a practiced routine by both Navy and merchant vessels, the convoy broke up off Ambrose Light and individual ships made their ways as best they could to their assigned berths.

The Narrows, the cramped strip of water through which ships had to pass to enter into New York's great lower harbor, was a special trial. Entering convoys had to squeeze down their fronts almost to single file. This meant a good deal of pushing and shoving as ships jockeyed for position. In the case of large convoys there was sometimes a shortage of harbor pilots as well, leading to a scramble for their services. As a column leader, most often near the center of the convoy front, we enjoyed an advantage from all this. We almost always worked our way in early, but some of the trailing ships might even have to anchor and wait, all within sight of New York's remembered delights. After a hard westbound passage, that was not nice at all.

I don't know now if Mac's Marj had stayed in New York during our absence or if she had gone home to Nebraska and returned. She was there when we tied up at a Hudson River pier. The four of us—Mac, Marj, Tommy, and I—often had dinner together. Then we would go to a show or have a few drinks. I stood what watches Mac might have had, and Tommy never had watches to stand. Our times in port were thus very comfortable, but they seldom lasted long. The buildup in Britain was going into high gear by that time. We were usually in harbor less than a week.

That was all right with me. Since the Tea Drinker's priest had effectively excommunicated me, I was at loose ends anyway. Tommy accused me of carrying a torch, and I guess I was. I was still pretty naive in such things. But I noticed Tommy had no regular girl either. "Why buy a cow when the milk is free," he explained, with more truth than originality. Sometimes, after Mac and Marj had gone to their hotel, Tommy and I would sit morosely and drink—with all those millions of ready women swirling around us. But we do many things in youth that we regret later.

Our second trip took us to Scotland, as would most of our other voyages that long winter. Usually we anchored in the Clyde, off the small ports of Greenock or Gourock, but one time we went all the way to Glasgow and entered that port's famous King George V Dock, known more often as KG5. The word "dock," incidentally, has a different meaning in Britain than we give it in the States. Here, it means the structure at which ships tie up. In Britain, it means the water that is caught behind gates at high tide. Ships may come and go only at times of high water. The rest of the time they float on a pond of water held behind closed gates.

After all I had heard and read of the Clyde River, I expected it to be a much larger stream. In reality, it is narrow and so twisted I wondered how ships as large as the *Queen Mary* could have been launched into it. The answer lay in the way the launching ways were placed at bends in the river so that big hulls were slid into the water along the length of a relatively straight reach and not across as was done in other places.

When we passed Leith, a small port in the Clyde, with well-rusted building yards, I remembered seeing the name once before on the builder's plate in the *Moa*'s wheelhouse. The *Moa* had been built and launched into the Clyde at Leith, only to sail halfway round the world and be sunk in the soft warmth of Solomon Islands waters. Seeing the Clyde brought things full circle for me and the *Moa*.

September was coming to a close by that time. The air was, to say the least, nippy. The eastbound crossing had been downright rough. It was good to slide into the lee of hills in the Firth of Clyde. The wind was a little less—though certainly no warmer—but the endless battering of high seas was over. Thus we steamed to our anchorages in relatively smooth water.

The hills showed the colors of fall, including the famous purple of heather. The trip upriver, in fact, made a good run for sightseeing, what with the gray stone farmhouses and red cattle and black-faced sheep of Scotland. It was a lovely countryside, at once rural but with a settled and tended look. It came of the long centuries of cultivation the land had known, I suppose. It was interesting to realize that Oklahoma had been a state for only thirteen years when I was born there whereas this country had been settled for thousands of years.

The town of Glasgow itself was little more impressive than Belfast had been. A good deal larger, of course, but with the same coal-blackened buildings and tall once-red brick stacks working hard to make them blacker still. There seemed, though, to be more stone than brick in the buildings of Glasgow. There were sizable vacant areas, too, which, we were told, were where bombed neighborhoods had been. There had been neither time nor materials to rebuild them for so long as the war lasted.

KG5 Dock itself was crammed full of ships. "It's going to take Vaseline to get us into that mess," Mac said when he saw the mass of ships. But it didn't. Somehow, the docking pilots worked us in. Ships from every non-Axis country in the world were crowded in, and the gates closed behind us. We would be thus trapped until some succeeding high tide.

Here, as in New York, there was little need for a signal watch. We piled ashore in the early dark of a high latitudes autumn. A tram let us off in the big coal-blackened square in front of Queen's Station. It was full night, by that time, and the town was blacked out in a way that made New York's and San Francisco's modest blackouts look like carnival midways. Even the headlights of cars and buses were painted over, leaving only a thin blue-tinted slit to show the way and warn of their coming. Buildings themselves showed no light at all, except, sometimes, for a furtive glow as a blackout curtain was lifted at a doorway to let someone in or out.

The standard Scottish storefront was painted black in any event, with names and identifying signs lettered in old gilt paint. Windows were small paned and apt to be dirty enough to make the blackout job relatively easy so far as they were concerned. Inside, the shops were small and cramped and cluttered, though their stocks were pitifully small. Britain had been in what—to that time—had been a losing war. They knew the cost in men and ships of getting goods across the Atlantic. Totally unlike the Belfast Irish, though, the Scots were as friendly toward us as they reasonably could be. Even the men—who in Britain at that time could be a bit stiff with what they saw as well-fed and lavishly paid Americans—were friendly in Glasgow. They were pale and tired looking and dressed in bedraggled woolens, with sagging cloth caps and heavy leather shoes they called boots. You had to remember they had not been eating well for a long time. I came to have a great respect for them. They built good ships.

As for the women—our feet had hardly touched the curb (spelled "kerb" in Scotland) in getting off the tram when we felt a firm feminine grip on an arm and heard the interesting—though nearly unintelligible—Glaswegian-accented voice of an invisible woman suggesting, "Come on, Yank. Let's have a go." I don't know how they knew we were Americans. I guess their eyes were better adjusted to darkness than ours.

Naturally, it was raining. A standard joke among the Scots was, "We had a right nice summer—a couple of days last June." This was inevitably followed by laughter. Unfortunately, we were never there in June. And every time we were there, it rained. Only the steadiness of the rain varied. Still, I liked Scotland more than any other place I saw during the war. Maybe it was the people.

All seaport towns have a sailor street. In Glasgow it was Sauchiehall Street, pronounced by sailors as "Sucky All." It was one pub, cinema, or dance hall after another for what seemed a long way in the dark. To me, the atmosphere along Sucky All was much warmer than along other such streets I had seen about the world. There were seamen, naval and merchant alike, from all over what was then called the free world. They drank, swore, and whored as best they could in the short times they had. I don't remember ever seeing a fight in Sucky All, though I'm sure there must have been some. Sometimes, raised voices, in any number of languages, and the crash of broken glass might be heard from behind a drawn blackout curtain. But the big Scottish Bobbies were both experienced and adept in their duties. Nothing ever got out of hand.

I liked the Sucky All pubs. They were teeming blocks of humanity, most of it male. The sounds were those of foreign languages in hoarse voices, of laughter and banging bottles and glasses. I don't remember ever hearing a juke box, or even a piano. A piano would have taken up too much valuable floor space, for one thing. For another, there was no point in trying to attract further trade to establishments already full to bursting. The smells were those of beer and wet wool, of bodies and burning tobacco, all imposed on a base of soft coal smoke, the smell of which became, for me, the single most evocative sensation of the Scotland I came to know. I cannot smell coal smoke to this day without recalling Glasgow and Sucky All Street in the war.

We walked back to our ship that night. The Scottish night was black as ever, but there was a surprising lot of foot traffic in the narrow streets, most of it male and more or less unsteady of gait. Drunken laughter and raucous calling back and forth echoed off the dark stone fronts of the buildings, all of which stared back with blank windows at our foolishness. The big Bobbies were forgiving in most cases and lashed out only on provocation. But, once provoked, they lashed out with a will, as poor Jack Choner found out to his considerable pain.

Luckily, we did find our way back. I remember—vaguely—a tunnel connecting some of the docks. It was used by what the British call "navvies," or yard workmen, in their moving about the dockyard. It was floored in wood that had become furry from the chewing of generations of hobnailed boots. There were few lights, and what lights were there were dim. It was a spooky place on a dark night of rain and strange surroundings.

The tidal docks of Britain had one peculiarity that struck me as unsettling. Even the calmest of ordinary harbors have some movement of their waters in sympathy with the great waters of the oceans outside. But the water of KG5 dock, closed off as it was by iron gates, was flat and motionless as any mirror. It just didn't seem right.

The next day, while Mac, Tommy, and I were exploring Glasgow in the light of its short wintertime day, we came upon a group of lassies, all of whom had the pale faces of northern latitudes, with the bright red spots over their cheekbones which are so common there. They all had jobs of one kind or another, but they felt it would be peachy if we all got together after work for a go at the pubs. They gave us an address on Arlington Street and cautioned us to be sure and "knock them up" at six o'clock.

The expression occasioned a brief pause in conversation for it had an entirely different connotation in America. But once that misunderstanding was clarified—with much good-natured laughter—we continued on with our sightseeing. Since there was little else of interest in Glasgow, we spent much of our time studying the scenery of backbars until time for our date.

Arlington Street, as I recall it now, was not far from Sucky All, but its atmosphere was totally different. It was a fairly bleak curving street of gray stone houses with slate roofs shining in the wet, each with its own wee front garden behind a low wall of equally gray stone. Wooden trims were painted a startling white, and lace curtains hung at almost all of the windows. Multiple chimney pots, like fixed antiaircraft batteries, on the roofs broke the murky skyline, many of them doing their best to make Glasgow blacker even than it was.

Inside our girls' house we found the rooms small, but with high ceilings that had the odd effect of making them seem even smaller. Furnishings were heavy, numerous, and badly worn. Knickknacks and curios of all kinds cluttered every horizontal surface. Most of the pieces were from India and Egypt and other outposts of empire.

There were also lots of what I took to be family photographs of men. Many of them posed stiffly in uniform, both Army and Navy, all of them staring out from their frames accusingly, as though resenting our moving in on their women. That interpretation may have been owing to a guilty conscience on my part. The photos did not seem to bother Mac and Tommy.

The girls made themselves as presentable as their poor resources allowed. Their heavy woolens were drab and well worn and their stocks of cosmetics severely limited. I always felt a great sympathy for the Scottish women I saw. They had so little, and they had suffered for so long that my own privations, such as they were, seemed petty in comparison. And they lived in such a bloody awful climate.

Most of all, they could feel their biological clocks ticking, and there was nothing they could do about it. Life was slipping away from them. Their men, for the most part, were gone far away. And we were there. I could never find it in me to blame the women we met during the war—either in America or away—for what sometimes seemed a collapse of morals.

Once the girls were ready, we set out on our great Celtic romantic adventure, pairing off in what seemed a natural order. I don't even remember the girls' names now, but they did what they could to entertain us. None of them was a raving beauty, but for what we had in mind, beauty would have been no more than a nice fringe benefit to be appreciated if present, but easily overlooked if not, a fact the girls seemed to take for granted. After visiting a pub or two, one of them suggested we get a black market bottle and go back to Arlington Street. "Ever so much more comfy, don't you see?" was the way she put it.

So, that is what we did. When we had been there earlier we had seen no one else in the house. But, when we returned, we found a redhead who was a ravishing beauty. I never did find out who she was, but she was a glowing standout in wartime Glasgow. In the first place, she was English rather than Scottish. She was wearing real nylons and had on an interesting dress made of some kind of clinging material. She was indeed a beauty—and completely aware of the fact. Tommy gave her a go, out of pure sporting instinct, I suppose, but he didn't get far. I suspect the girl was saving herself for something better. She looked like what we used to call officer gear.

I later learned from my girl that she was a distant relative who had left London to escape the draft. I resented it when she treated the Scottish girls almost as servants, but they did not seem to mind at all. They fell all over themselves catering to the English girl as though it was no more than her due. It was odd, but it was also none of my business.

I don't remember our ever coming back to Glasgow in the ship. We usually anchored off the Firth of Clyde ports and took the funny little train to Glasgow. I remember one rail passage especially. The car was one of those with individual compartments that could be entered or left only when the train was standing in a station. The luck of the draw gave us a compartment occupied only by a moderately elderly lady in mannish tweeds and a dignity as hard as the Scottish winter, which was, by that time, in full force over the snowy hills outside.

It is not a long ride from the Clyde ports to Glasgow, but well before we got there our companion was down on her wool stockinged knees and entering into our craps game with as much abandon as she could muster, given the handicap of her breeding, I suppose. Weldon tried to introduce her to the language of craps, but that proved a total failure. She insisted on taking everything literally and simply rolled the dice, relying on us to tell her if she won or lost. We saw to it that she won, of course, and we parted at Queen's Station in Glasgow as firm friends, though both sides reverted to proper frostiness when she was met by an equally tweedy old gentleman who regarded us with a stare that could have been used to chill beef.

Despite the presence of the redhead from London, I came to feel comfortable in the house in Arlington Street. So did Mac and Tommy. We used to bring from the ship little gifts for the girls—butter and cooking fats especially. And when we sailed for home each time we asked if they would like anything from the States. I expected them to ask for such things as cigarettes and cosmetics or nylons, but they didn't. All they ever asked for was onions and cotton wool, their term for batt cotton. I don't know what they used it for.

Such was our life for all of that winter of 1943: the glitz and glitter of New York at one end and the hard wool and leather of Scotland at the other—with the stormy North Atlantic in between. And, although Hitler's submarines proved to be of little trouble—except for causing us the nuisance of zigzagging and steaming in convoy—the ocean itself proved enemy enough.

I had seen storms as bad in the Pacific, I think, but they weren't so unceasing. And certainly not so cold. For our first truly winter passages, in fact, we were not equipped with proper clothing at all, and we suffered cruelly. There were times when outside watches were relieved every fifteen minutes, even though we piled on whatever we could find to wear. The wind still cut. Ice froze on the hair in our noses, and we learned to breathe with our mouths closed to keep the cold air from causing the fillings in our teeth to contract and hurt like hell. Later, we were provided with highly effective three-ply clothing—hard-finished twill on the outside, a layer of waxed paper under that, and a lining of warm woolen fleece inside that. We had close-fitting helmets of the same material. There were even masks to cover our faces, but those first few crossings were not pleasant at all.

The sea seemed always in torment. When it was not rough it tended to be smothered in fog and the ships would stray from their positions with very good chances for collisions. But, for the most part, it was just plain rough. For a couple of voyages we had a small ship named the *Evangeline*, a former Fall River liner, in our column next astern of us. There were times when we could not see even her masts. Then she would emerge in a great leaping surge that saw her bows reach high into the sky, white water pouring from every scupper and freeing port she had. It was hard to imagine what life must have been like in that little ship. It was bad enough in our larger one.

Conrad once wrote, in one of his famous descriptions, that a sea in storm looks old. Indeed it does. The huge marching waves are themselves intricately wrinkled with smaller waves like the creases in an old man's neck. The water is gray and white with blown spray and spume so that it has the color and tone of an old man's skin. The wind howls and screams as though alive, tearing at the ships and causing them to heel sometimes from the force of wind alone. The sky overhead is churned and roiled into one gray, shroudlike pall racing overhead at little more than masthead height. In this terrible and violent scene, men and ships alike are endangered intruders.

Coming west, we were usually butting into the storms, and the ships were likely to be light in ballast. The *Florence Nightingale*'s high merchant ship bow would rise in a great swooping lift to meet the rushing seas, sometimes so strongly it could cause a man's knees to buckle. Then, at the top, the bow would hesitate for a beat or two before dropping down to crash into the trough with a shuddering shock that set the masts and rigging to jiggling. Huge bursts of white spray would explode from under her bow and be whipped back across the ship, splattering against vertical surfaces with the stinging force of bird shot.

Sometimes solid green water would come right over the bow and thrash about among the lashed down boats and against the hatches and deckhouses with force enough to twist steel. The propeller, with the bow thus down so low, would rise clear of the water and race wildly, adding its own rattling vibration to the overall chaos. The ship would toss and roll as though in living torment.

Once, in such conditions, the *Nightingale* split her hull. We were inbound for New York, some hundreds of miles at sea. It was early in the morning, and I was still in my sack. All of a sudden, with a crack like that of a 5-inch gun, the ship split across the main deck and down the side of the hull just forward of the superstructure. I can't tell you how quickly that got our attention. We had for so long been in the overall commotion of the storm that it had become no more than background noise, but the sudden snapping report of steel plates parting brought us up, full standing. And it was followed by an ominous screeching and grinding of steel plates scraping against each other to make us uneasy about the chances of our staying afloat. As it happened, the two ends of the ship did hang together and we crept safely into New York at low speed, but the incident served as a topic of conversation for some time.

Eastbound sailings, on the other hand, found the storm seas taking us on the quarter or from right astern. Either way, the effect was almost as bad for us, though not so hard on the ship. The stern would rise. Then, as the moving hill of water passed beneath the ship she would skew off to one side or the other and slide in a sickening skid down the great watery slope heaving up from under her stern.

She would roll even more in a quartering sea, with wild gyrations made even more attention-getting by long pauses at the end of each lurching roll. Sometimes she would seem to hold a pause for what would seem a long time, and we would come to wonder if she were going to come back at all. Everything not tied down below would go clattering off to the low side of the ship. When it was all over we would sometimes find the black marks of rubber heels on bulkheads two feet or more off the decks where men had put up their feet to keep themselves from falling.

Going east we would be heavy loaded too, causing the ship to labor even more so that the weather decks were all but constantly awash. The troops, locked below as they were in bad weather, made a god-awful mess of vomit and other emissions in which they had to live, eat, and sleep as best they could. It would take the deck force most of the return passage to clean the troop spaces, by which time we would load another lot and endure the whole process over again.

Once in the lee of the Scottish hills flanking the Firth of Clyde—or in the Hudson at the western end—we could relax somewhat, lick our wounds, and prepare for the next sailing. The lee of land might not do much against wind and rain, but it at least blocked the mighty march of storm seas. I remember once, for instance, when we lay at anchor in the Clyde off the small port of Gourock, a storm came up so severe that boats could not make the short passage between ship and shore. Those of us ashore had to stay ashore—we had what the Navy calls a Shanghai liberty, whether we wanted it or not.

We slept that night in the cold stone lobby of a cold stone hotel, without bedding or other comfort. The next morning the Red Cross fed us an educational breakfast of cold oatmeal—they called it porridge—and kippered herrings, a meal entirely lacking in charm for me.

This then became our seldom varied routine. One time we made a brief run to Iceland, but we were not allowed ashore there. The Icelanders did not want us polluting their culture, I suppose. Or their girls. But with our long glasses on the signal bridge, we could see virtually everything there was to see in the small city of Reykjavik. The public and commercial buildings of the town seemed solid enough in stone and brick. But the residential structures were wood-frame in Scandinavian styles. Some were painted in startling colors, as though to counteract the overall drabness of the landscape, which in winter, as it was when we were there, was mostly snow, with a few outcroppings of black lava. It didn't look like much of a liberty port. We were there only briefly in any event.

Although we came that time within only a few miles of the Arctic Circle, the weather seemed no worse than that farther south where we usually ran. That is not to say it was good at all.

On the west end, we sometimes called at Boston rather than New York. I liked Boston. It was not so garish as the parts of Manhattan we most often saw. But by that time I had met Joan, and New York had become more appealing. Joan lived in Pontiac, Michigan, but she used to come to New York when we were there.

Midtown Manhattan during the war saw the rise of an industry of pleasure palaces designed to draw money from sailors' pockets as efficiently as possible. One of these establishments was Rogers Corner on Eighth Avenue at West Fiftieth Street, as I recall now. Entry was through wide corner doors onto a broad open lobby, in the middle of which Tommy managed to fall flat on his face one night. He argued during the entire following round voyage to Scotland that there was a step-down in the lobby floor over which he had tripped. Anyone could trip and fall, for Christ's sake. We made book in the quarters on whether there was a step-down in the lobby floor or not. None of the rest of us could remember one. A good deal of money was bet. The first order of business upon returning to New York was to send a delegation ashore to settle the question. The lobby floor was flat as a table top.

The first room off the lobby was a bar, long and shaped like a racetrack with harried bartenders inside and clamoring sailors three to four deep all around its outside. A small band alternated service anthems with rousing renditions of Irish marching songs. Tiers of booths with little nightclub-sized tables rose about the central bar like bleachers. This is where the women, both escorted and not, sat. It was very much like the trading pits in Kansas City and Chicago where cattle and hogs are bought and sold. And its function was not all that much different.

It was actually a good way to do the business of the time. Sailor and girl could handle the preliminaries at a distance and save a lot of wasted time—and sometimes embarrassment—before commitments were made. That is where and how I met Joan.

I was standing at the bar—as near as I could get to it anyway—and she sat at one of the bleacher tables. We began playing eye games. She was with a large young sailor, and I let caution be my guide. In fact, when, a few moments later, I felt a hand on my shoulder and turned to look up at that large young sailor, I thought, "Oh, Christ! Here we go." I had seen enough barroom fights over women to know what to expect. But this guy just smiled and said, "My sister wants to know if you would like to join us, Chief."

There were no flashing lights or bells or any of the other stuff that is supposed to happen, but Joan and I came together in what at the time seemed a perfect meshing of needs. She was a tall, slender brunette—very much like the woman I would eventually marry—with striking black eyes and a shy smile. Her voice was soothingly soft when she spoke, which was not often. We could go sometimes for long periods without speaking at all, content to sit and watch the others making fools of themselves. Still, we seemed always in perfect communication.

I think now Joan must have been older than I was. Though, God knows, there was no hint of physical deterioration in what was a spectacular body. But she owned her own beauty shop in Pontiac, for instance, and moved with an easy self-assurance wherever I took her.

Her brother proved an understanding type, and so Joan and I had dinner that night at the Coconut Grove, a posh nightclub in one of the big Manhattan hotels. She was later my date when we had a ship's dance in a Waldorf Astoria ballroom one time. Being expert as she was in makeup and hairstyling, she made a striking figure in a simple black dress and wearing white gardenias in her hair, which was the style then. I remember being very proud of her.

At any rate, Joan and I were good friends, I think. When I got leave for the Christmas holidays of 1944, she invited me to stop in Pontiac on my way home to Oklahoma. It was a couple of thousand miles out of the way, but what the hell. Wartime rail travel was not much in the way of fun, but I did enjoy being with her. In my admittedly limited experience, I had never really been comfortable with a woman before. I suspect I was beginning to realize just how sterile my drinking and barhopping had become. I was ready for Joan, I guess, when she came along. And she for me.

She met me at the station in Detroit and drove me to Pontiac—twenty miles or so—in her car. We stopped at a florist's shop on the way and bought a large poinsettia for her mother. There was snow on the ground, and the weather was cold. The florist's windows were all frosted over inside. The store was a mass of red flowers. I had never seen poinsettias before, except in magazine illustrations. Everything was very Christmasy.

Joan lived with her mother in a small brick house in a Pontiac complex called Ramona Terrace. Both she and her mother did all they could to make my brief stay pleasant. With them I had my third taste of what middle-class life could be. (The first had been with the family in Honolulu; the second with my cousin in Kansas City.) I got my first indication of what life might be for normal men. It was good, but it also made me uneasy in some strange way. It was as though I realized, even then, that it was not meant for me. Honk, Sandy, Nations, and Jordan returned again and again to my thoughts. And the dark ships then so far away in the Pacific.

I went on to spend Christmas Day with my family in Tulsa. That was not totally successful either. Everything was much as I had left it on my last visit. I had grown still further away from my family, and the disillusionment I had felt upon first coming back to the States returned. No one seemed to be taking the war very seriously, and I came again to feel guilty for not being with the fast carrier task forces. I did not feel I had contributed much to the winning of the war in the past year. Hell, I was supposed to be a regular.

By that time I had left the *Florence Nightingale*, but my new ship was not yet commissioned. I was at loose ends, living in the receiving station on Commonwealth Pier in Boston. But I remembered the *Nightingale* with a festering bitterness I had never felt for a ship before. Or for its captain. For almost eighteen months I had been in a ship that did not need me, and I had been under a captain I did not respect. Nelson did not respect me much either.

We had gotten off to a bad start. Shortly after I reported on board the *Nightingale*, the captain had the exec order me to take off my Presidential Unit Citation (PUC) ribbon. I had it for nothing more heroic than simply being in the *Enterprise* during the Battle of Santa Cruz Islands and for various actions in the Solomons. Being young and foolish, I wore it—along with all the other ribbons and stars I rated. Old Chain Gang argued I didn't rate the PUC because I wasn't in the *Enterprise* anymore. I had to point out to the exec—for relay to Chain Gang—that there was a goddamned star on my ribbon. That star meant I had been in the *Enterprise* when the commendation was won and that I, therefore, was entitled to wear it in whatever ship I might serve—forever, if I lived that long.

I guess the exec made the point to Chain Gang because he came back to say I could continue to wear it. Once that was established, I took off all my ribbons. That really upset the captain. He personally ordered me to put them back on. The whole thing was petty as hell, but I guess I showed Chain Gang that a lowly chief petty officer could be every bit as petty as any chicken-dropping four-striper in the goddamned Navy.

At the start of our last sailing from New York the captain almost did something that would have been far more serious. We all drank in those days, but Tommy was the worst of us all, I think. This time, he was not on board when sailing time came. The colors were still flying aft, but the gangway had already been pulled in, the pilot was on the bridge, and our lines singled up. Except for Tommy, we were ready to shove off.

Missing his ship is a serious offense for a sailor, and we knew Tommy could expect little mercy from a captain like Chain Gang. We all—including the exec—stalled as long as we could. Choner asked for more time to secure the booms for sea. McNulty lost a key chart. But we could hold up the sailing only for so long. We had an assigned place in the convoy. If we were late, other ships would be held up. Hell, the whole goddamned war might be lost.

At the last minute, Tommy came running around the inboard end of the pier shed, topcoat tails flying in the wind. The exec quickly took the captain into the wheelhouse on some pretext or another before he saw his missing chief yeoman. But that still left the problem of getting Tommy on board without a gangway.

Choner took care of that. He was on the main deck aft, where he had been loading bagged flour with a cargo net. Without hesitation, he swung the working boom with its empty net over the side and let it down. Without pause, Tommy stepped into the net and was hoisted neatly aboard. He was in blues, and the cargo net closed about him like a shroud. Whitened with flour as it was, it left him a bleary-eyed ghostly figure, not too steady on his feet as the net fell away from him and he stepped out on deck aft.

Choner's men hustled him out of sight, and so far as I ever knew, the captain suspected nothing. If he had, Tommy would have suffered a good deal, I suspect. Chain Gang's standard response to chiefs who gave him a report or answered a question was, "Will you bet your buttons on it?" This meant that if the chief were wrong, he would lose his pretty brass buttons and be back in what we called the low-neck gowns of ordinary enlisted men. He did bust a couple of the younger chiefs.

Once in Scotland that time, we were ordered to the Mediterranean. It was April, as I recall, and the North Atlantic weather was beginning to be tolerable. Steaming conditions became almost bearable. That couldn't be allowed, of course. So, after freezing off various appendages through a long winter, we would go to the Med where—by all accounts—we would sweat them off. I never saw Arlington Street again.

17
The Med

OUR LAST PORT OF CALL IN BRITAIN was Cardiff in Wales. We were anchored off the Clyde ports when we received our orders to the Med, but we were told off to stop in Cardiff to load troops for the passage. The port, behind lock gates, was on the north shore of the Bristol Channel. We were in Wales, but we could see England, misty and blue, on the other side of the river. We entered at high tide—necessarily—because at low tide what seemed miles of mud appeared between us and the sea. We were kept afloat in water pooled behind the closed dock gates as we had been in Glasgow's KG5 Dock.

All my reading about Wales—*How Green Was My Valley* and the like—had led me to expect dirt and squalor, but I remember it now as a green and pleasing land studded with gray stone buildings and towns that looked much like those we had come to know in Scotland. On leaving the Firth of Clyde for the last time, we rounded Ailsa Craig, the famous rounded rock that had seen so many British seamen get away to sea, and turned left to coast down the east side of the Irish Sea, sailing the same waters John Paul Jones had raided in an earlier war. With our long glasses, we could tour the countryside as we went, seeing fat cattle and sheep munching the green hills. I remember no coal mines at all, nor even any sign of them.

Cardiff itself did have substantial coal shipping facilities, but the grime was no worse than that of Belfast or Glasgow, as I recall. The residential districts, in fact, were cleaner. Neat, though small, houses of stone or brick with white stone stoops and brightly polished brass door knobs and knockers. I remember seeing housewives on their knees scrubbing the stone stoops with hand brushes. Commercial shops and other buildings were much like those of Glasgow, and the dockyards were not much different from KG5, though somewhat cleaner.

We were in Cardiff overnight, long enough for only one liberty, but it was a memorable one. An oddly exhilarating sense of freedom came over us in Cardiff.

In New York and the Scottish ports we had come to know people and were expected to make calls when in harbor. In Cardiff, we were free again. We knew no one in the town, and no one knew us. We could come and go as we wanted, with no feelings of guilt or responsibility at all. It was much the way I had felt through my first years in the Navy.

Of course, there was damned little to do in Cardiff. The town was utterly blacked out at night and seemed to have fewer pubs and cinemas even than Belfast. I remember no Welsh counterpart to Glasgow's wonderful Sucky All Street. But Cardiff did have the charm of any new and different port. Our last crossing of the Atlantic had been an unusually gentle one, and the passage down the Irish Sea little more than a sightseeing excursion. A group of us from the quarters went ashore in a party mood, spiced with the sailor's titillating knowledge that in any port something might happen.

We made the requisite pub calls and found the locals easily as friendly as those of Scotland. Since we—the chiefs—were operating as a group, we had little expectation of serious romantic involvement. But, oddly, we didn't seem much to care. I suppose our recent calls at New York and Scotland had quieted our most urgent gonadal urgings, and we were left free to enjoy the more innocent, but no less delightful, pleasures of female company. In Cardiff I met a girl named Lal.

She was a sweet-voiced girl whose face and form I can no longer remember. But I do remember our holding hands and walking together in the black streets of Cardiff. There were five or six of us from the ship, and we had become attached to an equal number of Welsh girls who seemed more animated than their counterparts we had known in Scotland. They laughed more and chattered in what, to me, was a charming accent. Lal and I lagged behind, saying little, but enjoying the skylarking of those going ahead. It was a strangely innocent evening, but I remember it now with a poignancy I associate with few other liberties I had in the Navy.

As usual, Doc Weldon—the ship's chief pharmacist's mate—was the star of the show. There was a square, I remember, in Cardiff where the trams came. The black ruins of an ancient castle loomed to one side, and a large and ornate stone fountain or monument rose in the middle. There was a moon that night, and a scud of low clouds that made an illusion that the moon was racing through a black sky of stationary clouds. Everything earthly, of course, was black with the coal smoke of centuries past. The blue slits of the tram lights and the occasional car or lorry, by accenting the overall blackness of the night, made the scene dramatic as hell.

The pictures were letting out and the pubs closing, when we came to the square. Masses of people—sailors, soldiers, and the local Welsh alike—flooded through the square, which was washed over with the redolence of soft coal smoke we had come to associate with all British towns. It was a warm night and still not late. Everyone seemed reluctant to give up and go home. That was when Weldon took over.

Once before Weldon had gotten us into trouble with his musical talents. He, Mac, Tommy, and I had spent all of an afternoon in New York's Blue Angel nightclub, one of the city's most popular at the time. It consisted of a forward bar and lounge separated by a screen of blue glass etched with a stylized angel from a more formal nightclub and dance floor in the rear. There was a piano in the forward area, and Weldon had been chording it and singing his risqué parodies all afternoon.

At first, all went well. We were there for hours, and the other patrons seemed appreciative. So was the management, who invited the lot of us to dinner on the house when the time came. The show that night was three actors in ludicrous drag and gaudy wigs who played Andrews Sisters songs on a backstage phonograph and mouthed the words on stage. When the master of ceremonies introduced the act, he announced that the house was honored to have the real Andrews Sisters in the audience that night. We thought it a gag, and a part of the hype, and paid little attention until, wedging his way through abutting tables on a trip to the head, Weldon glanced down and saw the famous wartime trio. Startled, he yelled across the crowded room, "Jesus Christ, guys! They *are* here!" This, along with some other indiscretions, resulted in the management's suggestion that we take our dinner in the forward lounge.

But that night in Cardiff Weldon had more room in which to operate. He climbed onto the monument in the center of the square and led the throng in singing. His biggest triumph came when he taught the Welsh the words to a nonsense song then popular, "Mairsy Doats." The crowded square rang with the silly syllables, and the old and blackened buildings all about echoed back the rise of the singers' voices and the laughter.

It is odd that one incident can come to stand for an entire period, but that night before Cardiff Castle did come to represent for me my whole British experience. Just as that other night of singing on the decks of the *Indianapolis* came to represent for me the serenity of my time in the Pacific before the war.

I walked Lal home that night and went back to the ship, strangely content and ready to return to the sea. We sailed the next day. I would not see Britain again for the remainder of the war. Nor did I ever see Lal again.

The Bay of Biscay is a notoriously rough part of the Atlantic Ocean, but it was bland when we crossed going south. Each day the weather was warmer and the sea bluer. It was a mark of the war's progress to that time that, though we went in convoy with escorting destroyers, we passed the Strait of Gibraltar in daylight. During the hard times of the submarine war, convoys passed the narrow strait at night to avoid being reported by German agents in Spain and Africa. The water there is so narrow ships could be seen from both continents at the same time. Tommy noted that the Rock of Gibraltar, if seen from the right angle, looked exactly like the Prudential insurance company logo.

Our first port of call in the Med was Oran in French Algeria. It was what we came to know as a typical Mediterranean port, protected for the most part by a man-made breakwater of stone or concrete. In the case of Oran, the breakwater was of stone and extended for what must have been a mile and a half, with only a very small opening to the northeast. The old port—all French ports seem to have an old port—was but a small corner of the harbor and was used mostly by fishing boats.

Ashore, the immediate harbor area was low and flat, with the usual clutter of railroad sidings, warehouses, piersheds, and shops. The main part of Oran—certainly the most impressive part of the city, sat on level ground at the top of high cliffs. This is where the ruling French had their homes and businesses. The streets were wide and handsome avenues set in the shade of plane trees, and the buildings strikingly modern. I thought I saw a vague similarity between Oran and Nouméa in New Caledonia, but that may simply have been because both were French.

Oran's *casbah*, or native quarter, was not nearly so impressive. There, the houses were plastered stone that shined white in the African sun and made hard-edged shadows in the narrow streets. Some of the streets were actually stairways, too steep and rough for wheeled traffic. The scents under the hot Mediterranean sun were unpleasant because a good deal of the sewer system consisted of little more than an open window and the law of gravity. We learned to walk in the middle of casbah streets.

The people of Oran, though they lived in the same city, were of at least two different worlds. The French colons were well fed, well clad, and seemingly prosperous. They also had the surly, pouting expression I had come to know of their countrymen in Nouméa. They looked right through Americans as though we were not there at all. The French in my admittedly meager experience of them were considerably less than charming.

Oran's native Arabs were not much more cordial—but they had more reason for resenting us since we were white. They had learned from the French to fear whites, I suppose. Many of them at that time still wore turbans or fezzes and the flimsy white cotton robes of the country. Incidentally, a considerable black market in the sale of mattress covers from American naval vessels developed when the locals discovered that the covers enlisted sailors used in lieu of bed sheets could, with a minimum of alteration, be made into excellent robes. The practice became so rife that sailors were required to turn in their old mattress covers before they could be issued new ones.

The Arabs had dark faces with glittery black eyes that tended to avoid ours if at all possible. Once they did meet our eyes, though, their faces would split in a ready smile, showing startlingly white teeth. The women, of course—many of them veiled—would not meet our eyes at all, and we were warned to stay away from them, except for those in licensed whorehouses. We heard the same warnings about knives we received in Juarez and Honolulu's Aala Park. Altogether, the French treated the Arabs in such a way that I could easily understand why the oppressed people revolted after the war and, after a bloody struggle, won their independence.

The attractions of Oran were quickly run through. I remember one pleasure palace with the French chest-high zinc bar along one wall and a scatter of rough tables and chairs filling the ground floor. There was a dance floor and one of those rotating mirrored balls that once hung from the ceilings of such places to reflect darting shafts of colored lights about the room. Oh, it was a swell joint. The bar glasses were well-rusted Army C-ration cans. A blowsy old woman patrolled the scene with a funnel and a large bottle. In the unlikely event anyone left without finishing his drink, she used the funnel to pour what was left of it into the bottle. I did not like even to think of where that salvaged alcohol wound up. The drink of choice—or necessity—was a villainous *vin ordinairre*, which could have had any number of disgusting things in it without the fact being noticed at all. There must have been better places in Oran, but I never saw one.

One day while we were in Oran, Weldon—who else?—somehow got hold of an Army weapons carrier, a kind of small truck, complete with driver. We drove it to Sidi bel Abbes, some fifty or sixty miles inland from Oran. Sidi bel Abbes was the longtime headquarters of the French foreign legion in Algeria. It was a relatively small town, dominated by the yellow plastered buildings of the legion. Its casbah made up a comparatively larger part of the town than did Oran's, but the French homes—perhaps through contrast—seemed even richer than those of the larger city. The legion's officers' club was especially noteworthy, set in watered green gardens under sprawling trees that left both buildings and garden in welcome shade.

We naturally were interested in seeing the legion barracks, and a red-headed Pole with fair English showed us around. We asked if any Americans were there, but he said all the Americans and British had been allowed to leave the legion and to return to their own forces upon the outbreak of the war. It was hard to tell from looking at them which countries the legionnaires we saw came from. It was said a large part of their sergeants were German, even during the war. They were not a physically prepossessing lot, but their picturesque uniforms helped. They wore short swords that reminded me of the heavy cutlasses our company commanders had used against us in boot camp. They wore these weapons even when off on liberty.

The legion barracks were Spartan to an extent that made our old boot camp quarters in San Diego look damned near palatial. Low, continuous wooden shelves lined the walls. They were slightly higher at the walls than toward the center of the large room but not separated into individual bunks at all. These were the bunks where the men slept. Many years later I saw photos of the same sleeping arrangements in Hanoi's notorious Hanoi Hilton prison during the Vietnam War. Smaller and higher shelves over the bunks were neatly arranged with the men's toilet articles. Crude wooden footlockers and rifle racks flanking the door completed the furnishings. The only light was from shallow horizontal windows placed high under the ceiling. These, too, were like those in the Hanoi Hilton, which had been designed by the French to cage Vietnamese rebels.

It must have been a holiday routine the day we were there for the men lolled about with no sign of the harsh discipline for which the legion is so famous. We did notice, though, that they snapped to an exaggerated attention when their officers were about. They were almost as respectful of their sergeants. In all, they had the furtive watchfulness of men who have been systematically kicked around. But, in a classic example of the battered-child syndrome, they got even at the cost of the poor bloody Arabs.

Once I saw two legionnaires strolling down a narrow street, apparently on liberty. They came upon two Arabs who were so lost in animated discussion they did not notice the approach of the legionnaires. With no word of warning at all, the legionnaires unhooked their short, heavy sheathed swords and knocked both the Arabs flat. Still without speaking, they replaced their sheathed swords at their belts and moved on, not bothering to look back at what they had done. Remembering that violent scene, it was easy to understand the later Algerian revolt and how brutal it became.

The Arab residents of Sidi bel Abbes lived in obvious terror of the legionnaires—who were tough. We stopped in one establishment for a drink. The day was hot. The room was a large hollow cube of a place, with a chest-high bar to one side and a loose scattering of tables and chairs in no particular order. A rough stairway led up to a wooden balcony running around all four sides of the room. It looked like a stage-set saloon for a low-budget American Western movie. Doors led off the balcony to rooms we could not see. A staggering parade of legionnaires and haggard, hard-faced women of assorted colors and races passed up and down the stairs.

Not all the legionnaires bothered to go upstairs. I saw one grab his woman and lift her bodily to sit on the chest-high bar. There he hiked her skirt and did something I would not have believed only a few months before. The woman continued to drink and to smoke her crude cigarette with an air of bored unconcern. No one else in the place—legionnaires, women, bartenders, and swampers alike—seemed to notice. "Let's get out of here," Tommy choked. His voice was pretty tight.

None of us had much to say on the ride back to Oran, watching the country we saw in silence. I had always thought of Algeria as desert. I had seen too many foreign legion movies, I suppose, and read too many adventure stories in the old Blue Book and other pulp magazines. Actually, the part inland from Oran was much like the country between Los Angeles and San Diego in California. The grassy hills even had the same sunburned blond look to them. One noticeable difference was a scattering over the land of small white cubelike structures with rounded domes on their tops. From any distance they looked like blank dice with halved golf balls perched on top. We were told they were the tombs of holy men. It was a Muslim country.

It all appeared to be grazing land. I remember no tilled fields at all. There were leggy sheep with skimpy fleeces, not the squarish Scottish black faces we had seen on the banks of the Clyde. Given the Arabs' reputed love for horses, it was strange that we saw so few of those animals and that those we did see were so poor in appearance. There were many little donkeys, though, most loaded to the gunwales with bundles and bales or bearing with dainty steps some Arabian gentleman sitting sideways on their thin hip bones and absentmindedly beating on them with long sticks. The donkeys were so small their riders had to hold up their feet to prevent their dragging on the ground.

Back in Oran, we found the ship already freed of the troops we had brought out from Cardiff—and boarding those we would take to our next port. To us, soldiers were soldiers. We could see no reason the ends of the war effort would not have been served equally well by keeping on board those we already had, but there was bound to be a reason somewhere, I suppose.

Altogether, we must have carried thousands of troops across the Atlantic. I always felt vaguely sorry for them. Most were very young, and by that time, virtually all were draftees. I had nothing but pity for draftees, and I even then questioned the institution of the draft. There were practical reasons for it, I knew, but something seemed lacking in any country that had to force its young men to defend it. It was as though old—and sometimes young—politicians were forcing young men to do things the country had not sufficiently inspired them to do voluntarily. Those of us from the regular peacetime forces had no one to blame but ourselves. As Sandy had reminded us, "We wasn't drafted." But I figured the poor bloody draftees had plenty of people to blame.

I always felt guilt when I watched them disembark. Even if it were not off an invasion beach, they were still on their ways into battles they did not understand, under conditions that left little room for personal glory or even dignity. And they went so unprotestingly, even waving feebly to us sometimes as they went. Then we returned to the States for another load to deliver into the fire. I was never comfortable hauling troops. Someone had to do it, I suppose, but I didn't want it to be me. I was not very happy in the Med.

North Africa, by that time, had been held by Allied forces for some time. There was a substantial infrastructure of training facilities in place. I suppose the soldiers we brought out would be given additional training in Algeria before going on to the fighting fronts.

From Oran, we went next to Naples in Italy. The Sicily and Salerno campaigns were, by that time, over—but only just. We entered Naples Harbor only a few days after the Germans had left. Sunken ships clogged the piers and docks, and we saw for the first time serious and recent damage in the European war.

The departing Germans had left a massive bomb in the basement of the Naples post office, for example, timed to explode several days after they were gone and the locals were beginning to feel safe. And, explode it did, killing some hundreds of people and filling the streets of the city with a powdery white dust of shattered stone and concrete. We made a game of trying to find an unbroken window pane anywhere at all. Even with our powerful long glasses, we could find but a handful. Wonderful people, the Germans. They had already lost the goddamned town; they didn't have to kill a lot of innocent people who could no longer hurt them.

Blocking the harbor was more justifiable, I suppose, but it proved remarkably ineffective. American engineers and Seabees with cutting torches went onto the ships sunk at the docks and cut them down to dock level. Our own ships then simply tied up to the sunken vessels and off-loaded over their decks. The work was actually made more efficient because the docks, in effect, were made wider, with more room for maneuvering trucks and cargo. The Germans, bless them, must have been chagrined to see the port they had thought wrecked in virtually full operation so soon after. "That must have frosted their goddamned balls," Choner said.

For several round voyages then, we moved troops from Africa to Italy. We came to know Naples fairly well, and Weldon arranged a number of excursions for those of us not needed in the unloading. Our boats were in the water anyway in order to free the hatches, and one time Weldon somehow got the use of a tank landing craft (LCM) for a day trip to the Isle of Capri, the one of song and legend.

The Germans had used the beautiful little island as a rest haven for their Luftwaffe. The Americans would use it for the same purpose for their airmen when they got around to it. But, for one blessed little while, neither side was there, and our little party of chiefs had the place to ourselves. Physically, it was untouched by the war, though the natives were suffering economically from a loss of trade. They greeted us—and our dollars—with open delight.

Capri is a small island of very high, all but vertical limestone cliffs, with a small waterside settlement and a larger town in a shallow valley above. A funicular—cable car—joined the two, rising abruptly through a rough, nearly vertical landscape of rocks and thorny growths. Small, cubelike plastered stone houses were scattered wherever footing offered. The hardness was softened only by latticed grape arbors and brilliant flowers.

We hired a little stunted figure of a man as a guide and set out to explore the island. Our guide's English was much better in his pitch for business than it proved in execution for the rest of the tour, but we made do. He was big on the villas of notables on the island, pointing out those of various ancient Roman emperors, as well as those of more recent British and American movie stars. I remember Gracie Field's pleasant place. And Ginger Rogers'. That is where I got married.

Our little guide paused before a black wrought-iron gate in a stone wall, all well covered by bougainvillea and other subtropical growth. "And this," he said, somewhat breathless with the enormity of the fact, "is the villa of the American film star, Ginger Rogers." We were gathered in a group before the gate, eager to hear about this figure of our celluloid dreams. But Weldon, with his steel-trap mind, aimed a good deal higher. "Ginger Rogers!" he blurted. "Why, we've got her husband in our ship. Here he is. Right here."

Without bothering to look, he hooked his thumb over his shoulder. By chance, he pointed at me. I was pretty slack-jawed. The other chiefs, too, were taken aback by this turn, but they recovered quickly and added some lurid details in support. None of it was necessary, though. Our little guide had bought the whole scam from the beginning, with no reservations whatsoever. After gaping at me in awed silence for a moment, he sprang at the gate and pounded on it with his stick.

After what seemed a long time, an old man in a black satin vest with a black-and-white striped back came out and engaged our tour guide in a noisy crackling of more and more excited Italian, which none of us could understand. It ended in complete surrender of the fortress, and we were ushered in with a good deal of hand clapping and calling out for reinforcements in the form of maids and cooks and others whose functions were not clear from their dress.

It was not an extravagantly elaborate villa, but it would do. Nicely. It had white plastered walls and cool tiled floors. Slatted wooden shutters sliced a magnificent view into little horizontal strips. A stone terrace, shaded by a lush arbor of pendant grapes, opened off a wide double door.

I was becoming a little nervous about what was going to happen when the truth came out, but Weldon and the others showed not a care in the world. Our little host settled us into some nice white wicker chairs on the terrace and brought us soft, sweet cherry herring from Denmark, which must have been too tame for the German aviators' taste since they had taken everything else. Our little guide happily settled in with us, but the old guy in the vest hustled him away and left us to drink while he rustled up something for us to eat.

I later felt guilt for forgetting entirely about my old shipmates in the fast carrier task forces, but, oh god, it was nice there on that terrace overlooking blue Naples Bay, with the stony beige shores of Ischia and Sorrento in the background—and, over all, the blue symmetry of Vesuvius. After a while shyly smiling Italian girls brought us heaped platters of pasta with several other dishes, most of which we did not recognize. And, to top it all, a little man in a velvet jacket came—breathless from his hurried summoning—to play his violin for us.

The cherry herring must have been more potent than it seemed. We melted down into a warm alcoholic bliss. Since we were having fun, the time flew. But someone did notice the time, and, like Cinderella fleeing at the stroke of midnight, we rounded up our little guide and ran back down the mountain. "I got to get this goddamned boat back," Weldon screamed, "or my ass is mud."

That effectively broke the spell. It was an inelegant way to end an unlikely idyll, but the Navy did not keep LCMs around as excursion boats for chiefs. We were, I thought, unusually quiet on our ride back to Naples. I suppose each of us was lost in his own thoughts of the contrast between what we had just known and the bloody truth going on in the Italian hills not far away. The contrast was just too great. I know I felt guilty then for burning diesel fuel brought at such great cost and risk across the ocean for nothing more than my own pleasure.

Oddly, more than thirty years later, while Ginger Rogers was on a book tour in San Francisco, I met her and told her of the incident. She laughed and said, "I was always puzzled by that. My housekeeper wrote and told me about it, but I didn't understand because I was between husbands at the time."

Weldon got us into another, more prosaic, situation another time as well. He promoted a car from the Army, and we went to Pompeii, the ancient Roman city buried by an eruption of Vesuvius centuries before. There were thunderstorms over the great volcano that day, with black clouds and darting lightning and the echoing mutter of thunder. We were the only people there. The crippled guide we hired showed us one chariot-rutted street after another, and the ruined houses with their amazingly preserved painted walls little faded from what they must have been when new. Some had the huddled, petrified figures of people lying where they had fallen that awful day. Others made modern pornography seem tame in comparison.

A surprisingly large area of the town had been excavated, but even more intriguing were the abrupt endings of streets in rubbled cliffs of ash and stone. What must lie, still undiscovered, in the parts not yet excavated!

Most of the time, though, we made brief liberties in Naples itself. Although there were some pleasant tree-shaded residential streets on the heights overlooking the city, most Neapolitans lived in six- or seven-story slums at sea level. Shops were small and ill stocked, and the people glum and dispirited. Most of the women, especially the older ones, wore shapeless black bombazine dresses turned, like their faces, a dull corpse-gray by the stone dust left from the German post office bomb and kicked up by pedestrians' shuffling feet.

One of the saddest things I ever saw in my life was a funeral procession making its slow way through Naples' narrow streets. The mourners trudged behind an ornate black glass-windowed hearse drawn by plumed black horses. Hearse, horses, plumes, and mourners—all were stained the same dead gray by the stone dust from the Germans' goddamned bomb.

At night, we used to see family groups huddled by little fires of burning scrap lumber, cooking tiny fish over the flames in black and filthy streets. The streets and walks were slick with the slime and old soap of too many pans of greasy dishwater thrown from upper floor windows. Naples' people were poor. I remember seeing little kids come down to the waterfront with empty burlap bags tied to lengths of line. They would throw the bags into the water and let them settle to the bottom. After a few minutes, they would pull up the bags and pick off the small, snail-like shellfish that had attached themselves to the rough cloth. The kids ate those things, raw and unwashed, straight as they came from the filthy harbor water. They were hungry.

This led directly to a rare flare-up in the chiefs' quarters one night. One of the older chiefs whose name I no longer remember had come in from a run ashore. He had loaded too much *vino* and was giving the Italians hell for their low moral standards. "This goddamned broad laid me right in the same room with her goddamned family," he growled. "They were eating their goddamned supper, with just a goddamned blanket hanging from the ceiling between us and them. And she did it for a lousy pack of cigarettes."

That was the only time I ever saw Tommy lose his temper. "It's no worse to sell than it is to buy, you dumb son of a bitch," he said. "She did it to feed her family; what the hell is your excuse?"

Another time some of the ship's junior officers, fine young American gentlemen that they were, rented a nice little sailboat of twenty feet or so. They had a fine sail on beautiful Naples Bay. But, when they returned to the ship, they stepped gaily onto the landing platform at the bottom of the accommodation ladder and shoved the boat off to go where it would. God knows whether the Italian owner ever got it back or not. Not all Americans were charming.

This all may sound as though we were doing nothing else all that time, but we were making regular round voyages between Naples and Oran. Sometimes, if the wind were right, we could use the ash and smoke from then-erupting Vesuvius all the way to Africa as a smoke screen against the diminishing but still real threat of German bombers. We might choke to death on the volcanic ash, but we didn't get bombed.

On the African end of the trip, we more often called at Mers el Kebir, a small French naval base just around a stony point from Oran proper. At Mers el Kebir the British navy slaughtered the French ships lying there after the fall of France in 1940. The British were afraid the Germans would get their hands on the French ships. When the French refused to meet British demands, the British sank them where they lay. Scars from British shells still could be seen in the breakwater and on the beach when we were there.

Mers el Kebir, like most Mediterranean ports, consisted of a man-made offshore breakwater curving out from an otherwise unprotected shore. On land, it was reached from Oran through a tunnel cut through the solid rock of the point. The marks of hand chisels could still be seen in the rock. It must have taken years to build. But slave labor is cheap.

After a month or so, we were ordered round to Arzeu, a small open roadstead a few miles east of Oran. It was one of the landing beaches in the 1942 invasion by British and American troops and was being used as a training area when we were there. We anchored offshore, and green troops were brought off in landing craft to climb up cargo nets let down over our sides. Once they had done that, they climbed back down again and were landed through the light surf. Then, once they had done that, they came back and climbed our nets again. This went on for a long time. I had not realized how complicated climbing up and down a net can be. The trick lay in resisting the natural impulse to grab the horizontal ropes of the net, and to hold to the vertical ones instead. That made all the difference for soldiers burdened as they were with rifles and packs and all the other gear they carried or had strapped to them.

It was damned boring for us. We were not allowed ashore. The little town didn't look much as though it had anything to offer anyway. There was a French seaplane base there, though, and it was interesting to watch the airplanes. One day there I saw the biggest single-engine airplane I ever saw in my life. In circling to land, it dug a wing tip into the water and crashed in much the same way I remembered the PBY had done that time off Guadalcanal.

Maybe out of boredom, I began to clash more and more often with Chain Gang. There is little hope of winning in an enlisted man's clashing with his captain, even if he is a chief. But there are limits to what a man can accept with much grace.

It was our job to carry landing craft to invasion beaches. Those landing craft carried one signalman per boat. They had the merest of training and were used in controlling the boats at the line of departure and for the dash in to the beach. One of these signalmen, a blond young man from New Jersey, asked me one day if he might stand watches on the bridge when he was not in his boat. I thought it a great idea. He could learn something and get some experience in real signaling. His name was Hartwig, and he was a bright young man. But one day on his way to the bridge, Chain Gang got him.

Boat crews were not issued black shoes when they were embarked. They wore the high-top rough shoes we called sand shoes. Unfortunately, at Chain Gang's insistence, the uniform of the day for bridge personnel in the *Nightingale* was black shoes. Chain Gang seized on the opportunity to strike a blow against the Axis. He put Hartwig on report, a charging procedure against sailors who do wrong.

Because I was responsible for letting him on the bridge in the first place, I had to stand up with him at captain's mast. I pointed out that Hartwig did not have any black shoes but that the Navy stood to gain through his improved proficiency, which might eventually lead to a better prosecution of the goddamned war. I didn't use the word "goddamned," of course, but I guess I was sarcastic enough to get Chain Gang's attention. He sprang his usual ploy of wanting to know if I were willing to "bet my buttons" in the matter. What he meant was that, if I kept on, I was going to lose all those pretty brass buttons I wore. I would be back in the ordinary enlisted man's uniform. I just had to point out to him that I was, by that time, a permanent appointment chief and that I could be demoted only by sentence of court-martial. This infuriated the captain, and he sentenced Hartwig to thirty days of extra duty—which I was careful to see he never performed.

Chain Gang did later bust an acting appointment chief. (Chiefs, when first appointed, are given what are called acting appointments. For one year they are on what amounts to probation. The captain under whom they are appointed can demote them during that period for anything he likes. If the new chief performs satisfactorily, he is made a permanent appointment chief and can be demoted only by court-martial.) The young chief Chain Gang demoted happened to meet his brother, an Army second lieutenant, in Naples. The brother invited the chief into a nearby officers' club for a drink. The chief was in khakis, virtually identical to Army khakis, but he knew he was not supposed to put his enlisted ass on any officers' club barstools. His brother solved the problem by taking off one of his gold bars and pinning it to the chief's collar. This made both of them out of uniform, of course, since neither had the prescribed two bars, you see. It probably would have worked had not the chief, upon entering the club with his brother, run face-to-face into our beloved Chain Gang.

The most serious thing Chain Gang ever did, though, was order our red truck lights turned on off the landing beaches of southern France. Red truck lights are at the tops of ships' masts—"truck" is another word for masthead. They are usually shown in harbors when friendly aircraft are operating in the area and are meant as a warning to air crews. Of course, if there are any enemy aircraft in the area, they are an invitation.

It was dusk of the first day of the invasion, and German airplanes were circling far off on the horizon with radio-guided glide bombs. The task force commander had ordered chemical smoke to hide the ships. Chemical smoke, by its nature, lies close to the surface, sometimes shielding only the hulls of ships and leaving their masts showing. Distant airplanes are not likely to see anything so small as a ship's mast. But, if you stick nice bright red lights on those masts, they can damned well see them.

Chemical smoke hides ships from each other, as well as from airplanes, and our Chain Gang became upset at what he took to be an overriding danger of collision. That is when he ordered the red truck lights turned on so other ships could see us. The problem was that the goddamned Germans could see us too. Those two red lights on our masts were probably the only visible lights between neutral Spain and Vatican City, for Christ's sake!

The exec argued against the order, but Chain Gang would not listen. The lights were turned on—briefly. Soon a bull-horned voice roared out of the darkness ordering us to "turn off those goddamned lights!"

Chain Gang, standing in all his formidable dignity, announced back that he was a "four-stripe captain in the United States Navy." The voice out of the darkness was unimpressed. "What the hell do you think I am, a seaman second?" The voice from the darkness turned out to be a four-stripe captain in the U.S. Navy too. He was in a Beachmaster's control boat and had a good deal more authority under the circumstances than Nelson did.

Anyway, I had had just about all I wanted of the son of a bitch. Enlisted men, even chiefs, don't have many weapons in conflicts with commissioned officers, but they do have some. They can request transfers, for instance. Their commanding officers may either approve or disapprove such requests, but they are required to pass them up through channels. I had already requested transfer several times. The ship didn't need two chief signalmen in the first place. But Chain Gang disapproved my requests as quickly as I could write them. Finally, after the Hartwig affair, I requested transfer to "any other ship or station in the United States Navy."

Now, I knew the Navy did not particularly care if I was happy or not. But chiefs, even then, enjoyed a certain amount of respect from senior officers, and I knew Chain Gang would not want the brass seeing a request from a permanent appointment chief for "*any* other ship or station."

The invasion of southern France came along before anything came of that particular request. Chain Gang never mentioned it to me. I suspect now that Tommy probably intercepted and destroyed the letter. If I remained in the Navy, it would not have done my career any good to have something like that in my record. And, at that time, I was still planning to stay in the Navy after the war. Tommy knew all that, and the request would have had to cross his desk.

We were in Naples when the invasion orders came through. We moved immediately to Castellamare, an industrial port not far from Pompeii, to combat-load elements of the Forty-Fifth Division, my old Oklahoma National Guard outfit. We anchored offshore and brought the troops off in our own boats. The coming invasion would be the closest I would come to actual combat since leaving the Pacific, but it would be entirely different from anything I had ever known before.

The types of ships, for one thing, were different. I don't remember seeing any combat ships in the Med until then—except for a few escorting destroyers. Everything else was a converted merchantman or the unhandsome and awkward new landing craft, large and small, that swarmed about us in their hundreds. One of a signalman's jobs is to keep track of ships in company—and, in that regard, we were busy indeed. The ships all were virtually identical and could be distinguished only by numbers painted on their bows.

Fortunately, there was not a great deal of signaling after we were under way. Communications people, at that stage in the war, were not very well trained, especially not those in landing craft. Simple course and speed changes were about all we tried with them. But we did arrive, all present or accounted for, off the coast of France near the small town of Frejus.

It was a misty morning, I remember, with the Maritime Alps seeming to hang in the sky, all blue and white, above the haze. We did see combat ships that morning: battleships, cruisers, and destroyers, both British and American. They did a little bombardment, but the main softening up was done by what was said to be a thousand heavy bombers flying from Italy and Africa. The very air trembled with the sounds of four thousand powerful engines and the beat of their propellers.

I tried to imagine what it must have been like to have been under that mighty fleet of airplanes when it dropped its load. There were bound to have been civilians—including women and children—in the area. We in our ship were several miles at sea, but we could hear and feel the explosions of the bombs, a distant shuddering rumble that seemed to shake the earth itself. Not long after, we could smell the sharp turpentiney smells of shattered pine trees on the light offshore breeze then blowing.

The LSTs, LCIs, and other ramped landing craft proceeded right onto the beaches before unloading, but the big transports like the *Florence Nightingale* lay to, four or five miles offshore, and sent in their troops in their small LCVPs and LCMs. Except for the German bombers lurking on the horizon with their radio-controlled glide bombs, we saw no enemy aircraft at all. Nor were we shot at by shore batteries. There was not much resistance. The Germans had the Normandy landings in their rear and retreated early on to avoid being cut off by the Allied forces landing in the south. One British LST did pass us on its way back from the beach with its bridge structure pretty well banged up by an 88-mm direct hit. But, for the most part, the landings went smoothly. We could see none of it from where we were anyway. Of course the few men who did die were no less dead for being so few. But few is better than more.

That night was the night Chain Gang distinguished himself in the chemical smoke. The next day we moved around to Marseilles to bring out a British paratroop unit, the Red Devils, which had jumped in the initial assault. They were large, rough men, but surprisingly genial. One of them gave me a beautiful little hand bearing compass, which I have on my boat to this day.

There was time for only a brief run ashore in Marseilles. I remember it as a typical Mediterranean city, with a picturesque old quarter and a chapel filled with hanging models of fishing boats whose owners had left them there for luck before setting out onto the sea. The women were remarkable for what, for me, seemed unusually coarse faces and dyed hair. They tottered unsteadily in tight skirts and rough shoes with high wooden platform soles. The men were little more impressive, most in blue work smocks and limp berets. They were no friendlier than any other Frenchmen I ever had met. I didn't mind leaving Marseilles.

We took the paratroopers back to Naples. On the way, we served as mother ship for a group of little LCIs whose college-boy navigators sometimes had problems in finding their way if left too long on their own. Before darkness came, I made a count of the number we had with us. I think now it was forty-eight. When light came the next morning, we had forty-nine! In the big Atlantic convoys we had become used to losing ships overnight sometimes, but I don't remember our ever gaining one. Obviously, some stray had stumbled upon us in the night and had simply tagged on at the end of the line on the assumption we were all going the same way.

For the next month or so, we continued on in the Med, doing whatever chores we were assigned. Once, we took a load of German prisoners of war to camps in Africa. The exec, a notably practical type and not given to taking chances, rigged live steam lines in the holds where the Germans would be kept. Predictably, one of the German officers set up a howl about something, and the others joined in. The exec pointed out the steam lines to our disaffected passengers and explained what they could do—if turned on—to human flesh, whether it was German or not. His words had a remarkably calming effect that lasted the rest of the trip.

Then—it must have been around the end of September—we were ordered back to New York. My orders to a new ship were waiting for me when we got there.

18
Next, Okinawa

THE USS *MEDEA* WAS A NEW ATTACK cargo ship (AKA) then being built in Providence, Rhode Island. AKAs were much like merchant freighters except that they, like the *Florence Nightingale*, carried landing craft and had a few guns. They did not carry troops. Their cargos were ammunition, food, toilet paper, bombs, and any of all the thousands of supplies an invasion force might need. They delivered those supplies over the landing beaches in the ship's own boats or at piers in captured ports. It was still an amphibious ship, though, and I took the assignment as a continued putdown from the fast carrier and cruiser duty for which I had been trained.

But at least I was getting away from Chain Gang. That would be a plus—for both of us, I suspect. Our animosity toward each other lasted to the end and was as petty in its conclusion as at any other time.

Chain Gang almost never came to the signal bridge. He much preferred the relatively sheltered navigation bridge with its closed wheelhouse, especially in cold weather. But all-around vision was better from the signal bridge, and he did come up there sometimes for getting under way or docking the ship. Not that he had anything to do with the work at all. We had a pilot on board for that, and the exec was there to take care of any problems. Still, he was there when I came up to say good-bye to Mac and the signal gang. I intended to be over the accommodation ladder the minute it was rigged. Maybe Chain Gang had come up to tell me good-bye, which is to laugh. It was childish, I suppose, but I made a bigger show than was necessary of shaking hands and saying good-bye to all hands, including the exec, except Chain Gang. He was equally cold to me. It was a bad scene.

Except for the exec, in fact—and Chain Gang—the only officer I remember with any clarity in the *Florence Nightingale* was the ship's communications officer, a lieutenant named Lowell W. Budlong, who was said to be a member of an "old New England family." Biological facts being what they are, I never understood how one man's family could be any older than another's, but that was the way good

271

families were described sometimes. Budlong was a mild-mannered, slightly built man whose life in the *Nightingale* was made miserable by Chain Gang.

At any rate, while we were still in the Med, Lieutenant Budlong recommended me for a commission as an officer. He put it in the standard military hyperbole. If all he wrote about me had been true, I could have relieved Admiral Nimitz, for Christ's sake. Still, it was nice of Mister Budlong to say what he did. But Chain Gang was unimpressed. He disapproved the promotion, and that was that. It may well have been that he—for good and ample reasons—honestly felt that I was not officer material, but I always suspected it was because of my experience with the dread social disease.

My reaction to this development was odd since my motivation for entering the Navy in the first place had been a determination to be an officer. But I don't think now that I would have taken a commission even if Chain Gang had approved. My whole attitude had changed. For almost two years I had been kept on a ship where I was not needed and had little to do—at one point I was even assigned to read the daily news over the ship's speaker system!—under a commanding officer for whom I had no respect, a commanding officer who had soured me on the idea of being an officer at all. Honk and Sandy—along with thousands of other enlisted men—were commissioned during the war and proved to be good and effective officers. But I don't think now that I would have been a good officer at all.

In light of my future career as a minor—very minor—corporate executive, I suspect that I subconsciously recognized myself as not being the executive type. I had always rather do things myself than tell others to do them. Certainly, I would never have been the officers Sandy and Honk had become. Or perhaps I had simply been frustrated for so long, and for what I took to be such arbitrary reasons, that I didn't give a damn anymore. Old Chinese proverb: "That which is wanted, if wanted long enough, is no longer wanted."

The crew for the *Medea*—a ship named for a remarkably nasty woman from Greek mythology—was being assembled in Boston. I took the first train north and reported in to the receiving ship there. As was New York's, Boston's receiving ship was not a ship at all. It was the cavernous shed of Commonwealth Pier, which had been partitioned off into quarters, messes, and offices in the same pattern used at Pier 92 in New York. I was assigned a berth in chiefs' quarters and set about seeing Boston.

In the *Florence Nightingale* we had called sometimes in Boston at the western end of our Atlantic crossings. I was not a total stranger in the town, but it was different being alone rather than with shipmates. I knew no one at all, and given my mood at the time, I quickly tired of the place. The *Medea* would not be ready for manning for several weeks yet to come. I requested and was granted leave.

That was when I saw Joan in Pontiac on my way to Tulsa. It was midwinter, and the land was in a cold and silent sleep under snow and ice. From frosted train windows, the whole world was white and misted shades of gray over the drab backsides towns show rail passengers. Joan had always been good at putting me strangely at ease. She was no different this time. She sensed the trouble in me, I suppose. The time I had with her was about the only good thing about my leave.

Seeing my family was good too, of course. We still loved each other, but we had been apart then for five eventful years. I could not relax with them and accept the love they so freely offered. I had become irritable and short-tempered, and they could not see why I should be. They all were working, and their lives had never been easier. They tried to close the gap between us, but I did not make it easy for them. I did not even telephone the blonde with the Plymouth convertible.

In the end, I returned to Boston before my leave was up—and found I had been reported to the *Medea* as having died while on leave. A replacement chief already had been requested in my place.

This was the second time during the war that I had been reported dead. After the *Lexington*'s sinking my family was told I was among the killed. This probably was because the ship's company had been confused with the Flag allowance. I don't know how the second false report came about. At least my family never knew about that one. I left it that way.

It was while I was in Boston that I got the British navy's Oak Leaf Emblem, a small bronze oak leaf to be worn along with the other campaign ribbons on my uniform jacket for the war's duration. It signified what the British called a "mention in dispatches." In the old days, when a man did something nice, his name was included in dispatches sent home to the king—hence the name. In my case, Captain Phipps had awarded me the emblem for my alacrity in ducking behind the Lewis gun shield in the *Moa* the night we tangled with the Japanese armed barges off Guadalcanal.

I had no inkling the award was on its way, but the awards ceremony was not embarrassing at all. That may have been because there wasn't one. I was called to the receiving ship office where a WAVE yeoman handed me a small brown envelope with the offhand comment, "Here, this is yours."

It didn't mean one hell of a lot, but I wished I might have had it while still in the *Florence Nightingale*. It would have been fun to see Chain Gang's face when I showed up on the bridge with the little metal leaf on my chest. Life is full of little disappointments.

Chiefs in the receiving ship were given little to do. The only memorable assignment I got was to take a general court-martial prisoner to Rikers Island Prison in

New York. Four or five of us were issued loaded .38-caliber pistols and handcuffed to an equal number of prisoners. We rode in a crowded day coach along with regular passengers. We either were handcuffed to our charges or we chained them to a seat arm. The prisoners gave us no trouble, but I have often wondered since if I could really have shot my prisoner if he had tried to escape. It could have been messy in the crowded car. He was very young but had a disturbing look in his eyes. I never did find out what he had done—he wouldn't say—but it must have been something serious to rate a general court-martial.

We dropped off our prisoners at Rikers Island and were free to do whatever we liked until the next day. The other chiefs had families or "shack jobs" in Boston and took the next train back. (A shack job is a woman a sailor is living with without benefit of marriage.) But I stayed on in New York. It was the first and only time I ever made a liberty with a loaded gun on my hip. I wore it under my topcoat so it wouldn't show.

I was still pretty morose. Although she had occasionally written letters to me, I had not seen the Tea Drinker for a long time. But I guess I was not as over her as I had thought. After a few drinks—well, maybe more than a few—I went up to the residence club where she lived, and one of the other girls told me where I could find her.

Her theatrical career must have come on hard times because she was working as an instructor in an Arthur Murray dance studio. She made a big show of welcoming me before the other instructors, but before I left she told me she had a ballroom dance partner named Rocky. They played resort hotels. She never said so in words, but she made it clear that Rocky was a partner in more than dancing. That didn't do one hell of a lot for my morale, but I couldn't do much about it. The *Medea*, once she was commissioned, would be off to the Pacific, anyway. God knew when I would see the Tea Drinker again. As it turned out, I never did. But, in a final futile puppy-love gesture, I gave her my little British Oak Leaf Emblem. Let her goddamned Rocky match that.

Back in Boston, I was coming to know some of the other *Medea* chiefs and set out on a joyless career of nightclubbing and pub-crawling. There was one basement club in downtown Boston called the Cave. It became the *Medea* chiefs' home ashore. It was all right, I guess, but I had become tired of the whole scene. The Cave was nothing like the Log Cabin in Honolulu. And it sure as hell was not Trader Vic's in Honolulu or the Cock-and-Bull in San Francisco, where a beautiful woman had sung "As Time Goes By" to me. Hell, it wasn't even the Piccadilly Hotel bar in New York. Frequently I went back to Commonwealth Pier long before my liberty was up to read or brood in my bunk.

It was still winter. We used to watch the fishing boats come in with their crews using axes to knock ice off their rigging to reduce weight aloft. One night, after leaving the Cave, I walked for a long time all by myself in the Boston Common. There was snow on the ground and more falling, deadening the sounds of the city and making yellow haloes around street lamps. That became my most lasting memory of Boston: the winter-dead trees of the Common made misty by falling snow and the lamplight behind shaded windows in old redbrick houses across the way. I tried to play my old game of the windows, but the pictures would no longer come. It was a gentle and calming scene, but nothing worked for me anymore.

There was not the slightest sign a war might be going on. Dark figures of strolling men and women were probably as they always had been in that place, and the houses were just as peaceful behind their drawn shades. Mr. Budlong's family probably lived in a house like those surrounding the Common. It was all both soothing and troubling to me. I started back for the Commonwealth Pier, confused.

I was waiting in front of a big hotel, watching for a cab in what was becoming a heavy snowstorm. Naturally, there were no cabs to be found. As the whiskey fumes wore off in me, I became aware the night was cold. Damned cold. I stamped my feet and cussed. That didn't help.

Then, all of a sudden, where there had been no cabs at all, there were several of them. Seven or eight pulled up before the hotel and their doors flew open, letting loose a noisy, laughing crowd in mussed theatrical makeup and evening clothes. It was the cast of an Olsen and Johnson musical comedy that opened that night in Boston. The people knew they had a hit on their hands and meant to celebrate.

Willy-nilly, I was swept up in the crowd and found myself in a large suite on an upper floor. Champagne and other booze flowed in great abundance. Glasses were pushed into my hands. But I was soon forgotten in the general theatrical exuberance. Some of that exuberance was sliding off into sexual entanglements, which were becoming a little embarrassing for me. I remembered that French Foreign legionnaire in the Sidi bel Abbes bar. The party never got that raw, of course, but it was well past the level of a Methodist Church social.

Finally, a middle-aged lady came and asked if I didn't think I would like to leave. I looked a lot younger than my age at that time. I guess she recognized my discomfort and thought I was in over my head. I saw that woman later in character roles in movies, but I never knew her name. She led me out, to a chorus of lewd shouts about cradle robbing and the like. Once out in the hall, she kissed me lightly on the lips and shooed me away. She was a nice lady.

The only other adventure I had in Boston was considerably gentler. I met Megan one Saturday night when she came into the Cave with a laughing group of girls. She lived in Gloucester, a town a few miles up the coast from Boston, and before the evening was over, she invited me to her house for dinner the next day, a Sunday. It was the only time that I was in a private house on the East Coast.

Gloucester was an old town. It was the town where the movie of Kipling's *Captains Courageous* was made. There were numerous picturesque piers and sheds along the waterfront where big powered fishing boats, called schooners even though they carried no sails, were moored. Megan's father, she told me, owned two of them.

She lived with her family in a big square white wood-framed two-story house that was typical of the town's houses. Her mother, father, and a number of brothers and sisters greeted me warmly and did all they could to make me feel at home with them. Only the brothers looked awry at my fancy uniform. They were crews for their father's boats and had the weather-burned faces of real seamen. I suspect they didn't think much of Navy sailors. I knew a lot of merchant seamen and fishermen didn't. But it felt good to be inside a family home again. I was grateful for the day.

I was not so grateful for the food though. A typical New England boiled dinner, it had all the color of a white sheet draped over a snow bank. Beef, potatoes, clam chowder, and turnips—all boiled to the same pasty white and bland as the apparently total lack of salt could make them. Tall glasses of milk added little to the rainbow.

After dinner, which was around noon, Megan's mother shooed the two of us out, and we walked through the town. Megan showed me the ruins of a Revolutionary War fort and the town's famous statue of an oil-skinned fisherman leaning into the wheel of a schooner under sail. But that is about all there was to see in Gloucester—except for the waterfront itself and the winter streets of the town.

We walked until after the early winter dark and did not return to the house at all. Megan saw me off at the station, and I went back to Boston alone. It had been a strangely gentle episode, and I was left with a fond remembrance of the girl and her family. I often thought later what it must be like to have spent all one's life in the settled security of such a town and in such a family. I never saw Megan again.

I know it must seem that I use those words a lot, but that is the way it was during the war. Megan and I didn't really know each other, but she clung to me with a kind of desperation at the station. It must have been hard for young women then. Their nesting instincts were in full cry and with damned few male voices to listen. When they did come together with a man, time was apt to be compressed and reality tilted.

Not long after that the *Medea* was ready to take her crew. We were shifted from Boston to barracks at the training station in Newport, Rhode Island, which was not far from Providence, where the ship was nearing completion. It was still winter, and the Newport training station was bleak, lacking even the spare amenities of Boston's Commonwealth Pier. Newport is an old-time Navy town and, even during the war, clung to some of its old ways in its treatment of Navy enlisted sailors. It was not a pleasant time for us.

I remember busing across white snow fields to Fall River, Massachusetts, where the chiefs' club of some naval installation had invited the *Medea* chiefs to a New Year's Eve party. The winter's early darkness was broken only by the yellow glow of windows in isolated houses, which, in their loneliness, made us feel more alone than ever. The host chiefs had invited a few WAVES for female company, but the party still was less than exuberant.

The *Medea*'s commissioning ceremonies, when they came, were both brief and perfunctory. The Navy had commissioned many ships in the war years. The novelty had largely worn off. Besides, the weather was so cold that brass players in the band kept their mouthpieces in their pockets until the last minute. Most of the music, as I remember it, was drumbeats. The traditional reading of orders and commissioning oratory were gone through at a dead run. When the time came, on a signal from the captain, I gave the order to break the commission pennant at the main masthead, and the USS *Medea* became an official part of the U.S. Navy.

The *Medea* was a new design built by the Welsh-Kaiser Company. Medium sized, with two centerline stacks and trim lines, she was a pretty vessel but never very efficient. Few of the class were built, and they were hardly noticed in the great mass of ships the Navy had become. I remember seeing some of them in newsreel shots of the sacrificial fleet gathered for the A-bomb tests in Bikini Lagoon, but I was not long enough in the *Medea* to develop much feeling for her one way or the other.

Her chiefs' quarters were comfortable enough and, being new, they were clean, but she was an awkward ship for signaling. Her halyards, for one thing, were run to her triatic stay, making flag hoists hard to read from either ahead or astern, which just happens to be the most common position in which a ship will find herself in formation at sea. Triatic stays are those strong wires that connect the mastheads of fore and main masts for their mutual support. Flags, when hoisted to them, fly on inline halyards, one behind the other, and become an unreadable fluttering of colors to ships either ahead or astern. I requested that an athwartships yard be rigged, but it never was. We went to sea with signal halyards rigged like those of merchant ships.

The men of the signal gang were typical of the time. I don't think any of them ever had been to sea before. But they, for the most part, were cooperative and tried to learn. Fortunately, we would be of such humble station that little serious signaling was ever likely to come our way in any event. When we sailed on our maiden voyage, in fact, we bothered neither to zigzag nor to wait for a convoy. We sailed alone without escort of any kind.

I don't remember why now, but we moved around through the Cape Cod Canal from Providence to Boston. Probably for fitting some last-minute gear or the correction of a discovered shortcoming of some kind. We were not in Boston long before being ordered to the amphibious training base at Solomons, Maryland, to pick up our boats. That was all right with me since Boston was so blinking cold. I remember thinking, "Thank God! At least that far south, it will be warm."

Well, like hell it was. When we rounded up into Chesapeake Bay, coast guardsmen were out in their boats chopping ice off channel buoys to prevent their capsizing. Our bluff-bowed, ramped landing craft, when they came off to be hoisted aboard, were heavy and awkward with the ice of frozen spray. The ice was so thick sometimes it had to be knocked away before the boats could be nested on board. Oh, it was fun.

We didn't even bother to anchor off Solomons. We hoisted our boats in while moving slowly ahead. And, when all were aboard, we moved immediately to Norfolk, Virginia, where we loaded several thousand tons of flour. It came aboard bagged, in cargo nets. I could not help remembering the time Choner had lifted Tommy aboard in a net like that and how funny Tommy had looked with his blues all white with flour. I wondered where he and Choner were.

Loading did not take long. I remember it mostly for the padeyes fitted along the tops of the pier sheds. We rigged yard-and-stay, with the ship's own booms serving as anchors for one end and the pier shed padeyes as the other. I had never seen that arrangement before anywhere else, but it worked well.

I did not even go ashore in Norfolk. It too was an old Navy town that was notorious with peacetime Navy sailors for its coldness to them. Towns like that had lost a good deal of their enchantment for me by that time. Besides, the weather was still cold as Billy Hell.

Once loaded with our boats snugged down on deck, we sailed immediately for Panama and the Pacific Ocean. We sailed at darkened ship, but again, we did not zigzag and steamed alone, with neither convoy nor escort. The war was winding down in the Atlantic by that time. We would learn that there was still some left in the Pacific.

The first night was pretty bumpy as we rounded Cape Hatteras, but within a day or two, the sea began to behave itself, and the weather to warm. We slipped gratefully into the semitropical waters off Florida. There, we shifted into summer uniform. We had warm following winds and seas all the way to Panama, and the *Medea* proved herself a fairly good sea boat, though the sea offered little challenge to her on that passage. I suspect she would have labored a bit more in the North Atlantic.

It was good to see again the soft white of tropical clouds instead of the gray mists stretched tight by the cold winds of high latitudes, and the incredible blue of tropical water. The green and rounded hills of Central America, when they did rise from the sea ahead, looked, for all the world, like the islands I had known in the South Pacific. I felt at home immediately. The snows and bitter winds of a New England winter became dim and fading memories.

I drilled the signal gang hard. They needed it, for one thing. And, since we were steaming alone, they would have had no practice at all otherwise. It would have been embarrassing to have joined a task force in the state we were in upon leaving Norfolk. I had little hope of bringing the gang up to prewar standards, of course. There simply was not time. And I am afraid I had lost a good deal of my own motivation. I didn't really give a good goddamn. I suppose I had seen too much of the home front. I knew the guys in the fast carriers and cruisers were still catching hell—from the bloody kamikazes, if nothing else, but that no longer seemed to have much connection with me.

Since we were a relatively small ship, the passage of the canal was simple. I don't think we even anchored at the Atlantic end. There were many merchant ships waiting their turns, but it seems to me now that we were taken immediately into the locks. I suppose Navy ships were given priority. After that the passage became a sightseeing excursion for those of us on the signal bridge. With our powerful long glasses, we could look right into the jungle and see the monkeys, alligators, and birds. That was one advantage signalmen had. If we got anywhere near a shore, we could get a pretty good look at whatever it offered. We called such examinations "long glass liberties."

We stopped at the Pacific end of the canal. We tied up to a pier whose shed was paved with a rough parquet arrangement of wooden blocks. We even had time for a brief liberty in Panama City. I remember the place for its rain- and sun-weathered wood-frame buildings with rusted tin awnings extending out over the teeming sidewalks. Sailors, either merchant or Navy, were no novelty to Pana-manians who had devised extremely efficient amusements for them—especially in the areas of sexual sin. The girls were a wildly exotic mix of nationalities and languages.

For those leery of intercourse itself, there was a product the little boys who hawked it in the streets called "Exhibish! Exhibish!" This offered, for a fee, the privilege of watching through a hole in a wall some other poor jackass wrestling around with a woman on a primitive bed. A variation was the spectacle of a gyrating nude dancer smoking a cigarette in her labia major. Uplifting as hell! Well, in a way, it was.

From Panama, we made an uneventful passage up the coast to San Diego. The only thing of note was our meeting with a fleet of four dingy Russian ships. They were small and appeared to be trawlers or minesweepers of some kind. They were just outside the long buoyed channel ships must transit across the inshore shallows of the Gulf of Panama when we saw them. They diligently ignored our friendly signals and plodded on their way. Through our long glasses, we could see their sailors staring at us, but that is all they did.

San Diego, when we got there, was much changed from the way I had known it before. A man had to look close, with a good glass, to find all the buildings I had known at the training station. The Marine base was grown almost as large. Although I was then only twenty-five years old, I felt like an old man.

We stayed only long enough to offload our flour—and to load an equal weight of bombs—big 500- and 1,000-pounders. It was unsettling at first to see how nonchalantly the big bangers were handled by the guys on the dock. In slings of two or three at a time, they were lifted up from the dock and lowered into our holds, bumping and banging against things every inch of the way. It was not pleasant at all to think of what little pieces of us would be left if the lot suddenly decided to save itself a long ride and blow up right there in San Diego. At least the death would have been a quick one.

I don't remember exactly how long we were in San Diego that time, but it must have been several days. I didn't go ashore at all—not even to Sherman's. I had lost a lot of weight and was irritable and morose much of the time, all of it probably an omen of what was to come later. It is a measure of my mood at the time, I suppose, that I now do not remember even the names of the men in the *Medea* with me. Not even the captain's. The only name I remember is that of the ship's doctor, Jack Sharp, a short and much opinionated man from Cincinnati. That, too, is probably only because of what happened to me off Eniwetok as we steamed west for Okinawa.

In a given latitude the waters of the world are remarkably much alike, either north or south. But there are subtle differences, and the islands to the west of Pearl were beautifully clean and brushed with fresh winds. As I have said before, I've often thought that, if heaven has a counterpart on earth, for sailors it must lie somewhere in that part of the world's oceans. There I had spent the happiest days of my life to that time, in the *Indianapolis* before the war, days that then seemed as remote to me as history.

We stopped at Pearl for refueling. There was one of the new *Essex*-class carriers—the first I had seen of her kind—in the harbor, along with two or three cruisers and some sea-worn destroyers. I felt better simply for seeing such ships again. The familiar sights of Pearl Harbor itself were much changed, though. The algaroba trees on Magazine Island, our old berth, were all cut down, for instance, and replaced with buildings and paved areas. The Navy yard parade ground—where Sandy had suggested Bogeman's ass as a strategic diversion against the other cruisers' landing forces—was gone as well. At least I couldn't see it from the ship.

One highlight was the arrival of the *Florence Nightingale* while we were there. I saw the tracery of her masts and booms beyond Hospital Point as she came in. There were many converted C3s in the Navy then, but this one seemed somehow familiar, Sure enough, when her hull became visible as she cleared the point I could see her number: AP-70.

Immediately, I stepped out onto a clear area and short-armed a greeting. We were not supposed to do that. Every signal from a naval vessel is presumed to come from its captain. Or, at least, to be cleared through him. But signalmen often short-armed when in harbor. It was one of the ways scuttlebutt was so efficiently spread through the ships. We did not use semaphore flags and moved our arms only from the elbows so as not to be conspicuous. That is why we called it short-arming. Most officers let us get away with it if we kept it within reason.

At any rate, Mac himself answered. It was good to see his Irish face and to recognize his somewhat jerky style of semaphore. The *Nightingale* passed close aboard of us in making her way to a berth. Mac and I had time to catch up and to make a date to meet in Honolulu. I had not yet been ashore. I hadn't called Ilse since the war began. I hadn't even gone out to Trader Vic's, but seeing Mac made things different. We agreed to meet at the Log Cabin. Mac had been in HAWDET destroyers before the war. He had been in one of them—the *Cummings*—the morning the Japanese attacked Pearl. He knew the Log Cabin.

It was good to be with Mac again. We had had some good times in the *Florence Nightingale*. It wasn't his fault that I had been stuck in the goddamned ship for so long. But it was not a successful liberty. Benny Newman, one of the cooks, came with Mac. They told me Tommy and most of the others had been detached in New York shortly after I was. Even Chain Gang had left the ship, I think now.

We had a couple of watery drinks in the Log Cabin. They did not help one hell of a lot. I remember we walked along Hotel Street—waded would be a more accurate term, so crowded with sailors was the street—past Wo Fat's ornate multistory joint. I remembered how we had called the kid, Moffat, Mo Fat, in what seemed a long time ago. I even have a couple of the cheap snapshots we posed for that day in a stand on Hotel Street. The three of us look lugubrious as hell, peering out from the phony grass shack. As I remember it now, we returned to our ships early. It was the last time I saw Honolulu during the war.

From Pearl, we steamed west to join in the great invasion fleet that would take Okinawa. Although still mired, as I saw it, in a noncombatant ship, there was a considerable picking up of emotions as we sailed nearer and nearer to the Japanese. Lookouts came to pay a good deal more attention to the horizon, and gun crews did not sleep so much. And, since we were steaming in company with a considerable number of other ships, there was signal work to be done as well. Green as they were, our gang did fairly well.

I do not mean to imply from any of this that I anticipated being bombed and shot at with any real pleasure. But there was a kind of satisfaction in knowing that I was beginning to earn my keep again. I had taken the king's shilling; I owed him something in return. As Sandy had used to remind us before the war—we wasn't drafted.

I always felt guilty upon seeing drafted men killed and wounded. It was the way I had felt in the Med when we were delivering drafted soldiers to the landing beaches. And, oddly, I always regretted most the loss of the least favored. Most people seem to sorrow most for the loss of handsome young men from good families who had everything to live for. I sorrowed more for the poor bloody bastards who had never had anything and who—if they did survive the war—would go back to having nothing for the rest of their lives. Some of them might even have to work in grocery stores.

I remember the young ROTC officers bitching sometimes about the perceived preference given to what they called trade school boys—their name for Annapolis-trained officers. But I don't remember ever hearing any of them comparing their own privileges with those of the enlisted men, many of the old regulars of whom contributed one hell of a lot more to the war effort. Oh, well. Out of step again.

All this sophomoric maundering came to an abrupt end one morning a day or so out of Eniwetok. I went into the chiefs' washroom to shave and woke—God knows how much later—in sick bay with Doctor Sharp standing beside my bunk with a medical book in his hands and a worried look on his face. Except for feeling weak and a little shaky, there did not seem to be much wrong with me. All of my vital signs were good. But the muscles of my hands and forearms ached like hell. Doctor Sharp told me I had been paralyzed for some time with my hands and fingers hyperextended and my arm muscles locked.

He did not know what to make of it, but for the next few days I was hit with the same kind of attacks every few hours or so. Even more often, Doctor Sharp would burst into sick bay with hope in his face and a finger marking a place in his medical book, confident he had found the answer. But, each time, after poking and feeling and smelling me over, he would slam his book closed and storm back to his room, frustrated.

In the meantime, we had come to Eniwetok. As an interim diagnosis, Doctor Sharp settled on a rare condition called tetany, which usually attacks infants. It is marked by a lack of blood calcium, and he rationalized that I had been for so long in the tropics, drinking distilled water and sweating like a horse, that my calcium balance was knocked askew. I didn't mention it at the time, but I had sweated damned little for the year and a half I had spent in the North Atlantic.

Doctor Sharp decided he could not do much for me in the ship. It was preparing to sail for Okinawa, where there would be even fewer resources available. He put me ashore in an Army hospital on Eniwetok, where I lay for a week or two with liquid calcium dripping into my arm from a bottle hanging over my bunk. The Okinawa invasion would have to make do without me.

Eniwetok still showed signs of the heavy bombing and shelling that had led to its capture from the Japanese. The island's blindingly white coral sands were pocked with everything from small dents to large craters. Palms were shredded where shells and bomb fragments had made direct hits, leaving stumps that looked like old-fashioned shaving brushes stuck, bristles up, in the sand. Wrecked buildings and equipment—already rusting in the island's salt air—lay wherever they had been pushed to be out of the way.

It was not a pleasant sight. Unpleasant stinks made the place even less enjoyable. And the volume of air traffic on its strip made for little peace and quiet, even in the hospital, which was not far away. Nothing was far away from anything on Eniwetok. It was a small island on a large lagoon. The most memorable sights there were the men's improvised washing machines. All along the beach on the island's windward side, men had placed five-gallon buckets, each fitted with a windmill connected to a crank and a plunger so that when the wind blew—which it did constantly—the plunger was worked up and down. Soap, water, and dirty clothes were put in the buckets and—voila—in a little while the clothes were clean and hung from lines strung between the stumps of shattered palm trees.

The hospital itself was a series of Quonset huts, the rounded metal structures used wherever the war was fought throughout the world. Screened windows pierced the sides of the huts, each sheltered by a metal flap like an eyebrow to keep out the rain. It was pleasant enough, I suppose, with trade winds humming through the window screens and the busy clacking of wind-powered washing machines keeping time. But I was preoccupied. It is not normal for healthy young men to collapse into paralysis. I was more worried then, I think, than I had been at any other time in the war.

The Army doctors kept me busy with their tests and questions, many of them repetitions of Doctor Sharp's. The most interesting was when they stuck pins and needles into my arms and I could not feel them. Finally, they put me in a C-47 and flew me to Kwajalein, where there was a larger and better-equipped hospital.

That was one of the most spectacular flights I ever made. Kwajalein was at the opposite end of what was said to be the biggest coral atoll in the world. We flew low and for what seemed hours over the shallow lagoon waters, one fantastic pastel color replacing another for the whole distance. Incredible.

The doctors on Kwajalein were no more successful than those who already had poked, stuck, and felt me on Eniwetok. After a while, they put me on a hospital C-54. It was the first four-engine airplane in which I had ever flown. I felt guilty for being strapped into a bunk. Hell, I wasn't hurt—by that time I wasn't even sick—and many of the other guys on board had horrible wounds. The Iwo Jima operation was still going on, and most of the wounded on the plane had come from there. But my stock of options was low just then and off I went to the Navy's big new hospital at Aiea in the hills overlooking Pearl Harbor.

Interestingly, we made a fuel stop at Johnston Island, where I had been in the *Indianapolis* the day the war began. It seemed a long time ago. I remember little more than an airstrip at the place. It was a short runway. When the pilot ran up his engines for takeoff, I could look out the window beside my bunk and see water under our overhanging tail. When we went off the other end, we were so low I could see propwash on the water there as well.

By the time I reached Aiea my attacks were beginning to taper off. They were less severe, and they came less frequently. But I was kept there anyway on a high protein diet of steaks, ice cream, and milk. Aiea was a modern hospital for its time, with all kinds of fancy equipment, but they couldn't make any better diagnosis than Doctor Sharp had in the *Medea*. Finally, in their frustration, they sent me around to the squirrel robbers, which was a name we sometimes gave psychiatrists.

By coincidence—and without much hope of anything coming of it—I had taken the Navy's flight physical examination when passing through Pearl on the *Medea* only three or four weeks before. That examination has a heavy component of psychiatric measurement in it, but I was found to be "physically, emotionally and psychologically qualified for command of aircraft in flight." If I had gone off my mental rocker, I had done it damned fast.

The only psychic malfunction the psychiatrist could find, he said, was my repeated requests to rejoin my ship. "Quit while you are ahead, Chief," he said. "They can fight this goddamned war without you."

I didn't doubt that for a minute, but I didn't much like the boredom involved in sitting in a hospital room until they did. I was completely ambulatory by that time, but I spent most of my time in the ward moping. I didn't even read, and I could not think of much to say to my fellow patients. It was a stinking time.

The only bright spot was a letter from the Tea Drinker. It had been following me for some time. It perked me up a lot. She had written from Boca Raton, a resort town in Florida, and seemed much as she had been when we first met—young and vulnerable. Her Rocky had turned into a rolling stone, it appeared, and she was alone. I kept the letter for a long time, but I never answered it.

Then, one day, I was bused to the Honolulu waterfront and put on an American merchant ship for San Francisco. It was better than the *Tabinta*, the Dutch ship I had ridden from New Caledonia, but not much. At least it had bunks. And the ride was not so long. That is all I remember of the ship. I don't even remember her name now.

We tied up, upon arrival in San Francisco, near Pier 35, as I recall—the pier where the fancy cruise ships tie up now. There we were loaded into a gray Navy bus with a blond driver. She was the first woman bus driver I had ever seen, but, it turned out, there were a lot of them in San Francisco at the time. We were taken to a temporary receiving hospital the Navy had established then, somewhere out on Geneva Avenue, not far from a big indoor arena called the Cow Palace, which had been built by the Works Progress Administration (WPA) during the Depression to make work for the unemployed. There we were sorted out by destination. It was the Navy's policy then to send men to the hospital nearest their homes. For me, that meant Norman, Oklahoma, but we were held in the receiving hospital until onward transportation could be organized.

I was fully recovered by that time, although my weight was down to 130 pounds. My blues hung on me, and my eyes looked out from some pretty deep holes. As I recall, I was in the receiving hospital three or four days and was granted liberty if I wanted it, but I went ashore only once. I wanted to see Suzanne—hell, I wanted to see anyone with any sanity at all—but she no longer worked at the Cock-and-Bull, and I didn't bother to look any further. I went to a Market Street sailor dive and got as drunk as I could, as fast as I could. The only thing I remember of the liberty is that a cab driver got to me for twenty dollars. That was a lot of money in those days.

After only a few days, we were bused down to the Third Street yards and put on a hospital train for Fort Worth. We arrived there in the middle of a summer night. Those of us who could walk were in blues. I remember the blast of hot Texas air that hit us when the train doors opened. We could smell dust. The ocean seemed a long way off.

After no more than the normal confusion associated with any naval operation, we were put onto another train for Norman, Oklahoma. There was a Navy air station in Norman during the war, and an associated hospital in prefabricated wooden buildings. Tulsa was only a hundred or so miles away, and I was free to come and go as I pleased. I did not realize it then, but my war was over.

I did get in touch with the blonde with the yellow convertible this time, and she came down often. She would let me drive her car. That was fun. Once, when we were returning from Tulsa and were almost to Norman, I looked up to see three of the Navy's Yellow Peril Stearman training airplanes circling overhead and coming lower with every circle. We had the car's top down, of course. From the air, I, in my chief's blues and white cap, must have looked like an officer and, therefore, socially acceptable. Blondes in yellow convertibles were always acceptable.

But, if anything, I felt lower than ever. The ships off Okinawa were taking a pounding from kamikazes. The *Medea* and *Florence Nightingale* were probably off Okinawa at that very time. And I was sitting on my ass in the middle of what had not long before been an Oklahoma cow pasture. I wasn't very nice to the blonde in the yellow convertible during that time—nor to anyone else for that matter.

The Navy had refused my request for flight training originally because it would have had to train someone else in my place, but it would not have taken one hell of a lot of training to replace me in what I did for the last two years I was in the Navy. That college boys were constantly overhead in pretty yellow airplanes did not help worth a damn.

I had a private room at one end of a ward and spent most of my time there. The relaxed standards of wartime sexual morals in Oklahoma still applied, I suppose, but a lot of the fun was gone even from that. I did go to a couple of parties at the Skirvin Hotel in Oklahoma City, but I returned to the hospital early each time. I was stronger than a housecat, I suppose, but not much more than that.

One day I happened to remember the woman whose son had died that time in 1940 when the two torpedo planes collided over the *Yorktown*. If you recall, she had written to me for a long time, but I had not kept up my end of the correspondence and she finally gave up. I remembered one day that she lived in Norman. I found her address in the telephone directory and went to see her.

She was very nice. Her house was a model of Oklahoma modern, with highly polished furniture, clean carpets, and religious pictures and embroidered scrolls on the walls. There was a photograph of her son on the mantel. He was posed to show the single golden stripe of an ensign on his sleeve and the bright golden wings of a pilot on his chest. He was obviously proud of his uniform, the same uniform I had so fervently wanted to wear. It was eerie. I had seen that smiling young man die, but I had never thought of him before as having a face.

I became very uncomfortable and did not stay long. The woman—she was getting old then, possibly as old as fifty—cried when I left. I guess I reminded her too much of what was lost and had reopened old wounds better left covered by their scars. I never went back.

Not long after that, the war ended. The word came at night, as I recall. Nurses ran up and down the halls, their rubber-soled shoes squeaking on waxed floors. Corpsmen stuck their heads in the door and yelled the news. Over at the air station some flares were fired and some guns let go, but for the most part, the hospital remained quiet. I closed the door to my room and went to the window.

A warm night wind hummed through the screened window, and the Oklahoma prairie outside lay pale and colorless in moonlight. So, it was over. In a way, it was as though nothing at all had happened. Except that Honk, Jordan, and Allen Nations all were dead. I didn't know where Sandy was or any of the others I had known in the *Indianapolis* all those centuries before. For a moment, tears came to my eyes, and I didn't know why. The rest of the world was laughing.

⟨ Appendix: Biographical Details ⟩

Floyd Beaver, CSM (PA) 356-13-29
Born: 20 March 1920 in Tulsa, Oklahoma. Enlisted 6 June 1939 in Dallas, Texas
Years of service: Six plus, June 1939 to September 1945
Shore duty: Naval Training Station, San Diego, three months
    Naval Communications School, San Diego, four months

Ships:

    USS *Indianapolis* (CA-35), 6 January 1940 to 12 May 1941

    USS *Chester* (CA-27), 12 May to 6 August 1941

    USS *Louisville* (CA-28), 6 August to 19 September 1941

    USS *Indianapolis* (CA-35), 19 September 1941 to 5 January 1942

    USS *Lexington* (CV-2), 5 January to 7 May 1942

    USS *Chester* (CA-27), passage to San Diego and onward to Pearl

    USS *Saratoga* (CV-3), temporary duty with Kinkaid Flag

    USS *Hornet* (CV-8), temporary duty with Kinkaid Flag

    USS *Enterprise* (CV-6), 8 October to 1 December 1942 (Kinkaid Flag)

    USS *Argonne* (AG-31), 3 December to 8 December 1942

    HMNZS *Matai/Moa,* 8 December 1942 to 8 May 1943

    NAB *Noumea,* 17 April to 29 April 1943

    USS *Florence Nightingale* (AP-70), 23 September 1943 to 22 November 1944

    USS *Medea* (AKA-31), 10 January to 15 April 1945

    Various military hospitals, 15 April to 24 September 1945

Actions:

    Battle off Bougainville, in *Lexington,* February 1942

    Lae/Salamaua raids, in *Lexington,* April 1942

    Battle of the Coral Sea, in *Lexington,* 7–8 May 1942

    Battle of Santa Cruz Islands, in *Enterprise,* October 1942

Battles off Guadalcanal, in *Enterprise*, October–November 1942
Actions off Guadalcanal, in *Moa*, January–May 1943
North Atlantic convoys, in *Nightingale*, September 1943–June 1944
Invasion of southern France, in *Nightingale*, August 1944

Sinkings:

USS *Lexington* in Battle of the Coral Sea
HMNZS *Moa*, 8 May 1943 in Tulagi Harbor

Woundings:

"Battered about head and shoulders" in Battle of the Coral Sea
"Multiple minor gun[shot] wounds" in *Moa*
Injuries to right foot in sinking of *Moa*

Promotions:

Routine from apprentice seaman to signalman first class
Promotion to chief petty officer for "meritorious conduct in action against the enemy" in *Moa* off Guadalcanal
Recommended for promotion to commissioned ranks (1944 letter from Lt. Lowell W. Budlong, USNR, in USS *Florence Nightingale*)

Awards and Commendations:

Routine letters of commendation for battles listed
Presidential Unit Citation for service in *Enterprise*
British Oak Leaf Emblem for Mention in Dispatches for "meritorious conduct in action against the enemy" in *Moa*

Discharge:

Medical discharge as "unable to meet demands of the service," 24 September 1945

Life after Discharge:

Graduated from University of Tulsa, BS
Service as faculty member in Economics Department of University of Tulsa
From 1948 until retirement in 1981, San Francisco advertising man
Married in 1947; four children
Community activist and various local government posts
Freelance writing, both fiction and nonfiction

∽ Index ∽

⤙ About the Author ⤚

Floyd Beaver spent one year at Tulsa University before joining the Navy. He served in fifteen different ships—four separate Admirals' Flag allowances as a signalman. He also performed liaison duty with the British and French navies. He served in both the north and south Pacific Ocean, on North Atlantic convoys, and in Mediterranean landing forces. He was awarded the Conspicuous Service Medal (CSM) for Meritorious Conduct in Action and received a British Mention in Despatches. He became an advertising executive after the war, and his writing credits include books, magazines, and other media. He currently resides in California.